Secrets of Stage Hypnosis – S Hypnotherapy – NLP – Comp And Marketing For Hypnotists

MW01148824

With Contributions from Jonathan Royle
& Many of His Colleagues

Compiled By: Dr. Jonathan Royle

© 2013 – Dr. Jonathan Royle

www.UltimateHypnosisCourse.com

www.EliteHypnosisBootcamp.com

www.MagicalGuru.com

www.HypnotherapyCourse.net

VERY SILENTLY I CREPT FORWARD, I HEARD A SNARLING GRUNTING SOUND FROM ABOVE ME, NOW I LOOKED UPWARDS, THERE WAS THE TIGER, ITS MOUTH OPEN WIDE SHOWING LARGE TEARING FANGS, THE BLACK PATCHES ON THE ROOF OF ITS MOUTH STOOD OUT WITH STARTLING CLARITY, WITHOUT ANOTHER SOUND, IT LEAPT DOWN TOWARDS ME, I CROUCHED LOWER, AND IT PASSED OVER ME, BEFORE THE TIGER COULD TURN, I LEAPT ONTO ITS BACK, CIRCLED ITS THROAT WITH MY LEFT ARM, AND RAISED MY RIGHT ARM WITH THE LONG DAGGER IN IT, VERY HIGH, READY TO STRIKE INTO THE TIGERS JUGULAR.

THAT SENTENCE HELD YOUR ATTENTION, THAT IS WHAT A HYPNOTIST DOES, GRABS YOUR ATTENTION THEN HYPNOTISES YOU. A LESSON BEFORE YOU HAVE EVEN STARTED TO READ THE BOOK.

SECTION ONE

THE KEY TO HYPNOTIC SUCCESS

By: Dr. Jonathan Royle – www.EliteHypnosisBootcamp.com

As is well known within the Psychotherapy world **"We are all products of our environment"** or to be more accurate:

"We are all products of our environment, unless we are given the tools and opportunities to positively expand beyond the confines of our direct environment"

You see to function Positively, Happily and Harmoniously in life (on all levels) we need to as human beings (especially as we are growing up) to feel:

Loved – Wanted – Needed – Appreciated – Cared For – Cherished and Valued

If there is a lacking of or disruption in any of those 7 Positive Pillars then it will most likely lead to that individual suffering a negative impact on their:

Self-Confidence, Self-Esteem, Self-Image and/or Self-Control (Willpower)

And sadly when there is a disruption or negative impact on one or more of those 4 vitally important Foundations of **"Self-Worth"** then this can and often does regretfully lead to the individual feeling…

Negativity, Trapped, Worthless, Like A Failure, Angry, Resentful, Frightened,

And even more depressing is the very real fact that when one or more of those 7 Negative Pillars is in place that it can often lead in one or more ways to the individual going into

SELF-DESTRUCT MODE

And that combined with negative environmental factors can be the straw that breaks the camels back so to speak and can lead to a downward spiral which could include things as extreme as them turning to a life of:

Crime, Self-Harming, Drugs, Alcholism, Domestic Violence, Prostitution, Homelessness or even worse in extreme cases **Suicide…**

These are most always destructive behaviours and actions that manifest themselves either as an extreme reaction to or negative result of the Emotional impact of what has been going on in and/or lacking in their life's.

Often for example Youngsters can get involved with a "bad crowd" as this gives them a sense of belonging and despite the negative consequences of such "gang culture" can help to fulfil the gaps they may feel inwardly in those 7 Positive Pillars and those 4 vitally important Foundations of "Self-Worth" which I mentioned earlier.

And once the downward spiral starts it can and often does lead to a lifetime of destruction which negatively impacts not just the individual, but also their family, friends and even often many members of the community as a whole (in the instances of crime etc)

**HOWEVER THERE IS A WAY WE CAN HELP
STOP THIS HAPPENING**

But the great news is that when an individual is helped to discover ways to expand their horizons, try new things, gain a sense of achievement, given a chance to grow as a person and starts to realize that there are better options available for them and that a brighter future is a possibility for them then this can work wonders in helping them to positively impact and develop their:

Self-Confidence, Self-Esteem, Self-Image and/or Self-Control (Willpower)

And when they grow in these areas, the 4 vitally important Foundations of **"Self-Worth"** they can then start to feel a sense of:

Positivity, Personal Freedom, Positive Self-Worth, Success, Courage, Achievement, Happiness

And perhaps not surprisingly as a positive side effect of these beneficial changes they will finally be able to learn to **LOVE THEMSELVES** and of course gain **SELF-RESPECT**

This can lead to a whole new perspective and positive approach to life, can help the individual to gain a whole new positive support and positive social network and so ultimately can also lead them in the long term to a more **Positive Environment** and thus consequently help them to gain the 7 Positive Pillars in their life's of positively feeling:

Loved – Wanted – Needed – Appreciated – Cared For – Cherished and Valued

Now fortunately for the majority of people, a lacking in one or more of the Positive Pillars does not usually lead to such negative results as the few examples given earlier, however it is my experience that this is always without doubt or exception the Ultimate under lying reason and cause that people develop Bad Habits, Addictions and other personally Negative and also Self Destructive Behaviours.

A lack or imbalance in one or more of the Seven Positive Pillars will always in some way lead to some kind of less than beneficial behaviour and/or thought patterns and thus it is true to say that a lacking or imbalance in one of these area's starts to lead the person away from Pleasure and sets them on the road towards Pain.

Therefore it is also true to note that doing therapeutic work in order to enable the lacking or imbalances in those areas to be eliminated so that the person feels fully 100% Positive and Complete in the areas of:

Self-Confidence, Self-Esteem, Self-Image and/or Self-Control (Willpower)

Will then ultimately mean that any previous lacking or imbalances in the following Seven Positive Pillars will set themselves right and thus enable the person to be the Perfect Them:

Loved – Wanted – Needed – Appreciated – Cared For – Cherished and Valued

It is with this model that I created (as outlined above) that I formulated my creation of "Complete Mind Therapy" and is exactly what the "Non Specific Treatment Script" which you will find later in this book is all about targeting.

In a nutshell it is my belief and experience that when you consider the above and put things right in those areas that everything else will fall positively and permanently into place for your clients.

If you think deeply about this, you will, I am sure also realise that offering a person the chance to be the centre of attention and creating an On Stage environment where they feel:

Loved – Wanted – Needed – Appreciated – Cared For – Cherished and Valued

Is also the True Key Motivating Secret of how and why a Successful Stage Hypnosis show works and when you bear this in mind I am sure your shows will become more successful, just as your results with therapy sessions will also.

To fully understand this further consider that one end of the scale is Pain (lacking or imbalances in these areas) and the other end of the scale is Pleasure (balance and completeness in these areas) and then consider when reading about "Pain and Pleasure" therapy later in this book in my section about Complete Mind Therapy how this can be used to so easily help the client to make changes in their life, or with a little thought to make your Stage Hypnosis Shows more successful than you may ever have thought possible.

Consider that the negative end of this scale can also be called "Out of Control" and the positive end termed "Self-Control" and perhaps things become even clearer for you?

And then consider that the negative end can be termed as "Trapped" and the Positive end as "Freedom"

Or indeed it could be "Unhappy or Depressed" at the Negative End and **HAPPY & JOYFUL** at the positive end.

In all cases however the route from one end of the scale to the other is through and by dealing with the personal attributes and feelings that I have repeated several times during this introduction.

And now I have to say that without doubt to understand this fully and the sheer possibilities of what I have just taught you, right now you would be wise to go on Amazon and order a copy of the excellent book **Psycho-**

Cybernetics, A New Way to Get More Living Out of Life by Maxwell Maltz.

Also consider that in life **FAILURE** occurs because of:

F – rustration

A – ggressiveness

I – nsecurity

L – oneliness

U – ncertainty

R – esentment

E –mptiness

And as you should by now realise all of those things relate back to what I have discussed already. Then at the other end of the scale **SUCCESS** in life occurs due to the following:

S – ense of direction

U – nderstanding

C – ourage

C - almness

E – steem

S – elf – Confidence

S – elf - Acceptance

Again I am sure you can see how that all relates back to the Positive Pillars I mentioned before.

Read **Psycho-Cybernetics, A New Way to Get More Living Out of Life** by Maxwell Maltz and consider it in light of what I have discussed in this opening introduction and I feel certain that on all levels you will become a far better Hypnotist.

The following are Six Further Books that I also consider vitally important to your success in Hypnosis and would say that you should read as soon as possible:

01) They Call It Hypnosis by Robert A. Baker.

02) If This Be Magic – The Forgotten Power of Hypnosis by Guy Lyon Playfair.

03) Monsters & Magical Sticks – There's No Such Thing As Hypnosis by Steven Heller.

04) Bad Medicine: Misconceptions and Misuses Revealed, from Distance Healing to Vitamin O (Wiley Bad Science Series) by Christopher Wanjek.

05) Trick or Treatment: The Undeniable Facts about Alternative Medicine by Edzard Ernst & Simon Singh.

06) Influence: The Psychology of Persuasion (Collins Business Essentials)

by Robert B. Cialdini.

And of course if for some Strange reason you got your hands onto this, Volume Two of "The Encyclopedia of Hypnotherapy, Stage-Hypnosis and Complete Mind Therapy" before having read Volume One then it goes without saying that you should order a copy of Volume One as a matter of Priority in order to make your Hypnosis Education complete.

The simple truth and very real fact is, that much within the pages of this, Volume Two, will only make total sense to you when you have read, studied and understood Volume One.

NOTE = The Above Was Extracted from "The Encyclopedia of Hypnotherapy, Stage-Hypnosis and Complete Mind Therapy" Volume Two by Dr. Jonathan Royle which is available on Amazon.

"BACK TO FRONT"

By: Dr. Jonathan Royle – www.EliteHypnosisBootcamp.com

"Scientists say that we only use 10% of our brain power, well in that case what do we do with the other 47%?"

Seriously though, the potential of the human mind is literally unlimited and far greater than the average person could ever imagine.

As you will discover in this chapter the key secret to hypnosis is the belief and expectancy within your subjects mind, may the general public remain ignorant to the way their minds work otherwise we hypnotists will be out of business!

COURSE IN COMPLETE MIND THERAPY

"The Professional Art of Stage Hypnosis and Hypnotherapy"

IMPORTANT WARNING TO ALL WHO STUDY THIS COURSE.

In order to have purchased this course and enrol as our pupil you will have had to have sent the supplier who sold it to you a signed declaration to state that the information enclosed will only be used for legal purposes.

We would not wish this course to get into the wrong hands as Hypnosis really is a far more powerful force than you could possibly imagine, as such anyone studying this course and putting the enclosed contents to use do so at their own personal risk. The publishers of this course, the supplier who sold it to you and the author Alex Leroy in no way accept any responsibility whatsoever for other peoples actions and/or uses of this courses contents.

In this part I will reveal all the key secrets of Hypnosis. In other words, within the next few pages you will find everything you require to become a professional Stage Hypnotists and/or Mind Therapist like myself or Paul McKenna.

However as you will have, I presume, no previous knowledge of the subjects in hand you may think that the next few pages over simplify the art. The idea of this however is to show you the key points and then to explain to you why these are the key points.

As such when you have read the last part of this course you will then realise and more importantly understand just how easy and simple it really is to hypnotise someone. So this is if you like what most people would have made the last chapter of this course, but for reasons you will understand later, it has been presented "Back to front!"

The main advantage of doing it this way is that you will learn both the cause of what you are doing and also the effect it has upon people. This will mean that you will automatically know more than a great number of Stage Hypnotists who just know the outcome of what they do and not what has caused it to happen. So always remember EVERY CAUSE HAS AN EFFECT and EVERY EFFECT HAS A UNDERLYING CAUSE.

•<u>STAGE HYPNOTISM</u>

Boiled down to the basics Stage Hypnosis is IDENTICAL to all other forms of Hypnosis. The only difference being the way in which it is PRESENTED and the speed at which the volunteers are placed into a DEEP hypnotic trance state. There are seven key points to follow for Therapeutic Hypnosis and below I shall explain how these key points also apply to the use of Hypnotism on stage.

•SEVEN STEPS TO THERAPUTIC HYPNOSIS

1 Introductory talk to the client in order to obtain "rapport."

2 Induction of the hypnotic trance state.

3 Deepening of the trance state.

4 Ego-strengthening Therapy.

5 Carry out the necessary Therapy on the client.

6 Implant the major post Hypnotic suggestion.

7 Awaken the client from the Hypnotic trance state.

•SEVEN STEPS TO STAGE-HYPNOSIS

1. Obtain rapport (done through one liner jokes at start of act).

2. Induction of Hypnotic trance. (Any fast method after handclasp).

3. Deepening of trance (giving suggestion that each time they are told to return to sleep they will go deeper.)

4. Ego strengthening Therapy (butter them up/compliments etc).

5. Do the Therapy (in this case the comedy routines of your act).

6. Implant the major post Hypnotic suggestion. (N.B. This is done at stage two when they are told that when you tell them to return to sleep they will go deeper and is done so that all suggestions given to them are cancelled before they leave the stage).

7. Awaken them from trance (awaken them and ensure they feel ok).

So you see, the basic structure is the same. In fact to be honest the best piece of advice I could ever give you is to go and see a Stage Hypnotist performing when they are in your area. Study them and also consult a Hypnotherapist and then you will see with your own eyes just how similar the two forms of Hypnosis really are.

This will also be a most valuable learning experience as you can learn an awful lot by emulating (not copying) the style and manner of established experienced Stage Hypnotists. Basically speaking if you did what they did word for word and with similar actions on someone whom had been made to believe in your abilities then they would go into a trance state and react to your various suggestions.

•<u>THE KEYS TO HYPNOTIC INDUCTIONS</u>

When wishing to place someone into a Hypnotic trance there is also a set procedure to follow which is:

A. BELIEF and EXPECTANCY

B. DISORIENTATION and CONFUSION

C. SUGGESTION and REPETITION

D. RELAXATION and SLEEP

Step A means that if you instil into them a belief in your powers as a Hypnotist and as such they believe that you are able to place them under trance, and they also expect to go under if you were to try it upon them, then they are in the correct state of mind to be very successfully and rapidly placed into a Hypnotic trance state.

Step B means that once they are in the correct state of mind to be Hypnotised you then use methods of disorientation and confusion to convince them they are starting to go into trance, and that's why they are feeling these strange effects. As such if they believe this to be the case then they will expect to go under deeper and as such they will, as in the end its all down to their personal state of mind.

Step C means that once these things are starting to convince them they are beginning to slip into trance then you use methods of suggestion and repetition to confuse and disorientate them even further and also to convince them that they are going under more. If they believe this is the case and expect what you are doing to have an effect upon them, then indeed, in turn it most certainly will.

Step D is the end result of carrying out steps A, B & C and should be that if they believe what you have done to be Hypnosis and expect it to work then this will have the result of relaxation and sleep. And as all Hypnosis really is, is deep relaxation they will then be in the Hypnotic trance state.

So you see the secret to all induction's of any kind whether Stage or Therapy and whether slow, rapid or instantaneous is that if the subject sincerely believes that what you are doing does work and they also sincerely believe and expect it to work on them, then the end result will always be that it works on them.

Basically, the key secret to all induction's is to have instilled into the prospective subjects mind, the belief in your powers and the 100% expectancy that should you as the worlds greatest of great Stage and/or Therapeutic Hypnotists picks upon them to be Hypnotised then it will work and as such they will enter a trance.

BELIEF AND EXPECTANCY EQUALS HYPNOSIS.

•<u>THE SPEED PROBLEM</u>

Generally speaking if you place a person into trance via a long induction then they will remain in trance longer and go into a deeper state of relaxation. By the same token if you place someone into trance via a rapid or instantaneous induction then they will slip out of the trance state very quickly.

The general rule of thumb in the Hypnotism industry seems to be that:

•<u>"QUICKLY IN EQUALS QUICKLY OUT"</u>

AND

"SLOWLY IN EQUALS SLOWLY OUT"

However, from experience I have found a solution so that instant induction's can be used to place them into a trance with the end result of them going into a deep state of relaxation and not slipping out of Hypnosis as might occur otherwise when you don't want them to! The solution is simply:

1. Use your instant induction's and place everyone into the trance.
2. Then use the group deepening method as detailed later to deepen the trance to such a level whereby they will not slip out of it.

So remember that if left to their own devices and a group deepening method is not used, then the subjects of an instant induction would probably slip out of the hypnotic state in a very short space of time indeed.

•THE SECRET OF SPEED

The secret of speed induction's is just to make sure that you follow the keys which I have mentioned already and also to have an enormous amount of confidence. This confidence must be in your abilities.

You must also carry out the instantaneous induction's with no doubt in your mind that they WILL work!

This is so that this personal belief is transmitted to the subjects and they are then in no doubt in their minds that it will work. You must do instant style induction's with conviction, also a very commanding tone of voice and attitude and you must transmit to the subject that you expect to be obeyed by them.

An element of shock is also used with instant induction's in order to catch them off guard and as such "shock" them into deep hypnosis so to speak.

•THE THREE STEPS TO HYPNOSIS

An even simpler way to explain how Hypnosis works to place someone into a trance state is like this:

A. They must know that you are a Professional Hypnotist and can therefore do as you claim.

B. Ask them to close their eyes and to breathe deeply and regularly.

C. Suggest ideas of heaviness, sleep, tiredness and relaxation to them for a few minutes and then THEY WILL BE IN A HYPNOTIC TRANCE.

Once again I'm sure you can see how it all relates back to those two key words/secrets which of course are belief and expectancy.

•PEER GROUP PRESSURE

A small percentage of people will react to your suggestions due to peer group pressure and the fear that if they don't then they will be tormented and subjected to ridicule by their friends as they are unable to at that time be a good Hypnotic subject.

•THE I.I.C. SYNDROME

A phrase which I always use in my opening patter is this: "If you've got good powers of intelligence, imagination and concentration then you will be a good Hypnotic subject!" The psychological effect of this is that if they come up to try and be Hypnotised and did not react, then they think it will make them look an even bigger fool by not reacting than by taking part and being a "good" subject in the show.

As if they were to return to the audience their friends and family would ridicule them for not having good powers of intelligence, imagination and concentration to be a good Hypnotic subject. So again in a way, this relates back to peer group pressure.

•<u>THE KARAOKE SYNDROME</u>

The life of an average person is the set 9 to 5 routine, they lack attention and appreciation in their lives and would love to have the chance to be the centre of attention and to be given some appreciation by lots of other people. In fact the secret dream of many people is to perform on stage even if they do make a fool of themselves. It's the Karaoke syndrome and is exactly the reason why Karaoke nights are so successful. Those people that get up know they are awful singers and are making a complete fool of themselves and yet to them, its an escape from everyday life, a step into the world of fantasy and the chance to be a star! The fact other people are also prepared to make fools of themselves brings the sheep effect into play, so it then doesn't bother them either to make a fool of themselves. In just the same way a high percentage of people who volunteer for your act will have the Karaoke syndrome at work on their mind and as such you have got several more good subjects to partake in your act.

•<u>THE SHEEP EFFECT</u>

The sheep effect is such that if one person is prepared to do something or make a fool of themselves, then others will "follow the leader" and they become one of the sheep following the crowd and doing what all the others upon the stage or in life are doing. (Never allow yourself to become a sheep!)

•<u>THE EXHIBITIONIST</u>

These come in two forms, the first is the positive one who likes to have a laugh, be the star of the show etc and as such although not actually under Hypnosis, plays along and hams it up so to speak. As entertainment is the key word on stage, if they look convincing you would of course allow them to remain on the stage. Then of course there is also the negative form which manifests itself as the person who has a need to show off to his friends/family just how great they are and what an idiot you are. These people of course should be dismissed from the stage at the earliest opportunity. It is a wise idea to have a friend stood in the wings (side area of the stage) who can keep an eye on the subjects whilst you are facing the audience and have your back turned to the on stage volunteers. This friend can then, if they spot anyone, give you a hand signal which you would of course have prearranged between you to indicate which person is and in which chair they are sitting. You then return them to the audience and by so doing, are now in almost the same position as having eyes in the back of your head. By the way if this observant friend is trained in Hypnosis also, they can then also give you hand signals to indicate which of the on stage volunteers will be good to place into trance, which ones not to bother with and those which are under deepest when Hypnotised.

•PEOPLE HYPNOTISE THEMSELVES

The Hypnotist only tells them that they can do it! Until he told them, they never knew that they could do it. In effect we are "directors" of the film and the subjects become the "actors" doing as we say. We just guide them into what is really just a deep state of relaxation and should really be classed as "Self Hypnosis". So much for the 1952 Hypnotism act, 1989 guidelines and 1996 government review then! These are covered later.

●THE PLACEBO EFFECT

Most all of the previously mentioned rules also apply to the use of Hypnosis in a therapeutic context, although in this case the persons motivations rather than stardom are those of changing their lives for the better. One important thing that applies only to Therapeutic work, is that of the placebo effect. By the time your client has read your newspaper advertisement and/or been given a personal recommendation about you by a previous client, belief and expectancy are already going to work on their minds. It then takes a lot of courage to phone you and book an appointment for Therapy as this is then a conscious decision within themselves that things must change and will change for the better. The prospect of attending at your house or office is one that will fill them with much apprehension and this is why in some cases, clients will not show up for their appointments as the thought of change becomes just too scary. However when a client does show up as happens in 99% of the cases they are almost cured of their problem the moment they step into your consulting room, as they have already made a conscious decision by booking the appointment and attending on time that things must change! The other piece in the jigsaw is when you get them to hand over the payment for the session before you even start the Therapy. Most people do not like parting with money, especially not large amounts of it, such as the fee of around £40 per hour, which you will be charging them for your time and as such paying this fee makes them believe in your abilities to help them even more. The final 25% of the Therapeutic process is the actual treatment which you give them, although even if this were to be fundamentally worthless (which it is not), if the client is made to believe it will be beneficial then indeed it will!

•<u>GOLDEN RULES TO FOLLOW</u>

RULE ONE: Have total confidence in yourself and your skilful abilities.

RULE TWO: Exude that confidence so that others will then have total confidence in you and your abilities.

RULE THREE: Monotony and repetition is the trade of the Hypnotist so repeat, repeat and then repeat it again.

RULE FOUR: Learn to use your voice so that it can sound demanding and also commanding.

RULE FIVE: Follow the steps and instructions detailed within this course to the letter and your success is guaranteed.

YOUR HYPNOTIC TOOLKIT

As a Hypnotist, the only tools of use to you are self-confidence, which you must have in abundance, suggestion, commanding and demanding tone of voice, rhythm of speech (cadence), monotony, repetition, professional appearance, knowledge and experience. These are the only tools available to you. However, if you learn to use them all effectively then it will become a most powerful tool kit and will make your job far easier. So learn to handle these tools with finesse for they are the start, middle and end of all that you must do and know.

•<u>SOME OTHER MOST IMPORTANT POINTS</u>

1. Hypnotists are not Hypnotists, they are merely actors playing the part of the image of a Hypnotist which people expect to see and as such react to.

2. All Hypnosis whether Stage or Therapeutic is really just self hypnosis.

3. Hypnosis occurs due to co-operation and not confrontation or challenge.

4. As Hypnosis is just a state of mind and compliance based on the subjects levels of belief and expectancy, there is no such thing as a "Hypnotised" feeling and this is because each person experiences everything that happens during the course of their life differently.

5. Belief and expectancy are the most powerful keys of all to success.

6. Suggestion correctly expressed is Hypnosis.

7. The correct way to express suggestion is in a commanding and demanding voice, and to keep on repeating it to the subject.

8. One willing co-operative volunteer is worth more than a hundred pressed men.

9. To make life easy for you, use the suggestibility test of hands locking together to find those subjects who will be the easiest to Hypnotise and who are obviously in the correct co-operative state of mind.

10. A Hypnotist is perceived as being a person of authority and people in general expect to be ordered by and to obey as a person of authority says. Just remember your school days and you'll realise both what I mean and also the fact most all people are conditioned in this way.

11. For suggestions of sleep, slow deep tones of voice with words suggesting a downward motion are used.

12. For awakening suggestions, a faster, higher tone of voice with words suggesting an upward motion would be used.

13. The salesmen's techniques of mirroring and matching are used to put people to ease, make them relax and to establish rapport easily.

14. Hypnosis is a state of heightened awareness and as such subjects can taste, smell, see, feel and hear things better than they usually would be able and are more, rather than less aware of their surroundings.

15. If the mind is focused on one thing, or at least one thing at a time and is not allowed to wander, then as the normal worries of the day are not considered your subject will automatically relax completely.

16. When people relax they tend to lose a lot of their inhibitions and this could also explain why they are then prepared to do daft things.

17. Confidence begets confidence and as a man thinketh so he becomes, which proves that positive thinking is a most positive force.

18. It has to be in the mind first before it becomes an action (in every day life) and it has to be in the subconscious mind first to become an action during Hypnosis.

19. When the imagination (subconscious mind) and the will (conscious mind) are in conflict, the imagination always wins. So if you can get a person to focus their mind on something to the exclusion of everything else, you are then able to bypass the critical area of their minds and firmly embed a suggestion into their imagination without any conscious conflict! Then afterwards even if the conscious mind were to try and oppose the suggestion the far stronger force of the imagination would always win and the suggestion would be acted upon.

20. Hypnosis merely shuts down the analytical (critical) area of the mind that is located between the conscious and subconscious. It acts as a kind of "gate-keeper" and processes all incoming information from the conscious mind before it is allowed to enter the subconscious mind where it is permanently kept on file.

21. As we've already stated if the suggestion can be given directly to the subconscious mind (the imagination) then it will be acted upon immediately and as I've stated already all Hypnosis does is shut down that analytical (critical) area of the mind which in turn makes this action possible.

22. Talk success, think success, act success and dream success and then successful things will occur.

23. Remember positive thoughts breed positive actions, they are contagious and positive actions breed positive results.

24. Relaxation is the key, which opens the door to the subconscious mind. In this state, get the subjects to visualise your suggestions with implicit faith that it is so and so and it will be.

25. Co-operations with a highly developed imagination are the best qualities your subject can have for successful acceptance of your Hypnotic suggestions.

26. You want your subjects to have confidence, belief and faith with expectation of success, but it is no use just telling them this. They must be "sold" on Hypnosis and its effects to possess these real qualities.

27. Rapport, observation, recognition and leadership. These are the four stages of inducing a Hypnotic trance. All are lead by the subject and merely followed by the Hypnotist as will be explained later.

28. Rapport should establish three things, trust, comfort and of course belief.

29. Hypnosis is merely a form of communication. Tone of voice is essential in all communication and indeed in Hypnosis also. It is also possible to hide "secret" messages within a spoken sentence by changing your tone of voice so that they have an almost "subliminal" effect.

30. You must take the venue or consulting room over. Show that you and you alone are in charge. Demand instant respect, dominate your subjects, control the subjects and condition them to react to your suggestions even before they are in a trance. Give them orders and expect them to be obeyed, talk and act in an authoritative manner and look at ease with all you do. Keep their mind off what's happening at all times and then you'll be well on your way to Hypnotic success.

31. If they believe that you have special powers then your job is easy, if they expect to be Hypnotised by you then they will be!

32. They are in a strange situation and environment (whether on stage or in therapy) whereas you feel at ease. You have the microphone or seat and are at home upon the stage or in the room and therefore you are in charge. You make them feel important, needed and appreciated whilst also conditioning them so that they sincerely believe they are only clever and intelligent if they co-operate with you.

33. You know what's going to happen and they don't so you are already ahead of them. You act in a routine manner as though it always works and it will then work.

34. Ordering them around at the start conditions them to obey you. You are the salesman selling the great idea of Hypnosis to them. The sheep effect then makes them follow the leader and try to be a "better" subject than the others upon the stage.

35. Music which suits each routine in the background sets the correct style of scene and has a psychological effect upon them, that of making it all seem more real and easier to imagine.

36. The subjects who are in a deep trance are kept and used for the, harder routines. You then direct all applause to them and this reward makes them feel good and also conditions them to react throughout.

37. On stage always paint a verbal picture, so that the subjects know what is expected of them. They must know what you are saying as they cannot read your mind. The suggestions you give must also have one meaning only so that they cannot be misinterpreted.

38. A Hypnotist to be successful must be a self-motivated, strong minded, egotistical individual, who is confident in their skills. You must be a good showman and an artist par excellence. A smooth talker, persuasionist, salesman. Actor and adaptable at a seconds notice. In other words you must be able to think on your feet, use your common sense and have the gift of the gab.

39. Hypnosis is co-operation and not confrontation and the nature of your game should be imagination not humiliation.

40. You cannot see Hypnosis, you can only see the effects of it. This is my reason for saying that the use of props and music helps to make the whole show more attractive and more believable for both the on stage subjects and also for the watching audience.

41. Lastly for this part, allow me to explain how Hypnosis works between the subject and the Hypnotist in much the same way as a Bio-feedback machine. Also let me explain briefly how the human mind works, we'll elaborate later on.

THE HUMAN MIND AS I SEE IT

As I see it the human mind is made up of three separate layers making the whole, these three layers are as follows:

1. The conscious mind and/or human will.
2. The analytical and/or critical area.
3. The subconscious and/or imagination

We use the conscious mind to speak etc, the subconscious deals with the automatic actions of our blood circulation and breathing as well as being our imagination area of the mind. And lastly the analytical area analyses all incoming information before being allowed entry and storage in the subconscious mind as truth/fact. I will now make the analogy of the mind being a computer. The conscious mind is if you like the keyboard, which inputs new information. The analytical area analyses it for any mistakes in much the same way as a spell checker, then the "corrected" data, if of an acceptable nature, is allowed to enter the subconscious mind where it is stored forever in much the same way as storing data onto a floppy disc.

To briefly explain if you told a fully conscious person that when you snapped your fingers they are Elvis and then snapped same said fingers, they would not react! Why? Well simply because the analytical area processes it and then compares it with the memory bank record in the subjects subconscious mind of who they are before rejecting it as it realises the statement to be untrue. All this of course takes only a fraction of a second to occur.

Under Hypnosis the mind and body of the subject relax, and due to the disorientation, confusion and repetition of suggestion the analytical area shuts down or goes to sleep. As such when told that on a snap of the fingers they will be Elvis the mind is then unable to process the information and find out that it is untrue and consequently it is believed to be true. It goes directly into the subconscious as being true and so is acted upon as an automatic reflex action.

If only in a very light state of trance the will of the person may still go into conflict with the imagination or subconscious, but as we stated earlier when the imagination and will are in conflict the imagination always wins.

As such they will react and be Elvis or do whatever you have suggested without question. Just as with any computer, programs placed into the memory which in the long term could be dangerous or more harm than good MUST be cancelled out or erased so that things revert to normality. So it is also with your subjects mind, all suggestions must be completely cancelled out before they leave the venue after the Hypnotic show.

Otherwise they will remain in the computers memory bank to be automatically acted upon long into the future! Imagine the scene as the subject is driving home and Elvis comes onto the radio. This triggers off the memory bank association that upon hearing Elvis they must start to dance. They then do so and Crash! This is obviously an extreme example but expressed to implant firmly into your mind the importance of removing all suggestions and commands from your subject's minds except those of a beneficial nature such as in Therapy before they leave the room.

You should always aim to leave them feeling refreshed and as good if not better than when they entered the venue that night. If you do this and abide fully by the 1952 Hypnotism Act, the 1989 guidelines and the 1996 Government review and generally put the safety of your volunteers first then you should be a most successful performer.

This part contains all the keys you require for Hypnotic success, but I'll end by explaining how the mind is like a Bio-feedback machine. Observe Figure A and you will see the Hypnotist facing the subject. The final key to a most successful induction is as follows.

The Hypnotist suggests things to the subject who in turn accepts and reacts to these verbal suggestions. The Hypnotist then observes the effects of those suggestions and feeds back his observations as new suggestions to the subject. The subject accepts and reacts to these, the Hypnotist observes the effects and then feeds back the observations as new suggestions to the subjects and so the Biofeedback computer effect continues until the subject is in a deep state of trance. In other words the Hypnotist's suggestions are always made up of his observations.

THE BIOFEEDBACK COMPUTER EFFECT

An example of this so that you fully understand how it works would be as follows. The Hypnotist suggests that the subject will start to breathe deeply and regularly, this is then accepted by the subject and acted upon by them. They then start to breathe more deeply and regularly and perhaps also start to close their eyes.

The Hypnotist observes this and then feeds back the observation to the subject as new suggestions along the line of "That's great and as you continue to breathe deeply and regularly, notice how your eyelids are now so heavy and so tired, in fact it's so much easier, just to let them close!" The subject accepts and reacts, the Hypnotist observes and feeds back the observations as new suggestions and so the cycle continues.

This now means that you really do know how to Hypnotise someone, as with this technique the wording of your induction must always be ad lib and worded so as to contain your observations and as such capitalise upon them.

You would of course at all times be following the basic guidelines of voice tone and speed of suggestions etc. And remember the key words associated by most people with Hypnosis and a trance state are: sleep, relax, drifting, deeper, falling, resting, calm, heavy, tired and all other words associated which mean similar things to these.

Well congratulations you now know more about Stage Hypnosis, Hypnotherapy and Related Mind Therapies than most if not all of the "cowboy" Hypnotists who are currently flooding the industry. Now that you have the keys to Hypnotic success, lets look at them all separately and in depth so that your understanding and knowledge of the subject is total.

You will have noticed by now I'm sure, that throughout this course, I will repeat many key points several times, the reason for this is that the trade of any Hypnotist is repetition and you can only learn through repetition.

As such, this course has been written, not only to be enjoyable to read, but rather in a way that you learn the maximum amount possible in the shortest space of time possible.

The fields of Stage Hypnosis, Hypnotherapy and Related Mind Therapies have made numerous Hypnotic multi millionaires and many more of us very rich and financially independent indeed. I promise that after reading the last page of this course, listening to the instructional audio-tapes, viewing the videos and possibly attending your personal training day, you will be in a position to, if you so desire achieve this same level of financial freedom and success. And don't forget of course that should you ever require any additional help or advice I am only ever at the end of a telephone line and as my old grandmother used to say "Two heads are better than one, even if they are sheep's heads in a pan of barley!" For now I'll sign off and see you in the next chapter.

NOTE = The Chapter Above was extracted from "The Encyclopedia of Hypnotherapy, Stage-Hypnosis and Complete Mind Therapy" Volume One which is available on Amazon. Also Visit **http://www.UltimateHypnosisCourse.com** and http://www.elitehypnosisbootcamp.com for more details.

'Running The Numbers'

by Robert Temple

As hypnotists we are probably one of the luckiest breeds in the world. Not only are we self-employed (and therefore able to dictate our own hours, projects, salary and working conditions) but we are also able to change the lives of ordinary people, every day.

Whether you're a stage hypnotist or a hypnotherapist, chances are that you've been asked to stop someone from smoking or make them 'stop eating chocolate' on more than one occasion.

In fact, if you had a penny for every time you'd had these requests, you'd probably be able to retire, financially free, and simply enjoy the rest of your life on a yacht in the Bahamas.

That's precisely what I want to talk to you about here, today.

I think that all of us have some kind of 'dream' or some big goals which, right now, you may think will never be fulfilled. Maybe you want to buy a $1,000,000 home or drive a Lamborghini.

Perhaps you're looking for that paradise beach lifestyle. Or maybe you'd like to pay off your mortgage and not worry about the bills each month.

Whatever it is that motivates you to be successful and whatever you envision as true 'success', in this chapter I want to empower you and give you the tools that you need to 'make it happen'.

When you started out in hypnosis, chances are you had a couple of things in mind:

1 To change people's lives for the better and make a real difference;

2 To build your own business and make money for yourself, rather than working for 'the man'.

Would you agree?

Well, there is one fundamental 'flaw' with this business model which is limiting you from achieving both of those things to their fullest potential.

There is only ONE of you and only 24 hours in each day so, even with the best will in the world, there are only so many clients that you can consult with per day.

Unless you're charging many thousands of dollars and treating high-end celebrities or business people, chances are you're probably not seeing the kind of dream income that you desired.

Your income will always be obstructed by:

1 The amount of money you can charge per session;

2 The number of sessions/clients you can fit into a day;

3 The number of clients you can actually get per day;

4 The local radius from which you can realistically find clients.

So, without the capital and the business experience to open up a chain of top-notch hypnotherapy practices around the world, chances are your dreams of million dollar mansions are going to remain a far-flung hope.

Wouldn't it be great if there was a way that you could find, attract and treat literally hundreds of clients per day for dozens of different issues or problems, without taking up any of your time.

Imagine if you could be at the beach, in your local coffee shop, browsing the designer high street stores or on a 5* vacation and STILL be able to treat more clients that you ever dreamt possible.

Sounds too good to be true?

Well, it used to be... but it isn't anymore, thanks to an incredible tool.

I am, of course, referring to the INTERNET.

We now live in a world of digital publishing and internet marketing, where literally anything you need is available at the push of a button.

Some of the world's biggest companies are exploding into bankruptcy, whilst regular people are building solid 7-figure businesses from the comfort of their home Internet connection.

As hypnotists, we are in the perfect position to do exactly the same. Whether you'd be happy to make an extra few hundred bucks per month, or whether you're looking to build a multi-million dollar online empire, I urge you to read on - and consider what I'm about to share with you, very seriously.

A couple of years ago, I made the decision that I wanted to raise my fees, work less and make more money. So I set about learning, designing and perfecting a system to generate passive income online, which would allow me to work as much or as little as I wanted.

I soon stumbled across something golden. I realized that you can actually package, market and sell your hypnotherapy skills online for HUGE profit margins as 'downloadable information products'.

Let's face it, there are literally BILLIONS of people around the world who need our help in SOME way, but there's no way we can get them all into our offices for a hypnotherapy session.

BUT, we could easily give them some kind of virtual help, whether that's a hypnotherapy MP3, video training, an eBook or whatever the best medium to package your information is.

I'm sure you've seen those 'big-gun' hypnotists with their best-selling books and audio programs in your favorite high-street book store, right?

Well the truth is that a lot of physical book publishers are worried right now, as more and more people are turning to the Internet to solve their problems.

The cool thing is that ordinary people like me and you can now create their own fantastic products, get them up for sale online and start raking in big cash, for less than $100 and in under a week.

Let's run some numbers...

Imagine you could have a 'Quit Smoking' product, which sells for $67 on-line. If you could sell 10 copies per day, that's $670 in your pocket. Once the 'system' is set up, it takes NO effort to complete those sales.

That's with just ONE product. What if you had 5 of those products.?Or 10?

I call this 'Passive Hypnosis Profits'.

When I discovered this possibility, I knew that I had stumbled onto something that would change my life... and it did.

Over the past few years I've generated over $1.2million in online sales of this kind of information product. Best of all, the overheads and set up costs are super-low and literally ANYONE can copy my success.

Let me tell you, when you have an automated online system selling your hypnotherapy products and generating hundreds or thousands of dollars per day in hands-free income, it's an incredible feeling.

Not only are you helping hundreds of people worldwide to change their lives for the better but you're also making fantastic money along the way.

The truth is, the more money you have, the more resources you have to further spread your skills and help even more people - which, in turn, makes even more money. Cool, right?

All you need to know is the 'system', which I have conveniently broken down into 5 simple, bite-size chunks, ready for you to implement.

Step #1: Choose a topic for your product

This is the simple part. All you have to do is to choose one of your favorite, or most popular, issues that you can treat as a hypnotherapist.

It could be anything from smoking cessation or weight loss to phobia cures and stress/anxiety.

There are literally hundreds of issues which can be easily treated with hypnotherapy, so you can simply pick one of your preferred.

Perhaps there is a particular problem which you've had a great success rate with, or something you have noticed is requested a lot.

Either way, if you can make money from it as a hypnotherapist doing one-on-one sessions, then you can make 100x the money from it as a down-loadable information product.

Once you've chosen one, you can move on.

Step #2: Create your product

Most people have never (and will never) create their own product. Why? It's usually because the thought never crosses their mind or they don't think they can.

Truthfully, as a hypnotist, you are probably in one of the most powerful positions to create a fantastic information product effortlessly.

Think about it this way. Every single time you treat a private client for any particular issue, you are effectively creating an audio product, live... which is then instantly gone forever.

You're sitting, in a room, and talking for 60-120 minutes, hypnotizing, treating and re-awakening your clients.

Now, imagine if you were to purchase a simple, cheap $30 USB micro-phone for your computer or hire a local, basic recording studio for an hour, and you were to do a full hypnotherapy session... for a microphone.

Yes, actually sit down and run an entire session as if your client were there in front of you, but record it all onto a microphone.

An hour or two later, you have your very own perfect information product ready to sell. Simply save it as an MP3 and you're done.

That was easy!

If you wanted to take this a step further, you could also create a manual or video course to accompany the hypnosis MP3, detailing further tips, tricks and tools to help them beat their issue.

Your product could be as simple as a 60-minute audio file or as complicated as an entire multimedia program consisting of books, worksheets, videos, audios, etc.

With the product created, simply give it a snazzy name and it's ready for sale.

Never thought you could make a hit-selling product? You just learned how to do it in as little as an hour. Now what's your excuse?

Go make your product, otherwise you're missing out!

Step #3: Build an automated sales process

Once your product is complete, the next step is to build a simple online sales presence to enable you to convert visitors into customers.

Your online sales system will consist of a few different parts:

1 Sales page - this is a simple web page, which consists of some simple graphics and either a long, scrolling sales letter or a sharp, snappy sales video to sell the visitor on the benefits of your product. It would also have an 'Add To Cart' button, so that your customers can buy the product.

2 Order form - this page enables your customers to actually send you some money for your product. Whether it's $10 or $1000, you need some kind of merchant provider. Fortunately, with companies such as ClickBank, PayPal and JVZoo, who will actually handle your payments for you, this is really pretty easy.

You can simply create a free account with any of these services and create an order form to add to your sales process within minutes.

3 Download page - this is where your customers will be returned after they have purchased your product. It's a simple web page which contains a download link for the MP3, eBook or video course.

This kind of website is often referred to in the internet marketing as a 'minisite'. It's very straightforward to create and can even be entirely outsourced (recommended!) to a professional graphic designer.

If you turn to Google and search for 'Minisite Designer', you'll find a ton of really talented people who can create your entire minisite out for you, while you just sit back and put the individual pieces together.

You'll also need website hosting and a domain name for your product, but you can also find these with a simple Google search.

Step #4: Start driving traffic

With your product and sales process online, you simply need to flood it with traffic. The more traffic you receive to your site, the more sales you'll make and the more money goes into your pocket.

There are literally dozens of ways that you can get traffic to your site, but my personal favorite is to find affiliates and have them promote your product for you.

Affiliates are other internet marketers or information publishers who already have a business in your niche area. For example, if you have created a 'stop smoking' product, then you could search for blogs, product creators, mailing list owners and experts to promote your product to their followers and fans.

They could add a banner to their website or e-mail their subscriber list about your product. If anyone buys it, they receive a commission from the sale.

There are literally thousands of successful affiliates around the world who are hungry for quality products to promote, in every niche or topic you could possibly think of.

It's like having an army of sales people working for you all day, every day, and you only have to pay them when they make you money first. Cool, right?

If you use ClickBank or JVZoo to run your payments (see above) then you already have a built-in and ready-to-go affiliate program to handle all of the sales tracking and commission payouts, too.

Once your system is ready to go, your entire job becomes simply finding and recruiting new affiliates who can promote your product on a daily basis.

I'd recommend spending 20-30 minutes per day just looking for (and contacting) new potential affiliates. Even if you only bring 1 new affiliate onboard each day, that can be enough to generate thousands of sales per month.

Step #5: Rinse and repeat

Believe it or not, it's actually completely possible to have steps 1-4 up and running within 7-28 days, starting from scratch.

So what do you do next? That's easy, you do it again with a new product in a new niche market.

Literally start from the beginning and run through this entire system again. Each time you do it, you'll add a new product to your collection and bump up your potential income.

Why have 1 product making $100 per day, when you could have 10? The more products you have out there, the more money you could make, even if you put less work into each individual product promotion.

Plus, the more you do this, the better and faster you'll become. There is absolutely no reason why you couldn't release a new product every 2-3 months.

If your products sell for, say, $47 and convert at around 5%, if you get 100 visitors to those sales pages every day (this is not an unrealistic figure at all!) then you'll be making 5 sales at $47 = $235 per day.

That's an extra $85,775 per year in hands-free, passive income!

Oh, and that's only with ONE product. Imagine the damage you could do with FIVE or TEN products!

The truth is that the entire world is shifting rapidly to this new, digital marketplace.

People are becoming more and more familiar and comfortable with the idea of online purchases and downloadable digital products every day.

Some people will be buying those products and others will be selling them.

Which would you rather be?

As a hypnotist, you have one of the most powerful abilities to change people's lives and generate huge cash. Please don't limit your opportunities to do this on a global scale.

There is NO reason why you can't build your very own five, six or seven figure online income with the system that I've detailed in this chapter.

I have done it... my students are doing it... and you can do it too.

If you're interested in learning more about this system, you can check out our 100% free coaching on 'Passive Hypnosis Profits' by visiting: http://www.passivehypnosisprofits.com/free/

or http://www.elitehypnosisbootcamp.com/platinum/

Reg Blackwood's Ten Street Hypnosis Show Tips

http://www.regblackwood.com

Reg Blackwood is a British professional hypnotist, resident for most of the year in New Zealand. When he's not entertaining audiences around the world with hypnosis, mindreading and roving hypnotic entertainment, he practices hypnotherapy, manages an online training resource for performers, teaches other hypnotists and hypnotherapists and writes original effects for mentalists and other psychological performers.

1. Be clear of your purpose

As fun as it might sound, the idea of running around town, hypnotising people willy-nilly will soon wear thin. Look around at the number of people who start out saying "I'm a Street Hypnotist. I'm THE Hypnotist" and then within a couple of weeks, they're back doing card tricks, juggling or accountancy again.

Before you go out, be clear of your purpose.

Early on, don't aim for that amazing, funny and entertaining forty minute street show, complete with invisibility and wallet stealing.
Set yourself some simple goals and not only will your confidence and technique improve no end, but you'll also end up giving much richer experiences to the people you meet and you won't be boring or get bored.

For example, for the first month or so of going out, you might decide to just try one or two different fast inductions, give some positive, motivational suggestions and wake them up again. Nothing else.

Once you have that mastered, the next month, maybe add a hand-stick for each participant and leave them laughing.

Slowly, little by little, add different routines, find what works best, most of the time, what spectators enjoy most and before long you'll have a street show to be proud of and well worth watching!

One of your goals can be to practice some of the new inductions your keen to try as re-inductions.

2. Aim for groups of people

Stage hypnosis has been successful for many years, so don't make things hard for yourself by trying to reinvent the wheel. Adapt what you know about stage shows for a street environment.

The most obvious thing is the number of potential volunteers you will have to select from.

Do your homework and find the best days, time of day and locations to encounter groups of friends hanging out, with time on their hands. Lunchtime on weekdays is hardly ever good!

Don't approach individuals. Not only are you in danger of looking a little creepy, but with a group, you'll play the numbers game, increase your chances of being successful and have an attentive, ready-made audience!

Play some games and do some icebreakers to see who you might be able to work best with. It's not really about suggestibility testing, it's more about finding out who is best able to focus on and follow your instructions in the environment.

You shouldn't really be approaching anyone at all. Think of some creative ways you can set up and get people to approach you. You could make a sign or attach a poster to a nearby fence or window or you could start some other kind of performance to attract a crowd.

The first volunteer is always the hardest to get. Once your crowd see you treating someone respectfully and giving them an enjoyable time, you'll have no shortage of volunteers.

You could take your favourite somnambulist friend along with you and begin by hypnotising them.

3. Expect failure and deal with it

Too many trainers will tell you to go out there with balls of steel and an invincible, no-fail attitude.

They'll tell you confidence is king. Act as though you can hypnotise every man, woman, child and animal on the planet and you will be successful.

In reality, you won't be able to hypnotise everybody you meet so you will inevitably fail. Sometimes you will fail more than you succeed. You need to accept that and deal with it.

When you can't hypnotise them, don't stress about it. Act a little surprised, thank them, make your excuses and move on swiftly to someone else.

Remember, very few people out there know as much about hypnosis as you do. They don't know an induction from a deepener. By jumping between icebreakers and inductions, everything can be framed as an experiment (some of them entertaining in their own right) and nobody really notices or cares when you fail.

I'll tell you a little secret. When you fail to hypnotise someone, there is one response you will hear more than any other. One word:

"Sorry."

THEY apologise to YOU. Does this make you feel any better?

4. Don't go for dramatic inductions

So you've seen everything from arm-pulls to drop-backs, to neck-snapping head-twists and you're keen to drop people on the dirty ground to gasps from the gathered crowd?

Do us all a favour, stay away from hypnosis and go take some martial arts classes.

Instead, do gentle inductions with the participant seated on a bench, a low wall or that chair you remembered to bring along with you.

By gentle inductions, I mean something like a simple Elman Eye Closure or Magnetic Hands which relies on the focus, imagination and concentration of the participant rather than a shock induction.

If you do insist on having your subject stand at some point, remember when you tell them "Sleep!" they might fall over so get them to sit down again before saying it or say "Sleep and Stand!" instead but be prepared to catch them anyway.

5. Treat your subjects with respect

I find the best attitude to have towards those we can easily hypnotise (and utilise to entertain others) is to consider them very talented individuals.

That really is the best way to view those we call "somnambulist."

Without them, there would be no stage shows, no entertainment and let's face it, no hypnotists.

So treat them as such. Make their comfort, pride and safety of paramount importance and in return you will inevitably get the best out of them.
Try not to be annoyed with your star participant when suggestions aren't carried out successfully (which could and does happen) and keep your hypnotist/hypnotee relationship on an even keel by requesting simple acts of compliance between suggestions.

Make them smile, laugh and feel great and others from the crowd will soon emerge wanting to feel the same.

6. Define your performance area

Stage hypnosis has followed a successful basic formula for decades. It involves performing in a defined area (the stage) in front of a group of spectators (the audience) from which people are invited to join the performer in the defined performance area and become a part of the show.

So when you do a street performance, bear all this in mind but also watch other types of street performer to see how they do it.

As well as making for a safer performance in an area away from cars and other potential hazards (and by being able to tell your participant not to wander outside of the area) you'll look more professional and find it easier to attract a crowd.

7. Remember it is a performance/demonstration

Not much point speaking quietly or whispering in the ear of your volunteer.

People will quickly lose interest and won't stick around to watch you if they can't hear what it is you're saying.

So remember you have an audience (or soon will) and deliver suggestions so that everyone can hear exactly what's going on.

Also make sure you interact regularly with the spectators and maybe also get your volunteer to interact with them too.

8. Make it a personal experience for the person

Find out what kinds of suggestion they enjoy best or perform best, use their name, occupation, home town or other personal details.

If you're experienced in such matters then also offer to deal with something for them (motivation or minor issues without going into the underlying cause.)

9. Do a proper wake-up

You can't always be sure what's going to happen when the person has left you, so ALWAYS go through a clear and consistent wake-up procedure with them before they go.

A good wake-up will leave them feeling refreshed, happy and clear headed and remember to be smiling yourself when they open their eyes. Nobody wants to see a concerned or confused looking hypnotist during this still-suggestible time.Always be sure to give a general suggestion to clear any silly suggestions you might have given them. Even if you cleared each suggestion after it was carried out, do it here too, as an extra safety measure.

10. Give them a business card/contact details

What? You don't have one? Truly? How do you expect anybody else to take you seriously? Better go back to juggling, card tricks or accountancy!

Fun With Re-inductions – Reg Blackwood

http://www.regblackwood.com

Over the next few minutes I'll be covering the following things:

First I'll talk about exactly what a re-induction is and how it's commonly used. Then I'll talk about the best times to use a re-induction for entertainment hypnosis. Then finally, we'll look at how you can be creative with re-inductions and use them as the basis for an infinite number of street or stage hypnosis skits and routines.

So, once we've performed our initial induction and deepening and have someone hypnotised, we can instantaneously drop them back into hypnosis very quickly, usually with the single word command "Sleep." This is what's commonly known as re-induction.

Now I don't have to tell you that re-induction can be a great way to practice rapid and instant induction techniques, at least until we have enough confidence to use them first off, but really all reinduction is, is the subject acting on a post hypnotic suggestion.

In its simplest form, a post hypnotic suggestion can be broken down as:
When X happens, You'll do Y.

In a re-induction, the form of this post hypnotic suggestion is usually something like "When I say the word Sleep, your eyes will close and you'll instantly drop back into hypnosis, even deeper than before." (Why not put a bit of fractionation in there too?!) *Note: Ok, please let's just conveniently ignore for a moment the fact that the formal set-up of such a post hypnotic suggestion for re-induction isn't always necessary.*

In entertainment hypnosis, be it street or stage hypnosis, I've noticed that spectators seem to enjoy these dramatic drops into hypnosis almost as much as any other phenomena we perform. They enjoy seeing people, often their friends and family functioning fairly normally one second then the very next second, apparently slumped over in a hypnotic state.

In my experience, the most dramatic and well timed re-inductions can often get the occasional gasp or at the very least a bit of a laugh from those watching.

So knowing this, we can use our Post Hypnotic Suggestion for re-induction at times during the performance when we know we'll gain the most dramatic or comic effect from it. The more animated or louder the subject is at the point the "sleep command" is issued, the greater the contrast and the better the dramatic or comic effect.

Let's take the popular stage hypnosis routine of having a hypnotised subject believe they are not really hypnotised. We encourage the subject to protest that they're definitely not nor have they ever been hypnotised and then suddenly issue the sleep command when they're mid-sentence. Well, I like to take this one step further in a routine I call "The Critic" during which I encourage a particularly vocal subject to openly criticise the very show they're a part of. I get them to criticise the town, the venue, the spectators, I get them to criticise the other participants and then finally, building to somethig of a crescendo, I encourage them to criticise me

the hypnotist and my technique. Then, just when they're beginning to get really personal (as they often do) and the spectators are starting to show concern for my fragile ego: "Sleep!" I've managed to get an entertaining 5 minute routine for street or stage hypnosis out of what is essentially, if you look at the amount of work I had to do, just a simple re-induction.

Of course, you'll want to adjust the wording of this and any other suggestions I mention here to suit your own style of hypnosis.

Now, we can get really creative with this and really have some fun because, as a hypnotist, we can transfer that sleep command to someone or something else.

You might have seen an effect where the hypnotist "transfers his powers" (in quotes) to some other person. "When this person points at you and says 'sleep'" etc. etc.

Well, I have a teddy bear which I use for a re-induction during my stage show. The bear is a children's toy which has a voice recorder in it onto which I have recorded my voice saying "sleep!" I give him a theatrical introduction and he's brought onto the stage by an assistant. Then I reinduce each subject in turn by squeezing the teddy bears paw and making him utter "Sleep!" For extra comic effect, I'll suggest to one person they'll realise all of the other people on stage were just instantly hypnotised by a teddy bear, but oh no, not them. They are the only person who wasn't.

Then of course, when they're suitably animated about that fact, I use the teddy bear to instantly hypnotise or reinduce them. Again.

What I've done here, is started out with what could have been just a simple group re-induction lasting a few seconds. However, by giving hypno-teddy a dramatic, over the top introduction, introducing the conflict element described above, adding a little bit of coaxing, persuading and carefully crafted suggestion into the mix. I've managed to flesh it out out into a pretty funny 10 minute routine.

Let's consider some other ways the word sleep could be introduced to a subject with a carefully worded suggestion:

We could do this by giving a suggestion and then giving the subject a letter to open – a letter which contains the word sleep. This would give the appearance of being hypnotised by mail. We could have one of those LED message fans onto which we've programmed the word sleep – that's a nice visual one. With the right suggestion, we could even reinduce someone by text message. So. Not just by teddy bear.

Now, if we bear in mind (sorry I couldn't resist that one) If we bear in mind that re-induction is just a post hypnotic suggestion to sleep (when X happens you'll do Y) and Y in the case of a reinduction is the suggestion to instantly sleep, the X part of the equation doesn't have to even have to mention introducing or presenting the actual command "sleep." It can be just about anything.

You've probably already seen "When I scratch my nose, you'll sleep." but why stop there?

I like to transfer it to something external, something that might happen spontaneously or something that's outside of the subject's control.

Let's have a look at the variations of our post hypnotic suggestion for re-induction we have available to us, without even having to say or present the command sleep to our subjects:

We have:

"when I or you do X you'll sleep" or

"when I or person A does X you'll sleep" or

"when I or person A SAYS X you'll sleep"

but we also have the much more general "when X happens you'll sleep." And X can be an infinite number of things.

Here's a few examples:

When that door opens you'll sleep.

When that person lifts their glass, you'll sleep.

When this egg timer runs out you'll sleep.

When this remote control device moves, you'll sleep.

When this pop up toy pops up, you'll sleep.

Endless, entertaining routines just from a simple re-induction, limited only by your imagination.

Need a few more to get you thinking? Ok. How about these:

Dominoes re-induction – when the person next to you falls against you, you'll sleep. - You can start at one end of the line and create a nice chain reaction along the line, like dominoes or a mexican wave of hypnosis.

Count to 100 in your head, but whenever you reach 50, you'll instantly sleep, I'll have to wake you and you'll have lost your place and have to start counting again from 1 – this is great to keep a subject occupied while you're working with others. The spectator's laughter will hopefully let you know when the subject has reached 50 and dozed off.

You could also have a reverse alarm clock – Normally an alarm clock wakes you up, but when this one rings or bleeps, you'll instantly sleep. Then set the timer and watch the fun.

Hold your breath and the instant you let any breath escape you'll instantly sleep. If you can make them laugh, they'll let out breath, follow your suggestion and down they go.

But even if you're not that adventurous you could just get someone to recite a children's nursery rhyme, suggesting that when they get to a particular word, they'll sleep.

Or a variation on that would be to react to someone else reciting a nursery rhyme, you could have a whole group of subjects reacting that way to somebody else's recital.If your interest is Street Hypnosis and you want to upload videos to really get people thinking, I would imagine you could create some nice looking videos from the following scenarios:

Give the following suggestion to a hypnotised subject:

When you walk past that public telephone over there, you'll be convinced you hear it ringing and want to answer it. But when you do answer it, after a couple of seconds you'll realise there's nobody there and you'll instantly sleep. (Now, you start recording after this and just overdub the sound of a telephone ringing during editing.)

Be careful with the safety aspect of this one as the subject is away from you, so be sure to suggest that they'll slip into hypnosis easily, comfortably and safely and won't suddenly fall over as there's a real possibility they could hurt themselves.

or

In a minute, I'll approach you and you'll greet me as if you've never met me before, as if you've never been hypnotised but whenever I hand you this plastic drink bottle, you'll be instantly hypnotised again, your eyes will remain open but you'll happily give me your watch, wallet, phone and house keys or anything else I ask for. Then when I say "you're fine" you'll wake up and wander off in the other direction, only realising what just happened when you get a few yards down the road.

Then, you send them off and only then do you start to record.

If you're really brave and clever, you could also film a companion video where the person you approach isn't pre-hypnotised and you'll almost definitely fail. But guess what? That doesn't matter because this will just convince your viewers that it's real and not always a sure thing.

In fact, some of you might have already seen some videos reminiscent of those last ones.

Obviously, as I've already said, if you do use any of these examples, you'll want to adjust the wording of the suggestions to suit your own performance style. For example I would usually also add "nod your head if you understand" and wait for the nodding response.

So, let's just summarise what I've talked about.

I've talked about what re-induction is and how it's commonly used. Then I gave you some tips about the best times to use a re-induction for entertainment hypnosis. Then finally I told you how easy it is to be really creative with re-inductions and use them as the basis for an infinite number of street or stage hypnosis skits and routines, limited only by your imagination.

Hopefully, through all of this, I've also helped to get your creative juices flowing.

(Transcribed from an audio recording.)

JENNAS THUMB THING

Description

With a few carefully selected words, the performer uses a magnetic influence to quickly and dramatically affect, from a distance, the hand movements of any number of people, from a single spectator to an audience of many.

The performer can decide for themselves whether they frame this flexible and visual effect as an explanation of genuine, ideomotor movement, an experiment in real subconscious and hypnotic manipulation or as a mysterious demonstration of psychic influence.

It can be delivered either to a single spectator or an entire theatre audience and can even be used as a demonstration on the television or radio where the home audience participate and experience it for themselves.

Completely hands-off and open-eyed, it is suitable as an icebreaker, a replacement for traditional suggestibilty tests or as a pre-cursor to an hypnotic induction, even in a therapeutic or client reading setting.

Explanation

This nice little hypnosis-style effect relies on eye fixation, imagination, suggestion and the ideomotor effect.

Although the spectator is entirely responsible for causing any movement, like with pendulum effects, because they are doing it subconsciously on such a minute level, many remain consciously unaware of that.

The following is delivered confidently, noting where the language used encourages disassociation by referring, for example, to *the* thumb or *that* thumb, not *your* thumb.

Script

Take your non-dominant hand and put up your thumb like this, just as if you're giving somebody the 'thumbs-up' sign.

Keep your elbow bent and relaxed, away from your body, lean forwards slightly and raise the thumb to eye level.

Let the fingers relax slightly so the fingertips are no longer pressing against your palm and let them part slightly so they're no longer in contact with each other.

Keep your eyes focused on the the thumb-nail or the creases of the knuckle and don't look anywhere else.

Ordinarily, that thumb would start to lower as muscle strain sets in. However we can counter that by handing the thumb over to your subconscious mind with some disassociative thoughts.

All you need do, as you focus on that thumb, is imagine you're looking at somebody else's thumb. It's no longer your thumb.

See it as if you are focusing on somebody else's thumb and as if you're seeing that thumb for the first time.

And notice that it just floats there in space in front of you without any conscious effort and already it doesn't even feel like it's yours any more.

And because you've done such a good job of imagining that it's somebody else's thumb, you've handed it over to your subconscious mind, it could just stay there all day, without any effort at all.

So watch what happens when I speak directly to your subconscious mind and simply say:

IT MOVES LEFT, *left, left, left, left.*

That's right! It moves over to the left, as you follow it with your eyes.

Are you making that happen yourself?
No. You're really not are you? Isn't that amazing?

Keep focusing on it. And I can also say

Right, right, right, right, right

and watch as that thumb begins to move in the opposite direction!

And I can say

Up, up, up, up, up

and it follows that suggestion too.

So when I say **stop** *you can just look away from your thumb now and give your hand a good shake as your thumb returns to your conscious control.*

Great!

Note

Because this effect won't work for everyone, it can indicate those in a group who might make good hypnotic subjects and make for interesting discussions about why it worked for some and not for others.

While delivering the directional suggestions, if the performer is in close proximity to the spectator(s) (or a camera) the movements can often be enhanced by making encouraging, beckoning gestures to guide their hand.

The experienced hypnotist will also see how this can lead naturally into an induction by encouraging the thumb to drift down toward the lap, the spectator closing their eyes and drifting down with it.

Many thanks to the very magnetic Jenna Fewings for devising this piece for a recent radio appearance and for allowing me to publish it on her behalf.

Reg Blackwood October 2012 http://regblackwood.com

Two Minute Handlock – Reg Blackwood

The Hypnotic Handlock is something of a "Waking Hypnosis" classic which is often used as a "selection test" for audience members at the beginning of a stage show. It helps convince a participant of their ability to be Hypnotized and can easily be converted into an instant induction.

For the Hypnotist and subject, it is an effective icebreaker, a demonstration of acceptance of suggestion and an indication of what can be achieved using the singularity of thought required for Hypnosis.

Here is the transcript for the Two Minute Handlock:

All Hypnosis is, is concentration, imagination and focus.

Can you focus and can you concentrate?

I want you to focus on the knuckles of your thumbs.

Don't focus anywhere else.

What I want you to do now is lock your mind around a single idea.

And that single idea is that these hands are becoming tighter and tighter and tighter.

That's right and you can feel the fingers on each of the hands pressing against the backs of the opposite hands.

Let them become tighter and tighter and tighter simply by you using the power of your imagination and focusing on those knuckles, those fingers become tighter and tighter, locking those palms together.

Bonding them together.

And now it's like I've spread glue over all of those fingers and under here under the palms and it's just locking those fingers tighter and tighter.

Just by listening to the sound of my voice none of the sounds around you bother or concern you as you continue that level of focus.

Brilliant. Wonderful job!

And now it's almost like they're carved from a single block of wood.

Fantastic.

A single block of wood and they just get tighter and tighter and tighter and tighter.

And now it's like they're steel, like they're made of steel and you can feel those fingers pressing even harder.

Getting tighter and tighter and tighter so in a second, even if you want to take them apart.

What happens, as soon as you try, is you find they just get tighter and tighter and tighter.

On three.

1

Feel them getting tighter now as that moment approaches.

Feel them getting harder and harder because you know on 3 as soon as you try, try and seperate them they just get tighter and tighter because of the power of your imagination.

2

Getting even tighter now because on

3

Try and find that you can't pull them apart, they just get tighter and tighter and tighter.

That's great you're doing a brilliant job, now look at me.

Stop thinking about it and they just relax. Pretty cool eh?

•SUGGESTIBILITY TESTS

By: Dr. Jonathan Royle – www.UltimateHypnosisCourse.com

"I want you to imagine in your minds eye that I've just cut a lemon into two halves. I have then picked up one half of this bitter, sour, horrible, juicy lemon and placed it into my mouth at which time I've sucked all the bitter, sour juice from inside it and now all that bitter, sour, citric lemon juice is now running down my throat!"

"OK now, TRY to whistle! I bet you can't, in fact I bet your mouth is now awash with saliva making the action of whistling impossible. In fact if you truly imagined what I suggested for you, this will indeed have occurred in reality and by the way this is an example of a most simple suggestibility test!"

•<u>THIS IS AN EXAMPLE OF THE POWER OF SUGGESTION</u>

In this short chapter we will deal with the subject of Suggestibility tests. All of these work due to the word TRY as detailed in the previous chapter and indeed also due to the law of reversed effort, an element of pure suggestion and the persons ability to be suggestible to this comes into play also.

These suggestibility tests are used whilst the subject is fully conscious at the start of your act or therapy session if desired in order that you can easily and quickly decide which of the people will make the best hypnotic subjects. Some hypnotists perform these tests upon the entire audience at once and then ask those it works on to come forward to the stage and these people are then narrowed down to the best subjects who are then used in the show.

Others who are more confident of their skills ask for volunteers to come up to the stage and then they do the tests only on those onstage volunteers, the logic behind this being that one sincere volunteer is worth one hundred pressed men. So either way should be most successful for you if presented correctly, confidently and believably.

I would however in your early days advise you to do these tests upon the entire audience, as then the law of averages will be in your favour. Don't forget, the more people there are in your audience by far the more chance you have of getting more people under hypnosis.

It really is all just a numbers game at the end of the day. Incidentally, as in your early days you will be working in pubs and clubs to audiences of about 80 to 150 people you will not have the advantage of 2000 people in a theatre to choose your subjects from and so in these situations the suggestibility tests are an essential part of your show and should be done on the entire audience.

When your career develops and you move onto larger capacity venues, you will then be able to safely and confidently ask for volunteers who wish to be hypnotised to come forward to the stage before you have even done any suggestibility tests.

Once upon the stage these volunteers are subjected to the tests and the best reacting subjects are singled out to be hypnotised. Remember that in a theatre which seats 1000 to 2000 people when you ask for volunteers at the start you will get around 80 to 100 people coming up to the stage. Not only does this look dramatic and impressive to the rest of the audience, but also effectively it means your volunteers each of who is worth a hundred pressed men wants to be hypnotised.

In a theatre situation, you will have almost as many volunteers on stage as would be in the entire audience during the early days of your career in pubs and small clubs! So you see, it really is all down to the law of averages and the numbers game. In general your shows will always be more successful in large capacity venues such as night-clubs and theatres than those held in pubs and social clubs.

Don't let this deter you though, as upon having read this course you WILL be able to do an excellent show in pubs and clubs until you progress to the larger venues. The only problem, or should I say difference there is really between working in a pub and a theatre, is that in a theatre they have paid to come and see you and so you are the main thing of importance and alcohol comes second and will only be available in the interval anyway!

●WHEREAS IN A PUBLIC HOUSE

They have come to have a few pints and you the poor entertainer have got to work really hard to keep their attention. Also in pubs it is not wise to let your show start too late as, due to the drinking and the fact people who are drunk cannot be hypnotised, it is wise your show starts before they have all had one to many to drink.

Some of the components that make up these suggestibility tests or the induction's which follow later are of a physiological and/or physical nature. In other words, in many of the cases if you got them to do as I describe then it would be physically impossible to separate their hands or open their eyes even without the verbal suggestion element coming into play!

However as these tests are all presented in a manner which makes the subject believe that whatever occurs is due to our suggestions, when these things do occur for whatever reason whether physical, physiological or suggestion, the subject comes to believe that it was all due to your suggestions and so will more readily accept and react to any future "genuine" suggestions that we may give them.

In other cases such as in the induction's detailed later, due to natural physiological causes, they may be made to feel dizzy or disorientated and because we know this always happens and is a natural feeling we can suggest that it will happen before it actually does happen of its own accord. Then when it does occur, as indeed it will, the subject always believes our verbal suggestions to have been the cause of what they now are feeling and/or experiencing and so in turn this compounds their belief in our powers even more and from that moment any "genuine" suggestions will always get a successful response as the subject is now conditioned to belief they will and expect they will work and so in turn they will.

So hopefully, you now see that little known naturally occurring phenomenon are used by the hypnotist to make the subject experience strange sensations which the subject then connects to your suggestions and as a direct result, increases their belief in your powers and takes them further down into the trance state.

Examine closely all the suggestibility tests and induction's which I teach you and you will, without fail, see that each one has an element of it either being guaranteed to happen or of some part, feeling or sensation being guaranteed to occur which the subject then comes to believe are due to your verbal suggestions and in turn cements into their mind the belief and expectancy that all future suggestions will indeed be 100% effective also.

These suggestibility tests also get the subjects to focus their attention and concentration onto one thing which of course you will also command them to do later when inducing the trance state. This conditions them to react in a certain way when asked certain things and makes your overall job easier.

So I suppose we should really call these suggestibility tests pre-induction's or light induction's as when anyone is focusing or concentrating on one thing they are in effect in a very light hypnotic state. This is because the key element of trance is fixation of attention and concentration on one point of focus.

It almost goes without saying that the people who's hands lock together are better subjects than those whose don't! So what? Well in a pub or club situation you will probably have only about 8 or 10 people come up with their hands locked together and so it would be wise here to hypnotise as many of these as possible before asking for other volunteers if needed. On theatre shows however you will have loads of people with their hands locked together so how do you choose which will be the best subjects to use?

Well very obviously those people whose hands are shaking violently as opposed to just locked together are by far the most suggestible subjects, as indeed they have so far reacted better to your suggestions than anyone else.

To narrow down the numbers even more remember always that one volunteer is worth a hundred pressed men so first of all return anyone to the audience who does not wish to remain there.

Next you would of course eliminate people who seem drunk or high on drugs, people who appear under the age of 18, anyone who looks petrified being on stage and lastly if there are enough people on stage with their hands locked together those people who just volunteered without their hands being locked together. However, where numbers are smaller than usual, the volunteers without hands locked together are used as potential hypnotic subjects also.

From the remainder, the "handshakers" are excellent subjects. Next, those people who have been hypnotised before on stage or by a therapist are easy to place into trance also and then it's a matter of observation.

Although experience of performing will give you an almost sixth sense of who to pick here follow some important signs to look for which are indicative of a potentially good subject. Those that take what you say seriously and appear to concentrate on things when you tell them to, appear to do as you say when you tell them to and generally seem sincere in their efforts will also make excellent subjects.

The reason for this being that hypnosis is co-operation and not confrontation. Also during your initial banter/patter with the on stage volunteers, the answers they give to your questions will on many occasions give you an indication of who will make a good subject and who won't! For example those who have been hypnotised before in the past can usually be made to enter trance just by commanding them to close their eyes and Sleep!

If the people have been hypnotised successfully before, even if it was not by you, then as they have entered the state of trance before, know how it feels and know what to expect and how to react they will make the most excellent of subjects and can be placed instantly back into trance as their belief and expectancy in the powers of hypnosis is 100% complete and based on prior practical experience of being hypnotised.

They have experienced the state of hypnosis before so they know it exists and now they just need a catalyst if you like, to renter the state and you serve this purpose for them. With these kind of people it is often as easy as snapping your fingers in front of their face and saying sleep to make them enter trance with ease.

So what actual visual clues are there that people are indeed doing as you suggest and taking it all seriously? Well basically, it's a case of using your common sense here. If they do as you say the moment that you suggest it, then obviously they are taking it seriously and are concentrating on your instructions and so in turn are a potentially very good subject. For example, if you suggest that their hands are getting tighter and tighter together all the time and you can visually see that their hands are turning red with the pressure they are using to squeeze their hands together then obviously they are reacting well to your suggestions.

Having given you all this guidance, it is however true to say that the selection of who to use is something that each person must master for themselves through practical experience.

Body language plays a part, those that will be good subjects will usually have similar patterns of body language which of course you will learn through hands on practical experience. Basically however, having used the correct patter to open the show and due to all the other psychological elements in our favour as discussed earlier, if you are adaptable and suit your induction to the personality of your subject then you can hypnotise given enough time EVERY PERSON that steps onto your stage.

Anyway, enough about what the suggestibility test is used for or how to spot potentially good subjects, lets now explain a few actual suggestibility tests, which can be used to narrow down the selection process. This is all "Waking State" hypnosis if you like and does demonstrate to the watching and participating audience that all suggestion correctly expressed does have a most powerful effect.

THE ARM DROP TEST

This test, if used at all, is used right at the start to find which people in the audience are already in a nicely relaxed state and as such would make potentially good subjects for use upon the stage, it also shows you which members of the audience are able to relax when they want to, as once again these type of people make excellent subjects. You get everyone to close their left hand into a fist and then to extend their left forefinger so that it points up in the air. They are then told to place the lower part of their right arm (near the wrist) resting upon the top of their extended left forefinger. They are told to allow the full weight of their right arm to be supported by the forefinger of their left hand. Next they are told to relax every muscle in their bodies and especially in their right arm so that all the weight of the right arm rests upon the left forefinger. You explain that you will now count to three and that on the count of three they are to pull their left forefinger away from under their right arm rapidly. You count 1,2,3, and on the count of three they take their fingers away. The people who are able to relax best and have followed your instructions to the letter will find that having allowed the weight of their right arm to rest fully upon the left fingertip, that upon removal of the left hand's finger, their right arm will immediately fall into their laps like a sack of potatoes.

Their arm will have fallen, as it will be limp, loose, relaxed and heavy and that's what you are looking for, the people who have relaxed easily in this manner. Those who did not react due to not relaxing enough will probably have remained with their right arm still suspended in the air upon removal of the finger or at least it would have fallen far more slowly into their laps than the really suggestible people. So in this test the idea is just to see who can relax quickly when asked to and indeed those people whose hands fell into their laps rapidly have passed this test with flying colours! This one is not a suggestibility test as such it's more a way to see who follows your instructions to the letter and who can relax easily. I would therefore use at least one actual suggestibility test such as the handclasp after this experiment prior to inducing the Trance State in order to ensure success.

FINGERS CLOSING TEST

This is a suggestibility text of a natural type. By "Natural Type" I mean that what occurs would do anyway for most people automatically without any suggestions, so it's a physical trick, if you like, but this instils more belief into them prior to the handclasp test. You ask them to interlock their fingers so that the fingers of the left hand are against the back of the right hand, and the fingers of the left hand are against the back of the left hand. Palms pressed tightly together and thumbs resting on top of their interlocked fingers just as in the handclasp text, which is fully detailed with complete explanation and patter in the "Know your lines" chapter of this course.

You then ask them to extend their two forefingers, so that the tips of each outstretched finger are touching. They are then told to separate the tips of the fingers by about an inch and a half, and lastly they are told to stare directly at you and not at their hands. You yourself have got your hands in the same position as their hands, as you suggest that by the count of 3 their fingers will be touching just as they were beforehand, that should the try to keep them apart then the fingers will just draw nearer and nearer together. You then count as follows:-

A It's almost as though there are strong magnets on the tips of your fingers, drawing them together, more and more, bringing them nearer together.

B They are getting so close now, that they are almost touching as those magnets become so powerful and pull your fingertips together. And on,

C The magnets are so powerful that your fingertips are now touching.

N.B.

As you do this, you close your own two fingers together slowly, so that by the time you say the number three, your own fingertips are touching. Many will take this as a non verbal suggestion that their own fingers are getting closer together.

You then get the people who's fingertips were touching by the count of three to place a hand up, this makes it easier for you to gauge the response level which with this test is usually extremely high. At the end of the fingers closing test, you can then go into:

THE HANDCLASP TEST

The way to do this is fully detailed in the "Know your Lines" part, so it is not necessary to repeat it all.

I will however, mention how it can be used differently when working in smaller venues where there is not enough room to have lots of people coming to join you on the performance area.

In these cases, you would carry out the test as described in the earlier chapter until you have counted up to 20 and given all the suggestions. At this point, you would say, "OK now, everyone, still believing in the worlds strongest superglue which sticks your hands tightly together, I'd like you to try and separate your hands (law of reversed effort takes effect here), but you'll find the harder you try to separate them the more they will stick together tightly. OK, now, try. (give them a few seconds then say) Right, that's enough, just relax your hands now and stop trying." Those people who's hands are now still stuck together I'd like you to stand up, because if you don't, your hands will be like this for three weeks, when they'll turn blue and drop off. Also anyone else who just found their hands difficult to separate who wishes to experience the state of hypnosis, please come this way towards me.

N.B.

In this way of using the text, obviously fewer people will end up with hands locked together. However, it solves the limited space problem. Those who's hands are shaking are usually the best subjects, those with hands just locked together, next best and those whose hands separate, but it was harder to do than usual come next in order of preference and lastly, those people who just volunteered to take part anyway. Remember though, as with anything in life, there will always be exceptions to the rules and as such, you must always use your common sense and learn to think on your feet.

In all methods of using the test, here is how to separate their hands for them. You simply suggest that the moment you tap them on the back of the hands their hands will spring apart, as if two magnets were repelling each other. You then go round to each person whose hands you wish to separate and touch them on the back of the hands, whilst at the same time, saying to each of them, "It's O.K. now you can separate your hands, you CAN separate your hands."

Just as imagination allowed them to stick together due to suggestion, so it will also allow them to part due to suggestion. Usually most people would separate all the subject's hands and then do the induction's on them. As you will have noticed in the "Know you Lines" chapter, on large theatre shows only, I separate their hands straight away, if I wish to return them to the audience, or, if I wish to use one of the induction's from the next chapter which requires them to have their hands separate at the time. Otherwise, I would place them into trance via the falling backwards induction, using the patter as detailed in "Know your Lines". Their hands would still be locked together and they would be held against their chest area. This being to case, the top half of their body would now be much heavier than the rest of their body, and, as such, they are now going to find it much harder to stop themselves falling backwards into your arms, when you start the induction of falling backwards. Once on the floor with their eyes closed, I would suggest to them, that their eyes will remain tightly closed at all times until I say otherwise and then, that when I take hold of their arms, their hands will immediately separate. The moment you have said this you take hold of their arms, one in each hand and say, "OK just separate your hands now." The moment they separate their hands, you use this as an opportunity to deepen the light trance they are in by saying, "The moment I drop your arms to the floor, it will not disturb you, in fact, it will serve to send you deeper to sleep, 10 times deeper to sleep" (then drop their arms to floor as you say) "Sleep and Relax".

LIGHT AND HEAVY HANDS TEST

With this test, the audience is told to close their eyes and extend their two arms out straight in front of themselves at the same level. You now suggest to them that their left hand has got a pile of heavy books upon it, which are so heavy, that their hand is being pushed downwards.

You then suggest that tied to the middle finger of their right hand is a large helium filled balloon which is pulling their right hand high up into the air, as it floats ever upwards.

You keep suggesting things along these lines, that the left hand holds the heavy books and right hand is being pulled up into the air by the helium balloon.

You will find that the people who really are open to suggestion, will allow their arms to react accordingly. As such, their left hand will move downwards, as if a heavy pile of books is upon it, and their right hand will move upwards, as if tied to a helium filled balloon. You then tell everyone to open their eyes, and many will be amazed to find that their arms are now in very different positions with a huge gap between them both.

THE PERFUME BOTTLE TEST

You remove a fancy cut glass bottle from your pocket and explain that it contains the most powerfully scented perfume in the world. You state that, in a few moments, you will remove the lid of the bottle and allow the scent to travel around the room for everyone to smell, as it really is that strong.

You tell everyone to raise their hand into the air the second they smell the scent come their way, which, as it's so potent, will take only a few seconds. The bottle's lid is then removed and the people start to raise their hands, once several hands are in the air you explain that the power of suggestion has worked upon them, and in fact the bottle contains nothing more than water, with a little added food colouring. You then drink the contents to prove your point and people will be amazed as they will swear they smelt the scent travel around the room, trust me, this does, if presented convincingly, work.

WARM FINGERS TEXT

This is sometimes used prior to the handclasp text. You have them place their arms outstretched in front of them, and get them to place their hands flat against each other, you then command them to start rubbing their hands backwards and forwards against each other, as quickly as they can. You say you'll count from 3 to 1. All the time they are to keep rubbing their hands together and, if they concentrate, then by the count of 1 their hands will be getting hot and sticky, as if coated with superglue. You then say 3, getting hotter and hotter, 2, the hotter they get, the more sticky they become, and the more sticky they become, the hotter they will get, and on 1, just interlock your fingers like this (you then demonstrate how they should put their hands for the handclasp test, which you immediately go into). OK everyone, as you hold your hands interlocked, the warmth and stickiness you felt, is already locking them tightly together (you then go into normal patter for handclasp).

Now just to explain briefly, the idea of his test is that if you rub your hands back and forth against each other rapidly, they do indeed become hot and sticky. But, as this is so obvious, people don't realise this to be the case and attribute it to your suggestions, which not only gives them a greater belief in your powers, but as they feel their hands are hot and sticky, do not be surprised if it becomes easier for them to believe that there is super glue on their hands, sticking them together tightly.

THE ORDER OF TESTS TO BE DONE

So, in your very early days when you lack confidence in yourself, you may wish to use all the tests, if you do however, please ensure you do them rapidly, as you're meant to be a dynamic showman and not a boring lecturer. So the order of tests would go:

1 Arm drop text
2 Finger closing test
3 Warm fingers test
4 Handclasp test
5 Actual induction of Hypnotic Trance

The psychology behind them being placed in this order being that:

ARMDROP TEST

This shows you which can relax easily and quickly, and which do exactly as you tell them to, it's just a relaxation exercise, however it gets them used to doing as you say.

THE FINGERS CLOSING TEST

It is natural for the fingers to close together anyway and, you will have a high success rate with this, the success of it then increasing their belief in your powers.

WARM FINGERS TEST

This takes but a matter of seconds to do prior to the handclasp and should, as just described, take the belief in your powers, another step further.

THE HANDCLASP TEST

By now they BELIEVE in you, and EXPECT it to work, so you should have a high success rate here.

THE ACTUAL INDUCTION

As the people you are using, have probably reacted successfully to tests 1, 2, 3 and 4, you can be sure as they are now conditioned to do as you say, they will enter the Hypnotic Trance.

GAIN PRACTICAL EXPERIENCE A.S.A.P

Do as many shows as possible, as soon as possible and once you've gained confidence in your skills, you will then be able to speed up the whole process. By then, just coming onto the stage, doing your opening talk and then going straight into the handclasp test from which you induce the Hypnotic Trance state in your volunteers.

The only thing which you may not quite have now, which will enable you to do this, is 100% faith in yourself and your new skill. But, if you have already got this faith, then start out like a master and just proceed as if you're a very experienced hypnotist (after all the audience doesn't know). I will end this chapter by telling you of a "Handclasp" style test in which it is, if they do as you say, physically impossible for 99% of people to separate their hands. This art which is unknown to the general public means:

A   You are guaranteed a high percentage of people who can't separate their hands when asked to try, and

B   It ensures that their belief in your powers is then greatened, so that it becomes extremely easy to place them into the trance state.

I personally use this method of "Handclasp" at the start of the second half of my theatre show, in order to get some new people upon the stage, whom

I can then use to demonstrate how I am able to place between 12 and 40 people or more into trance in less than sixty seconds. Have fun using it, it's also a great way to quickly establish your credentials and a volunteers belief in you when at a party etc. before placing them into trance to demonstrate your art.

THE GUARANTEED HANDCLASP TEST

With this you stretch your arms out with palms facing yourself. Fingers wide open and thumbs up in the air. Bend wrist, so that although arms are out stretched, palms are facing your body. Interlock your fingers and push in together as closely as you can. Turn thumbs towards you, until back of your hands are facing you. Now push arms out hard, until elbows crack, and push your palms away from you as much as you can. Now I will count to three, and on the count of three, your hands will be stuck fast together, and in fact, the harder you try to pull them apart, the more they will stick together tight so on 1, staring directly at the backs of your hands as they stick together, tighter and tighter. 2, just lift your hands up above your head now and push your palms up towards the clouds, as high up into the sky as you possibly can and on 3, keep pushing your hands up high into the sky, and now just try to separate your hands, the harder you try, they stick tighter together.

(GIVE THEM A FEW SECONDS THEN SAY)

OK, just relax and keep your hands together as they are until I say otherwise. OK, everyone, firstly I'd like you all to stand up where you are so that we can all have a good look at each other, now walk this way, towards the stage, and I promise you, I will not keep you up here if you don't want to take part.

N.B

At this point, loads of people will come towards the stage and as they do so you say:

"OK everyone, the moment I touch your hands, they will immediately spring apart and it will feel as though you've received a slight harmless electric shock in your arms."

You then quickly, go to each person and knock the underside of their arms firmly and sharply, so that their hands do indeed spring apart. For anyone who still keeps their hands together, just get them to reverse the procedure which got their hands into this position in the first place. From those who do come up to have their hands separated, you ask for volunteers to take part in a quick 3 minute test after which they may return to the audience. You get between 12 to 24 people to come up, dependant on the stage size etc. and the rest of the people are now returned to the audience to a round of applause.

It is at this point, that the 12 to 24 people are lined up in a straight line, when you can follow the details in the next chapter, in order to be able to place all of them into a trance in less than sixty seconds. That's about 2 to 3 seconds per person only to get them into an instant deep hypnotic trance. And that's where this chapter ends. In the next chapter, I will reveal what you have all been waiting for, and that's the secrets of the actual induction methods used to place people into trance. So hold onto your seats and leave your misconceptions behind, as we enter the hypnotic world, where there really are NO LIMITS.

For now, good luck practising the art of suggestions and the tests, as outlined in this chapter,

NOTE = The Section above was extracted from "The Encyclopedia of Hypnotherapy, Stage-Hypnosis and Complete Mind Therapy" Volume One by Dr. Jonathan Royle which is available from Amazon.

Www.UltimateHypnosisCourse.com

Ten Reasons Most Street Hypnotists Are Doing It All Wrong

By: Reg Blackwood

http://www.regblackwood.com

Back when I first started doing Street Hypnosis, there were only three or four of us in the entire world doing it. Now it seems there are Street Hypnotists everywhere and looking at the way most of them do it, that's really not a good thing.

On a recent trip to the UK, I managed to get licensed by a local council to perform Street Hypnosis legally, under the 1952 Hypnotism Act, in designated areas of the city. I'm highly trained, highly experienced and (I like to think) highly entertaining, so never thought it would be an issue. But as I'm only resident in the UK for short periods, the legality of Street Hypnosis is for someone else's soapbox. My issue with it Street Hypnosis is a completely different one.

I used to spend a good deal of time defending the practice of Street Hypnosis as a legitimate form of street entertainment. After all, the way I do it and teach it, there's no reason why it shouldn't be. However, in recent times, I've begun to see the other side of the argument and realise that most so-called Street Hypnotists deserve the bad rap they've been getting.

Here are ten reasons why, in my view, most Street Hypnotists are going about it the wrong way.

Don't Be A Creep

Most street hypnosis is just plain creepy. Seriously, you're making all hypnotists look bad. Stop creeping around squares, parks and pub tables and do some real performance.

You're meant to be a street performer, entertaining crowds of people, not molesting individuals.

Go It Alone

Gangs of hypnotists? What kind of message does this send?
Everyone's a hypnotist these days. Anyone can do it. It's nothing special!

You're killing the industry and suffocating the artform.

Entertain A Crowd

What's the point of being THE Hypnotist if nobody is watching? It's meant to be entertainment.

Be entertaining and entertain someone other than yourself. Even better: Get paid for doing it.

So You Can Hypnotise. So What?

Big deal. My nine year old daughter can do it too. The question is: What are you going to do with it? Where to next?

Everything Old Is New Again

There's a so-called new wave of hypnotists saying there's no such thing as hypnosis, there's no such thing as a hypnotic state.

Well somebody obviously forgot to tell the millions of clients and volunteers getting hypnotised daily throughout the world.

Clients and volunteers don't want to be educated, they want to be hypnotised. Hypnotise them! Audiences don't want to be educated, they want to be entertained. Entertain them!

Take your new, highly researched, evidence based model of hypnosis and stick it where it belongs: In a text book.

I Like Derren Brown But I Don't Want To Be Him

I also like The Amazing Kreskin, I really do, but it's high time everybody stopped trying to be them and just moved on. Being "a bit like that bloke off the telly" isn't going to get you anywhere.

Embrace The Trance

Nobody cares what phenonema you can achieve without trance. Audiences love the mystique behind inductions and re-inductions. Embrace the trance state, don't shy away from the word sleep.

YouTube Is NOT An Audience

Stop performing only for the camera, you're not on TV and probably never will be. Oh. And your mate's bedroom? It's neither a street nor a TV studio.

Get Out Of The Classroom

People you hypnotise on a course do not count as volunteers and a training course is not a show. Get out of the classroom and get some real experience. That includes you hypnosis trainers too.

Don't Be A Clone

A scripted approach to hypnosis makes you look like a pale imitation of the script-writer.

Stop trying one thing over and over and expecting it to work on ten people. Much better to have ten things that will work on one person.

The Bar-room Svengali
Alex D. Fisher
MagicAL EXcellencE

This has been a stock item in my mix and mingle act for over a dozen years, and not once has ever been questioned nor disputed. Never ! From the initial handling, it has grown into a polished routine with all the wrinkles ironed out. The intent of this routine is to bridge the gap between magic and hypnosis allowing the performer to effortlessly lead from one to the other or to simply create the illusion that you can perform feats of hypnosis when you might not be ready to so.

BRIEF SYNOPSIS

Performer allows a group of people to repeatedly select a card , over and over again they change to the same card ! Cards jump from place to place and change in a number of ways. the deck is always shown to be normal. Finally , one member of the group is 'hypnotized' into believing that all the cards are in fact the same card! This is all done with one deck of cards, no switching out.

REQUIREMENTS

One Svengali deck of cards and plenty of confidence. (description below)

The Svengali deck is probably the most commonly know of all the fake decks available to magicians. Also commonly known as the 'short and long ' deck. It generally consists of 48 not 52 cards (though this is largely irrelevant) 24 'force' cards and 24 indifferent cards. The force cards are all the same, for the purpose of this description , we shall refer to the force card as the 9 of hearts. (9H). These force cards are all minutely shorter in height than the indifferent cards and are arranged force card, indifferent , force card, indifferent throughout the entire deck. In this way, , if you flick the cards one way they will show all indifferent cards e.g. a normal deck . If you flick them the other, then you'll see a whole deck of 9s. (DONT BE TEMPTED EVER TO DO THIS) You will need to familiarise yourself with the handling of this deck prior to performing this routine.

ROUTINE

Approaching a small group of people , , I always do this with a group that has at least one lass in it. You ask the first to select a card as you riffle through the deck. when they say stop , you allow them to take the card. By the very nature of the deck this will be the 9H. Ask the guy to show everyone the NINE OF HEARTS! This will get a laugh immediately, as the person to put the card back in the deck, holding the same break from whence they took the card, so he puts it back in the same place, somewhere near the middle of the deck.

Now tell them to watch closely as you flick the deck ,"DID YOU SEE THAT ?" they will respond "NO" . Immediately lift the top card and reveal it to be the 9H !

Allow this moment to sink in, it's a very strong psychological moment and sets up what is still to come.

Place the card back on top and cut the deck.

"OKAY, WHEN YOU SEE YOUR CARD IN THE DECK , PLEASE SHOUT STOP !"

As you do this, lift the deck and riffle through it so that everyone can see the faces of the cards. (Obviously the indifferent ones). They will not see their card . Repeat this a few times, turning the deck upside down too.

"DID YOU LOOK IN THE MIDDLE ? ' they will answer YES

" YOU SHOULD HAVE BEEN LOOKING ON TOP !" as you do this flip the top card over to reveal the 9H.

Again cut the deck a few times and collect it all together.

By riffling down the deck , cut small packets of cards onto the table, 5 maximum.

each one of these piles now has a force card on top .

"WOULD YOU LIKE PILE NUMBER ONE OR WOULD YOU LIKE TO **_MOVE ON"_**

The first part of this sentence should be spoken quietly with the last two words almost shouted as a command!

Normally they will choose to move on, if not and they choose pile number one " JUST GOES TO SHOW , REVERSE PSYCHOLOGY WORKS !"

If they choose to move on, repeat the sentence this time emphasizing no.2. On the third pile just ask QUIETLY " would you like pile number three?" at this point normally one person will say yes but the rest will say no take number 4 . it really doesn't matter. gather up all the piles that are not selected and say " A FREE CHOICE " and turn over the top card on the selected pile AGAIN THE 9H !!

Collect the deck together again , cut it a few times . DOUBLE LIFT the top two cards to show an indifferent card on top. Slide off the actual top card (9H) and table it, ask several of the people to place their hands over the tabled card covering it completely. Riffle up the deck and stop around half way, pull out the card at this point it will be the 9H. Closing the deck, the position you should now be in is as follows, a 9H on the table covered by several people's hands (they all believe this to be an indifferent card) , you holding a squared up deck with a 9H sticking half way out of it.

Grip the deck and tap the 9H back into it by tapping it onto the hands of the spectators. turn your hand over , with the deck , face down in your open palm grip.

" I COULDNT DO IT ANY SLOWER !" slowly reveal the top card of the deck to show it to be the indifferent card that the group believes to be under their hands.

Let this sink in ! allow them to realise what must be the case and to remove their hands and turn over the tabled card ! Don't say a word just smile . you cannot follow this , it really is the most powerful single effect with the Svengali deck.

HYPNOSIS STAGE

Table the deck and , turning to the female of the group , ask if she's ever been hypnotized. Regardless of the answer, say something like GREAT.

Ask one of the group to hold the deck tightly so that no one can do anything with it. Now focus on the lass. From my own personal view I prefer her to be stood on my right hand side.

"I'D LIKE TO TRY SOMETHING REALLY COOL WITH YOU , DONT WORRY , I'M NOT GOING TO EMBARASS YOU IN ANY WAY SHAPE OR FORM, AND I WOULD NEVER MAKE YOU DO ANYTHING THAT YOU WOULDNT NORMALLY BE WILLING TO DO !"

Turn to the crowd and wink at this point.

Have the lass hold out her left hand and get her to relax , supporting her forearm with your left hand, Using your right hand , point to the lines on her palm and explain how if she focuses enough , she will begin to see these lines start to move. She will generally begin to giggle a little and say no .

At this point , with confidence, say "TRY RAISING YOUR HAD A LITTLE " as you do this , bring her hand up to approximately 9 inches from her head. Your left hand now moves from her forearm to her elbow with the fingers on the outer of her forearm and the thumb behind the elbow.

" NOW, I WANT YOU TO IMAGINE THAT YOU HAVE A SET OF SUPER MAGNETS BOTH SET IN THE ENDS OF YOUR FINGER TIPS AND IN YOUR EYEBROWS. NOW THESE MAGNETS ARE GOING TO PULL TOGETHER , DONT TRY TO STOP IT , IF YOU RESIST IT WILL GET 10 TIMES AS POWERFUL AND THEN 100 TIMES ,THEN 1000 TIMES, THEN 10,00 TIMES. "

Initially use your right hand to direct this motion and then place it on the nape of the neck of the lass ,palm open , flat onto the nape.

"AS YOURE FINGER TIPS REACH AND TOUCH YOUR FOREHEAD , YOUR EYES WILL CLOSE AND YOU WILL ALLOW YOUR HEAD TO FALL FORWARD AND SLEEP . "

as you do this use your left hand to guide the lass's forearm towards her head. this action should go unnoticed as actually you are simply contracting your grip with the left hand. As her fingers do touch her forehead simultaneously move your left hand to her left hand to act as support and use your right hand on the nape of her neck to move her head forward and down. (Do this gently)

"NOW, IN THIS STATE IM GOING TO GIVE YOU A SIMPLE PIECE OF INFORMATION, IM GOING TO TELL YOU THAT EVERY SINGLE INDIVIDUAL CARD INTHE DECK OF CARDS IS IN FACT THE NIE OF HEARTS, ALL THE SAME . AND WHEN I BRING YOU UP I WANT TO PROVE THIS TO YOU . WHEN I COUNT TO THREE YOU WILL COME BACK TO US"

THREE, YOURE BEGINNING TO THINK OF THE CARDS,

TWO, YOURE FEELING SOBER AND AS WSIE AS YOU EVER HAVE BEEN

ONE, BACK WITH US .

Use your left hand to raise her head back to normal position and then remove hands immediately.

YOU OK ?   of course she will say yes , probably burst into giggles.

Now , draw attention to the cards being held by the other member of the group.

NOW, NOONE HAS TOUCHED THOSE CARDS NO ?

they will agree

Take the cards of them and turn to the lass, and explain that your now going to show her and her alone the cards, take the deck , and holding it up so that only she and you can see it, riffle through the cards in such a way that you are showing the deck as a complete deck of 9H's. riffle through a few times, turning the cards upside down and back again. ONLY she can see this , tell her to take a good look all the way through the deck . then place the deck back in the hands of the previous spectator (cutting it as you do).

turning to the lass,
THANKS VERY MUCH FOR AGREEING TO DO THAT ,
extend your left hand to hers.

As she goes to shake your hand with her left hand , immediately grip it and raise it back to her forehead, your right hand moving back to the nape of her neck , bringing her back to the 'hypnotised' position ,
AND SLEEP !

This must be done smoothly and quickly firmly but gently.

NOW, WHEN I BRING YOU BACK , YOU WILL WANT TO TELL
EVERYONE PRECISELY WHAT YOU SAW, YOU WONT FEEL
EMBARESSED , YOU WILL WANT TO TELL EVERYONE JUST
WHAT YOU SAW!

THREE, THINKING ABOUT THE CARDS

TWO, FEELING HUGELY POSITIVE

ONE READY TO TELL THE WORLD

AND ,,,,,BACK IN THE ROOM . again raise her head to normal position,
remove your hands .

take the cards back of the person who was holding them,
NOW AT ANY TIME DID ANYONE SWAP OR MESS WITH THOSE
CARDS ? he will say no.

Look at the lass, and say NOW TELL EVERYONE WHAT YOU SAW .
as you do this openly riffle the cards sop that the whole group can see it .
this should coincide with the lass telling everyone that the whole deck was
the nine of hearts.

Ask her to repeat a few times, as you show the deck to be perfectly normal
over and over (by riffling in a manner that shows the indifferent cards
throughout) . packet the cards and put them away. thank them very much
and move away.

Post Script.

Hypnotists will recognise that in the hypno section you are actually conducting a basic hand to eye induction. It is just that, but in this case it is not intended to actually induce the person. At the end , do NOT be tempted to hang around, this will destroy the overall effect. you want the maximum disbelief and confusion to be established.

I know it's been a bit of a bind to read, but for those that chose to work this , you have a real gem in your hands. please let me know how you got on with it.

Alex D. Fisher -   alex@alexdfisher.co.uk

INDUCTION METHODS

By: Dr. Jonathan Royle –
www.UltimateHypnosisCourse.com

"The simplest things are usually the most effective in life and hypnosis is no exception"

"The process of hypnosis is so easy to carry out, that, for most, it's hard to believe it works and yet, that's exactly the reason why it's so effective as people believe you must be doing something complicated to place them into trance."

"But you should have learnt the true secret off by heart now and that's the fact it's all down to belief and expectancy and following the simple steps, which I am explaining to you in this course, then success will be yours."

Well welcome to the chapter which you've been waiting for, how to place people into the Hypnotic Trance. By now, you will have hopefully assimilated all the other knowledge which I have revealed to you, if not, then please go back to page one, read through it all again and digest until you do understand what I've said. As you must understand what I've said in order to understand how these hypnotic induction's actually do work.

Basically speaking, the success of the hypnotic induction relies on the belief and expectancy within the mind of your potential hypnotic subject. All the other elements of the suggestibility test, your opening patter and the fact that people are already 90% on the way to already being hypnotised before they step onto the stage, due to your advertising etc. also help in a huge way.

If you have followed all these points and the subjects on stage or in your consulting room believe you are a professional hypnotist, with the skill to place them into trance and they also expect whatever you do to work, then as hard as it is to believe at this moment in time, it will work.

So step A is the belief and expectancy within the volunteer's mind. Step B, of disorientation and confusion is catered for in the way which these hypnotic inductions have been designed. They themselves, if carried out as instructed, will either confuse them, disorientate them, or in some way do both. When this element is combined with step C of suggestion and repetition, you will almost always get the end result of relaxation and sleep, which of course is step D.

So follow the guidelines and you'll have great success with your hypnotic induction's. There are two general rules of thumb I should mention at this point, and these are also applicable to every hypnotist on earth.

1   The more confident you are in your own skills and talents, the more successful you will be as a result in all that you do. As it says in the bible "As a man thinketh so he becomes"

2   The more experience you get of actually hypnotising people, the faster and more effective your induction methods will become and the greater a percentage of people upon the stage or in the consulting room you will be able to get into a trance easily and effectively.

So practise, practise and practise some more. Remember this though, don't try it out on family and friends and expect a huge success, as they knew you when you weren't a hypnotist, so that most vital element of belief and expectancy will not be there.

Instead practise on new faces in bars etc. in conversation say what you do, and present them with one of your business cards to establish belief and expectancy and ask if the group wants a free demonstration, then go ahead and practise your skills. But remember this, you are the only one that will know this is the first time you've ever done this, as far as they are concerned, you've been doing it for years and are a true master of your craft. So once again belief and expectancy come into play here.

Anyway, I've tried to dispel any doubts which you may still have and hopefully I've done that, if not, you'll have to pluck up the courage to try it all out and then hindsight will tell you that what I'm teaching you is 100% true in every way.

As a hypnotist, the most important thing you could possibly need is supreme self-confidence, so here goes with an induction method which can be used very successfully on stage and in some cases even in the consulting room situation.

FALLING BACKWARD INDUCTION

You get the subject to stand with both feet together on the floor, hands down by their sides unless this is being done after the locked hands in which case they are told to place their hands closely against their chest. This means there is then more weight at the upper area of their body and they are even more likely to fall back than usual. You stand to the left of them and place your right foot flat against the back of their heels so it can act as a pivot if required. Your right hand middle finger pushes onto their forehead, as you say, "and tilt your head well back as you close your eyes." You have now still got your right middle finger on the centre of their forehead, just above the bridge of their nose, as you count from one to three and give the suggestions of relaxing and falling back, as I will describe in a moment, you draw your middle finger lightly across the centre of the subjects forehead, so that by the count of 3 it is almost ready to slide towards the top of their head. This acts as a non-verbal suggestion to fall backwards, and believe me, even without the verbal suggestions, it usually has the effect of the person falling backwards. When you have given your suggestions and the person starts to fall back, all you need do is lower your right arm from their head, down to their upper back area and just cushion their fall back so they don't hurt themselves. In actual fact, you are just lowering them down onto the floor at which point they will be in the hypnotic trance.

On some occasions, if I feel it is a difficult subject, I will prior to getting them to tilt their head back and close their eyes, get them to take some really deep breaths in, hold them a few seconds and then out. This has the effect of slightly "hyper-ventilating" them. This means that when you tilt their head back and tell them to close their eyes, they will then feel a little dizzy already and this brings the self-hypnosis angle into play again. This will occur even more strongly if you, as they breathe deeply, knock them with your right hand on their back at the place where their lungs are. This has the extra effect of knocking them off balance and disorientating them even more. Remember, that you must read these instructions several times and get it clear in your own mind the whole process of physical actions and verbal suggestions, as they should take just a few seconds from starting point to the point at which they are lying upon the floor in trance. From a verbal point of view, the whole lot would go as follows:

"OK sir (or madam). Just stand there, feet together, hands down by your side (or hands against your chest). Tilt your head well back and close your eyes. I'd like you to take nice deep regular breaths in, hold them a few seconds and then breathe out as this will help you to relax more quickly.

In a few moments, I'm going to count from 1 to 3 and on the count of 3, when I say sleep, you will feel yourself falling back, but I won't let you fall and hurt yourself, instead you'll just fall into a beautifully relaxed state.

1 The deeper you go the better you will feel and the better you feel the deeper you will go.

2 You can feel yourself falling backwards now into a beautifully relaxed sleeplike state.

3 SLEEP (They fall) falling back, back, back and sleep and relax."

THEY WILL NOW BE IN THE HYPNOTIC TRANCE

If the subject does not start to fall of their own accord, you can always use the fact that your feet against the back of their heels acts as a pivot to tip them back gently, so that to the audience it appears as if they have just fallen back into your arms. Another point worth mentioning is that on the count of three, you immediately remove your hand from their head and tap them firmly on the back as you say SLEEP. This has the effect of knocking them even more off balance and as a result they then fall backwards into your arms. So your next step is to get your wife or husband and use them to practise the actions on, until you can do them without hesitation, then you will have one of the quickest and most effective inductions that there is available to you.

The great thing with this induction on a theatre stage is that all the volunteers can be lined up in a straight row and one by one, after each other, they can be placed into trance using this method. Once all of them are upon the floor under your spell so to speak, you then proceed by deepening the level of trance for the whole group at once, which makes it slicker and quicker. In this case, the volunteers would be face on to the audience and they fall backwards away from the audience. As with all the induction methods, which I will explain to you in this chapter, I will tell you the basics, and your own common sense would tell you the rest. For example, in a funny shaped venue, you might have to have the subjects standing sideways onto the audience before making them fall backwards. This is really an excellent induction to use. It's quick, safe and works well, I wish you much luck with it.

FALLING FORWARDS INDUCTION

This is, in essence, almost identical to the falling backward induction, except that they fall forwards. The reason it works is the same, and even without belief and expectancy being considered, if this is done correctly, then people will feel themselves falling forwards into your arms.

You stand facing the subject, they have their hands down by their sides, stand up straight rigid, feet together and stare directly into your eyes. They are told to keep staring directly into your eyes at all times and then you proceed as follows:

Verbally you say something such as, "I'm going to count backwards from

3 to 1 and on each descending number you'll feel yourself falling forwards, but I won't let you fall and hurt yourself, instead you'll just fall into a beautifully relaxed, dreamy, sleeplike state. So,

3, the deeper you go the better you will feel and the better you feel, the deeper you will go.

2, You can feel yourself falling forwards, more with every breath you take, ever noise you hear and every word that I say.

And on 1, you can feel yourself falling forwards, falling forwards, forwards and to sleep."

As you say this or similar, the physical element is as follows:

From the moment you start talking, your fingers of each hand are placed firmly, flatly and gently on the sides of their head in line with their forehead. As you talk you are gently pulling your fingers forwards in a smooth motion towards yourself and this has the effect of both distracting them and also disorientating them a little. But, perhaps more importantly, as your fingers are firmly against their head, it has the effect of gently pulling their head forwards towards you, and also acts as a non verbal suggestion to do the same. This as a result will mean their body will follow suit and they will start to move forwards. At the same time to promote this further, you take one small step backwards, as you count each number and as they are to stare into your eyes at all times, it will have the effect of their eyes following yours, and as such their body will move forwards more. Also bend your legs slightly as you get nearer to the count of one, so that your eye level becomes lower. This means that to keep their eyes in line with yours, they have to lean over slightly and when they do, they will reach that point of no return, and will suddenly be falling forwards into your arms. You must catch them and then very gently lay them upon the floor, so that their head is to one side. Combine all this with belief and expectancy and the shock element of you commanding SLEEP, just as they reach that point of no return and now I'm sure you'll be able to understand why this induction works so well.

THE FLOATING ARM INDUCTION

For this induction, have the subject sitting in a chair, feet together and hands resting upon their lap, with eyes tightly closed. You then proceed as I will detail in a second, although you'll have to adapt things for each person. The method of this induction is to first get them to lift up their middle finger of the right hand, due to suggestion, then to allow their hand to lift up, followed by their arm. The moment their arm has floated up to their face and touches their nose, it will instantly fall back into their lap and they drift into an instant deep relaxing sleep.

This is really all down to suggestion, and is a 100% genuine induction. The standard phrases, which are used by all hypnotists and which are detailed at the end of this chapter, are inserted at appropriate points, to relax them even more. This will give you a brief idea of what to say, but this is really a case of what suits your personality, you now know it's all down to suggestion and what you want to achieve, so now here's an idea of what to say.

"As you breathe deeply and relax more with every breath you take, every noise you hear and with every word I say, you'll notice that the deeper you go over the next few minutes, the better you will feel and the better you feel, the deeper you will go. I'd like you to concentrate on your right hand middle finger, and as you do, just notice how it almost feels like a helium balloon is tied onto it making it so light, so light, that it no longer wishes to remain resting upon your lap. And just notice that with each breath you take and ever noise you hear, your finger now becomes so light with that helium balloon attached, that it is lifting up off your lap and up into the air. Now just imagine that helium filled balloon, floating up higher and higher into the air, and as it does your hand is starting to rise up, up off you lap and into the air, as it's now so light, as light as air, in fact, so light it floats up higher into the air. (Proceed in this fashion until their hand is up off their lap, and starts moving upwards) You now notice that as your hand floats up higher, being pulled up higher into the air all the time by the helium filled balloon, that your arm is now so light and follows suit. (Continue in the same vein, until their finger, hand and arm are up in the air). Now just notice that your hand is floating towards your face, nearer and nearer to your nose, all the time (Continue in this vein etc.) And realise now, that the moment your finger touches your nose, your hand will suddenly become as heavy as lead, will fall instantly down back into your lap, and you'll sink instantly into a state of relaxation 100 times deeper and 100 times more enjoyable than that which you are already in. (Continue in this vein etc).

N.B.

If you follow this basic outline, they will do as you intend and the moment their arm falls back onto their lap, you will also have a visual indication that they have now entered trance. Remember, paint a picture with your words, leave no doubt in their minds what you wish to occur and as such belief, expectancy and the power of suggestion will do the rest.

EYES GLUED TOGETHER INDUCTION

This can be done with the subject standing up straight, hands down by their side and eyes closed, or whilst they are sitting down, feet together with hands on their lap and eyes closed.

You place your right hand middle finger, firmly onto the central area of the head, just above the top of their forehead. You explain that they must imagine, that there is a hole in their head at the point where they can feel your fingertip and as such, they are to stare through the hole in their head and up at your fingertip. To do this they will have to push their eyeballs upwards underneath their eyelids.

Once in this position, you then suggest that by the count of one their eyes will be stuck together and the harder they try to separate them, the more they will stick. As long as you make it clear that even when you ask them to try and open their eyes that they must in actual fact keep staring upwards with their eyes as if staring through the hole in their head, then this will work. The reason for this, being that when your eyeballs are in this position it becomes physically impossible to open your eyes anyway.

The subject will believe his failure in opening his eyes is due to your suggestions, and then so that it comes very unexpectedly, you suddenly tilt the subjects head forward onto their chest as you say, "Eyes tightly closed at all times and just sleep". They will remain like this now until you command to them otherwise, obviously the trance will be deepened along with everyone else a little later on into the act.

INSTANT INDUCTION

Here follows the wording of a very effective and quick, induction method. Having finally got you subjects lined up on the stage, you begin in a very strong and commanding voice, "Close your eyes, begin go breathe deeply and regularly, you will find that your eyes will begin to stick together. They will become tightly stuck, in fact, you cannot open your eyes. Then walk up and down the line speaking to each person in turn. Try if you want to, but you cannot open yours eyes." (Each of them tries and can't, they believe they are now under hypnosis and shock themselves into a deep trance).

Then continue up the line saying "And neither can you, or you, or you, etc. In fact the harder you try the more they stick together and the more you enter trance. OK, now everyone, eyes stuck together, but your feet are now stuck to the floor, yes your feet are stuck, rigid to the floor, you cannot move from where you are standing, however hard you try. OK just try and move from where you are standing, but the harder you try the more your feet are stuck solidly to the floor, (continue for a few seconds, then say). Relax, relax, stop trying and relax as you go down completely into trance. In fact, from this moment forward, you will listen to and respond only to my voice. Whenever I say, 1, 2, wide-awake you will instantly be wide-awake, and do whatever I have told you to do. In fact, you'll carry out everything I say as an automatic reflex action. And whenever I say SLEEP, as quickly as this, (snap fingers) a snap of the fingers, you will instantly return into a deep sleep, but each time you re-enter it, for you it will be 100 times deeper and 100 times more enjoyable."

N.B.

Now whenever you say sleep, they will re-enter the trance state, but each time go deeper and deeper into trance. It is for this reason, that the harder to do routines are left until near the end of the act, as by then everyone will have gone in and out of trance several times and now will be so deep that almost anything is possible. A last word here, and that's the simple fact that as a hypnotist who wishes to master rapid and instantaneous inductions, you must have 100% faith and confidence in yourself to be a success. I will also take this opportunity to give you the address of a company, who can supply you with numerous books on Stage Hypnosis.

If you wish to get more books on the subject contact: - Magic Books By Post, 29 Hill Avenue, Bedminster, Bristol. BS3 4SN. Send them an S.A.E and you'll get a catalogue by return of post.

HYPNOTIZING HECKLERS (CEREBRAL ANOXIA)

Allow me to point out here and now, that this method is included for information purposes only, I would never, ever dream of using it myself and anyone who does try it, does so at their own risk. THIS CAN KILL PEOPLE. BE WARNED. Do you know what Cerabral Anoxia is? Well it usually means a dead person, dead from a lack of oxygen to the brain. You may be asking what has that got to do with you? Well, it is very easy to render someone unconscious by pressure on the Carotoid Arteries, leading to the brain. Even until a few years ago some stupid idiots would pass this off as a quick way to hypnotise people, or a way to hypnotise hecklers, even today, the odd person uses it, but if I were you, I would not even contemplate its use. Under many byelaws, laws of a country etc. its use is now forbidden. In fact, part of a permission to perform in the UK will read that only psychological methods may be used to induce hypnosis. Well, cerebral anoxia, is what they are referring to here. It is absolutely forbidden, for any member of P.O.S.H. or A.P.H.P. to use it in any circumstances, any reputable person would never dream of using it on someone.

However, should you ever come across a "new method" from someone which resembles this, you will be aware of it's existence and avoid it at all costs. Here's how it is done for information purposes only.

Stand in front of your subject, then place the fingers of each hand at the side of their neck, just below the ears and slightly towards their throat. Do this with their head tilted way, way back. Whilst in this position your fingers should now be directly over the large veins in the neck. There is one on each side of their neck, you can often see them, and if not, you can feel them very easily as they pulsate and throb beneath your fingers. Press gently on those veins, but also firmly at the same time. Now ask the person to breath deeply, keep the pressure on until the person goes limp, if the word sleep is shouted at this time, as far as the crowd watching will be concerned you have just placed that person under hypnosis. The moment they start to go limp remove all pressure and allow them to fall to the floor or back into their chair, like a sack of potatoes. However, should you accidentally keep the pressure on a few seconds later, the person may end up dead or a cabbage for life, with permanent brain damage. You could be arrested for murder, at the least manslaughter. If you did not kill them you can be convicted of attempted murder or assault, with intention to endanger life, or grievous bodily harm. So the golden rule here is ***never, never, ever attempt this technique on anyone at anytime***. Should you ever see someone use this method then please report them to the Mindcare Organisation and we will investigate, as anyone using this method is not fit to call themselves a hypnotist.

This by the way is what is known in the trade as the "Carotid Artery Induction" and yet as I'm sure you've realised, it has nothing to do with hypnosis and, as such, should not be used.

THE CRAIG WILLIAMS MICROPHONE INDUCTION

This is an induction method, which is excellent and a very good up and coming hypnotist, by the name of Craig Williams, has made it a masterpiece in his hands. Anyway, here goes with the technical inside information on how it's done.

This induction is very quick and looks amazing to the audience, it is usually done whilst the subjects hands are still locked together. You get the subject to stand so that you're both facing each other, and yet, at the same time are both sideways on to the audience so that they get a good view. You tell the subject to stretch out their arms, straight out in front of themselves, this means that the distance between you must be such that it gives them room to do this. You take hold of their right arm with your left hand and make sure that you have a firm grip upon it. In your own right hand, you have got hold of the microphone. You explain that they should stare at the top of the microphone at all times and for no reason whatsoever should they remove their eyes from it. You also instil into them the belief and expectancy that the moment the microphone taps them on the head they will instantly relax every muscle in their body from the tips of their toes to the tips of their fingers and that their eyes will immediately shut and remain closed until you say otherwise. You then hold the microphone, which is in your right hand up in the air as high as you can comfortably hold it. It is held at a slanted angle, pointing towards the subject's forehead. They have been told to stare at the top of the mike at all times and in order to do this, as the microphone is above their eyeline they will have to strain their eyes in order to do this and here, once again, the belief factor will be taken a step further by the strange sensation which the will feel in their eyes. You then count backwards from three to one and use the standard phrases as you would in the falling backwards induction etc. With of course the addition that the moment the microphone touches their head, they'll fall back into a relaxed dreamy sleeplike state, as you won't let them fall and hurt themselves, and of course their eyes will instantly shut and remain closed until you say otherwise. Then on each descending number you bring the mike closer towards their eyes, so that by the count of one, and the word sleep, the microphone will tap them upon the head and act as the trigger to enter hypnosis. Also to keep their eyes upon the top of the mike as it gets closer to their head, they will have to tilt their head backwards a little. As they do so, if you take a small step towards them, then they will start to fall backwards anyway, but as you have a firm grip of their arm you don't let them fall, instead you just allow them to lower to the ground in a smooth, steady motion. With the combination of belief, expectancy, suggestion, eye strain and visual disorientation, plus the added element that they will, if you do this correctly, start to fall backwards anyway, means that you now have in your armoury of techniques, a most powerful and quick induction, which should only take about 30 seconds from start to finish.

Once again, as with all things detailed in this course, experience will teach you more in one show, than any book, video or audiotape ever could. A last point here is, that should you wish to place a person under hypnosis with this method whose hands are not locked together then for the sake of the induction just have them clasp their hands in to the correct position, then, in both cases, the moment they are in trance and lying upon the floor, you can separate their hands for them and so suggest that as you drop their arms down by their sides, they will sink 100 times deeper in trance, so it even has a built in trance deepening method.

THE BODY FLOP INDUCTION

For this dramatic looking induction, your subject is sitting in a chair with a low back, this is so that you will be able to push the upper area of their body forwards by leaning against their back area, so obviously if the chair back was too high then this would not be possible.

They are sitting in the chair, upright with feet and legs together, so that feet the are flat upon the floor, and their arms and hands are rested upon their lap, with palms facing upwards. You then get them to close their eyes and at this point you must be standing directly behind them and the chair in which they are sitting. You place a hand upon each of their shoulders in a relaxed fashion and then say something along these lines.

"OK, (subjects name here) just relax. I'd like you to take nice deep, regular breaths so you can relax a little quicker and I'll keep my hands upon your shoulders so that we can get our rhythm of breathing into alignment. (Here pacing, leading and rapport come into play strongly).

I'm going to count backwards from 3 to 1 and on each descending number, you will find that the deeper you go, the better you will feel, and the better you feel, the deeper you will go. The moment that I say sleep, you will instantly drift into a deeply relaxed sleeplike state. OK (their name) here goes.

Three : With every breath you take, every noise that you hear and every word that I say, you are relaxing more and more as you concentrate only on your rhythm of breathing which is now so deep and regular.

Two : Every muscle in your body becoming so heavy and so tired, each muscle now so limp, so loose and so relaxed, as you go deeper and deeper. And on……

One: Sleep, deeper, deeper and deeper to sleep."

Whilst this is being said you are massaging their shoulders which is a great stress reliever and will help them to relax very quickly, it also acts as a distraction for their mind. As you are coming to the words "And on one", prior to saying the trigger word sleep (drawn out), this is the point of importance. At this moment in time you must rest your chest area against their back lightly, as you lean over them from behind, very smoothly, but very quickly, your hands now move off the subjects shoulders and down to their lap ready for the sudden physical element which shocks them into hypnosis. As you say the word sleep (which is drawn out), your hands lift their arms up off their lap and sweep them off, so that they quickly fall off and down besides them hanging in mid air, at exactly the same time you lean forward so that your chest area pushes the upper area of their body over and their head flops down almost into their own lap.

This, by the way, must be practised so that you can carry out both actions simultaneously. This is a disorientation method par excellence, as one minute they are being massaged on the shoulders and the next second they are simultaneously flopping forwards with their head falling towards their own lap and their arms have fallen off their lap at exactly the same time. This strange combination of distractions for the mind acts as the trigger and into hypnosis they do go rapidly. To the audience it looks so impressive, as the subject suddenly seems to flop forward in their chair like a rag doll as you command sleep.

THE LOCKED HANDS INDUCTION

This is an instantaneous induction method which one of my hypnotic tutors Mr Peter J Fox has a great success with and which I have seen him use many times. This is 100% reliant on belief, expectancy and your supreme self-confidence as are all instantaneous induction techniques, which you will ever use.

In practise you get a subject, lock their hands together and just a few seconds later after you've said, "OK, just try and separate your hands, but the harder you try the more they will stick." You suddenly, whilst facing the subject, place your right arm on the back of their neck and pull them gently towards you, with the end result of their head being rested upon your shoulder. This is done at exactly the same moment as you unexpectedly say in a loud and commanding voice, "just sleep and relax, going deeper and deeper to sleep". As their mind is already on something else, it's already distracted (see keys to hypnosis) and with the shock element of suddenly moving towards you and commanded to sleep and very quickly followed up with commands to go deeper etc., it also acts as a disorientation and confusion method. The moment they do have their head against your shoulder, you must follow up immediately with a quick trance deepening method, as explained elsewhere. Then you awaken them, get them to sit down and the moment their bum touches the seat you click your fingers in front of their eyes and say sleep, and back under they will go. This induction works because of the shock element being so unexpected at the time it occurs and as they have been trying to separate their hands with no success they have no reason to disbelieve any further commands as such they will be acted upon instantly.

THE HANDWAVE INSTANT INDUCTION

This is the method which I have both used myself and have also seen Paul McKenna use with great success. You ask your on stage subjects, if any of them have been hypnotised before. Those who answer yes are asked when and by whom, you remember this information and then place 2 or 3 people into a trance with inductions such as falling backwards etc. During this, the people who have been hypnotised before are watching and this takes the belief and expectancy concept one step further. As, don't forget, it's easier to hypnotise someone rapidly when they've just seen you place other people into trance, and as such know that you can do the same to them. You then return to the subjects who have been placed under hypnosis before and ask three quick questions.

1 Do you wish to enter this lovely dreamy state of hypnosis tonight? (YES)

2 Can you remember that the moment you enter hypnosis, your eyes close, your heavy head falls forward onto your chest and you breathe deeply and listen only to the sound of my voice? (YES)

3 Well (their name) in that case, may I have your permission to use the fastest form of hypnosis known to man, to make you instantly re-enter this lovely dreamy sleep like state? (YES)

NB

The moment he/she has said yes to answer all three questions, you immediately, without any time delay at all, so that it comes as a complete shock, just do as follows:

"Well in that case (their name) just sleep and relax."

As you say this, your right hand is lifted up in front of their face and as you command sleep, in a raised tone of voice, your right hand moves in a downwards motion in front of their face, so that the fingers are outstretched and move down from above head, past their eyes and downwards, which in itself, is a powerful non verbal suggestion of sleep. It also gives them something to psychologically connect entering the trance state to and something for them to believe in. Remember, that as they've been under hypnosis before, they know exactly how to react and your three questions prior to the instant induction have done two things.

A   It has psychologically conditioned them to enter the trance state immediately that you say the word sleep.

B   It has acted as a brief reminder to them of how to act in trance. If they have been under before and have answered yes honestly to the three questions that you ask, then you can be sure that they will instantly enter trance.

Someone who has been hypnotised before is, by far the best type of person on whom to do instantaneous inductions, as they know how to act in trance and their belief is 100% complete, as they have experienced it first hand. Also, as a general rule of thumb, the more recently they have been hypnotised, the more easily that they can be made re-enter trance. I'm sure you can now see why you need to have enormous confidence in your abilities in order to make instant inductions work.

HANDSHAKE INSTANT INDUCTION

Before I describe how this induction is presented, allow me to make this point. As long as the subjects' belief and expectancy in your powers is totally 100% complete and as long as you truly have tremendous confidence in your skills, and this is transmitted to the subjects through your actions etc., they will then both expect what you do to work and also know that you expect it to work. As such the Handwave and Handshake instant inductions can be done without asking any questions. In fact, the moment a subject said that they had been under before, then you could just say:

"Well in that case, (their name) Just sleep and relax"

The hand movement, handshake or whatever was being used as the trigger would be just the same and of course, your voice must sound commanding and demanding. However, the point which I am trying to make here is, done with belief, they will instantly re-enter trance without any additional psychological conditioning. This even applies to "Hypnotic Virgins" who have never, ever entered trance before, as long as their belief is total, then when you command them to sleep, they would do so however the induction had been presented as it's just the trigger word, sleep, which they expect to hear to make them enter the state and, if this is what they believe, then for them, it's very true indeed. You of course would only use instant inductions on the most susceptible subjects (see elsewhere) this means the odds are then even greater in your favour of it working.

Anyway, to the handshake induction. This really is as simple as it sounds, you approach a subject, who you have observed will be very susceptible after having unlocked their shaking hands etc. You ask their name, and upon their reply you extend your right hand as though ready to shake hands as you say:

"Nice to meet you (their name)"

Still holding their hand as though ready to shake hands you quickly say

"Have you ever been hypnotised before (their name)?"

Then, whatever answer he/she gives you, immediately follow up by saying

"Is it OK with you (their name) if I hypnotise you right now, instantly?"

If they answer yes, it's an easy subject and all you need do is just say

"In that case (their name), just sleep."

As you say the word sleep, you lift their arm into the air slightly, and then move it down rapidly towards their lap, as you command in a loud voice, "sleep." This hand (downwards) movement acts as a non verbal suggestion of sleep and that's why this is called the handshake induction, as the audience just see you go up to a subject, shake that persons hand and say "sleep" and at that moment the person has gone under your spell. Incidentally, I have found from experience, that the downwards motion of the handshake is more effective when made on an outbreath of the subject (as they breathe out), all suggestions of relaxation and sleep are more effective also when made as the subject breathes out, as this psychologically implies letting go etc. This induction, can of course, with confidence and experience, be done in the way which is used by experienced hypnotists. In our version, we simply go up to a subject, ask their name, the moment they reply, we extend our hand and clasp theirs and then do the handshake motion, as we say "Ok (their name), just sleep and relax." This is all so sudden for the subject, that it shocks them into trance and they connect entry of trance to the handshake. Lastly, if the person says no when you ask if they will allow you to hypnotise them quickly, you simply reply by saying "Well in that case (their name), I can't be bothered wasting my time on you. Sleep". Because he feels he has one up on you by saying no, he suddenly feels small when you say you can't be bothered wasting your time with him and here, the shock/surprise factor comes in, as you shake his hand and in a raised voice command him to sleep. As with all instant inductions, they do work, but only if you have enough confidence.

CAN'T BE BOTHERED WITH YOU INDUCTION

This induction only works, because what you do comes as a real shock to the subject and because you do it with such faith, confidence and conviction, that they will instantly enter the trance. They sense your confidence and as such, belief and expectancy again comes into play. They would of course have just seen you place other people into trance and will be waiting, anticipating, almost rearing, when you'll come and do the same thing to them.

Proceed like this. You do an induction such as the falling backwards technique and prior to this you've had several susceptible subjects stand directly in front of their chairs, which you've said they will sit in. They are standing right next to the chair, so that when made to fall back they will fall into the chair, and not fall and hurt themselves. You have just placed someone into trance, and now walk along the line as if deciding whom to pick to hypnotise next. As you do this you must stare directly into each person's eyes and send the fear of God into them. You walk along the line and when you reach the subject whom you are going to use this induction upon, you stop for a moment which you did not do with the others, you say nothing and just stare at him for a couple of seconds, this will scare him to death, he will be so relieved 2 seconds later when you continue along the line, that he will relax more, and let his defences down. You then come back along the line, and the moment you reach him, your right palm is pushed against his forehead, and he falls back into his chair as you simultaneously say in a loud and commanding voice. "Oh, I can't be bothered with you, Sleep." This will come as such a shock, especially when he thought he had escaped. It works due to shock, belief and expectancy, in short, it's the power of the moment and the power of the unexpected which will make him close his eyes as he's seen the others do (he's been conditioned), and he then enters trance. Although I shall give you several more presentation examples for inductions, the bottom line is, that if belief and expectancy are 100% total, then any trigger can be used to make them enter the trance instantly. Remember this and you can always adapt to suit any venue, audience or show situation.

AEROPLANE INDUCTION

The moment you have just placed someone into trance, you turn to the person sitting next to him or her and say, "you wouldn't do anything daft like that, would you?" They, of course say no. You then tell them to watch the microphone as the moment is taps them upon the head, their heavy eyes will shut tightly, their head will fall forwards onto their chest and they'll breathe deeply as they go to sleep. You then hold the mike in front of their face as if it is about to tap their head, then suddenly, for a few seconds prior to unexpected tapping them upon the head with the mike and commanding sleep, you move the mike up, down, sideways etc. and make funny noises as if the mike is an aeroplane. This will cause the audience to laugh and the person upon the stage to think you're crazy, but as the beliefs already there and he expects to go under when the mike hits his head, guess what? As such he will go under. This "aeroplane" gag, can also be used when the person has already been placed under hypnosis and you just want to add a little variation, so, instead of using the trigger word sleep for them to re enter trance, you use the aeroplane induction which takes only a few seconds and helps add an extra little comedy elements to the proceedings.

Another comical way to make two people re enter trance, is to apparently knock their two heads together and then they go back to sleep. Of course, the real reason they've gone back under is because you've used a stage whisper to put them back under by quickly and audibly to them (but not through the mike) saying sleep. To the audience however it looks hilarious, as you appear to knock two people's heads together and they then re enter trance instantly.

Yet another comical way you make them re enter trance is to say to them

"You wouldn't go to sleep if you slapped yourself across the face would you?" (They say no) "Of course you wouldn't. I'll tell you what though, give it a try." He then slaps himself across the face and as he does, so instantly re enters trance, he would do anyway, but if in doubt, use a stage whisper to say sleep to ensure that he goes under as he slaps his own face. These few ideas are all very simple to put into use and all looks hilarious to the audience and as entertainment is the key thing on stage you are onto a winner here

THE FINGER STARE INDUCTION

This is also a very quick induction and should take no more than 40 to 50 seconds to have the person enter a deep trance state.

They should be sitting on a chair, feet together firmly flat on the floor, upright and looking directly at you, the hypnotist. Their arms and hands being rested upon their lap with palms upwards, you then proceed as follows. You extend your own right arm and then extend your own right hand index finger, whilst the rest of the hand remains like a clenched fist. This extended finger is then held slightly above the level of the subjects eyes and a few inches away from them so that they must strain their eyes to look upwards at your fingertip.

You explain that you want them to stare at all times at your fingertip, they must not move their head, only their eyes in order to follow the route which your fingertip will take. When you are sure that they have understood this full you say something such as;

"In a few moments, I shall count from 3 to 1, and by the count of one you'll notice your eyelids will be so heavy and tired, in fact the harder you try to keep them open the more they will want to remain shut. The moment that I say sleep, and tap you upon the head, you'll instantly drift into a deep, relaxing, dreamlike state. So on 3, the deeper you go, the better you will feel, and the better you feel, the deeper you will go. On 2, you can feel your eyes starting to strain as they get so heavy and so tired, it's so much easier to just relax and let go. And on 1, eyes closing tightly now, as with every breath you take, every noise you hear and every word I say, you go deeper and deeper to sleep. Now that you're asleep, in a few moments I am going to tap you on the head. The moment I do, you'll sink instantly 100 times deeper into trance, so just sleep (here head is tapped) and go deeper."

NB

As they start off staring at your fingertip, which is above their eye line, the key here is to strain their eyes as much as possible, as quickly as possible. To do this in a steady motion, during the count from 3 down to 1, you move your fingers both nearer to them (they go cross eyed etc) and at the same time in a downwards motion. So on 3 it starts above their eyeline, on 2 in line with their nose and 1 in line with their chin, which means by this time, as they will still be trying to keep their eyes on your finger, their eye lids will have shut naturally anyway, and because their eyes have been very strained, it's so much easier to leave them shut as you say sleep. Without pausing you follow this up immediately, with the quick trance deepening method, of telling them that the moment you tap their head they will go 100 times deeper into trance, you then tap their head and remove your finger quickly, as you say sleep and go deeper. This usually has the effect of pushing their head back a bit, they resist and as such push forward onto your fingertip with their forehead and then you suddenly remove your finger as you say sleep and go deeper, which means that their head then falls down onto their chest. If this does not occur, you can literally just place your hand upon their shoulder, as you say, "and your head is now so heavy, it falls down onto your chest." Whilst saying this, you simply use your fingers as a lever against the front and back or their neck to make them move their head down against their chest. In practise, the whole induction takes between 40 to 60 seconds maximum.

THE SWAYING HANDCLAP INDUCTION

For this induction you have the subject standing just in front of their chair. Their legs and feet are together, hands down by their sides, eyes shut and they must breathe deeply in through their nose and out through their mouth. You then say something such as:

"As you stand here, with your eyes closed, you notice that with each and every breath that you take your body is relaxing more each second that passes by. I'd like you to relax completely, so I'm going to gently sway you backwards and forwards in rhythm with your rate of breathing." (This you then actually do) "So breathe in and out, in and out." (They are swayed back and forward in time with their breathing) "Don't forget that the moment I tell you to, your whole body will relax, your eyes will remain tightly closed and you'll enter a sleep like state."

N.B.

Throughout all this talking, you've been progressively swaying them further backwards and forwards, so much so, that if you were to set them off swaying backwards again and did not stop them falling with your hand, then they would indeed, fall backwards into their chair, or at least it would be very difficult to stop themselves. You capitalise upon this fact, and the moment you've said, "and you'll enter a sleep like state," you have timed this as you will be ready to set them back on their swaying backwards direction movement. The moment they are moving backwards, you clap your hands by the person's ear, as you simultaneously and very loudly command sleep. This is immediately followed in a quieter tone of voice by, "and going deeper, and deeper to sleep." As you clap in the direction they are going anyway, the sheer shock of the noise knocks them off balance and they'll fall all the way back into their chair, it also quite literally shocks them into hypnosis.

THE PROGRESSIVE RELAXATION INDUCTION

This induction, as the title suggests, is a slower, more progressive style. It is the type of induction which can be suitably used in the therapists consulting rooms, as well as upon the performance stage. In a stage situation, it is usually used to hypnotise a group of several people simultaneously so although it takes longer, you are actually placing several people into trance at once, therefoe overall, there isn't too much difference timewise. For these styles of inductions the subjects must be sitting on their chairs, feet together and flat on the floor, with hands and arms resting upon their laps, with palms facing upwards and they should be sitting up straight, as comfortably as is possible. You will find that the wording for such an induction (with added subliminal effects) is in the verbal psychology chapter of this book, and basically, it just relies upon the principles of rapport, observation, recognition and leadership, which are also described in full elsewhere.

What you say to the subject/s will be different each time and dictated by the way in which the subject/s react to you suggestions. (Always use what the majority do as your guide.) Of course the standard phrases, which all hypnotists use at some time, and are included at the end of this chapter, will come in extremely useful during a progressive relaxation induction. Follow all that you've been taught, and the example induction as given in the earlier chapter and you will be able to carry out a progressive relaxation induction, both in the therapy room and upon the stage. As you will by now know, the basic techniques of what makes an induction work and of how rapport, observation, recognition and leadership dictate what you say to the subjects in a progressive relaxation induction, I will now give a few examples of additional distractions which can be offered to the subjects mind to promote the onset of trance more rapidly.

THE SIDNEY FLOWERS BLINK METHOD OF P.R.I.

This is in essence a progressive relaxation induction (P.R.I), which is also combined with a method to strain the subject's eyes. The subjects are seated as for other P.R.I.'s and are told to focus upon a spotlight, or a point on the ceiling, which they are not to take their eyes off (this also helps strain the eyes). You then explain that you will be counting, and on each number everyone will get more and more relaxed, and within a few short moments, everyone will find it so much easier to let their eyelids, which will become so heavy and tired, to shut, rather than trying to keep them open. You also explain that on each odd number as you count, they should close their eyes and on each even number, they should re open their eyes. For example:

On 1…….. eyes shut
On 2……. eyes open

On 3…….. eyes shut

On 4…….. eyes open

On 5…….. eyes shut

On 6…….. eyes open

On 7………eyes shut (etc)

So that on each alternate number, from one they have to shut their eyes and then re-open them on the next even number count. Combine this with the fact they are staring at one point all the time and I'm sure, you can understand why their eyes become strained so quickly. And as the littler muscles in the corner of the eyes do become tired, they will find it much easier to allow their eyes to remain shut. You use your normal patter, which is formulated at the time through a combination of the standard phrases and the things that come to mind, due to rapport, observation, recognition and leadership. Obviously you will also keep suggesting that their eyes are becoming so tired and that their eyelids are becoming so heavy, so tired, so limp, loose and relaxed, as each second passes by. By the count of thirty, most, if not all people, will have had their eyes closed for a while already, however, if their should still be the odd one or two with eyes open, this is now the time to command everyone to close their eyes, and you then proceed directly into your trance deepening patter, to take them all to a deeper level of trance, in a very short space of time.

SPOTLIGHT EYESTRAIN P.R.I.

To cut a long story short, the principles used are identical to any other P.R.I., except, that here, it is very bright spotlights that strain their eyes and disorientate them, as you deliver your suggestions of relaxation as usual. The lights should be in the fly's (the area above your head at front of stage) or front of house. For the consulting room, it can simply be a spotlight mounted on a wall. In either case, the lights should be above the subjects normal eye levels, so that they must strain their eyes in the first place in order to see the light. Add to this the intensity of the bright white spotlight itself and maybe now you can see why they become lethargic, their eyes glaze and then close and they do exactly as you say.

MUSCULAR RELAXATION P.R.I.

Very briefly, the principles are the same except here, they start with their eyes closed and you suggest that, as you mention different areas of their body, they are to imagine the muscles in that area of their body as ropes tied together in knots, and as they mentally undo the knots in their mind so that they become separate lengths of rope, so, in reality, all the muscles in that bodily area, will become so limp, so loose and so relaxed, as they also become so heavy and so tired. You start with their feet, and move around their body, getting them to imagine the same thing happening for their ankles, lower leg area, knees, upper leg area, hips and thighs, groin area, stomach, chest, back, spine, shoulders, shoulder blades, the whole arm area, wrist, hands, fingertips, neck, jaw, cheeks, brow muscles etc.

Each time getting them to visualise the relaxation and each time telling them that as the knots untie and the ropes become separate, so in reality all the muscles in that area, will instantly become so limp, so loose, so relaxed, so heavy and so tired, with each and every breath that they take. You also, at various intervals along the way, insert some of the standard phrases, such as "The deeper you go, the better you feel and the better you feel, the deeper you will go." By the time you've gone round their entire body in this vein and have reached their heads, you will find that they are in a deep trance, and at this point, you would immediately deepen the trance further in the standard way. At the end, you would then say "Sleep" firmly and implant your post-hypnotic suggestions. This induction when done nice and slowly, which is why it's called a P.R.I., should take between six to ten minutes, dependent upon your speed of delivery. Remember that the techniques, which you have been taught in this course in other chapters, can also be combined into any basic induction outline, which I may give now or later.

THE COUNTING BACKWARDS INDUCTION

To do this induction upon the stage to best effect, you should have your voice recorded onto the background music, which you would use for any normal style of induction. Upon this voice on music tape, you must say something such as that in the example induction given in the verbal psychology chapter. For example:

"As you stand up straight upon the stage, or sit comfortably in your chair, you will retain perfect balance at all times. From this moment forward I'd like you to listen only to the sound of my voice, and you'll find that with every breath that you take, every noise you hear and every word I say, that you will go deeper and deeper to sleep.

Now, you don't know if you will go into a trance quickly, or if it will take some time.

To really enjoy all those pleasant changes that are occurring in your consciousness."

YOU THEN CONTINUE, AS PER EXAMPLE IN VERBAL PSYCHOLOGY CHAPTER.

The whole induction, which should be changed by making the example of how to count backwards in their mind longer, so that you keep setting the pace of counting in their mind until you've gone back to 180 and then it's left to them to continue doing so in their minds, which distracts their conscious mind, so that all suggestions given go directly into the subconscious mind. Your pace of wording should be such that it suggests relaxation and then you end the induction as per the example in verbal psychology chapter. These are all dubbed over the induction music and reverbs is added to the voice, with an occasional "sleep" or "relax" added between each count backwards, to add an element of confusion too. This whole induction should last no more than five minutes in total, from start to finish and is "overdubbed" onto the induction music such as Jean Michelle Jarres "OXYGENE" or TRANQUILITY, which is a tape available from new age supply centres. This tape is set ready in the player and the moment the lights dim, as will be explained in a moment, is the exact moment when the tape is started.

Now imagine this, you have completed a few quick inductions and placed a couple of people into trance, but still have about 60 or more people upon the theatre stage, who have come up to have their hands separated. So why not try to hypnotise them all at once and then base your selection of the 12 best subjects, upon the 33 observable signs of trance and a few quick text routines?

To do this, you proceed as follows:

You ask everyone who is sitting down and not already in trance, to sit up straight in their chairs, feet together and flat upon the floor, with hands and arms rested upon their laps with palms facing upwards. Anyone who is standing up and not already in trance is told to stand with feet slightly apart, so that they stand firm and steady, hands down by their sides (unless still locked together) and then everyone in the audience is told to remain silent for the next few minutes whilst people enter the trance state or hypnosis, and then the fun will begin.

Everyone upon the stage is then told to close his or her eyes and listen to everything that you say and then imagine it as 100% total reality. You also say that should you touch them upon the shoulder at anytime they will pay special attention to what you say and ignore what you tell everyone else, whilst still counting backwards in their minds. At this moment, the stage lighting grows dim, so that the figures of people in chairs, or standing up can be seen, but only just, everything appears as a silhouette. This dim atmosphere in itself helps to promote the onset of trance. It also means, that for the next five minutes, whilst the recorded induction plays, you can go around the stage (with your radio mike switched off) pretending to talk into the microphone. The audience will assume what they hear coming out of the speakers at the time is what you are saying live, there and then. In actual fact, you are either just miming and know that the studio recorded induction sounds better than you could ever do it live, or you are saying other things to separate subjects whose shoulder you have got your hand upon. I will leave you to work some of this out for yourself, but they've already been told, if you look back through what I've said at the start, that should I touch them upon the shoulder they will ignore what you say to everyone else and will know you are speaking to them and them only. As such, they will then take special notice of all you say. This means that you can touch people on the shoulder, talk to them and as the radio mike is switched off, the audience will be unable to hear you and will assume that what you are saying, is what they hear coming through the speakers. This means, everyone is being hypnotised, to a certain degree, just by the voice upon the tape and for dramatic effect, you can go up to those you feel are very susceptible, place your hand upon their shoulder and speak audibly into their ear to do a falling backwards induction on those standing up, or a body flop induction upon those who are sitting down.

As the audience will only be able to see an outline of each person, it will look most impressive to them as they listen to the induction, which they assume is you speaking live, to also see people falling backwards onto the stage or flopping forwards in their chairs like rag dolls, it will look most impressive indeed. And the moment the "subliminal" style induction recorded on the audio tape reaches the point where the lights on the stage go brighter, the tape will now be playing just relaxation music, the audience will be amazed to see people scattered all over the stage, and you now go into your group deepening immediately, this being done for real through the radio mike, which by this time will have been switched back on.

The post hypnotic suggestions are then given to everyone and lastly, in order to narrow down the onstage 60 people to the best 12 subjects, you go through a quick process of mind imagination screening, which is also quite entertaining to the audience, as well as serving it's required purpose. Those people who are obviously not in trance are dismissed immediately, and then simple suggestions are given, such as, it's a cold day, a hot day, you're milking a cow, you're a washing machine etc. You will be able to tell visually, by the subjects reactions to these simple, yet fairly amusing tests, who will make the best subjects, and of course these are the people who are kept on stage, the rest being slowly dismissed, once fully out of trance. So, in other words, the show begins and continues, whilst the selection of good subjects and return of not so good subjects is still being made. This means that the fun, entertaining routines start a lot quicker and from the point of view of the audience, the show is much slicker and quicker than many I could mention.

If you ever get the chance to see Paul McKenna work live, in a large capacity venue, then you'll know exactly what I mean. You, at the end of all this will already have extracted many laughs from the audience, who will be thoroughly enjoying themselves and also will have selected your best subjects for use throughout the remainder of the evening.

So, here for your reference purposes, is the running order of events, which would make up a very professional and entertaining hypnotic stage show.

1 Intro music with voice over introduction recorded upon it.

2 Play on "Theme Music" as you walk upon the stage and take a bow.

3 Your opening comedy lines and talk about hypnosis.

4 The locked hands test, with suitable background music.

5 People have got to the stage area, whilst loud and exciting music plays.

6 Get to know the people etc. and establish rapport.

7 Do a quick induction, or two, such as falling back etc. to get about five people into trance very quickly and to establish total belief and expectancy.

8 Then go into the "subliminal" induction on tape procedure as detailed above, whilst you also do several more instant inductions on suitable subjects, whilst the tape with your voice upon it plays.

9 Group deepening of induction is done in normal way.

10 The major post hypnotic suggestions are implanted into everyone's mind.

11 Everyone is awoken and obviously unresponsive subjects returned to seats.

12 Everyone left is then put under again, at same time, by just saying sleep, and using the handsweep techniques below.

13 The mind/imagination screening begins and good subjects selected.

THE HANDSWEEP TECHNIQUE

This is a quick way to return everyone to the eyes closed hypnotic state once the major post hypnotic suggestion has been implanted in the subjects minds. It saves the time needed to go to each person in turn and snap you fingers prior to saying sleep, it also looks a little more dramatic than just facing everyone and saying "OK everyone, I'm talking to you all now, so just Sleep" (This is said as you snap your fingers in a downwards movement, facing the whole group, they then all go back under at the same time).

To do this, stand facing the audience and suddenly, you do a 360 degree turn on the spot, rather like a dancer would do and as you turn your hand is open, fingers outstretched and you say sleep (drawn out), so, that as you turn, each and very subject sees your outstretched palm pass by their point of vision as they hear command sleep and they all return to the eyes closed hypnotic state immediately. It's quick and very impressive.

Of course, anyone who does not react immediately is told to sleep and if they don't react this time they are, of course, dismissed as an unsuitable subject. This should not worry you however, as by this stage of the show, all the onstage subjects should be real diamonds and worth their weight in gold many times over. From a time length point of view the running order I've just mentioned would be as follows:

1	Intro music and voice over introduction to show	(3 mins)
2	Play on music, enter stage and take a bow etc	(3 mins)
3	Opening comedy lines and talk on Hypnosis	(5 mins)
4	Locked hands test	(4 mins)
5	Getting people on stage as music plays	(3 mins)
6	Getting to know them/rapport/one liners	(3 mins)
7	About 6 instant inductions, with more one liners	(5 mins)
8	Group subliminal induction of everyone at once	(5 mins)

9	Group deepening of trance	(1.5mins)
10	Group major post hypnotic suggestions	(1.5mins)
11	Return those not under to audience	(1 min)
12	Put all group under with handsweep and oneliners	(1 min)
13	Start the first sketch/imaginations screening	(30secs)

So, from the point when first piece of music begins for the start of show, up until the point where everyone is under and the first comedy routine begins takes :

A TOTAL TIME LENGTH ON THEATRE SHOWS OF THIRTY SIX MINUTES

Which, done in first half of the show, leaves about twenty four minutes for comedy routines, so that the interval comes one hour into the evenings' events. The interval in a theatre show realistically ends up being 20 to 30 minutes and then the second half of the show is done, which also keeps to the one hour each way format, this makes the complete theatre show, including intervals, two and a half hours inclusive, which for a stage hypnotism show is standard practise these days.

In the second half of the show you have, of course, only to come back on stage to do a few one liners (say 4 minutes) then you say "come and join the party" at which point all the subjects race back to the stage (2 minutes), you return them all to sleep after questioning them about the comedy routines they are still doing, which they did during the interval in and around the audience (4 minutes). This means 10 minutes into the second half, the show starts again properly, leaving 50 minutes in which to do comedy sketches. Or course, if you do the guaranteed handclasp text and the world record induction of over 12 people in 60 seconds, then this will take up about another eight minutes of the show. The end result being, however, that you have more volunteers to use if you wish, it kills time and there would then only be 32 minutes to fill up with comedy sketch routines. Obviously, the show would end by all suggestions being removed from the subject's minds and then them being awoken properly.

Please note, this is just an example running order, you are free to devise your own and indeed, I would advise you to do so. The point I am trying to make is this though. The hypnotic induction can be made as much a part of the show as the comedy routines you get the subjects to do. In fact, the general public are truly amazed watching people being placed under hypnosis rapidly, it does not bore them, so have no worries there. In a club or pub show you would have a smaller audience and you'd have less people to deal with, as result the whole procedure being much quicker. Ideally, in pubs and clubs, you want everyone under hypnosis with 20 minutes of your act starting, so that there is 40 minutes left for the actual comedy sketch routine section of your one hour spot, which incidentally seems to be the standard time required in pubs and clubs these days.

I hope this has not only given you an excellent idea for use of the verbal psychology induction, but also, I hope it has given you a better understanding in the way a hypnotic show is engineered and routined to make a "whole" that is both fascinating and entertaining whilst looking slick and professional.

THE LITTLE BOY INDUCTION

Yes, yet another different method of induction. However, I hope you have noticed that with all of the methods I've detailed, belief and expectancy in the subjects mind is the biggest factor which works in our favour.

This is a method which I would only use upon a very small in height subject, so that I could make a logical reason for what follows by delivering a few one liners aimed at how small the person is, and how they remind me of a little boy.

I would stand upon a chair, with the subject on the left hand side of me, with their right arm stretched up into the air, as high as they can get it. I would then take hold of their upstretched arm with both of my hands and tell them to stare forwards, preferably at a bright white spotlight, otherwise at a small point high up on the wall facing them. They are to stare at this point at all times, you are now ready for the induction. You explain that you will count backwards from 3 to 1, and that, by the count of 1, when you say sleep, they will find it so much easier to just relax every muscle in their entire body, let their heavy eyelids shut and continue to breathe deeply and regularly.

"So on 3, as you stare intently at the bright white light, your eyes begin to strain and you just want to fall into a beautifully relaxed state. On 2, you can almost feel your legs becoming so weak beneath you, that you feel as though you will fall to the floor in a heap. But I won't let you fall and hurt yourself, instead I'll just let you fall into a beautifully relaxed state. And on 1, you can feel yourself falling to the floor, your legs are like jelly and cannot hold your weight as you sleep. (the word sleep is drawn out.)

N.B. As this is said, all the way through, in time with their breathing, you pull their arm upwards as much as you can on their in breath and then let it go slack again on their outbreath. This does two things, it acts as a disorientation method and a distraction for their conscious mind and also, for some strange reason, it blurs your vision. There is a pressure point in the armpit, which if hit hard, can make you pass out or vomit. Well, obviously, we are using nowhere near that kind of pressure and the pressure which we are using is indirect, as opposed to being directly on the pressure point. I believe it is possible however, that this indirect pressure to the point in question is responsible for the blurring of vision, combine this with the straining of the eyes caused by the bright white spot light and the power of suggestion and that's where the disorientation element comes in, it's also the reason why they end up collapsing in a heap to the floor when you command sleep, which, as you imagine, looks highly impressive to the audience.

What I have said may seem hard to believe, in this case I leave it to your experience to give you a true picture. But, I do know personally from use of this method that, if done correctly, it most definitely does work. This method although effective, is really just included for completeness, although I'm sure at some point in the future a performer will make a masterpiece of it.

100% CONFUSION INDUCTION

We have already established earlier in this course, that confusion and disorientation, play a large part in the success of all hypnotic inductions. Well, now to an induction which relies totally on confusion and disorientation, I will only explain how to do this induction briefly, because if you've already really studied the rest of this course, then you will be more than capable of working the rest out for yourself. Basically, you would proceed with saying things such as:

"Just notice how your left hand is hot and your right hand cold, whilst you left leg is light and your right leg heavy.

Now experience the sensation of your hot, right hand becoming cold and your cold, left hand becoming hot, as your heavy, left leg becomes lighter and your light, right leg is becoming heavier all the time."

You would continue in this vein for a while and then suddenly inject your suggestions of relaxation and sleep amongst the illogical confusing statements, which confuse their conscious mind, as one moment a hand is meant to be hot then it's cold etc., all this becomes too much and within a short time the conscious mind shuts down and doesn't even bother to analyse the rubbish which you are presenting to it. It all goes directly into the subconscious mind of the subject and disguised suggestions of relaxation and sleep are then enacted upon. The rest, as I am sure, you can work out for yourself, to finish however, here's an example of how to start adding sleep/relaxation suggestions to the confusion script.

"And notice now, how as your hot right arm tingles and your cold left leg feels heavy, that you relax more and more and your heavy eyelids start to shut."

SHOCK HYPNOSIS

This is just literally finding a most susceptible subject, whose hands have locked together well, observing their body language to check that they feel uneasy upon the stage, and then suddenly and most unexpectedly going up to them and both loudly and firmly, shouting sleep into their ear as your right arm pulls them back from a standing position to the floor, which disorientates them. Or you can literally just throw them back into a chair, as you make the command sleep, the end result will be the same.

I have seen a very well known adult stage hypnotist do this very successfully, on a regular basis, but believe me, it takes enormous confidence and works because you shock the person into hypnosis, you literally scare the person so much by your sudden actions, that they do everything you say and are in fact then scared to do otherwise.

I'll end this explanation of "shock hypnosis" by telling you how one well known stage hypnotist uses this method. To the audience it looks as though Mr? just walks up to the subject, who is staring at their shaking locked hands and knocks them on the back of the neck with the flat part of his right palm, as he commands in a loud authoritative voice "sleep." The subjects legs then fly up into the air and they literally fall in a backwards motion to the floor. Yes, your absolutely right, it looks very impressive, one moment they are standing up, the word sleep is said, and suddenly their legs fly up into the air and they fall down to the floor like a sack of potatoes, asleep.

Well, how? Firstly, let me say, that this is not a method which I condone or recommend any one to use, as it's very easy for someone to get hurt doing this. However, for information purposes only, here's what you do.

Your subject would be standing on the right hand side of you, staring at their hands, which are shaking (sign of good subject), you then simultaneously bring your right hand up, flat against the back of their neck and your right foot literally just knocks the back of their ankles very firmly, causing their legs to fly up into the air and, as such, they'd normally fall straight to the floor with a thud and hurt themselves. You however, have got your right hand on the back of their neck and can "cushion" their fall to the floor. To the audience however, all they will ever remember seeing is a person standing upright one moment, who, the next minute, goes flying in the air as you tap their neck and command them to go to sleep. It should go without saying that this is a very dangerous stunt to use and my advice would be not to use it, anyone doing so, does so at their own risk.

Obviously, as you knock their legs from beneath them is the moment when you shout sleep, which acts as a misdirection so that people do not realise what you've done. As I am sure you can imagine the shock of hearing the word sleep shouted into your ear is very extreme to say the least, let alone the shock of flying up into the air and then down to the floor. This is a very extreme form of disorientation and the rest, once again, is down to belief and expectancy. Impressive as this looks, and despite the fact I have, in the early days of my career, used this technique, USE AT YOUR OWN RISK.

THE RUBBER LEGS INDUCTION

To the audience, this induction appears as follow:

The audience see 12 or more people standing on various parts of the stage and all are staring at their hands, which are locked together and shaking violently. As you verbally suggest that the people are relaxing etc., people start to fall to the floor "asleep" all over the stage, almost as if their legs had turned to rubber beneath them. Yes, just imagine that, you are standing nowhere near them at the time, but they all start to collapse to the floor "asleep" as if their legs have turned to jelly or rubber. As I'm sure you can imagine this looks a real showstopper and absolutely unbelievable from the audiences' point of view. So how is this miraculous induction done, I can hear you say? Well, you would proceed as follows:

You choose the 12 most susceptible subjects from those whose hands locked together and they are spread out around the stage, so that there is room surrounding each of them when they fall to the floor "asleep". They are all told to stand so that their right foot is on the left hand side of their left foot and both feet are flat on the floor. By that, I mean their feet are crossed over and are placed next to each other in this position, whilst flat upon the floor. They then have to stare directly at their locked hands, which by now are shaking violently. Once all of the people are in this position, you explain that this is one of the fastest and most powerful forms of Hypnosis known to mankind. Very loud and exciting music, such as the Bladerunner Theme, or music from the Witches of Eastwick, begins to play at this point. As this music is loud and exciting and as we know excitement breeds excitement, the onstage volunteers will be getting more apprehensive all the time about what is to occur (belief/expectancy). As you will have, if you're sensible, already placed a couple of people under hypnosis with quick inductions, their belief and expectancy levels will be high and working in your favour. The lighting should also change to suggest that something dramatic is about to occur. Verbally, you now suggest to all the subjects who are standing in this strange position, something along the following lines:

"I'm going to count backwards from 3 to 1, and as I do, many of you will find that as you stare directly at your hands, which will continue to shake more violently, the harder you try to stop them, the more they will shake. In fact, the more they shake, the more you will be going deeper to sleep with every breath you take, every noise you hear and with every word I say. Many of you will find your legs will turn to jelly and give way beneath you, when this happens you will not fall and hurt yourself, you'll just fall into a beautifully relaxed, deep, dreamy, sleep like state. You'll enjoy every minute of it, as the deeper you go, the better you will feel and the better you feel, the deeper you will go to sleep."

N.B. At this point you then turn to the audience and say. "Well, ladies and gentlemen, be prepared to be amazed, as this one of the most powerful and dramatic forms of Hypnosis know to mankind. Your attention please."

(Turn back to the subjects and say) " OK, now everyone, so on 3, already many of you will be experiencing that rather strange sensation as your whole body becomes so relaxed and as you stare intently at your hands, your legs are becoming like rubber, so weak they cannot hold your body up any longer and you just want to go to sleep. And on, 2, as you hands shake so violently now, you notice also that your whole body begins to sway. You cannot keep your balance, you can feel yourself falling, as your legs become more weak and rubbery with every breath you take, every noise you hear and every word that I say, so it is so much easier to relax and sleep. And on 1, your whole body so relaxed now, it's hard to keep your balance, now all you want to do is relax and enjoy that feeling of serenity as your legs turn to jelly, as your whole body begins to sway, as you feel yourself falling and you all go to sleep (say sleep in drawn out fashion).

N.B. At this point, anyone who may be standing up is approached from the rear, so that they don't see you coming and you hit the upper side area of their right leg sharply with the side of your hand, as if doing a karate chop. This is enough to knock them totally off balance, so that they do fall to the floor as you once again shout sleep and shock them into hypnosis. Most people will have gone under and fallen to the floor by then however and of course, this additional "push" can be given to those that you feel may be resisting a little, as you actually deliver the count back with patter from 3 to 1. If you are unsure that anyone would fall to the floor, then stand as I've detailed, place your hands as if locked together, and shake them around violently whilst staring at them as the onstage subjects will be doing, I'm sure you'll see that in less than a minute you will fall over too. Then see what happens when someone knocks you on the side of the leg as detailed, whilst they also shout, sleep, firmly into your ear, this time I'm 100% certain you'll end up on the floor. Now do you believe me?

WHY WON'T THEY BE HURT?

Well, the reason is simple, any intelligent person will, as they start to fall to the floor, feel this is occurring and probably try to stop themselves. As they move towards the floor, their legs will naturally bend at the knee, which brings them nearer to the floor, before they "fall" properly, which means they will not freefall as far. When you combine this with the fact that they will probably fall sideways down onto their knees, and then sideways to the floor, this means that their journey to the floor will be far more gradual than it actually appears to the audience. Try it yourself, and you'll see what I mean, it's almost an automatic thing to "fall" to the floor in this way, which is very similar to a sideways fall which some stuntmen use, so that they do not get hurt. Obviously, there is still a small element of danger and this can also be eliminated by softening the surface which they are to land upon. To do this many hypnotists who work theatres regularly, have a nice soft carpet (size of an average stage) which they fix to the floor with gaffer tape, along all four edges, so that no one can trip up accidentally. This, then cushions that small final fall to the floor and the incident of people hurting themselves is practically non existent. However, as with all I describe in this course, proceed at your own risk.

THE ARM SPIN INDUCTION

For this one, the subject sits in a chair, feet together, whilst flat upon the floor, they interlock their fingers, as with the handclasp text, but leave them held loosely, so that when you wish to, you can immediately pull their hands apart and they will separate instantly.

They are then told to close their eyes and relax their arms, so that you are then holding the full weight of their arms and if you were to let go of them, they would fall down into their lap. Indeed you can do this suddenly to check that they have complied with your commands if you so wish.

All this should take but a few seconds to sort out and then you physically proceed by rotating their hands around in a circular motion, which in turn will move their arms in the same way also. This must be done in a steady circular motion, as you deliver your verbal suggestions of relaxation and sleep. The rotation must be done "rhythmically" and at the same speed throughout, so that it both distracts them consciously and also acts as a very low level disorientation method, whilst having a calming "rock a bye baby" affect. You then deliver your usual kind of verbal suggestions having already "conditioned" them to believe that the moment you say sleep their eyes will remain closed at all times until you say otherwise and that they will enter trance at the moment in time. The moment you command sleep, you simultaneously pull the subjects hands apart and, as you will be holding each of their wrists in a separate hand, you not only pull their hands apart, but also in a smooth motion you pull their arms slightly towards yourself and downwards at the same time. The effect you want to achieve is to have them move forward in their chair, with their head moving down towards their lap, as in the body flop induction, except here we achieve it by jerking their body forward by use of their arms (again it disorientates).

The moment you have done this, you allow their arms to drop down by their sides so that they feel lots of physical movements of their body which act as non verbal suggestions of sleep, as they are downwards movements.

All this should be practised upon a willing friend, so that at any performance, you are able to carry it all out so it just takes a matter of 2 or 3 seconds for all the end actions to be done with the result of them being flopped forward in their chair. In other words, you must be able to do it without any hesitation.

When done correctly the subject will start sitting up straight in their chair and the moment that you've said sleep and carried out the physical movements, their hands will be down by their sides and their head down in their lap with the upper area of their body slumped forwards, which, of course, looks most impressive to the audience. Verbally, you would do the normal thing of, "I'll count from 3 to 1 and on 1, when I say sleep you'll instantly enter a beautifully relaxed state and your eyes will remain closed at all times, until I say otherwise." Then you'd count from 3 to 1, usually using the standard kind of phrases along the way and on 1 when you say sleep, all the actions are carried out quickly. I hope you have noticed, that besides belief and expectancy, another reason why this and most inductions work is because of the ritualistic actions you carry out and the importance which you attach to them, which in itself also heightens their belief and expectancy. Also your verbal suggestions begin by explaining in a disguised form what you expect to happen to them when you say sleep, they then know how to react and belief will do the rest for you. As we said earlier, co-operation is a key word in hypnosis.

WORLD RECORD HIGH SPEED HYPNOSIS TECHNIQUE

What I am about to explain to you, is presented to any audience as the fastest and most powerful form of hypnosis know to mankind. And, indeed, to them, that is exactly what it will appear to be. You, as a knowledgeable hypnotist, will know that there is a lot of "psychological" conditioning done in your lead up to demonstrating this method of hypnosis, which is usually done at the start of the second half of the show, by which time everyone has seen you place people into trance rapidly and, as such, their belief and expectancy is complete. You do the "guaranteed hand clasp test" prior to getting people up to be instantly entranced for your world record attempt. The way you present this as a world record attempt, not only enables you to get free, large scale publicity at every large show you do, but also it makes everyone anxious to see you succeed and, as such, it puts them in the perfect frame of mind in which to do instant inductions upon them. The people whose hands are locked together, via the guaranteed hand clasp, are brought up to the stage and their hands are then separated, as detailed in the last chapter. You will no doubt, have many people who were upon the stage at the start of the show and wanted to be hypnotised but, as you sent them back, they missed their chance, or so they thought. So, when you ask for between 12 to 20 volunteers to remain on the stage and take part in the world record high speed hypnosis attempt, you will have many takers, as they will want to grab this second chance to be a star in any way that they possibly can.

The rest of the people are returned to the audience to a round of applause. The people are standing with a slight gap between each of them, in a straight row across the stage. They are standing so they are facing the audience and in a position ready for the falling backwards induction. You then use the I.I.C. principle to condition them that they might be an idiot if they don't enter the hypnotic state especially as this is the fastest and most powerful form of hypnosis known. You then make sure they are standing feet together and hands down by their side, as in the falling backwards test. Next, you get each and every person to stare at the bright white floodlight which should be high up front of house and facing the stage. All front of house lights are switched off and the stage lighting is also made quite dim, so that the light which they are staring at intently literally "blinds" them and blurs their vision. (So don't look at it yourself!). In fact, if you have a modern image, a pair of dark sunglasses would not go amiss during this routine, so you can continue with no risk to your own vision. Next everyone is told to stare directly at the bright white light at all times, and now the Bladerunner theme begins, which is a very loud and exciting tune, which will put a sense of fear into them. You then do your psychological conditioning of what will occur by saying something such as:

"Ladies and Gentlemen, in 1993, a famous television hypnotist, by the name of Alex LeRoy set a world record for high speed hypnosis. He placed over 12 people into a hypnotic trance in less than 60 seconds. Well, tonight, ladies and gentlemen, I don't intend to break that record, oh no, I intend to smash it.

In a few moments you will witness the fastest form of Hypnosis known. It is also the most powerful method of hypnosis. To this day, nobody has been able to resist it's most powerful effects." (Now turn to your subjects).

"OK, now I'm talking to everyone, as you stare directly at the bright white spotlight, listen only to the sound of my voice. In a few moments I shall touch each of you upon the forehead, and the moment that I do, you'll instantly fall back into my arms and enter a deep, deep hypnotic state, as this is the fastest form of hypnosis known.

Now, I won't let you fall and hurt yourselves though, you'll just fall back into a beautifully relaxed state."

(Turn to audience). "OK, ladies and gentlemen, prepare to be amazed."

At this point the induction starts and everyone is placed under hypnosis as I will detail in a moment.

(Once all under say) "Ladies and gentlemen, the fastest form of hypnosis know." (Here take a bow at your applause). At this point, you either awaken people and return them to the audience, or implant the major post hypnotic suggestion in their minds and use them in the second half of the show. Or, implant the post hypnotic suggestion that, when you say goodnight at the end of the show, they will all jump up out of their chairs and shout out loudly,

"WE LOVE THE WORLDS GREATEST HYPNOTIST JONATHAN ROYLE, OH YES WE DO!"

The moment they have done this and leave the building, all suggestions will, of course, then be completely cancelled out. Just imagine it, you say goodnight to end your show, and as you leave the stage 20 or more people jump up and shout out, "We love the worlds greatest hypnotist, Alex LeRoy, oh yes we do!" This is the kind of ending to a hypnotic show that guarantees a standing ovation.

OK, so what do you do physically? Well, quite simply, if the people saw you coming to touch their foreheads, then they would anticipate it occurring and could try to resist. That is exactly why we don't do that. Instead, we start at the left hand side of the stage, working along the row rapidly until we reach the right hand side. Always, when doing what follows, you must be standing on the right hand side of the subject as you stand behind them. Your right hand is then lifted up behind the subject's back and above their head. You then, suddenly, bring your hand down flat over their eyes, which they won't expect, and at exactly the same moment in time your left hand presses flat against the lower back area of your subjects. So as your right hand pushes your subjec's head backwards, your left hand pushes their stomach area forwards, they then very quickly reach that point of no return and fall back to the floor, with you cushioning their fall slightly.

To cushion their fall, you lift your left hand up at the last moment to their upper back area and lower them slightly to lessen the impact. All this, in practise, should take one to two seconds to carry out, as detailed. One moment the subject is standing up, staring at a bright white light and the next moment, everything goes dark as your hand unexpectedly goes over their eyes and they fall back to the floor as you shout "sleep" firmly into their ear, if that's not enough to shock anyone into hypnosis, then I don't know what is. Add to all this, belief, expectancy and suggestions and you really do have a most powerful technique to add to your repertoire.

As the timing of the induction, from a world record point of view, only starts when you touch the first subject by placing your hand over their eyes, it is easily possible to place 40 or more people into trance in less than sixty seconds. This is a very impressive demonstration of hypnosis, which can also get you much free, large scale publicity to promote your theatre show in each town you go to. It really is the fastest form of hypnosis known and will make you a lightening speed hypnotist, use it and be careful.

HYPNOTISING THE AUDIENCE

The induction used for this would be a progressive relaxation induction of an eye straining nature. The techniques of rapport, observation, recognition and leadership would be used with the majority being catered for, so that the end result of many people going into trance whilst still sitting in their seats within the audience is achieved. The standard kind of phrases are used as suggestions along with the classic suggestions of "Your eyelids are so heavy and so tired, that they want to close, in fact the harder you try to keep them open the quicker they will close."

The focus point for the entire audience is a large Hypno-Disc, which is a large black and white spiral effect disc with a motor rotating at a steady speed and giving a blackhole effect as if being "drawn" into the disc. The whole audience is told to stare directly at the spinning disc as your suggestions of relaxation are given in the usual way. The end result will be that as the disc both has the effect of straining your eyes and disorientating you, most of the people who do stare at it will fall to "sleep" in their seat and you will have to go out into the audience to awaken them and bring the subjects you want to use up onto the stage to take part.

I saw a hypnotist called Mark Maverick, use this method most successfully in early 1994 at The Garrick Playhouse in Altringham, and it was most successful for him, with a large majority of the audience going to "sleep" in their seat. These Hypno-Discs are available in a small size for the therapists office from Mr Kevin Gray, I am sure he would, however be able to make a large stage size motor operated Hypno-Disc for you to order, he can be contacted at:

Mr Kevin Gray (I.A.H)

2 Old Row

Burton on Stather

Scunthorpe

South Humberside

DN15 9DN

Tel: 01724 720706

Tel: 01724 720909

Fax: 01724 720877

When you contact Kevin, also ask for full details of all his other "Hypnoquip" products, which will be very useful indeed for your hypnotherapy consulting room.

THE EYE TO EYE FASCINATION INDUCTION

Watch the Jungle Book film and witness the snake staring at the young boy, as he says "look into my eyes", and you'll have an idea of how this eye to eye fascination induction works. I usually take hold of the persons left hand in my right, and this establishes an instant rapport and instant bond between you both. Then using the method explained earlier in the course, make them think that I am staring directly into their eyes and at no point do I blink or lose eye contact, this has a strong psychological effect upon them and, not only makes them feel slightly uncomfortable, but also makes their eyes become heavy and tired, via the eyestrain technique, already explained. I then start talking in a low tone of voice, at a steady monotonous speed, suggesting that they can feel themselves sinking into the chair, their eyes becoming heavy and they want to close them, as they feel warm, tingling sensations in various areas of their body, as they wish to go to sleep, etc.

Continue along these lines, only stopping for a second to take breath. The key with this induction being to keep their eyes fixed upon your gaze and bombard them with suggestion, after suggestion until their eyes close and they go under. At which point, you quickly deepen the trance, as usual, and they will then be your suggestible subject. The belief factor also comes in here very strongly, as people believe all you have to do is stare into their eyes, tell them to go to sleep and they will, well in this case, great, let them carry on believing, as it makes our job easier. The suggestion of sinking and a sensation of falling down a black hole creates powerful pictures in the imagination and, as we know, when the imagination and the will are in conflict, the imagination will always win. This method can have a person in trance in less than 60 seconds, and is ideal for use in a social party situation. It's funny, but I've noticed that lots of women want to be around you when they find out you are a professional hypnotist. Oh well, I suppose there must be some perks to the job after all.

INDIRECT INDUCTION METHOD

Another powerful technique, which I have found always seems to work, is to say the following sentence at the start of your show.

"If you do not volunteer, it does not matter, you have already heard the sound of my voice and many of you will find that you go to sleep by yourselves whilst sitting in the audience, but don't worry I will wake you up, as the deeper you go, the better you will feel and the better you feel, the deeper you will go."

By implanting this suggestion into the whole audience's mind, it will go into some peoples subconscious and in a short time have the effect of making them react to the sleep suggestions you are giving to the onstage subjects. On more occasions than I care to remember, I have had people enter trance whilst sitting in the audience and I've had to go out amongst them to wake up the ones who have gone under. This, too, is the reason why the full hypnotic induction cannot be shown on TV or broadcast over the radio, as people would most certainly enter trance around the country. Now you should be starting to realise just how powerful suggestion really is.

Incidentally, Mr Peter Casson, The Chairman of the Federation of Ethical Stage Hypnotists, was on BBC 1 many years ago, with the end result of cameramen and the production crew entering the hypnotic trance during the live broadcast, yes, it looked amazing and caused a sensation, but, it also lead to a ruling that the full hypnotic induction could not be broadcast on TV or radio.

<u>VARIATIONS ON INDUCTION</u>

The point that I wish to make here, is that, as long as you follow all the guidelines, which I set out in the first part of this course, then your induction's will still work, however you should decide to alter them to suit your own style. This in itself is a most important point, you must be relaxed in all that you do, then you will appear more confident and professional and so ultimately, you will have more success. An example of a slight variation or an induction is as follows:

You tell the subject, that you'll count from 3 to 1 and say sleep etc. Instead, you suddenly just say one and sleep, and they will, if a good, responsive subject, still fall back into your arms and enter trance. I suppose the shock element also comes into play here.

Another example, is they stand as with the falling backwards induction, but with eyes open, you tell them to follow the microphone with their eyes and the moment you command sleep to close their eyes, enter trance and fall back into your arms. You then move the mike towards their head at an angle, then continue past their head, so that in order to follow the mike's path of travel, they must tilt their head back more and so on, until they reach that point of no return and start to fall back into your arms, which is of course the moment when you command them to sleep.

CREATING YOUR OWN INDUCTIONS

By using the tried, tested and proven to work principles which have detailed in this course and the example inductions which are in this chapter, you should be more than capable of creating your own new unique to induction. Perhaps you yourself will write a book detailing your creations in years yet to come. A good source of material is any literature/books/tapes etc. which you can get by a gentleman from the U.S.A., called Mr Gil Boyne. Mr Boyne, is an American therapist, who specialises in instantaneous inductions. He has literally hundreds of quickie inductions and any literature which you can obtain detailing his methods would be of immense use to you. Another book, which I recommend, is one that was recommended to P.O.S.H. and after reading it, I too, wholeheartedly recommend it, entitled Trance-Formations, the book is by Richard Bandler and is very interesting reading on Hypnosis.

Another subject, which I would recommend you to learn, in order to become an expert at rapid induction, is anything on the subject of Neuro Linguistic Programming (N.L.P.) which is an extremely quick way to change perceptions of the mind and the way in which people think. It is also a very useful subject to have knowledge of for use in the hypnotherapist's consulting room, should you wish to pursue that avenue of financial gain. Remember, that old saying "Knowledge is Power", well, that is very true.

You may also wish to consider adding subliminal messages within the sounds of your induction music that you use to place them into trance. These verbal commands are not consciously audible to people listening to the music, but they are very quickly acted upon by their subconscious mind. How useful it would be to have suggestions of relaxation and sleep subliminally recorded within your induction music. A full kit, containing subliminal overmasks, sound effects, instructions and a full training manual are available to teach you how to make your own subliminal recordings. These can be used both as just mentioned, and also, to make therapy tapes, which can be sold separayely.

Details of the full kit are available for a S.A.E. from:

Mr Martin Windebank

6 Gwynne Close

Windsor

Berkshire

SL4 5PY

Another supplier of very unusual Hypnosis related items, which may be of use is:

Lifetools

Freepost KS1852

Poynton

Stockport

Cheshire

SK12 1FZ.

Tel: 01625 85885 or

Fax: 01625 850551

And ask for a free catalogue.

They supply relaxation music suitable for induction, subliminal tapes, books and training materials on hypnotherapy and mind control techniques. And devices, such as the lucid dream machine, which makes you have "virtual reality" dreams, their catalogue is well worth getting.

The very best audio tapes I have come across to date, which include countless different subjects for therapy including cancer treatment, childbirth, infertility, exams, esteem, alcohol abuse and much more are available (free catalogue on request) from:

PILGRIM TAPES PTY

P.O. Box 107

SHREWSBURY

SY1 1ZZ

I would also advise you to obtain, either from a book shop or your library, about 2 or 3 books by the following people:

Sigmund Freud, Carl Jung, Milton Erikson and anything, also by prolific psychology writers on the subject of personality types and the human mind. This will all be "heavy" reading, but will gain for you two things which are.

A You will have a thorough understanding of how the human mind works and how the damage caused by everyday stresses can be repaired in the consulting room and

B You will also have learned how to spot different kinds of people, how to get them to do different things etc., and this is the kind of information you need as a hypnotist.

So if anyone falsely accuses you of having no knowledge of hypnosis and psychotherapy, then having studied this course and acting upon my advice, will be a qualified hypnotherapist, with a sound knowledge of psychology and the human mind. This will set you far above most of the stage hypnotists who are currently at work, they, having been plumbers one minute and after reading just one book by Paul McKenna, they are stage hypnotist the next. You are advised by me to study several other peoples viewpoints on hypnosis and to then make your own decisions, then, and only then, will you be happy and confident in all that you do. The hypnotism industry is one of the most cut-throat and competitive area of showbusiness, then it's also one of the most lucrative. Should you join a stage hypnotism society, whether it is P.O.S.H., or some other, never be influenced by what other members say, they are no better than you, although they may think they are God.

Integrity is a key word in this business, which, unfortunately, many hypnotist don't seem to have. You must never talk about people behind their backs, you must never spread nasty rumours and certainly you should never try to stop a fellow hypnotist from getting work.

TECHNIQUES OF BRAINWASHING

Deprive a person of all sense of touch, light, sound and taste and they will very quickly become disorientated. Soldiers and police do it, when they make people stand with their hands flat on the wall and feet wide apart. It is not just a safety measure, it is also a hypnotic technique and that technique is disorientation. Another technique is to place subjects into a tank with warm water as the only support, deprive them of all external stimuli, they cannot see, hear or feel anything, and after short time, they will be at your mercy. Once in this disorientated state, you can then alter their personality, believes, in fact, anything that you could wish to change.

Place a microphone at the top of the tank, so that it is unidirectional in effect, now, giving any commands that you wish to have carried out, repeatedly, giving them in a slow, quiet, monotonous, firm tone of voice. After six or seven hours, you will have changed the victims' whole personality and can let them out of the water tank. Remove their blindfold and let them out of the dark warehouse. Male to Female. Nice to Evil. Or vice versa, with brain washing, anything is possible and you can get anyone to do anything.

Anything is possible with brain washing and that's why these details are included, for information purposes only, and have been kept deliberately vague, so that you will not be tempted to use them.

Relaxation aids are on sale now, from Lifetools in Cheshire (address elsewhere), for example, goggles that keep on flashing a red light in the wearers eyes at pulse rate, this will both make them enter trance and also start to brainwash them. If they were to then hear music, which contained subliminal commands within this, then the hidden commands would most certainly be enacted on.

PRESSURE POINT INDUCTION

These really have nothing to do with hypnosis, and if anything, are what has given hypnosis a bad name over the years. I detailed Carotid Artery induction earlier in the course and also the Little Boy induction, both of which rely on pressure, either directly or indirectly upon pressure points, which are all capable of knocking you unconscious. Unfortunately, if too much pressure is applied, or pressure applied for too long, then it can kill the person. So I wouldn't use these techniques. However, a book called "The Black Art of Death" gives full details of these kind of techniques and it's available by contacting the following company:

Coach Harness Books

C/O Haughley

Stowmarket (SFK)

1P14 3NS

Tel: 01449 673258

SELF HYPNOSIS BRIEFLY EXPLAINED

Self hypnosis is remarkably simple and the results can be absolutely astounding.

To hypnotise yourself, the easiest way is to use the audio cassette supplied with your course or alternatively make up your own on which you record the hypnotic induction, (P.R.I.) deepening and suggestion therapy, which of course, should be aimed to programme your mind that you have got 100% self confidence, then, at the end goes the awakening method.

Full details of all the components that make up the finished whole are contained within this course.

The tape would then be played to yourself whilst lying down on your bed, in a dimly lit sitting room/bedroom and will have basically the same effect upon your mind, as would be obtained, if someone else suggested the positive changes to you.

Just like medicine, although not dangerous in anyway, the tapes should only be used by the person it is intended for and as a hypnotic induction process is used upon these tapes, they should never be listened to in the car whilst driving or when operating machinery. Incidentally, these home hypnotherapy tapes are also ideal and in fact, I would say essential items, for a trainee hypnotist. Listening to them, you can learn first hand, how the hypnotic induction is correctly delivered verbally and how different suggestions have different effects. Also, perhaps most importantly, they enable you to experience the hypnotic state for yourself.

These tapes can be sold individually, or given to clients attending for therapy to help reinforce the treatment they receive.

The other method of self hypnosis, is to literally, mentally think the wordings of the whole therapy session through in your minds eye.

To induce self hypnosis, the procedure is similar to a guided induction and is as follows:

Make yourself comfortable somewhere warm where you will not be disturbed. Release all tight clothing and remove your shoes. Make sure your feet are not touching each other and your hands are resting slightly away from your body. Close your eyes, take a deep breath in and hold it for 5 seconds. Then release it slowly, all the way out, as far as you can, all the way to the bottom of your stomach. Repeat this a further 3 times. Each time you exhale, allow yourself to relax and just "let go". Let your body start to feel limp and heavy and let all the tensions flow away.

It is very important not to try too hard, as the secret is to allow things to happen naturally, with no effort at all.

Then start to count backwards, in your mind, from 10 to 1 and with each number you count, allow your mind and body to relax even more. Let your mind just drift away to anywhere you like and your body to become heavier and more relaxed with every number. Repeat this as many times as you like until you know you are physically and mentally more relaxed than when you started.

Next you need to bring in the visualisation technique. Imagine, in your "minds eye" the muscles in your feet and around your toes and FEEL them relaxing. Let them go limp and heavy. Let all the tensions fade away. Then move up slowly through your calves, the tops of your legs, your buttocks, your stomach, your chest, your shoulders and neck, down your arms and into your fingers and thumbs, up the back of your head, over the top and down your forehead. When you reach your face, pay special attention to allowing all the little muscles round your eyes, your eyelids, your cheeks, all round your mouth, your jaw and even your tongue. You may find, at this point that your jaw sags open slightly with the pleasant feelings of total relaxation.

Do not be afraid, as you will not loose control or become "fixed", but you may find that with the first few attempts you drift into a light sleep! Part of the knack is to stay more or less awake while being totally relaxed in order to give yourself positive suggestions. The idea is to program your <u>mind</u> to slip into relaxation to the trigger of backwards counting and physical relaxation.

The process can take a little time in the early stages – maybe 15 to 20 minutes – and sometimes needs quite a bit of practice to perfect. But when you have mastered the technique, the state can be entered very quickly indeed, in a matter of seconds with some people.

When you have entered self hypnosis, you can make any suggestions you wish to yourself eg.

I am gaining in confidence.

I feel relaxed and happy at all times.

Every day in every way I am getting better and better.

I will approach people and situations in a more positive manner.

I will be appreciative and receptive to people.

Should you have an event in the future to confront, an excellent way to approach it is by visualisation during self hypnosis, eg.

Suppose you have an important meeting or a public speech to make. You would induce self hypnosis and then go through the whole event from before the start to the finish in your mind BUT with the situation in a controlled and relaxed manner. Go through, in your mind, all the things you will do on that particular day, right from getting up in the morning, but this time you are calm, relaxed, in control and not at all agitated (almost a new you). Continue through the whole day, making special emphasis on the event, while remaining in this controlled state.

This is an accepted form of therapy and is equally effective when used with self hypnosis.

When you have completed your session, simply say to yourself that you will wake yourself up by counting from 1 to 5 and when you wake up you will remember all the suggestions and (importantly) you will feel refreshed, relaxed, revitalised, confident and full of energy (repeat these thoughts). Then simply say to yourself 1, feeling relaxed. 2, I am feeling refreshed. 3, feeling revitalised and starting to wake up. 4, I am full of confidence and waking up more with my eyes starting to open. 5, feeling full of energy, eyes open wide awake feeling on top of the world.

Practice this technique to perfection and you will be astounded at the results. It's almost like a wonder drug which will not go in a bottle but with no side effects!

STANDARD PHRASES WHICH HYPNOTISTS USE

To end this chapter on induction methods, I will give you some examples on the kind of "Standard Phrases" which would be used by a hypnotist during the induction process. The rules I explained in the verbal psychology chapter, would of course be followed when giving these suggestions to the on stage subjects, or the client within the therapy room. Firstly though, allow me to recap a little. Hypnotism becomes possible through five essentials:

1 The fixation of the gaze of the hypnotist.

2 The execution of certain passes that the hypnotist must know.

3 The delivery of commands of suggestions must be in a voice filled with conviction.

4 The ability of the hypnotist to concentrate on the suggestion which he wishes to impart.

5 The ability of the subject to assume a passive state, to concentrate on the suggestions given and their willingness to accept same.

Another piece of advice is this, your nose will tell you an awful lot about a person, very often, what they eat on a regular basis, do they smoke? Their place of work (eg. Mechanics smell of oil, nurses smell of ether etc.) Now go out and do the same, you will, with a little practice be able to smell the odour of fear, when someone is terrified upon coming to the stage, or coming to visit you in your consulting room. When you get close to a subject, it's all very well to be able to determine things about them, through the way that they smell, but always make certain that they cannot tell what you have eaten and always smell sweet. Bad body odour can, and will interfere with your image and you may not, at the time, realise why.

Let all your bodily senses work for you, not against you, train them all to perfection. You will then almost be psychic and will have mastered E.S.P.

(Extra Sensory Perception, training your senses to work better than most people) and not addition sensory perception as most people believe. These sorts of powers are within reach of all of us.

Another example of how your sense of smell can be used is to determine when any woman is on heat, this may sound unbelievable, but yes, it truly can be done, as they give out Pheromones, which I have mentioned elsewhere, so do men when they are feeling randy. Why do you think a dog smells the genitals? It tells him just how powerful you are, your position in the family group. So observe life and then learn from your eye opening observations. Atmosphere is another component, a successful hypnotist must use to best effect. The atmosphere must, as I explained earlier, always be such, that entering the hypnotic state seems obvious and easy to the subject. Let me present you with an example of how atmosphere works, then you will not be able to tell me that you cannot sense atmospheres, as you in fact do this every single day of you life. Have you never walked into a room where a terrific personal argument was going on, just before you entered? You knew nothing about the argument, in fact, you didn't even know that the couple could fall out. However, you could cut that atmosphere with a knife, couldn't you?

So ensure that the subjects are always seated comfortably, no tight items around the throat. You will have already informed them of what you intend doing, you state you will not give them any commands that are harmful, in fact, any commands that you give them will be only beneficial to their life.

The last subject I feel that must recap in, is something, which even some very experienced hypnotists seem to forget, and that is to cancel out all the commands which you have given to the subjects after they have been carried out. In other words, all commands must be cancelled out completely before a person leaves the building unless they are beneficial. This is a most important point and one which you forget at your own risk. In fact, I usually mention it in my opening patter and awakening speech in a similar way as follows:

"Whenever you leave this room/building/theatre/area etc., all my commands will be completely cancelled out."

Or

"When I awake you in a few moments, you will feel on top of the world, full of energy and optimism and in fact, you will feel better than you have ever felt in your entire life. You will not have any headaches or side effects of any kind. You will, in fact, feel really great. When you leave here tonight, all my commands and suggestions to you will be completely cancelled out, in other words, you will be as you were when you first came in here tonight."

Obviously, this only applies when on stage. During therapy sessions you should reinforce all suggestions as much as possible and encourage your client to REMEMBER the messages for the rest of their life.

Notice, the strong emphasis on "You", this tells the subject, that you are speaking to them and them alone. This kind of emphasis must continue all the way through, it is you, the hypnotist, that they must relate to all the time. If they start to notice what the audience is doing you will have lost them, unless it was you who brought the audience to their attention. Anyway, back to the original subject in hand, that of standard phrases which you can use during your hypnotic induction.

STANDARD PHRASES FOR HYPNOTIC INDUCTIONS

"The deeper you go the better you will feel, and the better you feel, the deeper you will go to sleep."

"With every breath you take, every noise you hear, every word I say and every thought that you think, you'll go deeper and deeper to sleep."

"Every muscle in your body from the tips of your toes to the tips of your fingers, now becoming so limp, so loose and so relaxed."

"Each and every muscle in your body, now becoming so heavy and so tired."

"Your eyelids are feeling so heavy and so tired, in fact, the harder you try to keep them open, the more they want to close tightly, as you relax completely."

As you sit (or lie) there in the comfortable chair, it almost feels as though every movement would be a great effort, as though you are sinking down deeply into the chair and into calm, satisfying, relaxation."

"This feeling of warmth and relaxation, is now travelling around your entire body and as you continue to breathe deeply and regularly, you are drifting deeper and deeper to sleep."

All the worries, stresses and tensions of days gone by, are leaving your mind and leaving your body now, allowing you to relax completely."

"In a few moments, when I awake you, you'll have an overwhelming desire to do almost everything I say, you'll find that you'll enjoy living your part in tonight's show to the full, and will carry out all that I suggest, as an automatic reflex action."

"Just as your subconscious makes you breathe at night, or circulates the blood around your body, in just the same way you can faithfully rely upon your subconscious mind to help you eliminate this problem from your every day life."

"It becomes habit in your subconscious mind to smoke (or whatever) and now your subconscious mind will make it habit not to smoke (or whatever)"

"Something that you thought would be difficult to achieve, will turn out to be ridiculously easy to do."

"Each morning when you awake, from this moment forward, you will awaken with an inner warm glow of confidence, a renewed optimism to life and a more positive attitude to get things done."

"Every day, in every way, things will be getting better and so much easier to cope with."

"You have made a promise to yourself to (whatever) and whilst it may be alright, on occasion, to break a promise to a friend, your subconscious mind will not allow you to break a promise to yourself and, as such, success is guaranteed."

NOTE: I hope these above examples will give you a much better idea of how on stage or therapy room suggestions, should be worded for maximum, positive effect.

Common sense and a little thought is all you require to word your own suggestions to give your own on stage subjects, just remember the golden rule, that there must never be any doubt in their mind of what you want them to do. Good luck with your induction's and enjoy "entrancing" people, but don't let the feeling of great power go to your head or else you'll end up like far too many other hypnotists in the profession, who have a Messiah complex and treat others like dirt, as they believe they truly are the best thing since sex was invented. This is OK on stage, but if it is carried over into your personal life, then you'll end up with no friends and your family will turn against you. To end this chapter, below are two little techniques, which can make life easy for you.

HANDSHAKE TECHNIQUE

This is basically just a way to tell, in the time it takes to shake a subject's hand, whether or not they will make a good subject. When you shake their hand press your fingers against the palm of their hand and feel how much moisture is there. The drier their hand is, the more relaxed the person is already and, as such, the easier it will usually be to hypnotise them. On the other hand, the more the subjects hand is perspiring, the more nervous they are and the harder it will be to get the subject relaxed for a normal style induction. These people, with waterlogged palms, are either not used to, or are shocked into hypnosis, as they are already too tense for the slow P.R.I.

TWO ARE BAD SUBJECTS PLOY

This is just a psychological ploy, which can be used to increase the chances of people wanting to be hypnotised and also the number of people who end up under hypnosis. At the start of your act, once the subjects are on stage ready to be hypnotised, you say.

"Well, I must say ladies and gentlemen, that there are two people on this stage who cannot be hypnotised, or at least I think they can't. The reason being, they don't have the correct powers of I.I.C. and we will not be able to use them. I won't point them out however, as they might surprise us and start concentrating a bit more." This, which you have just said to the audience, is pure waffle, however, as each person on the stage starts worrying if it's them, they'll all put 100% effort in to being hypnotised. Now your chances of success are considerably increased. Just imagine how daft people will feel, returning to the audience, having not gone under, when you have said something like that. My experience shows me they are more likely to remain on stage and act hypnotised and take part in the show before looking a complete fool and returning to audience.

See you in the next chapter.

NOTE = The Section Above was extracted from "The Encyclopedia of Hypnotherapy, Stage-Hypnosis and Complete Mind Therapy" Volume One by Dr. Jonathan Royle which is available on Amazon.

The $1000 Hypnotic Show Plan

By Devin Knight

Devin Knight is regarded as one of magic's most prolific inventors. He is also a highly sought after lecturer for both magicians and mentalists.

Most of his effects are run-away best sellers and have received rave reviews. Devin was a protege of the late Al Mann and currently works as a full-time Magician, Mentalist & Stage Hypnotist.

Some of his best known effects are *Blindsight*, *Farsight* and *Auto-BendSpoon*. Devin's work on *Al Mann's Glass Box* has been termed by many to be the most definitive work on headline predictions ever written.

In addition to over 50 marketed items, Devin is the author of three books; *Glass Box Revisited*, *The Blindfold Car* and *Cloudbusting Secrets* (with Jerome Finley).

Devin strives to create effects that not only fool magicians, but at the same time are easy to do. The majority of his effects rely more on clever ideas, rather than difficult sleights. This puts most of his effects within the skill range of most performers.

He is also an established authority in the world of Effective Internet Marketing and you would be wise to seek out his ebooks on Marketing for Performers, which along with his many other creations are available from most Magic Shops Worldwide.

Check out some of His Ebooks Here: **http://www.lybrary.com/devin-knight-m-86331.html**

This is a plan that you can easily use to make at least thousand dollars off one hypnotic show and possibly much, **much** more. This involves using certain venues that will be begging to book your show. This plan practically sells itself; you tell them about your comedy hypnosis show and they will be ready to book you on the spot! Comments about this have been mentioned in the past on online forums, but this is the REAL WORK and a proven method that will make you big dollars fast. If you follow this plan systematically, you will make big money and faster than you ever thought possible with your comedy hypnosis show.

If you wanted to, you could set this up in several different venues doing a show each weeknight. Doing this would result in a $5000 week for you. Please note this is not pie in the sky or pipe dreams, there are professional hypnotists working this plan right now and bringing home five to seven thousand dollars each week.

This is done without having to rent halls, promoters, or selling ads. You book the show, do a little prep work, show up on the day of the gig, and collect your fee.

You could do this part-time or if ambitious, you could perform full time, possibly making over $100,000 a year. It is possible and is easily done if you follow this plan and are willing to travel to do gigs.

THE TYPE OF SHOW YOU NEED

First, you must have a family-oriented hypnosis show, this cannot be an adult show, and it must be squeaky clean and contain a lot of clean comedy. Most important, your show must appeal to ALL ages. Positively no blue material or questionable material, this will kill your career in this venue almost immediately.

You need to do a professional show that is a minimum of 70 minutes up to 90 minutes or longer. Finally, you need many good references saying how great your show is.

Make sure your show LOOKS PROFESSIONAL. This means a professional sound system available when needed. When people come in to see your show, you want them to think they are about to see a professional show.

Once you have the right show and a lot of good references, you are ready to start making big bucks with your act.

What You Are Offering

This is a fund-raising show, but not quite like what you have heard about in the past, as this actually works. First, let's look at standard fund-raisers and why they do not always work. The standard method used in the past was to contact a civic club such as the Lions Club or a fraternal group such as the Moose Club. The hypnotist would try to convince them to sponsor his show with a 60/40 split.

The problem was that many civic clubs only had 15 to 20 members and most of them do not want to sell tickets. They hope people will show up at the door. This is not going to happen as a rule, unless you have lots of effective and expensive advertising. The performer would often book a show and discover later that only 30 or 40 tickets were sold. I know from experience that in most civic clubs, the members are lazy and it is difficult to get them to sell tickets. At best, some members pay for tickets out of their pocket for their family members, often resulting in low attendance. This looks bad on you, as low attendance makes it seem you must not be very good or popular.

Most of the time, the club has to rent a place to do the show, which adds more expense to the venture and often results in a loss for the club and performer. I do not recommend civic clubs for fundraisers.

Civic clubs used to be good if you had a professional promoter with a phone room calling thousands of people to sell tickets, but this has fallen out of favor and is seldom done nowadays.

Fraternal clubs are a bit better, especially if you have a Moose club, as these groups often have several hundred members and their own building in which to hold the show. Usually, enough members will buy tickets for their family to make it worthwhile, but the performer usually only winds up making a few hundred dollars for his efforts.

I know from experience, that I have tried both civic and fraternal clubs fundraisers in the past and been very disappointed with the money and the attendance.

Then one day I discovered the venue I am going to tell you about. It was the perfect set up and easily made a thousand dollars or more for every show. Civic clubs can be a HARD SELL, but this venue is an easy sell. So easy, that they will be jumping at the bait and eager to book your act.

So what is this fantastic venue that will be eager to book you and pay you a thousand dollars or more for every show? High school bands. That is right, high school band departments. Thanks to government cut backs on school funds, especially for bands and sports, schools are hurting for money BIG TIME.

Local high school bands conduct on average 8 to 12 fundraisers a year. Everything from car washes to selling candy bars that only give them 25 cents commission sometimes. Bands need money for school trips and a many other things. Here is where you come in.

This is an easy sell, because high school students think hypnotism is cool! They sometimes feel that a magic show is for little kids and beneath them. You will find the hypnotic show is MUCH EASIER TO BOOK than a magic show and there is less competition.

Depending on the school's size, most high school bands have from 80 to 200 student members, with the average being about 130 students. These students are going to sell tickets to your show and they will hit up their parents, grandparents, and other family members. Most students will sell an average of four to eight tickets each and that goes for almost every student in the band!

Band students are some of the best ticket sellers in the world. They do not mind asking their neighbors, and the neighbors buy tickets because it is a student and for their local school. Family members want to support the band their child is involved in and wind up buying almost everything the band has for sale. You could not ask for a better sponsor, and if you are not booking high school bands, you are leaving money on the table!

The cool thing is that the band has access to the school's stage free of charge, so you will often have a nice stage to work on. The worse case scenario is that you are stuck doing your show in the gym, but there is no rent for the group to pay, so that is an important selling point when you approach them.

You may wonder why not use another high school club, like the cheerleaders, or a sports team. The fact is these other clubs do not work as well. Most high school clubs have fewer than 20 members so that means each member needs to sell 10 to 25 tickets to make it pay off and to meet your show fee. This can be hard.

On the other hand, most high school bands have more than 100 members. All you need to do is get each member to sell two tickets to his parents and the fundraiser is already successful.

It is much easier to get 100 plus students to sell two or three tickets, than to get 15 or 20 students to try to sell 10 to 15 tickets each. Stick with the high school bands and you cannot go wrong with this plan.

Who You Approach

You do your sale presentation to the band director. He will be eager to have a meeting with you because he is always looking for ways to make more money for the band. Usually, he has to get permission from the principal or school board before he can sign an agreement, but this is seldom a problem. Sometimes a letter is sent home with the band members letting the parents know that the students will be conducting a show fundraiser.

If the school is in your area, I suggest calling and setting up an appointment with the band director. If booking shows outside your area, then you will need to conduct all the booking over the phone and through e-mails.

The Deal You Offer

This is a very good deal for the school and is an easy sell. The school makes no financial guarantee to you, but arranges for a place to do the show and for the band students to sell the tickets.

I recommend that the show be held on a weeknight at 7 PM. Avoid weekend shows if possible, as the school is normally closed and custodian personnel have to be paid to come in, open the school and clean up afterward.

By doing your show on a weeknight, the custodian personnel are already there and the school is open. Many of these people stay on after the school is closed and into the early evening cleaning the school.

You in turn, offer a professional show, 500 initial tickets, and full color posters at NO COST to the school.

The tickets to your show are priced at $10.00 each. Some of you may want to drop tickets to $8.00, but I recommend $10.00 because that is the average price people pay to see a movie. Live shows are usually $35 to $95 for tickets, $10.00 for a live professional show is a bargain. Do not undersell your show. If it is too cheap, people will think it is no good.

On the average high school plays, put on by the drama department, are going for $8 to $10 per ticket. Usually $10 for adults and $8.00 for students. No one is going to beef about a $10 ticket for a professional show.

The Split With The Band Department

Your deal with the band members is that the first $1000 of tickets sold goes to you for your show fee. This is easily done, as if the band has 100 members, each member sells one ticket and your fee is paid. This makes for an easy sell, as you point out to the band director that each member only has to sell one ticket. You tell him that your regular fee for the show is $1500, but you only require the first $1000 in sales.

After that, things really look up for the band, as the split is 80/20 with the band getting the 80% and you taking the 20%. Therefore, for the second hundred tickets sold, the band gets $800 and you get $200. If the band members sell 300 tickets, they make $1600 and you get $1400. First $1000 plus 20% of 200 tickets sold after that. Therefore, the band actually makes MORE THAN YOU, which is a great selling point.

With this deal, you cannot lose as you get a thousand dollars from the first 100 tickets and the band will not stop with only 100 tickets sold. Most bands with 100 members can sell four to five hundred tickets. This becomes a major fundraiser for the band. As I said previously, I like to give them 500 tickets to start with.

NOTE: Some people often ask me what you do if the band does not sell 100 tickets. This as a rule does not happen. If the band has over a 100 members, they will sell 100 tickets. If for some reason less than a 100 tickets are sold, you still do the show, but retain all the ticket sales. The band does not get a cut. However, the band can still make money from the door sales split, and from selling concessions. I have never had this happen. So long as you book schools with 80 or more band members, it will not be a problem for you.

The Door Split

The deal with the band department is that door sales are split 50/50. If you have promoted this properly at the school, then there should be a good amount of door sales from students who are not band members. Usually, I suggest letting other students in for $8.00

Tickets

The appearance of your tickets is an important feature in making this an easy to sell show to the public. Your tickets MUST look professional. Do not try to save money by printing cheap black and white tickets. Your ticket must be in FULL COLOR and preferably with a picture of you on it.

You will find that you can buy 500 full color glossy tickets at low prices from online printers. Do a search for show ticket printers and you will find a huge selection to choose from. Many of these printers promise shipping within 48 hours.

I cannot stress enough the importance of having a full color ticket. When the student approaches neighbors and shows them the full color ticket, and they see it, everyone is immediately impressed. They realize this is a professional hypnotic show and appears to be worth the $10.00 price. In other words, the full color glossy ticket projects the image of a high-class show with a perceived value.

Tickets are much harder to sell when they are cheap looking or black and white. Do not skimp here, as it is not worth it. You will sell far more tickets using full color printing than without.

POSTERS

You will also need a supply of full color posters. Again, do not skimp on this and make cheap looking black & white posters. You can make acceptable full color posters using your computer and printer if you have the right software. These posters MUST make your show appear professional and something the students will want to see.

Better yet, go online and search for large commercial web printers that will print you 1000 posters for a little over $200.00. Have these printed with a large white space at the bottom, so you can fill in information about the date and show location. The main body of the poster should be used for your photo and action photos of your show. Try to use photos showing people having fun. This will aid greatly in creating attendance for your show.

When you send the posters to the band director, DO NOT LEAVE them blank in the white space. He will fill them in with a marker pen and that will look tacky and make your show appear unprofessional!

Instead, buy a box of 8.5" x 11" stickers. These are blank on the front. Using your computer printer, print the show date, school sponsor, time and location on the label. Cut it to size and stick the label in the white space you left at the bottom of each poster for this information. This will give your posters a uniform and professional look

These posters are placed in the high school along the various hallways so you can sell the students on attending the show. I do not suggest wasting time putting posters up around town. That seldom works. Most people walk by and pay little if any attention to posters in store windows. Doing this is a waste of time and money. The only way you can get people's attention is if you plaster the town like a circus with big color posters in every window. This is costly and expensive and will not pay for itself for a small high school hypnosis show.

You want the band director put up a dozen posters throughout the school a week before the show. This has proved to be the most effective method way to use the posters. If you put them up too soon, the students see them, ignore them, and often forget the show date.

The only place I recommend putting up posters outside the school that has a fighting chance of the public seeing them are on church community bulletin boards. These are often found in the church's lobby. I have found that the congregation will take time to read these posters and it can affect door sales in a positive manner, especially if the band member's family attends that church.

For best results, have the poster put up the Sunday before the show and it will usually spark some door sales.

Sale Of Items At The Show

Both you and the band department sell things at the show to make additional money. The deal is you keep all your sale monies, and the band keeps all their sale monies. The band members can sell refreshments either before the show or during the show if you have an intermission.

The fact that they keep all the money from these sales is another selling point that makes selling this to the band department an easy sell.

You in turn can have back of the room (BOR) sales after the show. Here is where you can offer self-help hypnosis CDs and DVDs for sale, photos and other things.

The Plan In Action

Once you have booked the band department, arrange to have the show five to six weeks from then. Anything less is not enough time and normally anything more than six weeks away is too much time. You do not want people to forget about the show. The five to six week span gives the students enough time sell the tickets.

Print up the full color tickets as soon as possible and send them to the band director. He will then distribute the tickets to the band members. Make sure he keeps a list of which students have tickets and how many each student took. It is his responsibility to keep track of the tickets. Be sure to tell him that the band is responsible for returning all UNSOLD tickets and that they are accountable and must pay for any unreturned tickets, as you must consider them as sold.

I always suggest that each student be given five tickets to sell. This is an easy and realistic goal, as most students can sell five tickets to family members and neighbors. If the band has 100 members, that is 500 ticket sales for $5000.00 gross ticket sales.

Based on this, you take the first $1000 plus 20% of the other $4000. That gives you $1800 for doing the show! The band makes a whopping $3200! See why this is such an easy sell.

Do not get greedy and try to change the percentages and give the school a 60/40 or 50/50 split thinking you will make more money. The 80/20 split with the school getting 80% is why they jump on this deal. No one else has ever offered them such a deal. When the students know they are getting 80% for the band, they try harder.

The public has also heard about shows that come to town and take almost all the money, leaving little for the sponsors. Sometimes the sponsors have made only 5 to 10% of gross ticket sales.

People will often ask the band members selling tickets HOW MUCH THE BAND GETS. When the student can say that the band is getting 80% of the ticket sales, this will make the show look good and will greatly increase the ticket sales.

Once word gets around and it will, other schools, in other districts will be beating down your door, begging you to come do a show for them.

You should call the band director at the end of each week to see how ticket sales are going.

About 10 days before the show, send the band director the posters and ask him to put them up in the school and maybe give some to students who will put them up on their church bulletin boards.

Have the band director ask the students on Facebook to post on their walls about the show. This will help with door sales.

Have the band director arrange with the principle to announce the show over the intercom during morning announcements. This should be announced each day starting five days before the show. These announcements will help generate student door sales.

Have the band director ask the students to turn in their money and unsold tickets (if any) three days before the show. This way, it allows any students who forgot to bring the money or tickets an extra day or so to turn in everything.

A WEEK BEFORE THE SHOW, STRESS TO THE BAND DIRECTOR THAT THE BAND IS RESPONSIBLE FOR ALL UNACCOUNTED FOR TICKETS.

On the day of the show, arrange to have a meeting with the band director in the early afternoon after school and divvy out the money.

A few days after the show, be sure to get a recommendation letter from the band director that you can use to book other schools.

That is the plan, and you can do this year after year for the same school and have a steady route of shows to do. Since you are mainly selling your show to the student's local families, you will find you can do this several times in the same city. Most large cities have five to six high schools. You will find that you can book each school and the show will not interfere with the other school's show. Remember, this is a low-key show catering to that school and the student's family members.

Outside of the school's students and family members, most of the public will not know that the show is going on. This is the secret behind why this plan is so successful and allows you to work the plan several times in the same town with different schools.

Good luck with this venture. I will see you at the top!

Designing Your Show Poster to Maximise Your Audience

Stuart Cassels of Hypnotic-Consultants

Posters are a very important part of a Hypnotist's advertising arsenal – and a carefully considered & well designed poster can help bring extra audience members to a venue, ensuring a greater chance of repeat bookings.

Whether you are designing your own artwork, having it designed by a printing company or outsourcing the work to an independent graphic designer, there are a few things to consider at the beginning of the process, so that the final printed poster is as effective as possible.

Some of the following sections will be particularly useful if you want to design your own artwork, and many of the ideas will be transferable to other areas of entertainment.

Who Should Design Your Poster?

Choosing the right graphic designer is essential. Ideally they should have prior experience of working with other entertainers, and know something about your show in particular. Many graphic designers offering their services on the internet may have never seen a stage hypnosis show, so are not really in a position to be able to help you promote your show successfully.

Of course, the person that knows most about your show, your personality and what you are visualising will be yourself – and you may have suitable software on your computer to do the job yourself. But be careful that you are not too emotionally attached to your own act to create a design that fulfils the true requirements of the poster.

Similarly, if you have very little experience of working with software such as Photoshop, it can be tricky to master – especially if you want a professional finish.

One solution in this case would be to create a rough draft, which can then be sent to your designer for completion. If you don't have access to graphic design software, or have no interest in learning how to use it, don't be afraid of sketching out a few ideas on paper to send to your chosen designer to work with. A good designer will happily take on board ideas from a client, and develop these into a final design that works well.

Outsourcing design work can be a cheap option (although cheaper is not always best). Many sites such as Elance, Odesk and even Fiverr will connect you with an individual willing to take on a design project.

If you choose to outsource your design work abroad, be aware of cultural differences, which could affect the end product – and of course, if your designer doesn't have the same first language as you, be prepared to double check all spelling before sending your artwork to the printers.

Another option would be to approach a local college, to see if a student would work on the design, in return for payment and the right to use the final designs in their course portfolio.

Working With Your Chosen Designer

It is important to give your designer as much information as possible about you, your show, the intended audience, and how you think the final poster may look. The more they understand about the show, the better they can represent the show within the design.

Don't be afraid to have some input into the design, and if need be, tell the designer when you are not happy with something. After all, just as you are paid to provide a first class show every time, you are paying for a first class design.

Your Personality & Character Within The Design

It is always a good idea that your artwork reflects your on-stage persona. If your show is bright, lively and cheesy, then the advertising needs to reflect this. Similarly, if you portray a dark and mysterious "traditional" hypnotist, then ask your designer to promote this on your posters etc with suitable images, text, fonts etc. Giving your designer photos and video clips of recent shows may help them to understand your show better. Some designers may even agree to watch you perform at your next local show to experience the atmosphere.

Design Quality & Print Set Up

If you are designing your own promotional literature, it is essential that you understand the requirements of your print company. Every company will have their own specifications for bleed margins, file formats and sometimes even colour modes and resolution.

Getting these wrong during the design process can create extra work for you down the line, or worse still lead to a poor quality printed material which will of course reflect on you. It is always advisable to get all the specifications from your printers before starting a design. Many will have these details on their website, or be happy to email them across on request.

As a general rule, for posters and leaflets, we ask that artwork is provided as follows –

Resolution – 300DPI, Bleed – 3mm, Colour Mode – CMYK, File Format – JPG or PDF

If you are unsure on what any of the above means, and will be creating your own designs, we have a useful glossary printing terms on our websites at *www.hypnotic-consultants.co.uk* & *www.hypnotic-*

consultants.com & of course we will be more than happy to advise new customers on the best way to set up their artwork correctly for printing.

Now would be a great time to point out that as a rule, images from the internet are of a lower quality than those required for commercial printing. This means that photos and other images lifted from a website will look pixelated or blurry when added to a poster design. Wherever possible, provide your graphic designer with the original images at the best quality possible.

Sacrificing Your Ego for a Larger Audience

If you already have existing artwork for your show, consider the relative space you have assigned to each of the following – _Your Name, Your Photo, What You Do, Where & When You Are Doing It, Your Contact Details & Website, Any Other Information._

Now consider your artwork from the point of view of a member of the public, who may only spend a few seconds looking at your poster in a venue, shop window etc.

Just as a good website will capture the viewer's interest within 30 seconds or less, a poster should do the same in 5 seconds or less, from across a crowded room, AND share all the important information required for them to make the decision to attend an event.

Unfortunately, many performers see successful celebrities promoting their own shows and believe that the same format needs to be copied to become successful. This is far from the case, and because it's been happening for many, many years, it has now become the standard – and not just with hypnotists, but with other entertainers including magicians, singers, comedians etc…

It might sound harsh, but unless you are a very well known, recognised celebrity in your own field, your name is unlikely to fill a venue on its own merits. What will attract attention to your poster, and lead to sales of tickets, or "Bums On Seats" is more likely to be the word "HYPNOTIST" as large and as prominent as possible on all your material. Yet time and time again entertainers insist on using artwork to promote themselves where their name is two or three times larger than the description of the act.

The same goes for photographs. Unless you have a very distinct appearance, and the image on the poster is clearly that of you *in the role of a hypnotist* then you must ask yourself if it warrants the space being used, or if that space could be better utilised. How many people come to a hypnosis show solely because "the hypnotist looks handsome"? Very few I suspect… and that is assuming that you actually DO look good!

The truth is, the general public are after one thing – to be entertained. Even if they have seen your show before, it's not really you they are after seeing – *it's what you do*. In fact, in the majority of audiences, some will not remember your name, or your face, 24 hours after seeing the show. They will remember the fun time they spent watching a hypnotist on holiday over 10 years ago though. And for that reason alone, they will be attracted by the opportunity of seeing another hypnotist again. Use this to your advantage – and sell the word "Hypnosis" and the imagery associated with it as much as possible.

Yes there are certain exceptions to the rule. Those who have made a huge career, with big venues, TV appearances and massive advertising budgets, can afford to trade on their name and image as the primary attraction on their publicity. Similarly, those who are recognised in a locality due to their regular & popular performances, can do the same. But in the majority of cases, people seeing your show couldn't care less what your name is, or what you look like. It's just an ego trip for you, and wasted space on your artwork.

I'm not saying that your name or image is completely irrelevant, just suggesting that you consider how much importance you give to these on a poster compared to other items which may be more important to your audience.

Images & Symbolism

It is said that "a picture paints a thousand words"… although perhaps more accurately, a *carefully chosen* picture can paint a thousand words. Select any images (including photographs) carefully to maximise the impact of your poster.

As mentioned previously, a photo of you will only be relevant if it is you clearly recognisable in the part of a hypnotist. Perhaps the inclusion of some show props in your photo might help demonstrate what you do… or maybe a "posed" photo of you and some volunteers clearly taking part in a routine. Of course, there is always the option of using hypnotic spirals and / or the traditional image of the hypnotist with glowing eyes, holding a pocket watch. To you as an entertainer, in the hypnosis industry, it might seem very clichéd and "old fashioned", but to a member of the public, spirals and pocket watches are instantly associated with hypnosis.

If you want the image of your poster to convey everything about your show, spend some time listing the keywords that you want to get across before creating the design.

Fonts & Typography

The subject of fonts & typography is vast and has been covered more than adequately in other books. There are almost an infinite number of fonts to choose from, and some are most definitely better than others. So to keep this section brief – consider how the font you choose reflects on you, and your personality.

Handwritten Fonts – Applied correctly, these can look wild, edgy & impromptu, but be careful of over use. In the wrong context, they can look messy, amateur & cheap. Certain "Cartoon", Brush Stroke and Bubble font designs have been overused beyond redemption and are best avoided.

Calligraphy & Decorative Fonts – Unless you are "playing the part" of a 19th Century Mesmerist then it's probably best to leave these alone. They can portray an old fashioned image, and worse still can be so decorative, that they are difficult to read.

Essentially, the most important thing to remember when choosing a font is that it must be easily read, and that certain individual letters must not be mistaken for others. For example, it would be awful if your name on your final poster design was regularly misread as "Jerry" instead of "Terry" because the uppercase "T" was so ornate that it looked more like a "J".

Another way to ensure that the lettering in your design stands out is to use a thin dark line around the lettering, known as a stroke or keyline.

Sites such as 1001freefonts.com are a great resource for additional lettering styles.

Placing Your Printed Posters in Optimum Locations

So you have finally designed and printed your show posters, and now you want to ensure that everyone can see them at their best. If you are being employed by a venue, for a one night gig – or a short run of shows, and have the opportunity to drop the posters into the venue, it is worthwhile offering to help the venue out by offering to put the posters up, or at the very least suggest good locations in which to display the posters.

It is to both your and the venue's advantage that posters are seen and talked about. In a pub, club or nightclub, I would recommend placing a poster in the main areas where people congregate, visit and pass through. For example - behind the bar, so that it is seen every time a customer buys a drink; In any sheltered smoking areas, so that whilst smokers are stood having a cigarette, with no other distractions, they have plenty of time to absorb all the information; in both the ladies' & gents' toilets, usually above the sinks, and / or over urinals; and on the inside of doors leading out of the venue, so that they are the last thing seen as customers leave.

With an additional few posters around the main venue, you are almost guaranteed that nearly every customer passing through the venue, will have an opportunity to see your posters, and hopefully make the decision to come to the show.

For affordable printing of your posters, leaflets & business cards, plus more ideas, tips and tricks on promoting your shows, don't forget to visit our websites -

www.hypnotic-consultants.com & www.hypnotic-consultants.co.uk

GETTING STARTED IN HYPNOSIS

By: Cheryly Quinlan

Have you ever been thrown into the deep end of a pool without knowing how to swim? That's kind of how I felt when I started in the hypnosis business. My instructors were all very good and the techniques I learned were solid but there was always something missing. Sort of a 'Now what? What do I do next?' I'm hoping by contributing to this book, some of you will be helped by what I have been through to get started.

About me

I have always had an interest in hypnotism. My earliest recollection was as a child watching television. I don't remember the show or who the female hypnotist was but I do remember being fascinated while watching this woman in her large sparkly caftan knocking people out. As the years passed, this fascination remained but moved to the back burner while my life took many different paths.

Around the same time I 'discovered' hypnosis, my mother enrolled me in accordion lessons that lasted throughout my elementary and high school years. I was also involved in drama and music clubs. After high school I went to college as a music education major and began playing professional piano shortly thereafter.

Two times stand out during this early period. Our family went on a vacation driving across country. I decided to 'hypnotize' my brother by telling him to look into my eyes, waving my hands in his face like I'd seen done on television and telling him over and over 'you are getting sleepy, you are getting very sleepy.' After about five minutes of this, my dad stopped the car and yelled at me to cut it out because I was putting him to sleep. He actually had to get out and stretch his legs. A second incident happened in college. My two roommates and I were bored so I decided to 'hypnotize' one of them. It didn't take long before my 'you are getting sleepy, you are getting very sleepy' routine began working. Her arm became like a stiff rod of steel and the suggestion of 'at 10:00 you will start singing the Howdy Doody theme song' actually worked. And I was hooked.

I retired after a career with the Government but always kept entertaining as an outside interest and eventual full-time business.

When the opportunity presented itself to officially get into hypnosis I took it.

Getting Started

I've never been one to do anything half way and have actually been accused of being anal about things. When I purchased a camera, I didn't just get a camera, I got the best camera and the best lenses, and the best batteries.

When I started my DJ business, I didn't just get a cd player, I got the best cd player, the best computers, the best lights and lots of them, the best speakers, etc. I bought equipment I'll never use and never needed. This is only mentioned so you know where I'm coming from. Starting a career in hypnosis has been an exercise in restraint to say the least.

Having been in business, it has also been an exercise in laying the groundwork needed to make it successful. Unless the basics are done and done properly, the business will eventually fail. As I see it, there are two aspects involved; the business side and the hypnosis side and hypnosis HAS to be treated like a business.

One of the first things I did was to attend training. I am a firm believer in it. No matter how much you know, or how many years you have been doing hypnosis, leave yourself open to additional training. It's important.

Firstly, you just might learn something and secondly, you'll meet some other people in the same industry. Way back in 1624, John Donne said 'No man is an island' and he was right. You can't do it by yourself. You need a network of people who understand when you say the back of room sales aren't great, or people you can turn to when you need support. What better way to have open dialogue than in a relaxed training environment. So, attend training-if not every year; then every other year.

Depending on the type of hypnosis i.e. clinical or stage or both will require a little different groundwork. As my background is in entertainment, I am focusing on stage hypnosis as a primary career with clinical work as secondary. With that in mind, I took a 'Safe on Stage' course put on by Justin James (www.thehypnosiscompany.com/safety) in conjunction with the National Association of Mobile Entertainers (NAME). After passing the course, I purchased liability insurance through NAME. Insurance has been a much discussed topic through the years and people have their own opinions as to whether it's needed or not.

My feeling is we live in a litigious society and people will sue for anything. The cost of the insurance is nothing when compared to a law-suit.

Then I took a stand-up comedy class. This helped me in writing material for my hypnosis shows and helped me learn to focus and get the point across without being too wordy. Additionally, it helped me to be 'fast on my feet'.

Stage presence is utmost as is handling a microphone, both of which were reinforced through this training. You can see the final results at YouTube under Cheryl Q at the Improv (**www.youtube.com/watch? v=naEaO8Kwv3A**).

I would recommend this type of training for anyone getting into the business especially if you have never been on stage or performed in front of people before.

After deciding on the stage name of The Amazing Cheryl Q, I got what is called a URL (domain). This is the name used for a website. Some places to purchase a domain name is from Go Daddy or Webmasters. Then I built my website and submitted it to the search engines such as Google, Bing, etc.

Just prior to all of this, I registered the business name with the State and got a business license. (A lawyer or accountant can advise you whether to be a corporation or LLC. I am registered as a LLC.) You will need to check with your State and see what the business requirements are. Always remember, the way to be a Professional is to act like one.

There's More…..

I gathered up basic contracts from friends in the industry and talked to them about addendums. This is an addition to a contract that contains travel requirements, green room mandates, sound systems, stage and seating, and anything else that might be needed for a show. I then made my own contract. It was typed up with information I needed on it and is on file. Initial contracts should be reviewed by a lawyer to make sure you are protected.

Business cards were next on the list. They are fairly low in cost so what I did was get two distinctly different cards; one focusing on the stage/entertainment part with the second focusing on the therapy/clinical side. Depending on who the audience is dictates which card they will get. Companies offering printing service are all over the internet. The company I used was Vistaprint.

From there, CD's for back of room and on-line sales were made. The resale rights were purchased as part of a training package offered by Dr. Jonathan Royle. These will be used until my own are recorded. Available are Weight Loss, Stop Smoking, Stress Reduction, and Confidence Building. (If you are new to the industry and need something for back of room sales, contact me and I'll help you out.)

Finding scripts for therapy sessions have proven interesting. Here again, the training package mentioned above has helped immensely. It offered a couple of session ideas that I took and modified slightly. Release forms for clinical work are mandatory. If the client is under-age or mentally incapacitated a guardian needs to sign them.

Also needed is a worksheet the client fills out. This contains name, address, and other general information as well as a 'what ails them' section that will be used during the session. All of this has been researched, typed up and put in a special Therapy book that is taken with me for clinical sessions.

A good voice/video recorder has been purchased both for clinical sessions as well as stage work. If you are getting your own (you'll need one), make sure it is High Definition (HD) and make sure you purchase a video card that is 'fast' and long enough to record what you'll need.

You'll also need a long lasting battery. B&H Photo is where I purchase my professional audio and video supplies from. Some hypnotists make show DVD's for resale right at the venue while others take orders and send them out. If you decide to do them at the show, you'll need a good reproduction machine that can make multiple copies as well as DVD blanks, cases, and printing supplies. A good assistant or two is/are also needed.

One thing you will need to decide is what type of payment you will accept. Taking credit cards is up to you but it can facilitate sales. When you explore credit card processing companies, take a look at recurring monthly charges and the percentage they take. I currently use Intuit and have the ability to process cards either on line or through a small card swiper added to my cell phone. PayPal is another option for taking payments.

Their rates are reasonable and a business account can be easily set up. Of course there is always cash and checks, too. By the way, a bank account dedicated to your business is a necessity. Do not co-mingle your business finances with your personal accounts. It tends to upset accountants and tax auditors.

Royalty free induction music was purchased and will be used for my own CD's (when they are recorded) as well as for the clinical sessions and stage shows. Sometimes it's best not to leave anything to chance - you never know who or how your stage introductions will be made.

At the suggestion of the Incredible Hypnotist, Richard Barker, I hired a professional announcer to make my stage introduction. This has worked well and was worth the money. A promo video was then made and was posted on YouTube and put on my Facebook page.

(http://www.youtube.com/watch?v=jz7jaKyyfwk)

Using social media to promote your business is so very important. If you can take a few classes in this area, it'd be beneficial. Anytime you can get your name out there, do it. Look at various advertising sites such as Gigmasters for paid advertising. If you can get your name on sites for free, then do so. The more your name is on the internet, the more the web browsers will pick it up and will place you higher in the rankings.

Once you plan out your show, you'll need to figure out not only your music and sound effects but how you are going to play it. I've worked with hypnotists who use CD's and depend on the DJ to follow their cues (this is put in the addendum to their contract) while others load their show onto a computer and use a hand-held remote control to operate it. I bring both a CD and computer to a show and use a hand-held remote if I'm doing the show by myself.

Another useful item is a dry erase board which was a recommendation from Hypnotist Mike Valmar. I now have a couple of them that are put around the stage area as prompters to help keep me on track during the show. They can be easily packed and changed for the show's needs.

And Then.....

I always bring a 'mentalism' routine with me in case I ever get stuck and the show doesn't go right or just as an added something when I'm asked to perform longer. This is the anal me preparing for anything that may happen. I can also pull out one of my stand-up comedy routines. You might consider having something as a backup for yourself. Doesn't need to be elaborate or long but does need to be entertaining.

I'm sure I've forgotten to mention something like having professional promo photographs taken so I hope you will forgive me.

Once you get rolling, though, remember to keep really good records for tax purposes. Consider speaking with an accountant early in your career and periodically thereafter so you know what you will need for taxes. Never do a show without a signed contract. Make sure it protects you. If anything goes wrong it will be invaluable and will stand up in court.

Keep it business even for friends or acquaintances. If you don't protect yourself, no one else will. Trust me you will be respected more for it and taken advantage of less. Don't ever sell yourself short – charge what you are worth. There are a lot of decisions to make and lots to do to get started but if you do the groundwork you will be a huge success.

Cheryl Q

www.theamazingcherylq.com

www.facebook.com/theamazingcherylq

HYPNO-STAGE

(The First Ever Online Magazine For Stage Hypnotists)

Originated by – James Szeles – www.szeles.com

When the internet was not the common household word and addiction that it is to so many now, American Stage Hypnotist James Szeles was arguably the first Professional Stage Hypnotist to have a Website and indeed went on to design websites for many leading Stage Hypnotists to whom the internet was also something new and strange!

Seeing the opportunities that the internet offered and its vast potential, James Szeles soon set up "Hypno-Stage" an online magazine and newsletter for working Stage Hypnotists.

This ran for several years from the mid 1990's and indeed if you use an internet site such as "The Wayback Machine" or "Web Archive" you can type in James Szeles website domain name and look at it as it was then, thus meaning you can read at no charge all of the back issues which were filled full of useful information.

His domain by the way is **http://www.szeles.com**

He also has some amazing information available for Free which he has posted on Hypnothoughts here:

http://www.hypnothoughts.com/group/hypnosistrainings/forum/topics/ the-free-boot-camp-and

And you will also find some Amazing Free Videos giving Stage Hypnosis

Advice and Training on his You-Tube channel at:

http://www.youtube.com/jimszeles

I am delighted that James has given me the honour of within this book re-publishing a selection of the articles that appeared in the original "Hypno-Stage" online magazine.

Please remember that where Fees are mentioned, these articles were originally written in the mid to late 90's and thus generally speaking Fees are higher these days, however the principles for getting shows and all the other advice, in the main remains the same and bang up to date!

Stage Hypnotist Clones – James Szeles

If you watch enough stage hypnosis tapes you will see a trend in shows. There are some very talented stage hypnotists out there and then there are the clones. It seems there are some stage hypnotists out there that teach their act to an 'intern' and charge as much as $5000.00 to do so and then there are the people out there who get a tape of a show and copy the hypnotist word for word.

The problem gets worse when the clone gets cloned and then they in turn get cloned. I can think of four individual hypnotist's shows who parrot the same script, use the same music and the same skits.

The problem is, the show works great for the original hypnotist because it's tailored to that person, but when the second or third or fourth persons does it, it sucks because they don't have the charisma of the original hypnotist to carry it off successfully.

One skit the clones love to start out with is the hot/cold room. Now not everyone who does this skit is a clone, but it's a good indication that they might be. It's one of the most over used skits and in my option should be retired.

There's nothing wrong with a person learning from another stage hypnotist, but they should know enough about hypnosis to be able to change the show to fit their own unique personality and stage presence.

Letters to the Editor

From: C.J. Johnson, CHt.

.

In your HYPNOSTAGE article on Stage Hypnosis Clones you wrote:

"One skit the clones love to start out with is the hot/cold room. Now not everyone who does this skit is a clone, but it's a good indication that they might be. It's one of the most over used skits and in my option should be retired."

I believe that the hot/cold routine is in so many peoples acts for one very important reason, though many don't realize the reason. It's a deepening technique. As a subject begins to relax and is under the lights of a stage he/she actually becomes warmer.

They are having a physical response to the environment around them and by making the suggestion of being warmer the subconscious realizes that they ARE actually warmer.

Therefore they are having physical confirmation that the suggestion is working, thereby deepening the state of suggestibility (if this suggestion works, others will work) and their own belief in the process, which is crucial to accessing the desired state.

After having the subjects wave and fan themselves and then relax, stopping the action causes a physical change in their bodies and they DO actually feel colder, yet another suggestion confirmed by physical response.

This is why the routine, in a properly structured show, is one of the very first demonstrations of phenomenon I think the routine could actually be considered one of the final phases of the induction.

.

I would argue that the Hot/Cold routine is an almost essential part of an induction when properly placed in a show -- many hypnotists just don't realize this and use it merely as a routine.

.

I just thought I'd throw in my two cents worth for your consideration - I'd love to hear your thoughts on the matter.

Sincerely,

C.J. Johnson, CHt.
Master Hypnotist & Illusionist
Email: hypnotist@cjjohnson.com
Web Site www.cjjohnson.com

TEN THINGS YOU SHOULD KNOW BEFORE BECOMING A STAGE HYPNOTIST

10. There are too many stage hypnotists out there already and they all work for two hundred dollars less then you.

9. No one, no matter how good they are, no one can teach you how to be a stage hypnotist in three days or three weeks. They will take your money

and might, if you're lucky, show you some of the basics of stage hypnosis. But is what they teach worth from $500.00 up to $5000.00 dollars? No. You could learn just as much from several good books or even a good "how to" video tape for under $50.00. So how do you learn stage hypnosis? You can find a lot of great information on how to get started by reading Howard Morgan's and other stage hypnotist articles in HypnoStage, a FREE on-line stage hypnosis magazine. If you're lucky, you hook-up with a stage hypnotist who is willing to teach you. Then you work for him/her for a few years helping in their shows and working for little or no pay until they feel you are ready. Or, you teach yourself as I and many others did. Bottom line, if you waste your money on a weekend class don't quit your day job.

8. It's going to take at least one or two years before you make any money doing stage hypnosis and up to five years to make a good living at it. If your're lazy then this is not the job for you. You will spend most of your time trying to get bookings.

7. There is a Catch 22 in stage hypnosis. That is, you can't get a good show together with out doing a lot of shows and you can't get a lot of work until you get a good show. So what do you do? You start doing shows for your friends' partys and for anyone you can get to watch you. You might want to go to your local night club and offer to perform for free or for very little money once you feel you are ready for the next step.

6. You will do shows where no one goes under! This is a fact of life and when it happens it hurts your ego. Get used to it, your ego is going to take a beating. You are going to be performing at times for people who couldn't care less how long it took you to lean how to do a good show and sometimes everyone just wants to watch. When you ask for people to come on stage and no one does you know you have your work cut out for you. There is nothing that can beat a good stage hypnosis show, no band, comic, or magician But when it goes bad it goes really bad, twenty or thirty minutes into your show, when the induction is over and the two or three people you did manage to get on stage do not respond to anything you say and you still have sixty minutes of time to kill, you are going to know why most people don't make it in stage hypnosis.

5. The hypnotic induction is the least important part of your show. You will need a good induction but that is only a small part of the show. This is where a lot of people go wrong. Once they get them under they don't know how to pace the show and the show starts to drag. Respect the people who do volunteer for your shows , it's easy to get a cheap laugh by making them look stupid on stage. Keep in mind that they are the people who help you pay your mortgage.

4. Don't bitch when someone takes a skit you came up with, it happens all the time. Keep in mind that when you first get started at least part of your show will be skits you've seen other hypnotists do. Having them act like little kids or forget the number seven is a classic example of what I'm talking about.

3. Once you find a good gig there will be other hypnotist trying to under cut your price and take it away from you. Life in the big city, it's not the right thing to do but it does happen.

2. Never talk bad about a fellow hypnotist (at least, until their back is turned away from you!)

1. Should you be lucky enough to make a good living doing stage hypnosis there will come a day when a newbe will ask you to help him/her with a few questions they might have. Take the time to help them and teach them how to do it right. There is always room for one more good hypnotist. I hear people tell me all the time how they saw a hypnotist at their high school or college, and enjoyed the show so much that they booked me for their company event or party.

Getting in to the Zone

I'm going to address something very few hypnotists talk about, doing the difficult shows. I don't know about you, but I have performed under some very trying conditions.

Recently I worked a small fair in the high desert of Arizona and the first shows were at night outside on an open stage area. Arizona at night at that time of the year can be either very warm (in the 70's) or it could snow. The first two nights of the fair it was in the mid 50's with a very high wind and it was on a weekday school night so there were not a lot of people at the fair that night.

After about 15 minutes of working up a crowd, I had 10 people in the audience and 5 volunteers on stage. All 5 people were young girls who knew each other and I got lucky putting 4 of the 5 deeply under despite the cold and the wind.

On the weekend nights at the fair the weather was warmer, but like a lot of small fairs they had several events going on at the same time as my show and one of the events was a band that was playing very loud music. Of the 12 shows at that fair I managed to do 10 complete shows, one partial show and I had one show with 8 people on stage; 6 of the eight were young kids goofing off who didn't really want to try and they wound up waking up the other two on stage so no one went under!

I find that some of my performances are at shows were I really have to work had to get them going but every now and then I'll be performing and get into what I call "the zone". Here's what happens. I'll be 1/3 way into the show and have a group of volunteers under when everything falls into place.

The volunteers on stage are great, the audience is really into the show and it has a flow to it. It's a feeling you can't make happen and it comes at times when I least expect it. For example, I did a high school grad night show last month. It was the last of three shows on the same night and it was set to start at 3:00am. I arrived at the location only to see the DJ breaking down his equipment, so I have no PA system or CD player, the parents knew I needed the equipment, it was in the contract.

The hall they rented did have a house PA system with a cord mic that was hard wired in to the system so I could not use my wireless mic. It was my third show that night at three different schools and I was tired. One of the parents did have a boom box in their car so I used the house PA mic and placed it in front of the boom box so I at least had sound and talked as loud as I could.

The show started at 3:25am and a funny thing happened, once I got the show going the zone hit and things just fell into place. 18 of the 20 kids were wonderful subjects and went deeply under. The two hundred kids watching the show were very quite when I was talking so they could hear what I was saying and the show turned out great. I wound up doing an extra 20 minutes because the kids were having such a fantastic time. It's shows like that which make you forget all the times you really have to work hard to get it going.

It should be called Stage Entertainment

Many hypnotists new to the craft (and a few established ones) think that the hypnosis portion of the show is the most important element. While it certainly is the majority of the show, the induction is also an integral part of the show, as long as it's not boring to your audience any hypnotic induction will work.

People love to watch just how the hypnotist puts the volunteers under. Now I've seen several hypnotists who take forty five minutes to an hour to get people under and that is a little too long .

One such person does not even use an induction, he just tells the volunteers to "go along with it" and still takes twenty five minutes of faking it! My point being, do not focus too much on the induction and leave the rest of the show in the balance.

When you lose sight of the fact that you are there to entertain, and if you do not have a well planned, fast paced show, you will find the audience getting bored.

Your induction is only a means to an end and not the show itself.

So how long is too long of an induction? I would try to keep it under twenty minutes tops. Of course the length of the induction depends on what kind of a show you are doing. You would need a longer induction for a corporate show and a shorter one for a high school.

So now you have them under, what to do next? You want to structure your show so it starts out with the easier things to do like stuck to the chair, can't remember the number seven and work up to the harder skits like watching a funny movie.

Some hypnotists only do group skits and that's ok, but I like to interact with the people on stage on a one-to-one basis. Just keep your show well paced and lively. When working with a large group and you are taping the show for sale you want to try to work with everyone on stage so that you sell the most tapes.

Here is a little pet peeve of mine. I still see hypnotists making people bark like a dog. One of the first things people ask me before the show is will I make them bark like dogs or cluck like a chicken. My answer is always No. There are so many skits available to you which won't degrade or scare the volunteers on stage.

Here are just a few things people are doing on stage. Telling them there are rats all over the floor; there is a scorpion on your arm and it bites and last, but not least, the room is on fire. These are examples (in my opinion) of negative suggestions that have a potential of doing more harm than good. One should always try to keep a positive attitude in ones shows and help to dispel the erroneous stigma attached to our craft.

BEHIND EVERY GREAT MAN...
by Pauline Szeles

So the century turned and 2000 went out with pretty much the same enthusiasm it came in with. Time now to think about April 15 and Uncle Sam's cut of your business. For those of us who have been diligent and organized with our receipts and contracts throughout the year it's no big deal; for the rest it's a time to hunt for expense receipts and bills and hope that by some strange miracle we can find them all and satisfy both the taxman and ourselves! No easy feat, believe me....

One of my New Year's resolutions last year was to organize my husband's business. He's great at getting the bookings and expense receipts, but keeping them in one place, organized and having them relate to any one gig was another matter completely. We would literally spend days looking, sorting and stressing in an effort to get everything in some sort of logical order for the accountant. A new millenium to me meant a change in our business lifestyle. I was hell bent on having a stress free time of it this year!

I started out in December of 1999 by purchasing accounting and database management software. The best investment I have ever made! Realizing that show biz and not organization is in my husband's blood, I knew the burden of getting organized fell on my shoulders. So, software in hand and determination on my side, I stated out on my venture. Installing and learning the programs was the easy part, but how do you keep track of all those receipts when you are on the road?

I thought about this and came up with an easy solution, which may, or may not work for you, but it works for us. There are only 2 things I ask of my husband when it comes to keeping track of the receipts when he's on the road:

1)   Write the date and location on the back of each receipt
2)   Diligently put all of the receipts in a large envelope - and don't loose it!

When he gets back I enter everything into our accounting program and file the receipts in the appropriate hanging files. Thus, this year we know exactly to the penny just how much we've spent on everything business related.

Our accountant's fee will be less, because the accountant won't inherit a huge mess to sort through, we probably can deduct more on our taxes because we can account for everything and we have a wonderful sense of accomplishment; but for me the best part is no stress!

The database management software proved itself invaluable this year. I think both of us were somewhat stunned at the many functions, which it easily carries out. We loaded it onto the laptop took it to trade shows and entered our contact information right there at the booth.

We can track whom we talked to, about what and fees quoted. We now have a complete history of the last year compiled in such a way that we can pull up anyone in the database and there is their history with us!

When we got home, it took only minutes to print out our follow up letters. It has a really nice calendar function for keeping track of the booking schedule and other business related tasks. I really like the reminder function, which pops up on the PC desktop, so follow up calls or verbal confirmations are never missed or late. Learning the program was a snap – I don't know how we ever survived without it!

My advice to anyone is to get organized. It's a little overwhelming at first, but once you're on it and in the rhythm it's easy. Everyone works long and hard for his or her dollar, so why give Uncle Sam more than he deserves?

Who Cares?
Editorial by James Szeles

If you read the postings in alt.hypnosis or surf the internet, you will run across stage hypnotists who claim to be the "World's Greatest", World's Fastest", "World's Best" and "Official Hypnotist of the New Millennium". But what does that mean? When one goes to a comedy club or fair, does one really care if the hypnotist thinks he's the fastest or the best? After all, isn't it just that person's opinion.

Recently, in the alt.hypnosis posting, there was a group of hypnotists who were trying to out do each other with how fast they could 'put people under'. One even claimed he could get someone under in 3 seconds! Most of the fast inductions use a confusion technique that requires the hypnotist to pull or jerk the volunteer very quickly when the volunteer does not expect it. Sometimes the stage hypnotist will spent 15, 20 up to 30 minutes "testing" the audience before he/she brings the person on stage.

Most of the shows I've seen, it takes the hypnotist 20 to 30 minutes to get the show started and perform the first skit. In my option 20 minutes is ok, but when you reach the 30 minute mark it's a little long. When I got started I thought the audience would get bored watching my induction (8 to 15 minutes long depending on the group), but I found that the audience loves to see how their friends go from sitting next to them into a deep trance.

IAFE
International Association of Fairs and Expositions

By James Szeles

This article is purely my own personal view and opinion. I have just returned from the IAFE and had a chance to meet lots of hypnotists I had gotten to know solely by way of the telephone and/or email. I enjoyed meeting my colleagues and talking shop. Stage hypnotists are a unique group of people and when we get together we like to talk about one thing, money.

It seems there are a few hypnotists who will work far below the industry standard just to get the gig. We all need to work, but when some of us work for next to nothing, two things will happen:

1) By under cutting fees, it makes it difficult for seasoned hypnotists to get the fees their shows demand, and

2) As the novice hypnotists gain experience and exposure they are going to

find that it will become difficult for them to raise their fees, because their clients won't want to pay more for the same show they booked previously (if they get re-booked).

If you are new to this industry, please keep this in mind; think about the long-term and not the immediate. There is a need for all of us to set and keep standards not only for our fees, but also with the caliber of our performances. Remember that poor quality performances hurt our industry and damage our reputation as a whole. Will your performance be an asset to this industry or a detriment - the choice lays with you.

Grad Night Shows

- For many of us May and June are the times we perform at Grad Night parities at High Schools. They are fun and easy shows to do, the only drawback being many times the shows start as late as 4:00am. One of the things I'm seeing is the new high schools are not organized. This year I worked with two new schools, both schools have been open for less than a year, had their first grad night and both schools were not prepared. One school had no sound system at all, and the second school had to call the caretaker to set up the sound system at 3:30am!

- One school wanted to do the show outside, which is fine if you live in a warm climate. In Northern California it gets cold at night, even as late as July. I informed them of that and I was glad I did. The night of the show was very cold. I have gotten a few shows because the previous hypnotist the year before did something wrong. One of the shows I got was from a hypnotist who swore at the kids and still another show because the hypnotist was "hitting up" on one of the parents.

- Sometimes the shows are in the gym with a lot of other events going on around you. The kid's at the shows can be very rowdy and boisterous and you need to take control from the start. It can be a challenge to get the noise down and take control of the room, you have to be firm and make it clear that the quality of the show depends on how quiet they can keep it during the induction.

Are stage hypnotists going the way of the stand up comic?

In the 80's stand up comedy was all the rage and comics were in great demand. Every bar and bowling alley had a comedy room and soon there were more rooms than good comics to fill them. So, the comedy clubs started to use anyone they could get to perform and when people paid good money and saw bad comics the clubs went out of business.

In my opinion, stage hypnosis is reaching that point right now. Just as the clubs hired bad comics, the same thing is happening with hypnotists.

Everybody it seems, wants a hypnotist at their school or party and a lot of people want to be a stage hypnotist. The problem is, some inexperienced hypnotist's are selling themselves as pros and when they bomb at the events the people who booked them don't know they are beginners and never want to use a hypnotist again. This situation hurts all of us.

These new hypnosists perform a show or two at a school, or for a small groups of friends and think they are ready for the big shows. But then they run into trouble, the subjects don't go under as easily as high school kids, or don't go under at all and their show bombs.

A real pro knows what to expect and is able to handle whatever situation comes up and still perform a great show. I get calls often from people who have seen a hypnotist perform in college or high school and want to book me. I recently performed for a New Year's Eve party and did two shows. By the time the second show started at 10:15pm, many people in the audience were drunk and the room was very noisy. During the induction, people were popping balloons and blowing noise-makers. It was hard going, but I got the room under control and my subjects to go under. By drawing on my experience, I got the crowd to help me keep it quiet until I could get them under.

What will the future of stage hypnosis be? Only time will tell.

Putting my money where my mouth is.

If you read the posting in Alt.Hypnosis you've read about performing at corporate events and how hard they can be. Well, I just got back from performing two shows in Hawaii for a travel expo trade show and it took everything I know to make the show happen.

The shows were in a very large exhibition hall with a trade show going on at the time and several of the booths had hawaiian tribal dancers complete with drums performing dances every hour, the noise level was very high. On top of that, the attendees were very laid back and didn't respond to the skits I was doing on stage. I was told by the promoter that this is pretty typical of the island people, in fact he said when people like Ricky Martin come to town, they stop their concert and ask what's wrong with the crowd, why aren't they "into it".

I did one show per day for two days; the first show I had to beg the people to come on stage. There were only 40 people in the audience and I was lucky to get ten people on stage. I did a long induction and wound up keeping six of the people but only two were really deeply under.

The next day I had an idea of what to expect and the second show was much better. There were about 20 people in the audience, again I had to beg them to volunteer, but I got 6 on stage and got very lucky to get three of them deeply under. With two men and one woman under I started to get the crowd into the show. I told the woman that everyone in the audience was a long lost friend and she went thought the crowd hugging every one. This was great because the older people in hawaii do not like to be touched - the reactions were classic!

In the middle of the second show one of the two Hawaii drum bands started to play even though they had been asked to wait until my show was over. This was poor planing on the promoters part; he wasn't aware that some of the exhibitors were going to have live entertainment. The drums were very loud and I knew I could not talk over them so I had to think fast. I had my sound guy start my music for the male strippers and had him crank it up. This did the trick and they stopped playing. Several minutes later the second drum group started up and this time I incorporated their drumming into one of my skits. I did manage to do a great second show and was asked back next year.

Email: szeles@szeles.com

BEWARE THE OVER ANXIOUS.

by Michael Ray - Comic Hypnotist. Saratoga Springs, NY

.

Greetings to all who share a piece of the world of hypnosis.

Those of us who are performing, or soon will be, will experience (if they have not already) those who are more than willing to become a participant in your show. BEWARE!! Use caution while choosing your on stage candidates!They can cause much trouble for you.

.

The most common type is the natural show off. There are at least two problems associated with this type of individual.

.

First, they can disrupt your induction technique by over acting. When you ask for a deep breath from the group, this person is sucking air in the most animated way possible. This person is already trying to entertain his/her friends. Needless to say, this is the worst time to have your volunteers distracted. Distracted not only by the loud exhale of the volunteer, but also by the laughter of the few "buddies" in the audience.

.

Second, If the subject is actually kept on stage, he/she will tend to overact during every skit! Sometimes this can be very funny. (here is where the judgment call comes in) Other times it is often perceived by your audience that the person is not under but merely being their natural "actor" self!! The greater the CHANGE in character, the more convincing the hypnotic influence. Needless to say, if the comic is being funny..........

.

THIS ONE SCARED ME. At a recent show at a high school in Upstate NY, The president for the FBLA, who was female, almost killed my reputation!! Following the induction, direct suggestion deepening techniques were being used. (helium balloons, etc.) She slid out of her chair and onto the floor. A minute later she excused herself from the stage. I could see from the stage that she was upset for some reason. Though I hate to break the flow of the show, I went to her seat to investigate. She was in tears. I calmed her and returned to the stage. I addressed the audience explaining that some people make a conscious effort to fight the process and can be at odds with themselves.

.

Throughout the performance I could still see a problem in her area. The show continued. Following the performance, I was beckoned to her by her friends. She was still obviously shaken. I re induced her and calmed her. I let her know that she was scaring her friends and this worked to bring her back to normalcy. As I was breaking down my equipment, her friends came to me an apologized on her behalf. It seems that she had ingested a handful of UPPERS just prior to the show. NO WONDER SHE COULDN'T RELAX!!! To make matters worse, I was informed that the school was aware that there was a group of the extremely religious who already had a bad taste in their mouth for that "EVIL" Hypnosis. The school principal was sure that they would have representatives attend just looking for one hint that I too was evil and to justify their beliefs.

.

It was not in the least my fault but it could easily have been misconstrued as such. I later found that neither the audience or school administration had any misgivings regarding the incident and I was asked to return to the school to perform again.

Naturally, using your best judgement in choosing your volunteers is the best combatant. The only thing that will help you to create this character judgement is actually encountering these "problem children." It is only though experience that you will be able to gain the ability to make the spot decisions regarding this matter.

.

I look forward to meeting each and every one of you as our network of stage performers grows. Until then.....

Hypnotically Yours,

Michael Ray

http://www.capital.net/com/carnival/MIKERAY.HTM

Controvesies in Hypnosis by Ramelle Macoy
Central Pennsylvania—Mifflitown

.

Several years ago the Committee for the Scientific Investigation of Claims of the Paranormal (CSICOP) devoted a segment of its annual convention to a panel discussion titled "Controversies in Hypnosis". While I was unable to attend, I did listen to the tapes of the discussions.

.

Before commenting I should confess my own lack of credentials. I have done no studies--at least no formal studies with appropriate controls. I have been a stage hypnotist for the past thirty years and have hypnotized thousands of volunteers and while I am as disinclined as the next CSICOP member to be much impressed by anecdotal evidence, perhaps experience and observation is not without some value. It might at least suggest useful areas for research.

.

The woman in the audience who exhorted CSICOP not to deny the reality of the mystery was, I thought, right on target. There is a mystery and it is a mystery, I think, that will continue to be extraordinarily difficult of illumination. The variables are so numerous that in practice they may be impossible to control.

Suggestions that may have been given a subject prior to an experiment together with varying interpretations of the same suggestion by different subjects--or by different interpretations of the same suggestion by the same subject at different times--may well combine to render reliable replication impossible. Most of the routines that I do on stage I have done hundreds or thousands of times and yet in almost every show I encounter a reaction that I have never seen before.

.

The crucial and most important disagreement among the panelists seemed to be whether or not persons allegedly hypnotized are in any kind of special "state" or "trance". In passing I would like to suggest to Kreskin that he immediately claim his own $100,000 prize for himself. The man whom Kreskin reported as having thought he had been talking to him for three or four minutes when in actuality his arm had been "floating" in the air for one hour and twelve minutes was, I submit, in some sort of state or condition substantially different from what most of us regard as the normal waking state.

.

While the evidence is anecdotal, I assume that Kreskin believes it and I believe it (with appropriate allowance for some possible embellishment to which we entertainers are prone). I believe it because I know it to be a phenomenon common to hypnosis. Frequently when I have had a group of volunteers on stage for an hour or more someone will ask the volunteers how long they think they have been on stage and their estimates will usually be under ten minutes.

.

What we call such a "state" is not important. I call it a hypnotic state rather than a hypnotic trance because I think most people find "state" less mysterious and scary than "trance". But since "hypnosis" does imply sleep, and since it is emphatically not "sleep", I would, to satisfy the nit pickers, be happy to settle for "state of heightened suggestibility". What is important is that we try to agree on terms. I find it a little incongruous for people to deny the existence of such a thing as a hypnotic state while all the while referring repeatedly to "high hypnotizables".

.

For my own part I use the terms "hypnosis" and "suggestion" virtually interchangeably. The difference between a "hypnotic suggestion" and a "suggestion" is, I think, simply a matter of degree. One of the panelists argued that the apparent benefits of hypnosis had nothing to do with hypnosis but were simply the results of relaxation and suggestion. It was, I would argue, the hypnotic state that produced the relaxation and rendered the suggestions more reliably effective than an ordinary suggestion.

.

What's going on in hypnosis? My own guess is that through suggestion we can produce an extraordinarily relaxed state during which it is possible to reliably communicate with the sub-conscious.

.

Freud's theory states, if I remember correctly, that it is possible for the human mind to contain information--and for a person to act on that information--without being aware of the information. It was hypnosis that Freud pointed to as proof of the theory. I think there is additional evidence.

.

It takes an incredibly long period of time for us to consciously initiate many motor functions. Something like seven-tenths of a second (again, if I remember correctly; in any event, a long time) is required for my finger to begin to move after I make a conscious decision to move it. The reflex time for the same finger motion is a fraction of that.

Obviously all manner of seemingly simple but really very complicated activities like walking and riding a bicycle would be clumsy and difficult or impossible were they dependent on conscious decisions. Equally obvious, or so it seems to me, a great mass of data and information for automatically controlling and regulating such actions must be stored in the brain someplace and I don't think we have any direct access to that information or are even aware of its existence in any meaningful way.

.

Damage to specific areas of the brain can sometimes result in a "blind spot" in a person's field of vision. I am not talking about hysterical blindness. The person is actually physiologically blind in that spot or area. And yet in carefully controlled experiments it has been found that if objects are held in the blind spot such persons can, by "guessing", identify the objects with an accuracy approaching 100%.

.

One of the routines that I do on stage is to have a person negatively hallucinate a certain person, normally a friend who happens to be present in the audience. The subject will give every indication of being unable to see the invisible person (and have on occasion slapped me in the face when I had the invisible person pinch her on the fanny) and yet, on some level and in some way, must be able to see the person in order to identify whom it is that they can not see.

.

When the invisible person is seated in one of several otherwise empty chairs and the subject is asked to "imagine" who would be seated in each of the chairs if there were someone seated there, he or she will usually "imagine" the invisible person in the chair in which they are in fact seated.

.

I find it difficult to resist the conclusion that the visual information in both cases is stored in more than one area of the brain and that we have conscious access to the information in one area but not the other.

.

Can everyone be hypnotized? My answer would be a rather tenuous "yes". Given the right circumstances, a sufficiently skilled hypnotist and enough time (how's that for a "non-falsifiable" hypothesis?), I tend to think that everyone could eventually be hypnotized. I think so because I believe that everyone is to some degree suggestible and that people's brains function in very similar fashions.

.

I frequently hypnotize groups of from 20 to 30 people. I call it relaxation and it is very non-threatening and over the past several years my success rate with such groups has been well over 90%. No selection is involved. On stage, with groups of 10 or so, the success rate is frequently 100% but there is some selection--or at least I hope there is. I work only with volunteers and my untested assumption has always been that highly suggestible people are more likely to volunteer. But such is certainly not always the case. A goodly percentage of the volunteers are people eager to "prove" that they can not be hypnotized. Such people frequently turn out to be excellent subjects and it is interesting to me, if not to the audience, to see them struggling mightily--sometimes successfully; usually not--against a suggestion.

.

Can anyone induce hypnosis? The man from whom I learned the trade, Richard Hazley (whose claim to the title "The Amazing", incidentally, antedates and is more euphoniously valid than that of either Kreskin or

Randi), used to answer that question with a question: "Can anyone play the piano?". An excellent answer. Few of the tips to aspiring stage hypnotists that I have seen give sufficient stress to the importance of practice. I feel confident that I am a better hypnotist today than I was five years ago. After more than a quarter of a century, five additional years of practice has still made a difference.

.

Those who claim that "no induction" is fully as effective as an induction procedure are, I suspect, basing their conclusion on a comparison of "no induction" with an induction procedure by an unskilled hypnotist. In the first place, I'm not sure how the "no induction" portion of the experiment could be arranged.

If people are asked to volunteer, or are offered pay, to participate in an experiment and then given suggestions, that may in itself constitute an induction procedure. The induction does not have to be complicated or follow any particular format. One of several induction procedures that I use is simply to walk into the audience and tell a person that when I touch their nose they'll close their eyes and go to sleep. It is not a terribly effective procedure but for me, so far, it has been infallible and I take care that it remain so by employing it sparingly and only when I know it will work.

.

If you want to study the effectiveness of induction, first find yourself a good hypnotist. Simply saying the words is not enough. If you insist on doing it yourself, start off with several years of practice and then when you're fully confident that you have mastered the art, give yourself a test by walking out in front of several hundred skeptical people in an auditorium and giving a demonstration.

.

I agree fully with the reservations expressed about the unreliability and potential dangers of memories and testimony elicited under hypnosis. Many subjects do strive to please the hypnotist (others try equally hard to challenge him or her) so that memories may be unintentionally suggested or imagined and such memories may seem so real to the subject that they become very convincing when recalled in a court room. I would imagine that such a witness would pass a lie detector test without difficulty.

.

Past lives regression I regard as blatant nonsense. When people insist that such memories, even if inaccurate, must be evidence of reincarnation, I reply by suggesting to a subject that he has just returned from the planet Venus with a young Venusian girl who speaks no English but who has taught him Venusian. The two will then proceed to invent a language (mostly, but not always entirely, gibberish) and give confident answers and translations to all manner of questions about life on Venus.

I'm not sure that the demonstration is terribly effective with the reincarnation kooks, or that they even see my point, but it seems abundantly plain to me that past lives remembered under hypnosis are fully as unlikely as that the couple in front of me were really on Venus last week.

.

I would ordinarily place absolutely no importance on the reports of hypnotized subjects. Most subjects remember little if anything that happened. Others remember almost everything and many, I think, remember part and think they remember everything. The best and what seems to me the most accurate report I have ever seen is contained in the autobiography of one of my subjects, the late Richard Feynman's, "Surely You're Joking, Mr. Feynman".

.

Nobel Laureate Feynman, a man with serious credentials for both skepticism and critical thinking, reported that while he was fully aware of the absurdity of the suggestions I had given him and was convinced that he would not comply with them, somehow found himself complying and concluded that that was what hypnosis is.

.

Few people ever think they were hypnotized. To make that point to a class of college students, I once turned to a member of the class, Doug Smith, and asked him if he had ever been hypnotized. Doug was a super subject and everyone in the class had observed him when hypnotized. While I confidently expected him to insist that he had never been hypnotized, Doug surprised me by answering "Yes". I asked him how he knew and after a moment's reflection he replied: "I guess because of the things people have told me."

.

Mentioning Doug reminds me of another super subject, Ted Hansen, who provided dramatic testimony to the reality of the mystery. Ted was fond of cats and I had several times given him the post-hypnotic suggestion that upon awakening he would be petting a cat. One evening I decided not to remove the suggestion but to simply wait and see how long it would take to wear off. For more than half an hour Ted sat comfortably and contentedly in a chair stroking the cat before turning to me and, as he hefted the imaginary cat, saying: "This is mind boggling. I see the cat. I feel the weight of the cat. I feel the warmth of the cat. I feel the texture of the cat's fur. I feel the moistness of the cat's nose. And yet I know there is no cat."

.

Is it necessary for the subject to "believe" in order for hypnosis to work? I don't think so. It seems that with some subjects we communicate only with the subconscious while with others there is simultaneous communication with both the conscious and the subconscious. I assume that the former remember nothing of what is said while the latter remember some or all. With subjects of the latter kind I may give the post-hypnotic suggestion that when I touch my mouth they will be thirsty. When I touch my mouth a typical response is: "Oh, no. It didn't work with me. I wasn't hypnotized. I know that you said when you touched your mouth I would be thirsty. It didn't work with me. But, damn, I'm thirsty. But it doesn't have anything to do with you touching your mouth; I'm really thirsty."

.

And I think they are really thirsty. Just as I think the warts and migraine headaches really disappear and concentration and relaxation really improve and compulsions to eat or smoke or bite the nails really diminish.

.

To write it all off as "merely suggestion" seems to me to miss the point. I think it not "merely suggestion". I think it's all suggestion. I think that's what hypnosis is. And I think a lot of other things--acupuncture (which I frequently duplicate; using my index finger instead of a needle), placebos, transcendental meditation and witchcraft among them--are also suggestion...or hypnosis.

.

I also think there's quite a bit of suggestion (or hypnosis...or witchcraft, if you prefer) in modern medicine. Many nurses who have patients in intense pain but to whom they can give no more morphine, sometimes administer injections of distilled water and find that the suggestion of a morphine injection is often as effective as morphine itself. And several pharmacists have told me that they fill many, many prescriptions for placebos. "Take one before every meal"...and the suggestion is clearly implied that it will make you feel better...and sometimes it does.

.

Some medical doctors have told me that they would consider it a violation of medical ethics to prescribe a placebo. Yet the efficacy of placebos--for some people, for some things--is proven by a staggering amount of carefully documented data. Placebos are cheap and have no side effects. Why not use them? Because they don't always work? What medication does? I feel certain that hypnosis will remove warts and sometimes cure or relieve or prevent colds. Both are viral infections. What about other viruses? I have no idea but certainly think investigation is warranted.

.

I have a self-hypnosis tape (I call it a relaxation tape) that thousands of people use for a wide variety of purposes: smoking, diet, stress, migraine headaches and other pain, nail biting, insomnia, complexion, childbirth, phobias, etc. I will not bore nor strain the credulity of SCICOP members with a recitation of some of the benefits claimed. The tape is available from me.

.

Since I value skepticism so highly, I tend to be cheered, almost, by the skepticism of my audiences (why can't they be equally skeptical of such rubbish as astrology, ESP, reincarnation and water witching?). What they see is so very hard to believe that most audiences tend to explain it as "acting" or "faking".

.

I seldom encounter faking and if they're acting then my suggestion to any Hollywood talent scouts out there is to follow me around for a while. What talent they will discover. I recently gave a young man a pair of "X-ray glasses" that permitted him to see through people's clothing so that everyone appeared nude. I momentarily turned my attention to another subject and when I turned around found that the subject with the glasses had walked to the front of the stage, sat down with his legs hanging over the edge of the stage and was ogling the audience with lascivious and unconcealed delight. I asked him to return to his chair and as he stood up I saw immediately why he had sat down. He was wearing tight jeans and was in what must have been a most uncomfortable predicament. Faking? Acting? Please.

.

Macoy
Email macoy@nmax.net

Krisztina Hall

.

The Stage Perspective: Confidence to Success!

My experience as a stage hypnotist has been very trying at times. Perhaps it was because I lacked experience in the entertainment industry when I started. In the past few years I have made several observations while watching other stage hypnotists perform and found that they have difficulties as well.

One thing that I would like to express to all stage hypnotists and those of you that are interested in getting into this field is: You are there to ENTERTAIN the audience. That is your main objective and your main concern. Keep this in mind.

As I observe other stage hypnotists, I notice that they freeze or panic when there are small numbers of people at their show. As a result, the hypnotist will often back out of performing or they perform poorly. One hypnotist said to me that he has a better show but he blamed poor attendance for his lack of enthusiasm.

My point is that no matter what the circumstances are -- YOU are there to put on a show. You should use the same amount of energy (if not more) to entertain the crowd. Let the audience know that you are in charge. Take responsibility as the entertainer.

I was booked to do a show in a small town along the Saskatchewan border. I had no idea that there would be a blizzard. We set up to do the show in anticipation of a good turn out. I was amazed that there was a crowd of even 30 people given the weather conditions. At first I began thinking to myself that I wouldn't be able to do a show -- that there wouldn't be enough people to hypnotize. Of course, I started to panic.

Well, I took a deep breath and said to myself, "OK, I can do this," and I proceeded to do the show. I did it differently that night. I didn't do my typical up front material because of the small numbers. Instead, I talked to the audience individually and in small groups and explained the basics of hypnosis to them. By being a bit more personal with them, I gained their confidence and respect.

I didn't use the stage and instead I chose to put the volunteers in a circle on the dance floor. I proceeded to do my induction with five volunteers and four of them were hypnotized. I had to work extra hard and had to use extra energy to get the remaining crowd to applaud and cheer for the volunteers.

On the whole, I had a great show. After the show, I found out that there was a reporter in the room and later gave him an interview. The reporter was impressed at my ability to perform under these circumstances and said that it takes a great entertainer to do what I did. When I read the paper the next day, I discovered he had given me a great review and wrote a big article. The lead was even on the front page.

As you can see, it doesn't matter what the circumstances are. When you perform, always do your best! It's better to know that you did your best than to give up -- and you may never know who is watching.

I feel that this experience has made me a better entertainer. I am better prepared to take on the new challenges that come to me.

So remember, **YOU ARE AN ENTERTAINER!** Always do your best!!!

Happy Trancing,

Krisztina

.

Canada's Original and Best Female Stage Hypnotist

Stepping Up – Howard Morgan

Let's be honest. Hypnosis is fascinating. Not only do we love doing it, but to someone who's never seen a show, it's nothing short of amazing. Suddenly a person you know seems to have completely "lost it". The problem is, far too often, we ride the wake of the venue, and give up being showmen (and women for you politically correct types out there).

It was close to 25 years ago when I did my first hypnotic show. At the time I discovered that audiences were captivated by watching their spouses run from imaginary mice or forget their names. For a long time, I was satisfied to offer a list of slapstick "bits" back to back. At that time I was getting what would probably amount to $200 in today's money per show, and was ecstatic.

For a guy used to making $100 to spend 2 hours entertaining kiddies at a birthday party with magic and animal balloons that seemed like a lot of money. Then I started thinking, and a few simple changes in my routine suddenly made my show easily marketable at my current rate of $2500+ a show.

.

I remember my post grad years in theater when in college. I used to sit through endless "one act plays" that amounted to little more than someone's poorly written monologue being recited by two or more freshmen actors while trying to look like they were doing something on stage. Boring would be an understatement. Nobody in their right mind would ever consider paying for the "privilege" of being subjected to this torture.

.

Then there was community theater. Rogers and Hammerstein being massacred by the director's friends. Every now and then a few quality shows slipped in that kept the box office in business, but generally community theater offered the second rate version of what should have been a masterpiece.

These shows were usually performed for audiences of less than 200 people in small cramped rooms with no air conditioning. Ticket prices ran somewhere in the $10 to $20 dollar range (today's money) and rarely actually paid for overhead. If it wasn't for regularly scheduled handouts from overly generous patrons and city halls that wanted to boast of having a theater in their community, these places would never have survived.

.

And then there was real theater. It was a place reserved only for those who had taken the years needed to perfect every body motion and facial expression. Actors who had dedicated most of their lives to learning how to project and captivate. And once they "got the part" they had to earn it all over again. Countless hours memorizing lines. Days of practicing single hand motions and late nights trying to justify motivation.

The director then surrounded the cast with very expensive sets and special effects and spared no expense in promoting the show. The show was then performed only in elegant theaters with plush chairs and ornate lobbies. 2000-3000 patrons gladly lined up 5 or 6 times a week to each pay from $50 for balcony seats to $200 a person for private viewing boxes. And although the $30,000+ door they made per show more than covered overhead, the production soon found investors lining up to buy stock in individual productions. And audiences left convinced they had gotten a bargain.

.

Back in my $200 a show days I offered a show that probably fit somewhere in the community theater category. I dressed sloppy, and used a bunch of simple "bits" I had stolen from other performers. About the only time I actually thought about my show was when I was on stage having problems during an induction period. I usually sold an hour of interesting experiments in hypnosis, and even padded that with 15 to 20 minutes of explanation up front before even getting started. And only a very small portion of my clients ever called back.

.

Then I decided to make it a career. Oh, I had made my living doing hypnosis (and some magic) for probably 5 or 6 years by then, but never thought of it as my lifelong career. I started considering what made my show sell (as little as it did) and what might make it sell better. I started wondering what the "perfect" hypnotic show might look like. And suddenly I found myself slipping into the "real theater" mode.

I spent hours practicing walking on stage. I carefully considered when was the best moment to pull the microphone out of the stand. Should I pace or stand still? How should I dress? How could I tighten up my pretalk, so it became an entertaining part of the show instead of being a necessary evil. I remember spending hours trying to imagine myself sitting in an audience watching my show. What parts would I consider boring? What made the show drag (a word several of my theater friends seemed to use regularly when describing my show).

I even experimented with various concepts for streamlining the induction period and actually found you can do most of the induction "talk" before ever telling anybody to close their eyes, provided you can get their undivided attention.

.

I also overhauled my show. I began by lengthening my show to the industry standard of 90+ minutes. And instead of simply tossing a bunch of unrelated "bits" together, I started thinking in terms of captivating opening bits, exciting middles, and climactic endings. I also started combining routines together, which seemed to cut down on suggestion breaks, and seemed to make the show move much faster.

.

One such combination was what I called my "Out Of This World" routine. Instead of just having someone "Speak Like A Martian", I began by interviewing a deep south family (with a strong Southern Drawl) about a UFO that had landed on their property. Then quickly, without telling them to close their eyes or sleep, I would make the suggestion that they were all outside, on a hillside looking at the stars.

My body motion and "story teller" persona made it impossible for even the non hypnotized audience members to not see the stars. Suddenly, while staying in character, I'd point, as I suggested that a certain star seemed to be getting larger, and moving erratically. I'd guide them through seeing a space ship coming close enough for them to see the "creatures" inside. I'd get them all focused on a specific spot just over the audience heads, and then I'd assign reactions to each spectator. "You think it's funny", "you're very scared", "you want them to take you up as an abductee", etc.. I'd sit back and give them 30 seconds or so to establish reactions while the theme from "2001" played in the background.

I then had everybody imagine they were all Martians on the space ship, each doing their own weird body contortions and making high pitched squeaky sounds while landing and looking out of portholes at the "funny looking humans" in the audience. This was done complete with sound effects, background music and occasional bursts of smoke from offstage.

I even had people drop dry ice in hot water buckets off stage during some of my higher paying shows to get the eerie "smoke on the floor" effect. At the end I had the panel of Martians all sit down while an interpreter translated what they all had to say during an interview "on national television".

Watching each person trying to outdo all the others with facial expressions and body motions definitely offered a high quality "climax" to the 15 to 20 minute "bit" we had just experienced. And the fact that they were already into the moment (thanks to the logical sequencing of the routine) helped make each "bit" easier for them to understand and participate in. A sharp translator could easily make this one of the more memorable parts of the show.

.

Whereas my cheaper show usually sold only to one time buyers, once I took the time to do it up right, I suddenly found that my large number of repeat customers allowed me to cut down on promotion costs. I also discovered another hidden bonus.

Most corporate events are given for other corporate leaders. The audience usually includes the vendors and suppliers of your client. I found that it was rare for me to make it through a corporate event without having at least 4 or 5 CEO's or event planners ask for my card. Out of these, I could usually count on selling at least one show, meaning I now had doubled my steady clientelle. And as business got better, I could now afford to turn down lower paying shows (without offending my landlord).

I now begin my sales pitch with "You know, the truth is, you probably can't afford me. I make a point of charging enough so I can afford to dedicate my time to truly fine tuning the show. And I guess I sell enough of them to make this policy cost effective." I then go on and tell them what I offer. With that kind of leadin, most buyers spend the time while I'm doing my sales pitch trying to figure out where else they can afford to cut corners in order to be able to afford quality.

This is a far cry from a time when I was regularly stuck begging clients to believe I was worth $200 when deep down even I didn't believe it myself. And instead of getting the run around when I try to follow up after a show, I now get swamped by unsolicited letters of reference and personal referrals.

.

I can't tell you what's right for your show, but I can tell you that until you stretch to your limit, you're never going to reach "the big time". A few years ago we used to run an agency in Reno and worked pretty close with the Reno and Vegas markets.

I know for a fact that every Entertainment Director in the industry goes out of their way to find out and share information about entertainers. If you do a "great" job, all you'll need to "break in" is one private show seen by an Entertainment Director at a bigger showroom.

Word will get out quickly that you should be contacted. If, on the other hand, your show is less than top notch, you may not realize it, but soon after you leave the building, an Entertainment director is probably on the phone calling his buddies down the strip to warn them. And tightening up your show can't be done during the month or so notice you'll have before your "big break". Either you make it a lifestyle or you agree to settle for the leftover peanuts that fall after the elephants leave town.

.

Email:**howardmorgan@witty.com**
Web Site **http://www.merlynarts.com/hypnoshow3.html**

The Unknown Hypnotist
Behind The Scenes of an Entertainer

By Michael Giannantonio
.

I would like to take you backstage and behind the scenes of an entertainer. I am The Unknown Hypnotist, a stage hypnotist / Illusionist, and the questions I get asked most often aren't that of what most would think, they are of a more realistic nature, and it's time to put these questions to the test.

Have you ever wondered what was behind all the fancy costumes, the special lighting, even the smile that that entertainer wore when you shook his hand for the first time?

Let's start in the beginning, the life of an entertainer in the beginning can be summed up in a few simple words, a major struggle. The performances which are taken for a few hundred bucks, just to pay for hotel rooms, food and gas to get from town to town, the late nights and lonely days and for what you may ask?

To gain the experience and notoriety due as a performer in hopes of getting that big break? This could possibly be one of the loneliest occupation one can embark in. You see it's time that permits an entertainer from experiencing his / her life, specifically the lack of time, allow me to explain.

As an entertainer your first obligation is to your audiences, on a standard tour of we'll say three states and twenty-five shows in five to six weeks time. First let's consider the venue locations, let's say nightclubs, a five day fair (followed up by an adult show), and a corporate performance customized to the clients needs.

The nightclub run for instance would be extremely difficult, not so much for just a hypnotist who walks in with a boom box and a few tapes, however for an entertainer this can be a difficult task. Imagine this, time to rise, 8:00 Am Friday morning, the shows begin, to kick off the tour you have had it easy, two days to prepare the stage, illusions, and plenty of time for rehearsals.

The show begins at we'll say 9:00 p.m. and continues on until roughly 11:00 - 11:30, when afterwards you mingle with the fans, have a drink, relax for a bit and then the club is closed, so it's 1:00 a.m. and now time for you to tear down the stage, easy task for a 5 or 6 man crew, but let's face it, you don't have a 5 man crew, if you're lucky, you have a 2 man crew, that's you and someone else, after taking the stage props down and packing the vehicle (usually a large uncomfortable van with terrible suspension) you glance at you watch to realize it is now 3:30 a.m., and you need to be on the road at 8:00 a.m. to make your next performance at 10:00 p.m. that night.

As you can see even a short five-week tour can be enough to wear out even the most physically fit person. After five nights straight in four different cities, you get a night off, and believe me the last thing you want to do is go out for a night on the town, You tend to be more worried with getting the feeling back into your feet before the next group of shows comes up.

Then you do a short fair, ah, cake work, this is the easiest portion of the trip, virtually no set up or tear down, two or three forty minute shows a day for 5 days, one location, one hotel, and one city. Then the adult show, fun crowd, usually very late performance and wild and crazy audience, these shows tend to "drain" you as your energy level is extremely high. Time to pack up again, stop and do some laundry, run to the dry cleaners, buy some Dr. Pepper and hit the road again.

After a few more weeks of performing in clubs, It's time for you're corporate show, this is the show that funds the entire trip and pays the salaries. You have planned for this performance for 2 months and know exactly what you want to do, however the thing you didn't plan for was the fact that you have been on the road for four weeks and have set up and tore down all your illusions and staging somewhere around twenty times in the past four weeks, you have driven 2,000 miles, changes hotels 9 times and eaten Taco Bell for 3 weeks, not to speak of the fact that you average 4 to 6 hours of sleep per night. So you're just glad you had enough foresight to leave 2 days off before this performance.

After relaxing for a day, you decide to set up your stage and take your time rehearsing and making sure everything is perfect for the client. This is extremely difficult to do after going nonstop for four weeks and then getting the chance to slow down, you find yourself working at the same exhausting pace even though there is need to.

Once this performance is finished, it's time to kick off the final phase of the tour, three or four more shows in which you want to give your all to finish up a great note.

Now that all is said and done and the last show is over, you feel a sigh of relief knowing that it was another successful tour. This brings me to the point of the story, remember the questions I asked in the beginning?

Here's where it all pays off, because behind the lights, the costumes and the glitz is what you saw when you shook that hand for the first time, the smile, because without that, you can't go on, it's not the art that I push for, it's the audience.

When I meet someone after a show, that's what I remember the most. And you can believe that the smile is real, because the joy that a true entertainer gains from seeing an audience having a great time is unmatched by anything you could possibly imagine. All the work, the rehearsals, the late nights and lonely drives are all paid for when I see the smile on your face and shake your hand in friendship.

That is the payoff that I seek, be it a show for 150 people in a club, or a performance for 12,000 in an arena, the payoff is the same, and as we grow as entertainers and "make it" in the business, it is the true entertainer who never loses sight of what is important, the fans, because it is the fans who make you what you are and if there is respect to be given, don't feel it belongs to the entertainer, because the truth is, it belongs to each and every one of you, who support the cause and stand by in awe wondering what it would be like to be that entertainer.

To each and every one of you, from the bottom of my heart, I salute you and thank you for the years of good times that come out of all the work, the little moments that shine through and don't go forgotten, to all of you I say Thank You and I'll see you on the next tour!

Keep the faith and remember life isn't only what you see around you, just open your eyes to the reality you can make for yourself, and have the strength to follow your dreams whatever they may be, because you have the power to make those dreams a reality.

Sincerely,

Michael Giannantonio
The Unknown Hypnotist
http://www.unknownhypnotist.com/

The Very Best Advertising

Let's face it. Anything I say about myself, is just that, something I said about myself. I can tell you my show was great, that the audiences loved it, that people will be talking about it for years to come. But coming from me, most any accolade will sound like simple, arrogant boasting.

Of course, if someone else says it, it takes on a whole new meaning. And if that someone else happens to be the CEO for IBM or the Entertainment Coordinator for a Cruise line, now suddenly you have a prized possession that definitely means something. And the good news is, that if you know how to do it, getting quality testimonials isn't anywhere near as hard as most would think.

I honestly can't tell you how many testimonials I've gotten over the years. They've come from General Managers and CEO's of major corporations, The Activities Directors for world famous amusement parks, Sales and Catering Directors at 4 Star Hotels and Resorts, Doctors, Lawyers, Celebrities and countless others. They make anything I say sound believable.

When a potential client is busy considering whether or not to use my services, there are two things they're busy trying to find out. Is the show going to truly be entertaining, and will I be dependable (on time, well equipped, etc.). The logical place to find these things out is to ask respected people that have already experienced my show their opinion. Or better yet, rather than bothers spending hours trying to track down someone on the phone, check to see what they say in the quotes on my brochure.

The hidden secret that somehow seems to allude most entertainers when getting letters of referral is really very simple, just ask. That's it, simply ask for it. And there's more than one place in the process of doing a show where a well placed request is sure to get a letter.

Something you need to be careful about. Federal law says you aren't supposed to use quotes in your advertising unless you currently have copies of signed letters including them. It would really be great if we could quote every person that happened to walk by after a show and tell us we were great, but that isn't legal. It is legal, however, to quote sources, and even to use a simple trick I'll explain in a minute, to quote yourself, provided you can get someone important to sign the letter.

I have a stack of letters, including one of the few letters of recommendation ever written by the Activities Director of the world famous San Diego Zoo that say exactly what I want them to say. I know this to be true, because I actually wrote the letters myself, and then had these people sign them. But let's start at the beginning here.

Just this past week I did a show for a VIP Party (high rollers club) at Harrah's Casino just outside of Topeka, Kansas. Confidentially, the show didn't go that well. Everybody in the room was being honored as being part of the high class casino "elite". They had all put on their best and were walking around trying to act the part. And then I come up and tell them to bark like dogs. It took some doing just to get a decent group of subjects. But the show did go off, and the 5 people I ended up with worked out fairly well.

As soon as the show was over, I made a point of joining the Casino General Manager at the back of the room to say goodbye to people as they walked out the room. I'm not sure how the manager felt about the show on his own, but after having a few of his "high rollers" come up and tell me how great it was (what else are you supposed to say to the performer at the back of the room??) he developed a big smile and started congratulating the lady who coordinated the event on putting together a winning package. I waited till the crowd had died down and then turned to the General Manager, and asked simple, "So how'd you like the show?" Right after having heard all the positive feedback there really was only one answer he could give me.

He told me it was great. I thanked him and added, "I don't know if I'm overstepping my bounds here, but you know, I'm right in the middle of putting together a promo package, and it would really help me if I could get you to write me a note telling me exactly how you felt." He immediately assured me that he'd be very glad to draft up a letter and get it right out to me.

By itself, that commitment would buy me about a 50/50 chance of actually getting a letter. But I added, "If I know your letter is coming, I'll go on and hold up on putting my mailer together for a week so I can quote you if you don't mind." This statement happened to be true, but then, even if it wasn't, if I knew I'd have a current quote from the GM of a major casino coming in, you better believe I'd start putting together a mailer before his letter arrived.

He agreed to get right on it. My chances just jumped to 75%. But that still wasn't enough. I happened to be staying at the casino that night, so the next morning, right at about 9:45, I called the GM's secretary and casually mentioned that the boss had told me he would be glad to write up a letter telling me how he felt about my show, and asking her if she thought he'd have time to dictate it out before I left at noon. As expected, she told me he'd be busy, but assured me that she would see to it that he got it done real soon. I thanked her, and gave her my mailing address.

Yes, the casino's marketing department already had it, but it won't hurt for her to be able to casually walk in when he has a few moments and remind him about the letter. And then, without having to spend time tracking my address down, simply put it in an envelope and drop it in the mail. My chances just jumped to probably 95%. Well, the letter arrived 4 days later.

This is the traditional way of asking for letters. You might notice how persistent I was. Without being obnoxious, I'm willing to do all I can to get a good letter. They're worth it. Over the next few years, this one letter, which took less than 10 minutes of the GM's time, will probably sell $40,000 worth of shows for me. Every other casino in the world will stop and look when they see one of their own has something to say. And all the upper class establishments (cruise ships, resorts and the like) will definitely respect his opinions.

A simple way to get letters from past clients is, again, to ask. If you've already done a good show for someone, and you know they'll probably be calling you again, there's nothing wrong with calling them up and asking for references.

A little trick that works well here is to avoid simply asking them to "write me a letter". That will probably never happen. Instead, my approach is to explain that I'm in the middle of putting together a mailer, and would really like to include some of their feelings about the show. Once they agree, ask them if they'll mind giving you a few moments to answer some questions. In my case I also ask if it's okay with them if I record their answers so I won't misquote them.

I've never had anybody say no. Ask questions that require more than "yes" and "no" answers. Don't ask "did you like the show?" ask "how did you like the show, and why". Ask questions like, "What would you say made the show entertaining?", "What would you say to someone considering using my show?", "Is this the kind of show you might see recommending to others?", etc. This might also be a good place, as you're wrapping it up, to request a referral or two. Casually ask, as you finish, "By the way, now that we're on the topic, would you mind giving me a name or two of some of your peers I can contact who might be able to use my show?".

As soon as you finish the telephone interview, explain that federal law prohibits you from quoting him if you don't have his quotes in writing, so if he doesn't mind, you'll draw up a simple letter, reflecting his answers, and mail it right off to him. If he can simply initial it and return it, you'd greatly appreciate it.

When I do this, I also include a special thank you note and offer him an incentive as a way of showing my appreciation. It might be a copy of one of my books, or maybe a movie ticket I ended up trading for. It the letter is extra good, I might even toss in a night's stay at a local resort which I traded work for (I explain this in the next paragraph). Something he'll consider valuable. That guarantees that he'll get the note, sign it and place it in the self addressed stamped envelope immediately.

Truth be told, even if he doesn't return the letter, having a recorded copy of the interview is enough. But cassette tapes are a lot harder to save than letters are. These notes, obviously, won't be on the company letterhead, but you can still use these quotes in your brochures and letters.

Most of my larger shows get me letters of recommendation, and there's a simple reason why. When I quote them my standard price ($2500) they usually cringe. Their budget was more in the $1500 league and they're not sure if they can get this amount approved. Well I'll negotiate, but I won't cheapen my show.

Starting with $2500 and then letting them talk you down to $1000 is a sure way to convince the client that your show isn't as good as you think it is. I'll lower my price, but I'll always ask for something in return. And the first thing I ask for, is a letter of recommendation. Basically the discussion usually goes something like this.

CLIENT: "You know, I really would like to use your show, but the truth is, that price is a little out of our budget"

ME: "Well, Cathy, the truth is, I've been at this for quite a while now, and I have enough people that are very willing to pay that price. But I don't want to leave you high and dry. I'll tell you what I would be willing to do, though. If you'll agree to send me a letter within a week after the show, telling me what you thought of it, I'm willing to knock off $200 from the price."

CLIENT: "Even $200 won't be enough" (Notice I now have her negotiating for me. In essence she's saying, "what else can I give you in order to bring the price down to a number we both know will be necessary if you plan on working for us.")

ME: "How much do you feel you can afford?"

CLIENT: "I can probably go as high as $2000"

ME: "$2000......I'll tell you what. If you'll agree to get that letter out to me, and give me a week's stay at your resort that I can use any time I want, I'll knock my price down to $2000."

CLIENT: "Well, let me talk to the General Manager and see what I can do."

ME: "Okay, I'll hold your date for a week and expect to hear back from you by next Wednesday. Will that work for you?"

Considering the number of rooms most of these places comp weekly, and the fact that she now feels like 10 minutes of her time is worth $200, this is all but a done deal. I'll immediately fax her a contract with all the details of the show, and add at the bottom an extra paragraph that reads something to the effect of:

"Client further agrees to forward a letter to Howard, written on company letterhead, no later than one week (5 working days) after the completion of the show. Client also agrees to make arrangements for Howard, or a guest of his choosing to stay at the resort for 7 days at a future date."

I also have a bunch of these comped hotel vouchers. They're great for when I'm traveling, and more than a few wedding couples felt like I went overboard when I "paid" for their honeymoon. I also use them as "thank you" gifts for better clients at the end of the year.

Other things I'll often negotiate into contracts include advertising space in company newsletters (I sell a lot of tapes and books that way); comped airline tickets (when working for airlines); free meals (gift certificates at larger restaurants, etc. in exchange for lowering my price enough so they can sell it to their clients); traded performances (local DJ's etc. trying to impress their clients might agree to do 8 hours work in exchange for a half price show. I'm sure to need a DJ somewhere during my next holiday season, so I'll probably make a profit on the deal.)

There is a trick that can get you the ultimate letter of recommendation. And I have a stack of them. In fact, most of them come from people who don't usually write letters, because they're too busy.

The Director of Marketing at the San Diego Zoo is one of the busiest people in town. He's forever coordinating television appearances, warding off environmentalists, arranging special events and the like. He definitely does not have the time to stop everything and write a letter. Consequently, I don't know of a single entertainer that has ever received a letter written by him. My letter from him, on the other hand, is perfect. It talks about my incredible ability to hold and entertain a crowd, about the obvious experience and dynamic charisma. It says just what I'd want it to say, because I wrote it.

After a successful summer at the park, I called his office and asked him if he'd mind dropping me a note telling me what he thought of the show. He explained that as a policy he usually doesn't write letters because he doesn't want to get bogged down with a long list of people that all want his recommendations. I asked if the issue here was time, and he said yes. I then told him, if he didn't mind, that I'd be willing to write up a letter for him, send it out to him, and if he felt it adequately represented his feelings, all he had to do was sign it. If nothing else, curiosity alone pretty much guarantees he'll give it a try.

Typically, in this kind of situation, I begin by swinging by his office and ask someone for a piece of stationary because "Mr. So and So asked me to put together a letter for him to sign". They give it to me, I go home, write up something realistic but full of sound bites (he was captivating, I was amazed, the energy level was incredible, I've never laughed so hard in my life, etc.).

Once the person ends up with the letter in his hand, his main concern isn't whether it realistically reflects his opinion. What he's really wondering is whether anything you've quoted him as saying will be incriminating (stay away from comments like "there's no other entertainer in town that I'd recommend more than..." and so forth). If the letter is "safe" you'll get a great letter.

One final way to get a good quote from the media is to say it yourself. Personally I shy away from this method, because, although it's legal, the ethics are questionable.

I do know that a very large number of entertainers use it regularly. Basically, when you read one of those quotes from, say, the L.A. Times, that lists a person as "America's foremost Hypnotist", there's a decent chance the person isn't really quoting an editorial in the L.A. Times.

They're actually quoting their own ad.

They basically took out an ad in the paper, or ran a spot on the radio, and then quoted something they wrote about themselves. Again, it's legal, but it's the kind of thing that may eventually catch up with you. And considering how easy it is to get press releases published (which then do, officially, become the opinion of the paper) and the number of quality letters you can get elsewhere, personally I don't feel this method is needed. I include it here, though, for the sake of completeness.

It takes a bit of work, but after all is said and done, show business is like any other business. Either you work it with everything you've got, or it's just in it as a hobby.

Selling Therapy at Shows by Howard Morgan

Okay, let's be honest. Deep down, every one of us feels like a God when we walk off stage. We've just managed to take total strangers and somehow talk them into doing some mighty strange things. And to the average audience member, our power is just short of limitless. So why not take advantage and sell some therapy on the side, now that we've overcome the image issues?

I do it all the time. At the end of most of my shows I end up with a person or two in my hotel room working on smoking or some sort of phobia. And it's not uncommon for people to schedule sessions for the next morning, as well. Of course, there's a trick to making this work, and it goes a bit beyond just asking. But first, it's vitally important that we don't go around selling snake oil.

I know it's tempting. Once we have the induction part down, it's hard to not assume that means we qualify to cure all the illnesses of the world. Heck, if we can get them to bark like dogs, why can't we just tell them to stop smoking and then get on with our lives? There actually are several reasons, not the least of which is ethics.

We've all gone around telling people for years that Hypnosis is harmless, that nobody gets hurt, and many of us have even come to believe it, to some degree, ourselves. The truth is, in a therapy setting, it can be very harmful, if not done right. In a stage setting, where volunteers come to have fun, and don't expect any long lasting suggestions, most of what we're doing is, relatively harmless. There are a couple places where we can dive in over our heads, though.

We do need to be careful with time regression, and the possibility of taking someone back to some repressed memory. Suppose a person saw their father being crushed by a car on their 5th birthday, but soon managed, as a survival mechanism, to block the memory from their conscious mind. All the relatives managed to live with the distorted truth, because nobody wanted to see "little Johnny" suffer any more than he had to. Well, little Johnny is now Mr. John, a 45 year old manager for a major engineering firm.

His inner mind has that nagging feeling that there are things he hasn't completely come to grips with, but generally he's managed to live comfortably in his state of denial.

Now suddenly, during a show by the Magnificent Dr. Do It All, he's told to go back to a time in the past. In fact, he's now at his 5th birthday party. "Little Johnny" gets all excited, the way he actually did during the first hour of the party.

He's very expressive, and the audience is eating it up. Then he tells you he wants to go tell Daddy to come in so he could open presents. He mentally walks to the door, opens it, and suddenly, years of repressed fears and imagined monsters, all come flying out of your exposed Pandora's Box. Right there in front of him is the horrible truth. There lies his father, with brains and guts splattered all over the sidewalk. If you don't know what you're doing, this could easily lead to trauma, schizophrenia, neurosis and a hefty lawsuit.

Taking people back in time is something we all need to do with the utmost care, if at all. If you have a regressive bit in your show, be sure you remember to watch for the first sign of possible concern or worry. Even the slightest hint of an unexpected emotion is your signal to immediately move to a different time in their past.

Another possible problem on stage, is the possibility of exposing a schizophrenic to a traumatic experience. If, as you start to hypnotize a person, you find someone is having mild convulsive reactions to suggestions, you may want to send that person back immediately.

If someone who naturally suffers of a multiple personality happens to be told to "focus intently", you automatically create a logic loop in their inner mind. Which of them should focus? Should one of them listen in as the other obeys? Is it possible for one to focus completely, when in fact a full half of their thinking power is being used by a second personality? Don't play with this, it too is dangerous.

If you chance upon one of these situations, and they're not that difficult to spot. You'll see a person trying to focus, while at the same time, creating a troubled look on their face. You can almost see the conflict expressing itself in the changing facial expressions. It's almost as if a person were shooting back and forth from a trance to a faking it state.

If you find yourself dealing with this kind of person, don't bring them out traumatically. This can cause problems. Instead, pamper them back out. Make them feel safe. Use simple phrases like "everything is going to be okay, you feel comfortable with yourself, secure in who you are, at the count of three you'll wake up, feeling very relaxed, aware of all that's happened, but convinced you were never actually hypnotized. At the count of three, feeling alert and alive, One......Two....... aaaaaand..... Three".

If you choose to do therapy, be sure you take the time to understand what you're doing. Do some research. Be aware that the therapeutic setting is a lot more permanent. Clients walk in expecting long term results. One careless word can leave its impression.

I remember hearing about a guy doing an abductee session where he was trying to figure out what happened during a missing time period in a lady's recent past. The lady was very nervous, and obviously expected something terrible to happen. In an attempt to give her a secure anchor to work off of, he mentioned casually that "you're in a safe place. The Doctor is here and is taking care of you. He won't let anything happen to you. The Doctor loves you too much to let you suffer any pain." The session went well, and all the gory details were dealt with.

The woman came out of the session convinced not only that she had in fact been abducted and severely abused by probing aliens, but unknowingly the therapist had also created a causal response that made her assume that the only reason she had survived, the only reason these terrible "monsters" hadn't gotten the better of her, was because of the incredible love of her knight in shinning armor, the therapist.

Fortunately the therapist realized what he had done later on when he read the transcript of his session and understood the possible implications. It wasn't easy for him to call her up and ask if she had been feeling any misplaced love feelings for him. She told him she had, and that a lot of her recent dreams had involved him. He had her come in immediately and dealt with the potentially neurotic response. Be careful, and be sure you know what you're doing before getting started.

Figure out how to use metaphors and which ones to use. Try to stay away from negative reinforcement. Instead of telling someone that every time they see a cigarette they're going to think of a worm (I actually heard of a guy doing that), tell them they are a lot stronger, a lot more capable of taking control of their life.

They are able to overcome, and can now run long distances without loosing their breath, they can breath in and smell nature like they haven't smelt it in years, in short, they have become the masters of their lives. Where the negative metaphors might stop the smoking, in the long run, it will simply ruin their lives. Every time they see a person smoking, their inner mind is going to visualize a worm crawling on their face. It'll make them feel gross, insecure and unsocial.

Positive reinforcement, on the other hand, works wonders. Every time they take a breath, they'll be convinced it's a lot fresher, and they are more in control of their lives. Over the years I've kept track not only of my own success rate, but also of the hundreds who took hypnotherapy courses through my Mind Dynamix Institute in Los Angeles back in the 70's. Across the board, we had an 82% success rate, without ever having to ruin anybody's day.

This rate is measured based on call backs done 3 months after a two session treatment to see if the subject had gone back to smoking. Our successes with in other areas are just as impressive. In fact, in recent years, I've put on about 60 extra pounds. For a year or two after I gained my "40's" weight, I felt like a hypocrite offering to help others do what I obviously wasn't doing myself. But so many asked, that I gave in, and now, I still do a lot of weight loss clients, who accept that the methods work, even if I choose not to use them myself. Make sure you know what you're doing, and then start making plenty of extra money.

When I do private sessions back in my office, I usually charge $100 a session, for a one hour session. Smoking and weight loss usually take 2 sessions, phobias take 3 and most sexual issues take 3 to 4. When I'm on the road, I rarely have the luxury of offering more than one session. When I do therapy on the road, I usually sell a 90 minute session for $150, explaining that we'll need to really dig in deep and make this one session effective.

Because of the mystique surrounding a stage performer, these single session treatments do seem to do a lot more good than anything I can do at my office. Clients walk in convinced I can do anything, as opposed to wondering if I'm a con man who's only going to steal their money, as often is the case in an office setting.

The fact that I've already forewarned them that we're really going to have to "give it our all", tends to make them enter the room ready for business. And the fact that they've watched me do multiple rapid induction's on stage makes it acceptable to do a rapid induction rather than having to drag out a slow, full body, induction. Bringing a small Karaoke machine with earphones, and letting them lie on the hotel bed creates all the comforts of home, complete with music, a recorded copy of the session (for them to use again daily) and a relaxing setting.

So how do you go about getting all this extra money? It all starts long before you walk on stage. During the talk shows and newspaper interviews promoting the show you casually mention that you not only have fun on stage, but for x number of years you've also been doing hypnotherapy.

In that setting, it sounds like an endorsement for your competency as a hypnotist. In reality, it's a suggestion that you are as capable of helping anybody in this town with a problem, as you are of making them think they are Dolly Parton. Several locals who have always wished they could find the right "miracle worker" capable of helping them deal with, say, their fear of flying, may come just to meet you, wondering deep down, what they'd have to do to get you to help them.

Once your audience starts gathering in your showroom, make sure they have something to read. I use either small 1/3 page flyers or fancy table toppers (depending on the setting).

On these I write in 3rd person about myself. Comments like "He's performed in clubs nationally for over 25 years and has successfully practiced hypnotherapy for 27" again suggest that I know what I'm doing. I also include a line in there to the effect that "while Howard is on the road he is available to do private therapy on an appointment basis. Please talk to him after the show if you are interested."I back this up with tapes, CD's and books on self hypnosis at the back of the room. The flyer also suggests that clients can mail order therapy tapes at a future date. Not many do, but with that much pushing for my brand of therapy, there can be little doubt I'm able to do whatever is needed.

Then the show begins. Suddenly, all the skeptics in the room change their colors. People who entered believing hypnosis is a bunch of Mumbo Jumbo, suddenly watch their wives falling in love with brooms, and decide maybe it is real. Basically, the setup is perfect. Anybody who has ever wondered if a hypnotist could "heal them" is suddenly wondering if they can afford my services.

As I'm finishing the show, it's only natural to mention the tapes, books, t-shirts, posters, etc. available at the back of the room. I also usually plug copies of videos of the show and end by mentioning, almost as an afterthought, that "I'm going to be in town until noon tomorrow. I know after shows like this one I usually get quite a few people interested in private therapy sessions. If you're interested in sneaking in to one of the 3 time slots I'll have available before leaving town, let me suggest you come up and talk to me as soon as possible."

After that line, I've actually watched wives turn to their husband, quickly beg, and then start working their way up to the front of the room even before the show was over.

There are couple serious issues to keep in mind when doing therapy. First, most of your clients are going to be women. This isn't to say they are more sick than the guys are, just more willing to deal with it. If you happen to be a guy, you might consider adopting a policy I use where I refuse to do therapy on a woman where I'm stuck in a room with her alone.

There's just too much room for question there. With all the misconceptions about hypnosis floating around, I want to make sure nobody ever wonders what went on during our session. I invite them to bring their husbands or another female friend.

When they enter the room, I become a doctor. Quiet, sympathetic, concerned. I ask plenty of questions before diving in, and make sure she's comfortable with what's about to happen. I then do several in and out sessions, which let her experience it, and get over the "I expected a lightning bolt" issues.

I make a point of remaining unemotional even is she happens to be talking about personal sexual issues or some other potentially awkward topic. Basically I want her to rest assured I've heard it all, and I'm not here to get my jollies. She can be honest, and we'll soon get down to dealing with the issues.

The second, and the one that most beginning therapists end up ultimately discovering the hard way, is to be careful when dealing with pain. Remember you aren't a doctor. Those guys spend 7 years learning how to tell the difference between indigestion and ruptured appendixes.

As a hypnotist, you do have the ability to take away most any kind of pain, but that isn't always the advisable way to go. Someone who is convinced they are suffering from reoccurring serious stomach gasses may actually be suffering from an ulcer or damaged lung.

Without an actual written permission from a Doctor saying it's okay to relieve any kind of pain, it's usually a good policy to explain you really don't want to risk creating a dangerous situation.

Imagine finding out a week after you left a simple stomach ache victim that they smiled and had a great time until they keeled over dead from a ruptured spleen.

Remember, there's a lot of money to be make here, but along with any ability, comes a certain level of responsibility. Don't abuse it, please. It'll not only bankrupt you in the long run, it'll also make it impossible for any of the rest of us to do business in the areas where you've given hypnotists a bad reputation.

Promoting The Show, Part One

Several months ago I mentioned casually a few tips on selling shows. I must have hit a hot spot. I'm still getting emails from all over the world asking for more "how to" advice on selling yourself and dealing with specific marketing problems. So I decided to break down and offer some of the marketing tid bits you learn after making every mistake in the book (more than once) over the course of 27 years.

I should warn you before going on, I do not have an MBA and many of my methods might be considered questionable by Madison Avenue guru's.

Actually, most of my methods are probably considered "radical" by the mainstream, but they've worked for many others, and me. Personally I've managed to reach a point where my 90-minute private stage hypnotic shows usually make between $2000 and $4000 plus expenses. During the past couple months I've done Harrah's Casino just outside of Topeka (where I made $2600 plus expenses for a show), Cisco Systems (the internet giants) where they paid $3600 for a one hour show at Pinehurst, NC, and three other $2000 plus shows.

Most of my "Street Smarts" comes from 7 years as a theater major, 3 years as a Hollywood Casting Director (for Newport Pacifica Films) and 4 years as an Entertainment Editor for a Southern California magazine (Dawn). I was also a successful stunt coordinator and stunt man with the National Association of Stunt Actors for 2 years.

I spent 3 years as an Agent in Los Angeles, and then went on to run my own agency successfully for 7 years in Reno. But most of all, my know how is built on a bunch of scars and skinned knees I've inherited after years of false starts.

My company, The Merlyn Arts Group specializes in promoting events and entertainers, and I can pretty safely say that although some of my advice may not fit neatly into someone's corporate plan book, all of it has more than passed the test of time. Several years ago I used to do a seminar called "This Business Called Show Business" where I helped starting actors, magicians, clowns, stunt men and the likes get going in their careers. What are included here are the key points, if you will, of this 4-hour lecture.

In order to try and cover as much material as possible in the limited space I have, I'm going to move quickly here, so hang on.

We're dividing this topic into three sections. This month's section will discuss getting organized and choosing the market(s) you might be interested in. Next month we'll dive in deep into various marketing venues and how to best use them. Should you direct mail, take an ad out in the yellow pages or maybe pay for a billboard? It'll all be in next month's issue. Finally, the February issue will be entirely devoted to negotiating contracts and how to make the most out of every marketing challenge.

Before going any further, you need to be sure you know, without a question, what your mission statement is. What's your goal in life? Print it out in bold letters and hang it on the wall in front of you. If you don't know, without question, where you're hoping to end up, at best your career might succeed by mistake.

Working mission statements might be; "To make a six digit salary two years in a row within 6 years", or maybe, "To become a household name within 10 years". Or maybe, a bit more immediate, you might want to, "Sell at least one $1500 show next year." Other goals might include, "To travel Europe performing for a year" or "Get all my bills caught up, and achieve enough of a steady income to feel secure within two years".

My own personal goal is, again, a bit unethical. I want, "To consistently perform a show that commands enough payment per job to allow me the flexibility to spend time with my family and enjoy my daily life." Of course I also have goals as a writer (which I've done successfully most of my life) and a promoter.

Once you know where you want to go, determine how to get there. If you want to be famous in your community, then start donating shows around town. If you want your mother to think you're successful, then do a show for her card club. If you want to make a living as a performer, then stop chasing the poor.

It's that simple. If you're goal is to consistently command more than $1000 a show, then quit sending mailers to Civic Clubs. They're nice guys, but they don't pay much. If you're looking to build a reputation that will allow your phone to ring (as mine did earlier today) and have someone apologize because they can only afford $1500 for a one hour show, then focus all your promotion on the markets that have that kind of budget.

Now don't get me wrong. I'm not saying there isn't a place for lower paying shows, but you should only do them when they work in well with the bigger picture. I'll go into that pretty heavily in a moment.

Take a moment and consider what market you want to tackle, and PLEEEEEAAAAASE, if you get anything out of this article, be sure you get this. STAY FOCUSED. Most performers are so afraid of failing at any one of several ventures that they try to spread themselves out so thin that they never stand a chance of making it in any field. Pick a single market you're interested in and give yourself 3 years to master it.

That means one year to get them to know you well, another to get them to hire you and a third to get them to hire you again, while referring you to friends. Some possible markets for quality performers are:

1. **Local Christmas Parties**. They keep you in town and save a lot on long distance phone calling. If handled right (we'll go into that later on) you can get $2000 a show. The problem is there are only two, maybe three working weekends before Christmas (depending on what day the 25th lands). If you can sneak in two shows a night, you're lucky. But that still only gives you 12 to 14 shows all year. If you choose this route, start sending out mailers and making cold calls (a couple weeks after a mailer) in late May. You can add a few extra shows by working the colleges and military. They don't pay quite as much, but because all their "members" take Christmas breaks, they try to do all their parties during the first two weeks in December.

2.. **State Fairs and Public Events**. They happen year round all around the country. Your local Chamber of Commerce can direct you to events in your state. These aren't that hard to sell, but you'll have to be willing to travel. They don't pay as much per show (probably anywhere from $200 to $400) but you can usually sneak in a bunch of shows in a week's run. Back when I did fairs I usually gave them a minimum number of shows per week and bartered in a large booth space where I sold my books, t-shirts, posters and tapes, did some therapy and even booked a private show or two.

3. **Cruise Ships**. When you first get started with them, it's like selling your soul to the devil. They usually want a long term commitment, and they saddle you with a tiny room at the very bottom of the ship. You're expected to play PR 24 hours a day and the pay isn't great. It also completely pulls you out of circulation, forcing you to "start over from scratch" when you decide to go back to working on the mainland. The advantages include the feeling of being a "celebrity" (it's hard not to be when you have a captive audience). You also get all your living expenses paid for. Typically, you'll be working on board for 6 months, with no expenses, which means your $150 each shows done 3 times a week nets you a $12000 check as you get ready to take your month break before starting it all over.

4. **School Assemblies**. By themselves they pay nearly nothing. If you can get sponsors to promote a "say no to drugs" or "stay in control" kind of program, you can usually plan on $400 to $500 a show. When I did assemblies, I used to make some good money off the package. I began by selling all the Jr. High and High Schools in the area on a discounted show. Basically for $200 a single magic show and $150 for the second or third show, I'd agree to do an assembly and guarantee them their money back in a fundraiser. It'd then come in and do 15 or 20 assemblies in a larger town, all within a couple weeks. During the shows I'd mention a larger show taking place down at the convention center downtown during which I was going to do my hypnotic show (or we were going to have several performers doing a variety show). Tickets for this show were sold by the sponsoring organization (usually the PTA or SBTO or whatever the local parent teacher organization was. As part of the program, I was allowed to hand out flyers for all the students to take home (the only legal way you can advertise through the school system). With enough hype and a good enough take home flyer, it wasn't hard to sell a third or so of each school. If you average each school at, say, 800 students, which means roughly 260 students would show up from each school. You multiply that times 15 schools, you now have 3900 students. Of course, very few students come alone, so if you include at least one parent to drive and one sibling, we now have 7800 students and 3900 adults. I'd make $2 a ticket for students, $3 for adults. The school made $3 for any ticket they sold at $5 or $6. If this package sold, just the way it's outlined above, I would gross $15,600 at the door. Add to that 15 shows at $150 each (the assemblies) and your total goes up to $17,850. Even if you allow for half that amount (say there

aren't as many schools), you'd still make $8,925. You'd have to pay $1500 or so for the convention facility, and maybe another $1000 for lighting and sound, but regardless, for relatively little work, you just made $6,425. If you want to double that amount easily, find a local charity you like and offer them a dollar for every ticket you sell. Raise the overall ticket price by a dollar, and then hire a local phone mill company (telephone solicitors) to call every home in the neighborhood offering to sell them tickets to a show that will help benefit the local "home for abused children" or whatever. I know guys that travel the country promoting shows through local phone mills who make a fortune. Plenty of people will pay for tickets to help the cause; maybe a quarter of them will show up. If you take an intermission and sell nick naks, you can increase your net up to 150 or so percent of the door. Breaking $10,000 for this one night show is very doable. Not bad for a night's work, is it? I used to do these back to back. The week I was doing the larger auditorium I was busy doing the assemblies at the next town.

5. **High School Grad Nights**. They all happen within a little more than a month somewhere around June. The night after graduation, the school puts on a program for the graduating class. Again, these shows don't pay an awful lot, but they do seem to add up quickly. I still do Grad nights. I'll make $800 a show, but can usually sneak in at least 2 shows a night, 4 or 5 nights a week for 4 to 5 weeks. That basically ads up to $32,000 for a month of fun shows (High Schools are a lot of fun to do).

6. **Corporate Events.** This is where the big money is. It's hard to break into and it takes a lot of maintenance once you get there. This is one of my main markets. Most of my $3000 shows come from convention crowds or companies trying to wine and dine their clients or distributors. I have one company that flies me around the country monthly to finish off their weekend of marketing efforts to local banks. I can count on a steady $2500 here. Several others use me quarterly or biannually. Most of the buyers are very selective, and require very professional demo tapes and promo packages. Once you're doing it, you have to continue your marketing effort. I spend close to $2000 a month in marketing to this market alone (but then I can count on at least doubling that on a slow month with the corporate clientele).

7. **Comedy Clubs**. Again, this is a very competitive market. There are a lot of comics trying to get in, and most clubs will only use you, at most, twice a year. It takes a lot of phone calling and persistence to even get club managers to agree to talk to you. After they do, you're faced with the task of talking them into even taking the time to look at your tape. Because of the limited number of shows you can do in any given club, in order to break in, you need to establish enough "regular" clubs to keep you busy long enough to pay your bills. That usually takes 5 or 6 years. You also will have to be willing to do an inordinate amount of travel. I try to do as many of my clubs as possible during a yearly Spring Tour, which helps cover the otherwise slower Jan through May months. It also allows me to schedule smaller clubs near the Corporate events I know I've already booked in remote areas. Comedy clubs, again, don't pay that well. They usually budget based on a "per show" figure. A decent act can usually get between $300 and $400 a show. Once you're a bit more established, the bigger clubs might go as high as $600. That's provided you can carry a show without them having to pay for an opener or closer, which basically means you have to keep a very demanding audience entertained for a complete 90 minutes.

8. **Casinos.** It used to be that working a casino meant traveling to Atlantic City or somewhere in Nevada. Things have certainly changed in the last few years. Casinos are springing up all over the place. All along the Mississippi you can find major casinos and most of the Indian tribes have at least larger slot and bingo halls. Casinos are fun, but don't be fooled. They're like any other club. They usually have a larger room reserved for famous celebrities and at least on Cabaret room they have to keep full. Unfortunately management in these places is all too aware of the "glamour" associated with the casino industry. You can plan on working pretty cheap the first time or two, until you prove yourself. The good news is that once you're in, everybody knows about it. The entire casino Entertainment Directors know each other, and invariably discuss the good and bad acts that appear in their clubs. Casino shows can pay anywhere from $400 to $40000, depending on how well known you are, how much they think your act will draw, and how long you've worked for them. If you deserve it, they do have the money. I recently got $24000 from an Indian casino in Southern California to run a series of 3 magicians on shifts, each doing a 10 minute show at the top of each hour, 4 hours a day, for a month. It basically boiled down to 4 hours of sitting in the break

room waiting for your hourly "quickie".

9. **Working for Agents**. BE CAREFUL. Not all agents are as nice as they seem. Unless you know the guy (or gal) well, and you have no problem depending on them for your livelihood, stay away from signing exclusives. Tell agents you'll work for them but they need to understand that you're working for other agents as well. I've always done this and never had a problem. Agents are supposed to take between 10% and 20% of what you make. It doesn't always work that way, though. I know even in Southern California, where the movie industry has forced agents into some pretty strict guidelines, and they can lose their license for charging you 25%, it's a common practice for agents to take anywhere from 40% to 80% of your fee. Basically you go into their office and tell them you normally sell your show at $500. The agent calls you a week later to announce he managed to get you $600 on a show. Delighted, you don't bother to question how much he's getting. The truth is, he sold the show for $1500 and is pocketing $900. If it ever came up in court, he'd say he was contracted to help coordinate an event, and not all of the $1500 was exclusively earmarked for your performance. There are some good ones out there though. And if you find them, treat them right. I send out fruit baskets during Thanksgiving, cards at X-mass and birthday gifts to their kids. They in turn continue to fight among themselves to see who's going to fill my 8 holiday slots a year with $3000+ shows.

10. **Walling**. That's the industry term for "doing your own thing". You have to know your market and have the perseverance of a street performer. Basically you find a local auditorium and you put the whole package together yourself. You promote the show, sell the tickets, coordinate the show, and make money on drink sales, do the show, and consider yourself lucky if you break even within 2 months. When I 4 wall, I usually stack the deck in my favor. A favorite trick of mine is to negotiate with the Sales and Catering department of a well known hotel (Hilton, Marriott, etc.). I buy a banquet room for usage every Friday night for 3 months. I then go to every restaurant in the area and offer them a "dinner theater" package. Basically, if you bring your dinner receipt from one of these restaurants, we'll give you so much off at the door. We offer to include their name in our advertising, and the restaurant agrees to keep a table tent on their various tables announcing the show. I also get the Hotel to put in writing that

they'll place a flyer advertising the show in every room in the hotel, every morning. I then comp a big show to all the local theater people, magic clubs, clown clubs, etc. I make sure I have a room full of good natured "characters". I then offer all the local media free meals, on me (actually, I get Sales and Catering to spread out the cost over the 3 month run, as part of their package). Nothing will get a reporter in the door quicker than a free meal (I know, I've been in their shoes). One good show, a good press package and plenty of quick exposure make this an easy kick off. I then get local radio and TV stations to let me guest on their shows each week. We hypnotize co-anchors, do open lines, the works. If you keep it fun, they'll keep you coming back.

Obviously these are just some of the possible markets you can aim at, but hopefully it's enough to stimulate your imagination. Don't spend the rest of your life planning to some day get started. Just get busy and do it now.

Next month we'll cover the second half of this topic. We'll cover all the marketing possibilities (radio, television, yellow pages, newspaper, etc.) and how to best use each. We'll even include a section on how to get plenty of free or next to free publicity. Then in February, we'll discuss how to negotiate what to ask for and how to sell virtually any show. I know it's hard to believe, but if you know how to do it, there are very few shows you can't sell at a price well above the norm.

Promoting The Show, Part Two

.

Last month, in part one of Promoting the Show, we discussed the various markets where a Stage Hypnotist can work. This list, obviously, is far from exhaustive. Over the years I've found myself working everywhere. I've even found myself gathering my own crowds in Jackson Square in New Orleans and then passing the hat after hypnotizing 10 or so people. I can usually plan on making anywhere from $150 to $200 for an hour show done to a street audience. And during the course of a decent day, I can usually pull off 3 or 4 shows. There are definite advantages to street performing. There's very little, if any, overhead, you set your own hours and nobody feels offended if you try out new material. But it's hard to make a consistent living in a market that's controlled by weather and bus schedules.

In fact as you start looking at hypnosis (or magic, or comedy or any other form of variety arts) as a career, you soon find yourself looking for things like a steady income, regular clients, and higher ticket priced shows. And as you start pointing at specific markets, you suddenly find yourself defining the nature of your promotional efforts.

Let's begin with the obvious. How much should you plan on spending to promote your show? If I were trying to sell lollypops, where you'd probably make a 3 cent or so profit on each sale, you'd find yourself having to sell 13,333 lollypops to pay for each $400 newspaper ad you took out. A hypnotist, on the other hand, usually carries few, if any props. Basically, most of the overhead involved in your shows are covered by your client or the club you work for. Depending on how much you make per show, you can easily plan on spending much more of your profit on promotion. Personally, I plan on spending about 1/3 of my gross income promoting my show. All things considered, if you include advertising, promo packages, video tapes and the likes, I spend between $3000 and $4000 a month in advertising. It may sound like a lot, but in my case, my shows usually start at a low of probably $1800 plus expenses and a high of around $4000 plus. Considering the fact that I can easily plan on selling at least 4 or 5 shows on a slow month as a direct result of this promotion, it's a great investment.

And that's the first, cardinal rule, in promotion. ALL GOOD PROMOTION PAYS FOR ITSELF. It's just that simple. It's like working the stock market. If you try a venue and find that for every $100 you spend you make $200, then you can feel safe dumping as much money as you'd like to double into that area. As you get going you soon discover specific advertising mediums that get you the kind of business you're interested in. Once you do, work it like crazy.

Unfortunately, you eventually start finding yourself coming up against a time constraint. If, say, you're spending $10,000 promoting heavily for the Holiday Season, you're going to find that regardless of how good you are, you're still going to find yourself trying to cram as many shows as you can into the 3 weekends before Christmas. If you can manage 2 a night each

Friday and Saturday night, you're still only talking 12 shows. You'd have to make $834 per show just to break even.

Of course, another serious consideration here is quality. If you do the kind of show that keeps clients calling you back, it may be worth it to do a "break even" season. Next year, as you get going, you'll find a good portion of your season is pre sold, cutting your promotional cost down drastically. Referrals will also help push down the promotional cost. One final consideration you should keep in mind before we discuss specific advertising venues, is exposure. I recently moved from San Diego to Oklahoma City. Being new in town, I have, as a hidden agenda, getting my name out and about town quickly. To make my name recognizable locally, I'm a lot more open to high visibility ads, even if they don't seem to gather an immediate profit. As an example, the local AMC theaters are discussing having my company put together some packages for them. They can't really afford our cost, but I'm trying to negotiate in several of the large ads they run before the movies on their screens. On these ads I'll include maybe a couple full size pictures of myself and general biographical information about the show with a caption to the effect of "watch for him in and around Oklahoma City". I honestly would be shocked if I got a single call from these ads. In fact, it's debatable if I'll even have a phone number in the ad. But a lot of people will sit up and take notice when they see a hypnotist advertising at the movies. And the next time I do a show in town that's open to the general public, many of these people will already be familiar with the name. It'll also help me immensely when I go to sell these packages. Explaining to the Hyatt that we've been running these ads for the past 6 months will go a long way towards talking them into letting me do a stand up show in their lounge. Not to mention that several of their staff are probably going to remember the ads the moment the name comes up.

So where, exactly should you spend your advertising money? Let's take a look at most of the traditional, and a few of my own personal favorite non-traditional advertising venues.

The first concept to keep in mind as you plan a promotional campaign, is that fame is very fleeting. If you promote heavily, and people are familiar with your name, you need to keep the exposure up, so you don't end up throwing away all your past energies. In practical terms this means you need to begin by deciding which of the markets we discussed in last months issue you are interested in reaching. Once you know what your target goal is, make sure they keep on hearing your name.

Promoters usually agree that the typical prospect won't buy until they've had at least 6 exposures to your name and/or product. This means, that if you're looking to sell local convention shows, you need to find at least 6 excuses to get the person who pays for entertainment at the convention to see your name. Typically, if you're looking to attract the local convention business, you'll probably want to join your local "Visitors and Convention" Bureau. As a member, you'll get an automatic listing in their directory and possibly a web site listing somewhere. You can roughly consider this one line (or small ad, if you choose to pay for it) as your first exposure. People looking for entertainment during the Saturday night dinner at the end of the convention will begin looking under entertainment in the V & C directory.

As a member, you'll also get a list of everybody schedule to do an event in your town. Call the contact number and ask for the name of the person in charge of entertainment. At this point, try to avoid talking to this person. They may say they're not interested before they even know what you have to offer. Follow up your call by dropping a nice, brief, teaser package in the mail to them. Mine is usually a one sheet brochure that talks generically about myself and the show. The package should offer them the chance to request a demo tape, but don't expect any call backs. This is your second contact. Obviously, if anybody happens to call, you drop them a package in the mail ASAP. Most won't at this point.

For those that don't, wait about 4 days after they are scheduled to receive your information and then give them a call. Ask for the person you mailed the package to, and explain you are simply making sure your information is going to the right person. As you talk, ask casually if they are having a banquet or other function during their event where your services might be needed. If they are, and don't already have all their event booked, offer to send them out some more information and a demo tape. Don't try to sell anything here. You run the risk of developing a reputation as a high power sales person. Your goal here is simply to be a helpful friend. Unless they obviously are dying to buy right away, assume they'll need a demo tape in order to honestly come to a conclusion. It's also a good idea to assume if you're going to ask for higher ticket prices, you want them to be as sold as possible before you break the price to them.

If they ask for a price at this point I usually explain that I am one of the more costly hypnotists around, and if they're shopping price, I'm probably going to be out of their budget, but I'm sure , if they're interested in the show, that we can work something out.

In my case, I try to establish perceived value. If I can convince them that my show is worth $3000, they'll jump at the chance of getting it at $2000. I don't know your credentials, but this is where they come in handy. I usually explain that I've been doing my show for corporate clients for close to 27 years, and my web site is full of references and letters from satisfied clients. I explain that although my show does usually run for $2500 or more, I can guarantee it'll be an experience they won't soon forget. At this point I usually calculate how much they're spending on dinner that night and ask them if anybody really remembers what they had for dinner last year. "At 15 or so dollars a plate times 200 people, you're now paying $3000 for something most of your guests won't even notice." I ask them if they think anybody would ever forget watching their receptionist running around the room thinking she was Dolly Parton or Elvis Presley signing autographs. I then ask if $2500 is within their budget. They usually say no. I'm sure you realize that most of these guys are planning on maybe $200 max. I tell them I'd like to send out a demo tape so they can see why the show is worth that amount and then maybe discuss price. I always leave them with a statement that really is true. I tell them that after they look over the tape and see what I have to offer, we can talk price. I explain that I'm sure we can work something out that will bring it into their budget, but if we can't, I don't mind recommending quality performers that might be able to work at a lower rate for them. I even offer to give them my honest opinion about anybody they might be considering using, even if they choose not to use me. I explain that in the long run, it works to my advantage to have people out there seeing quality shows. If they love hypnosis, it's just a matter of time before someone will call me for a show.

Next month, when we talk negotiating, we'll discuss how to "bring it into their budget" without ever having to haggle or lower your prices.

With that kind of lead in, you can bet I'll get their attention. What would you do if someone told you they were mailing you a demo tape of a $3000 show? You'd probably wait at the mailroom each day, wondering what kind of show was worth that kind of money. And with my promise to help you find an adequate show in your price range, you'd definitely keep my phone number on hand.

If they don't ask price, I don't bring it up until about a week after they get my demo tape. At that time I call back to explain the price and details, realizing that more than likely, the person I'm talking to will have to go back and sell a committee or owner on getting more money. I try to avoid hard sells here. I simply ask if they're interested in the show, and wait for their answer.

Either way, when they get my promo material and demo tape, it better be good. Personally, I make a point of videotaping every show I do in a nicer room on digital (professional television quality) tape. I can usually find a local person who can do a "2 camera shoot" where one camera is stationary and the other one is hand held and roaming for about $250. I then edit these shows down to either a 10 minute or less tape (the one I usually send out) and every now and then a 30 minute more complete demo for agents and entertainment directors at casinos that ask for "a more complete copy of a show". The 10 minute or less tape is great because you can get blank 10 minute tapes for less than a dollar (I buy them in bulk for $0.65). It's also a lot easier to convince the average buyer to take "ten minutes" to see what your show looks like. This demo should look as good as one of those commercials for upcoming movies you see at the theater. Pay to have it done professionally, and plan on sitting in the editing room while it's being done, directing the editor concerning your needs and desires. I usually expect to spend around $1500 on a good tape, but considering the number of $2000 shows I get out of it, it's a real bargain. I end up with one digital master (for future editing) and a regular master. I went out and got myself a video tape duplicator (Price Club around $200) and make copies myself as needed.

That's the basic sales formula for probably 90% or my shows. Obviously different markets will have different specific needs. Cruise ships will be interested in the 30 minute tapes and more references. Grad nights and colleges will probably buy with just a simple call and a demo tape. You'll probably notice that I didn't pay a penny for yellow pages or magazine advertising. Over the years I've found that I do most of my sales without much outside advertising. In fact, quickly, let me give you a breakdown of the experience my company has had with various forms of advertising. Yellow Pages When you put in a business telephone line, you'll automatically get a one line ad in the yellow pages. I usually upgrade that to a small ($20 a month or so) "In Column Ad". You won't get many high ticket calls from yellow page ads although every now and then out of town conventions and events will check the local phone book, and every now and then some local secretary with the delegated responsibility of putting together the company holiday party might look here. Most of the calls you're going to get from your yellow pages ad are going to be local birthday party or civic group calls with itsy bitsy budgets. If you do magic or clowning, you may find it worth your while to use the yellow pages to draw the local, lower budget crowd. A $50 a month ad will probably pay for itself with the 3 or 4 bigger shows you book a year from the ad. Trade Journals These are the magazines that cater to the specific areas where you plan on working. Event planner journals, trade show coordinator journals, and so on. Most of these journals require membership in the organization to get an ad in them. If you're targeting a specific market and are willing to back up your ad with plenty of cold calling (using the formula shown above), then taking out an ad in these journals is well worth it. Coming across someone who remembers hearing about you "somewhere" is a definite $2000 shoe in the door. I usually spend some money here. $300 or $400 a month or $1200 for a yearly directory is reasonable, and more than pays for itself if you are willing to follow through.

Billboards, bus benches and the like. The rule of thumb here is: Billboards don't sell shows, they sell you. The odds of getting a call from a public ad are pretty slim. But if your marketing strategy involves a lot of plans aimed at local markets (grad nights, X-mas parties, local night clubs or extended local performances) making yours a household name may be worth the trouble. As a rule, I try to avoid the high cost of name recognition advertising until I have a reason to justify it. If, say, I know I'm planning to put up a billboard anyway, and I've talked myself into spending, say, $1200 a month, I might as well talk a local nightclub into letting me do an 8 week run at their club. The deal is I get 10% of the door. I also ask for $500 a night, but I agree to put all of it back into advertising. Most clubs would jump at this deal (provided they like your show and can afford a higher ticket price). You also insist that the club be required to do whatever advertising they normally do. This will get your name around town quickly. Not only will I end up with the $1200 billboard, but also an extra $800 which might buy me some good local coverage in the newspaper. 10% of the door, in, say, a club that seats 200 at $6 each, would make me (if we only sell 150 tickets a night) about $90 a night, plus plenty of exposure to leverage off of quickly. If you do this kind of deal, make sure you arrange to get 10 or so comped tickets a night to use for local agents, etc. I'm personally working on this kind of package for Oklahoma City aimed at this coming summer as a way of quickly becoming "famous" in my new home. It's sure to pay off in a solid row of $3000 holiday shows, and plenty of local leverage for seminars, self help cassettes and CD's and therapy, if nothing else. I'll also use it as an excuse to invite every local agent, event planner and sales and catering agent from local hotels to come by and see the show.

Newspaper Ads If you're looking to sell shows, newspapers generally don't work (unless you take out a full page ad). If you already have a show going and are looking to sell tickets, newspaper is a good medium. Check to see where all the other theaters are advertising (that's where people look to see what's going on around town) and place a good ad there. You can also get some exceptional coverage if you contact the layout person for your local paper and agree to buy "extra" space. They usually find themselves with a few extra blocks of space after placing all their ads. If you give them several different size ads and offer to let them use them to fill extra space, you can usually get ads placed for about 1/4 the cost. If you're looking for exposure (name recognition) try sending out press releases. Watch upcoming articles here for detailed explanations on how to write press releases that get published. Newspapers are also big on doing trades. Offer to do a show for their Christmas party in exchange for, say, $1000 worth of advertising. They'll probably jump at it, and give you a free review of the show you do in the process (if you discuss it with the local theater reviewer ahead of time, explaining you plan on doing a lot of local stuff quickly).

Radio Ads If done right, on the right stations, radio ads can work well. Basically, they're quick, hopefully memorable, and great for name recognition. You can usually end up with a package that includes 70 or 80 spots at about $4 or $5 a spot (on smaller local stations). If you do ads advertising yourself as a performer (aimed at Christmas Parties), try running them around June, and then follow them up immediately with a mailer and a phone call to the top local employers. You can get the list of top employers (anybody hiring over 1000 people better have a good Christmas party if they plan on keeping their employees happy) from the Social Science section of your local library. If you're selling tickets to a public show, it's hard to know for sure how effective your ads are, but generally, the name recognition won't hurt. If your goal here is to simply get your name out, then try doing a sponsor program. Put together a fund raiser for a local charity and arrange to have a local radio station "sponsor" your event. This means you agree to list their name in all your newspaper ads and posters. In exchange, they agree to run your ads for free. You then go to the local newspaper and talk them into running ads (including the radio station name and logo) in exchange for getting plenty of ads on the local radio station. The posters are put together for free in exchange for including one of the larger local printers as a sponsor as well. Find a local church or maybe scout group to help you put posters around town. Finally, if you're selling a good charity, phone sales will do wonders here. I explain these below.

The good news is that even though it's a fund raiser, you're still entitled to get paid! If it's a cause you believe in, agree to take a percentage of the door (20% maybe?), if not, sell it to them as a package, that costs them, say, $1000 for promotion and show.

Any time you work with radio stations, always try to get guest appearances on local radio shows. Even rock jocks have guests on. I probably do 300 of these a year promoting comedy clubs, books, events, etc. and never pay a penny for any of it. Again, watch for an upcoming article on how to book radio and television talk shows and what to do once you're on them.

Phone Sales Before trying phone solicitation, be sure it's legal in your area. If it isn't, you can always go across town, where city ordinances will make it legal and call into your town. The law only applies to the location from which the calls are made. Most comedy and night clubs depend almost exclusively on phone sales to sell tickets. Basically you get a directory that lists addresses in order with their phone numbers and start calling. Haines puts out a directory like this which you can probably photo copy down at your local library, or you can buy one of the many CD's that list home phone numbers nationally and cross reference them. Phone sales work well if you're working at a well known club or for a well known charity. Charity work allows many who actually have no intention of ever coming to the show to "donate" to the "save the whales foundation" or whatever. I remember several years ago getting hired by a group to do a magic show for a charity show. I walked in to a 300 person auditorium with about 25 people in it. I asked the promoter and he laughed. He explained the show was a sell out, but most people were simply willing to send in $10 to help the local "Say No" group. You can look in your yellow pages under Telemarketing Services for professional "phone banks" that will work for a percentage or price per call. RANDOM PHONE SALES ARE DEFINITELY NOT THE WAY TO SELL SHOWS. Unless you have a carefully prescreened calling list, don't expect to sell $1500 shows to the average person who's probably sitting at home because they don't have a job.

Networking If done right, networking is a very powerful tool in your promotional arsenal. Basically, networking means you've placed yourself in locations where potential buyers frequent, and you're getting to be their friends. Chamber of Commerce meetings, Better Business Bureau mixers, Lions, Rotary and/or Optimist clubs are all good places to meet people. I also make a point of calling the local health club (larger, more expensive ones) and doing a trade. In exchange for a show on an off time for me (Saturday afternoon or a weeknight) I get two one year memberships (one for me and one for my wife). Basically, members get to see my show during the Christmas party or Tennis tournament and then I have a year to hang out in locker rooms with company owners, etc. who have already seen the show. Country or golf clubs work well here too.

I'll cover networking more extensively in an upcoming article, but for now, here are the basics. Networking correctly is an art. This is particularly true at mixers and other group events where everybody is competing to sell products or services. The basic rule is, don't sell anything at the meeting. Just introduce yourself and get cards. You can do the selling later. Typically, I'll walk up and introduce myself with a line to the effect of "I guess we're suppose to meet everybody here, so hi, I'm Howard". I then ask what they do and spend my time digging (nicely) for facts about their company. What do they sell, how do they sell it, anything that will make me more familiar with their potential needs later on (do they do trade shows, conventions, company events, sponsor charities, etc.). Invariably someone will ask what I do for a living. Just saying I do Stage Hypnotic Shows guarantees me as much air time as I want. Don't give in to temptation. Just say enough to guarantee interest (don't burn them out) and then collect business cards. Simply asking, "do you guys have cards?" will get you a stack of them. Quickly find a quiet corner (or the bathroom) and write on the back of each card any important information you want to remember when you call next week to say hi and ask who you should send information about your show to.

Mailing List If you only use one form of advertising, this should be it. Let's be honest here. The average American isn't sure what a Stage Hypnotic show is. It takes a lot of selling to get these people in the door. Reaching people that already like you is a lot easier. Personally, I keep a list of national fans and contact them all whenever I'm in their area. During shows I have spectators fill out comment cards. If they bring back a completed one, I give them a free picture (which costs me about a dime). I usually autograph it, which guarantees it gets hung on a wall somewhere at their home, making me a "celebrity" at least in their minds.

I also keep a 645 name list of comedy clubs, casinos, resorts, and corporate prospects around the world that are solid potential clients (they can afford me and have the facilities or events that can house my show). I mail something to them every other month. A few months ago I mentioned a show I was doing at Harrah's Casino, and how much I worked at getting a letter of recommendation from them. Just yesterday I mailed a one sheet mailer to my general list that included a cover of the Harrah's Casino Magazine that featured me, a reduction of the article about me and a copy of the letter I got from them. On the outside flap was bulleted information about my experience, etc. and a note about my web site and contact information "to receive a free 10 minute demo tape, please call...". I just sent out 645 mailers, at a total cost to me (including postage, etc.) of $423 (I print out my own mailers on a Hewlet Packard 722 Deskjet color printer that's more than paid for itself [roughly $250 nowadays] several times over). From these I'll probably end up selling 2 or 3 shows. At $2000 a show, that's a great deal! And the ones that don't buy, will remember me and might buy next month when I send out a general article, written by me about how to use Self Hypnosis to achieve your company goals. Watch for an upcoming article about how to manage and make the most out of a mailing list.

Web Site If you don't have one, get one. There are plenty of on line services that let you put one together free of charge and if used correctly, web sites are a great way to promo shows. I regularly find myself with potential clients that have no information about me but have internet access. Just being able to tell them to look up my site helps validate my credentials immensely. I must leave at least 20 messages a week on voice mails where I tell potential clients that "I'm calling to see if you could use my services. I'll call back tomorrow, but in the meantime, feel free to look up my web site at WWW.HowardMorgan.com for more details about my show." It's not uncommon when I call them the next day to find someone who did look up my site and is ready to talk. In fact, I just had the Entertainment Director for one of the Mississippi River Casinos do exactly that a couple weeks ago. I went on to mail him a demo tape and promo package and we're now discussing doing an extended run this next fall. A simple site should include letters, background, at least one picture and general information about your show.

Finally, if you're in the process of selling yourself, remember that the effort has to become a way of life. This isn't about finding the one "magic" method that suddenly makes you a smashing success. There just isn't any. It's about keeping a steady flow of exposure to your potential clients and then delivering a show that's better than anything you offer. Any potential client that doesn't hear from you in 4 months might as well be a new client you're going to have to retrain concerning your abilities and the quality of your show. If you promote consistently, long enough, you'll find it easy to make a six digit yearly salary with relatively little work.

Next month, in the final part of this series we'll discuss negotiating. It's probably the most powerful stuff I can offer you. If there's any one thing that has made my company successful, it's my ability to negotiate. How to sell most shows or programs and how to get all kinds of extra bonuses tossed in with the package.

Promoting The Show, Part Three

.

So far we've discussed the various markets and various promotional venue's. All that stuff is obviously important to your success as a performer, but nothing can even come close to the importance of being able to negotiate. Without negotiating abilities, you'll forever be at the mercy of someone else's budget. You'll forever find yourself begging for a chance to prove yourself. A good negotiator, on the other hand, can create markets where there aren't any and have clients thanking them for the chance to pay $4000 for an hour of your time.

Someone once said negotiating was the ability to get people to give you things. Nothing could be farther from the truth. "Getting people to give you things" is extortion or larceny. Getting people to give you something and then thank you for the privilege, that's negotiating. Unless your client walks out of the deal feeling they got a real bargain, you might as well assume you're not going to get called back next year. Satisfied customers, on the other hand, not only call you back, but jump at the chance of spreading the word for you.

So what does it take to create the legendary "win-win" situation? How can you walk out of a negotiating situation and feel you got paid what you wanted while the client felt they got a great deal? Let's use a simple sales negotiation situation as an example to build on here. Suppose I was a portrait artist doing sketches in the park. You walk up and ask how much I charge. Chances are, you've already established a "perceived value" in your mind. You know you spent $8 last week down the street and you're comparing my cost to the other guy's. What are my options? I can offer you my time at the same price the other guy sold it to you and agree to do a portrait at $8. Or I can undercut the other guy's price and sell you the picture for $5. But suppose I wanted to make a bit more? Suppose I decided my time was worth, say, $20 a portrait? What would I have to do to get you to agree?

Even though the answer is pretty obvious, for some strange reason, few people seem to remember it when faced with a negotiating situation. You have to stop negotiating price. You need to increase the perceived value of your services. You probably want to begin with the "on hold" technique and explain to the client that you charge quite a bit more than other sketch artists, but if he'll give you a moment, you'll be glad to explain why. You've basically put the controversial issue "on hold". Now you need to convince them that they are going to get so much more from your services than they got for the $8 they spent last week. Show them samples of your work. Point out that it takes a bit longer, because you do a lot more detailed work. Offer credentials. Show pictures of exhibits of your work at the local art museum, or perhaps newspaper articles that proclaim you as a celebrity, a name worth hanging on their wall. You might also explain that you include, at no extra charge, a mailing tube with each portrait (which costs you $0.45 and just helped get you an extra $12).

I know personally, back in my street performing days, I really didn't take much note of the local sketch artists. Then one day a guy came out that did some pretty amazing sketches with pencil. In order to continue selling them on the street, he had to lower his price down to $40 a sketch. After seeing what he was capable of doing, and realizing it was at least as good as anything I had ever seen in a museum, I gladly "negotiated" a deal where he did 4 portraits from pictures for me for $600. Did I get taken? I don't think so. He took the pictures home and, judging from the fact that it took him a week to get them back, and the amount of incredible detail in the pictures, I feel I got a bargain. And at this point, if you enter my living room, you'll find three original "Patrick Hamilton" pictures, in expensive frames with track lighting showing off my masterpieces. Most who come in are shocked at how little I paid for them. I even considered offering to manage him for a while and get him a few museum exhibits, etc. going. So what does this all have to do with selling a show? The large majority of performers find themselves doing nothing but negotiating price. It's like the portrait sales person getting into a bartering mode and offering a picture for $20. The client then says $2. The artist comes back with $15 "and I'll toss in the mailing tube". The client offers $5 if the artist will include both the kids. Eventually you'll reach a "deal" but ultimately there is no way one or both of the parties won't come out feeling "taken". We get a call and the client says they need a show for the Saturday night of a convention. We tell them it costs $3000. They tell us they paid $200 last year for a comic. We agree to lower our cost to $1500 if they include expenses, and so forth. There are only two possible results to this kind of negotiation. Either you're going to give away your show and feel used (or worse yet, you're going to agree your time is only worth $200 an hour), or the client is going to be forced into paying way more than they wanted to and still get the show they originally bargained for.

If you expect to get 10 times what the client expected to pay for your show, you better be able to offer at least 15 times what they thought they were buying. So what can you do to increase your "perceived value"? In my case, I start by convincing the client that I believe I'm worth more than they thought. I'll start with comments like, "If you're shopping price, more than likely I'm going to be a bit out of your budget. This is what I've done professionally for the past 25 years, and I guess I have enough clients willing to pay a bit more for my services." If nothing else, this gets their attention. If, on the other hand, I get someone who can obviously afford the show, but merely needs convincing, I'll make opening statements like, "I'm probably one of the more expensive performers around, but if you'll give me a moment, I can probably show you why."

After making an arrogant statement like one of the above, I better be ready to back it up. I need good letters of reference that say I am as good as I claim, I need top quality promotional material (demo tapes, promo package, etc.). I need strong attention to detail. For example, I never mail packets out via normal mail. I always send my package out (each of which costs me about $15) by priority mail. It costs me $3.20 (with the new postal rates) as compared to $1.87 to mail, but the big blue and white envelope tells the client I'm serious about quality and I'm not planning to cut corners. And I do it quickly. Directly in front of my desk, that faces a wall, I have a map of the world, a map of the US, my general daily schedule, a calendar that takes me through Oct. of the year 2000, my schedule of upcoming shows and one other thing. A large piece of paper, right in the middle of it all that says, in large, bold letters "Three Hours Max". I put it there to remind me of a commitment I made to myself years ago as my personal way of dealing with a terrible problem of procrastination I've struggled with all my life. Basically, any time I promise to mail something out to anybody, I make a point of having it in the mail 3 hours after I've made the commitment. As I'm talking to a client, I fill out a work order that includes the time the call came in. Within 3 hours the requested item is either in the mail slot at my door (even if it means it'll get picked up in the morning) or in the case of a requested demo tape or press package, I'll actually drive down to the post office 3 blocks from my house, and priority mail a package out to them. All of these little details help back up the claim that I'm dependable and professional in all I do.

But we're still stuck with someone who budgeted $300 now having to figure out if I'm worth $3000. To get there, I usually follow a three step process in negotiating. And it goes like this:

1)   Get Information. Find out what they need and want. Find out what they're expecting. Look for unique bargaining chips you'll be able to use later on. This usually happens in the form of a simple question that gets them going. I'll usually ask something to the effect of "tell me about your event". That usually gets me a tiny bit of information. I'll then follow up with "tell me about your company". 9 times out of 10 people are all to anxious to brag about what they do. I'll usually find out that the company sells a certain product, and what kind of people they sell it to. I'll find out how long a conference or convention they're having will run and where my show fits into the overall picture. I'll usually find out what they've done in past years and why they decided to use a hypnotist. If they ask why I'm asking so many questions, I'll usually explain that I do several different packages, and I'm trying to figure out which one best works into their overall picture. What I don't tell them is that I'm also scribbling on a piece of paper by my phone a list of all the ways I can help them and all the "perks" I might be interested in getting from them.

2)   Make an opening offer. After I've gathered enough general information I usually make a simple offer presented in the form of a brief sales talk. A typical talk might go something like this: "Well, Cathy, after listening to you explain what your company does and what you're looking for, I think I can help you. I did mention at the beginning that I was kind of expensive, but let me explain to you why. Most people looking for

entertainment expect to hire the kid down the block to do "something" during their party. They don't realize that the only thing the average person might remember of your event is the entertainment, and then only if it's memorable. Think about it. You tell me you're feeding 500 people at the Marriott banquet hall. That means you're spending anywhere from $9.50 to $18 per person for dinner alone (I keep a list of the current prices for most of the major hotel chains handy for just such occasions). At $10 a head, that would mean you're spending $5000 on food alone. You're probably also spending another $500 on the room. My guess is you're also putting up a lot of your VIP's at the hotel, so I'm going to guess you're adding another $2000 or so to your bill for the night. So unless you're group is very unique, you're probably spending anywhere from $10,000 to $20,000 on your evening. And what will you get for it? A fancy meal? Do you really think anybody in that room will remember what you had for dinner a month from now? Do you really think that letting people dance after dinner will make this event any more memorable? Now, suppose your company president danced around the room thinking he was a ballet star, or imagine your accountant on all fours barking like a dog. Do you think anybody will ever forget that? That advantage of my show over, say, a good comedian, is that you end up paying for just my services but you end up with a stage full of performers. And what's really great about that is that everybody in your room will know who these people are. My show usually sells for about $2500, but a year from now, when people are still talking about it, you'll understand why."

At this point, I can almost always expect them to balk. They know it will take some serious selling to convince the planning committee or the CEO to spend that much. I'll usually give them a moment to let the shock settle in, and then I'll follow up with a question to the effect of, "Is that possible within your budget?" Almost without exception, I can expect them to try and negotiate. More times than not I'll get answers like, "That's way to much for us", or "We've never spent more than $400 on entertainment before". At that point I'll suggest that they let me send out some general information, so they have an idea of why my show is worth so much, and then I'll call back in about a week to talk. I'll usually leave them with a very powerful statement. I'll say something to the effect of, "Take a look at my demo tape and the promo material. You might also take a look at my Web Site while you're waiting for the information to get to you. Once you've looked it all over, I'm more than willing to discuss the price and try to figure out how to make the show affordable for you. If we can't bring it

within your budget, I'll be glad to recommend other quality performers in your area that are willing to work for a little lower price. In fact, even if you decide not to use me at all, I'll be glad to give you my honest opinion about anybody you might be considering. In the long run, it helps me immensely if people see good shows out there. If they enjoy hypnosis, it's just a matter of time before that translates into someone hiring me."
Notice here that I've done two things. I've hinted at lowering my price to "meet their budget" and I've agreed to help them find someone if they don't use me. Both are actually teasers that force them to not just cross my name off the list and go on to the next possible entertainer. 2 or 3 days later, when they get my package, they're curious and willing to keep the relationship open. Up to this point, no real negotiation has taken place. About all that's happened is that I've demonstrated that I'm willing to help meet their needs, and can do so in a professional way (something most would be performers seem to be pretty short on, and a quality you can easily use to stand out in the crowd).

3)   Close the Deal. After they've seen my demo tape and looked over the promo material, I wait about a week. If they haven't called me back, I call them. This is where the real negotiation gets started. Remember, the goal here is to stay away from arguing over price. I want them to feel I've given them a real bargain, while still getting my $2500 worth. The first rule I live by here is I rarely simply "lower my price" after a price has been quoted. Granted, the original price is on a sliding scale. A small construction company doing a X-mas party for it's 90 employees at the local Day's Inn will probably be quoted my rock bottom lowest retail price of $1500 where IBM can probably expect to start from a $4000 mark. Closing involves putting it all together, and ending up with a signed contract and deposit. Pick up a good book on closing techniques. There's a big difference between ending with, "So do you think you might want to do this show?" and " Well, if you're interested, I'll be glad to fax you a contract right away. I can hold that date and price for you for 2 weeks."

4)   Once they've established that they're interested in the show, and the only thing holding us back is price, I'll ask how much they feel they can afford. Most of the companies that even know about me, find out based on my mailings or cold calls (see last months article for information on running a mailing list). At least half these people come back willing to go

the higher price. This isn't as amazing as it sounds, considering I prescreened them before mailing to them. Of the other half, most will be intimidated by the $3000 starting point, and will quote the high end of their allowable budget. Most medium size companies will come in at around $800. I'll usually take a long pause, as if trying to figure out how to make that work and then I'll start negotiating perks. The truth is, the pause was pure theatrics. During my original, information gathering conversation, I was listing the very things I'm going to ask for here.

5)   The first "perk" I usually negotiate in is multiple shows. Suppose the company is an electronic firm. I would have asked early on if they do any conventions or trade shows anywhere. Now, when they tell me they can't afford the $2000 price tag, I tell them I'd be willing to knock $500 off the price if I could do more than one show for them. "If you can work me into any of your convention budgets, what I can do here is offer you two shows for $3000. And I'm willing to break that down any way you'd like. If you know you're company can justify promotional expenses better than it can entertainment at the company party, I'd be willing to do the Christmas party for $800 and one of your conventions for $2200." Considering that they can write me off as advertising during the convention, where they're interested in drawing crowds for their hospitality tent, many companies jump at this. If they do, I have them sign both contracts and send me both deposits (I always ask for a 50% deposit in order to hold a date) before I go on stage for the first show. If this isn't possible, or if they still can't afford the $2200 trade show, I look for things they offer, or can offer, that I might be interested in.

6)   I remember a few years back doing a show for one of the major airlines local office. They only had about 120 employees and could only afford $200 for entertainment. I offered to do the show for $200 plus 8 roundtrip tickets for two anywhere the airline flew. Considering that they give out vouchers all the time for overbooking and VIP premiums, these "tickets" cost them next to nothing. They jumped at the chance to get my $3000 show for $200 plus almost nothing. In my case, I took my 16 airline tickets and used them throughout the next year for all my longer airflights associated with shows. Basically I charged other clients the going rate for airfair and then used the vouchers. At an average of about $300 a flight, I ended up making about $4800 above the $200 on that one show. That

basically means I made $5000 for a show most people would have laughed at. I'm not complaining. And neither are they.

I remember a resort once calling me to do their company Christmas Party. Again, they begged poverty, and claimed to only be able to afford $300 or so. I ended up getting $300 plus 2 weeks stay at the resort. To a resort owner that was a steal, when you consider the number of rooms that usually go empty each night at these places. Considering that rooms there went at a minimum of $250 a night (this was one of those time share locations), I ended up with a $3500 value tacked on to the $300 cash I walked out with. I also made sure these days could be taken individually and I could transfer them to other people. Personally, I get to stay at a lot of fancy places each year while doing shows, so it really didn't mean much to me to get to go out for the weekend. So instead, I gave away 7 "2 night stay" gifts to some of my better clients in Southern California as Thanksgiving Day gifts. As a sidebar here, I always send out cards and give away holiday gifts during Thanksgiving. That way my package isn't lost in the crowd, and it gives clients the time to reciprocate rather than be in the embarrassing position of getting a gift from someone they forgot .to give something to. I'm sure the PR value of these gifts, and the guaranteed repeat business I got from them more than made up for the "sacrificed" 90 minutes of my time.

Over the years, some of the other "perks" I've worked into deals include; a) Advertising space in company magazines; b) Use of facilities (the Lions club might pay $300 and agree to let me use their hall 5 times this year, which I then use for seminars or sell to clients as part of a package, something I'll explain more in detail in a moment); c) Actual products (computers, furniture, down payment on car, jet ski, scuba gear and training, skydiving classes for my wife, membership to organizations, over the counter stocks, insurance premiums, travel vouchers, free printing at print shops or company print shops, video equipment, airtime on radio or television, newspaper advertising, etc.); d) Services (I actually had a dentist agree to do $1600 worth of dental work as part of a negotiation for a show done for a civic group he was a member of).

On the flip side of that coin, any money or time I can save the client, becomes another negotiating chip. It's not uncommon for me to put together complete packages for people. Back when I was first getting started I used to use this packaging technique a lot. A company would call and ask about my doing a show. I'd explain that my show cost $3000, but if we talked, I could probably get their whole night worth of entertainment in for just a bit over that amount. I would then offer a DJ (who I'd get for $500 and sell for $800), I'd have a balloon arch done at the door (which my wife would do for a couple kisses and a dinner out, and I'd charge them $300), I'd offer 2 roaming magicians before dinner (I'd be one of them and I'd pay a second guy $175 for an hours work, billing the client $400), I'd arrange for a palm reader (I'd pay her $30 an hour for 5 hours, the client would pay $50) and then I'd offer my hypnotic show at the end. If you itemized the entire package, including my show at $3000, it would work out to a total of $4750. I'd agree to offer my show at half price if they went with this package, which brought it in at $3250. Of this, I ended up taking home $2425, a lot more than they would have ever agreed upon for just my show. Granted, it did involve making 4 or 5 phone calls and doing an extra hour of tableside magic, but for the extra $1500 or so above their original "entertainment budget" I got out of the deal, it was well worth it.

I've also worked items into the deal I had negotiated with other clients. I mentioned getting air fare for comped tickets above. I've also taken rooms (like the Lions Club deal listed above) and offered them to clients as part of a package, charging them for the usage. I've also tossed in "perks" of my own. When things got really tight, I've often found myself tossing in totally unrelated items into the mix. I might take one of the resort rooms I got above and as a last resort make a comment like, "Bob, I realize we're hitting an impasse here. I understand that the money I'm asking for ultimately is money I'll be taking out of your personal pocket. Why don't I make it a bit easier to work out by tossing in a night's stay at the XYZ Resort. I have a few vouchers I got from them as part of a trade when I did a show for them last year, and I'm sure you and your wife would enjoy it much more than I would." I'm now asking Bob if he's willing to take a free vacation as a result of raising the entertainment budget on his event.

I remember talking to a guy once that owned a medium sized company in L.A.. We met at a restaurant, and spent quite a bit of time "chatting" before getting down to business. At the time my agency in Los Angeles was doing quite a bit of business with the Beverly Hills crowd putting together unique (very expensive) dates and 2 or 3 person events. We might have a helicopter pick you up at your home, drop you off on a yacht where a local chef had prepared a romantic dinner for two under the moonlight. The next morning, you docked and took a limo ride back home. This guy was fascinated by the concept and mentioned he had a lady friend he would love to do something like this for. I ended up suggesting he borrow a friends RV, and go camp out at a rustic (secluded) park just outside of town. He could have a local restaurant do some fancy meal to go, which he could pick up on the way to pick up his date, and heat up just before dinner. I'd bring in a violinist to play for them under the moonlight and then I'd join them inside for a private 1/2 hour magic show before leaving them alone for the night. A couple candles, a fine table setting and a good cassette player inside completed another "ultimate romantic evening". He loved it. I offered to toss that event in, free of charge, as a "perk" for him hiring me to do a $3000 show for his company. I paid the violinist $150 to play off to the side during a sunset dinner and I pulled up just before doing a 1/2 hour show. Basically, for 1/2 hour of my time and a $150 bill (the guy paid for everything else) I sold a show for $3000 instead of $800. Finally, another very powerful negotiating tool to ad to your arsenal is the ability to create markets where there aren't any. This is where true negotiating comes into play. Suppose you decide you want to do shows every Friday and Saturday night at the local mall. It's great for your own exposure, it will help draw people to the mall, and you can probably get a fairly decent weekly salary out of the deal. You begin by drawing up a proposal which you send in to the activities director at the mall. The proposal has to assume the person has never considered doing this kind of program before, so you need to begin by presenting a problem (you need to draw customers to the mall), offering a solution (my show offers you an added peg for advertising and has a great tendency to draw repeat customers), and make a proposal. The proposal itself consists of a package you offer to start negotiating with. A typical package I might put together for something like this might include: a) $300 per show payment for a guaranteed 4 shows a week (6 and 9 PM on Friday night and 2 and 6 PM Saturday); b) $200 advertising budget, per show. This is money they pay you and you agree to use entirely to advertise the show. c) One free use of the mall banquet facility offered in trade for each show done. d) Two mall billboards to use to advertise the show; e) You agree to publish a program to offer during the show that includes a half page ad for the mall on it (you also reserve the right to sell ad space to ANYBODY YOU'D LIKE in the program. Basically, you can make quite a bit of money selling space for coupons at mall businesses or even at the Wendy's across the street from the mall). e) You agree to provide a tent for the shows (in my case, I own 5 large, 20 X 40 foot tents I use for just such a program. I paid $350 each for the tubing and had elegant tarps made for about $800 each). f) The mall would agree to include you in their current existing advertising as much as possible, and agree to list you permanently on their marquee. g) The mall agrees to give you a kiosk to use to sell your therapy and self help tapes, books etc. for the duration of your performances.

Somewhere near the end of the proposal you should include a line designed to insure that you keep your negotiations open, something to the effect of: "Obviously this proposal is little more than 'thinking out loud'. In order for any program to be successful, both our needs would need to be addressed. Hopefully this proposal can stir up enough curiosity to merit a meeting where we can better discuss your needs and see how we can put together a final product we can both feel comfortable with. I'll be calling in about a week to see if we can set up a meeting."

Probably 50% of the larger malls in this country could be sold on such a package. The trick would be to convince the mall planning committee to let you come in and sell it in person. You'd have to bring in plenty of credentials that convince them you are worth $1500 a show and copies of a real sharp program. If they have a problem with it, you could probably afford to agree to use $300 of the $500 they'd give you per show for advertising. You'd basically end up taking home $800 a weekend, plus accumulate 4 meetings a week and get a small business (the kiosk) tossed in free of charge. You could probably plan on selling quite a bit of ad spaces if you make sure your tent is closed (has an entrance and exit) and you see that everybody gets a program. You could also be giving away programs from your kiosk all day long to people as they walked by. That way you could explain that you give away, say, 2000 a week to people roaming the mall. Setting up a larger television at the kiosk that shows videos of your show will not only get people to come in and see the show, but would also serve as a storefront agency to sell shows locally. If you use the conference space you've bartered for to do, say, a smoking seminar every Tuesday night and a Weight loss seminar every Thursday, you could plug these seminars and the kiosk from your stage during the show. With a little work and a fair dose of imagination, this could eventually ad up to a nice little business. Again, it'll take delivering a proposal, requesting a meeting to discuss it, convincing the board of the benefits of having a regular show on property, and then negotiating what perks you want, and what else you can offer them (more ad space in your program, a couple shows a year done in their name for local charities, free admittance to mall employees to the stop smoking seminars (they'd have to pay only for materials), etc.). I've made quite a bit of money over the years doing non traditional programs like these. Just remember to make sure there's enough negotiating chips on both sides of the table so it never comes down to just "how much?". As long as there's other perks either side can toss in, you're still working towards a solution. As soon as you've "resolved" everything but price, you're headed for trouble. Make price the given, and work around it.

Take the time to become a good negotiator. Trust me, there's nothing you could possibly learn that will be more useful for you as an entertainer. Not only will you quickly find yourself making far more per show, but you'll discover you can make money almost "appear" whenever you need to. I once put a package together at a swap meet where I offered free shows for the location in exchange for a lot of advertising and a free booth. I was allowed to sell ads behind me during the show, and in a program I offered people who came by. I then set up a bunch of local college students on commission sales for small placards that hung behind us. Between that and the ads we sold in programs (we did shows all day each day the swap meet was open and handed out about 15000 programs a week , guaranteeing good usage of coupons to neighborhood businesses), I ended up netting (after paying out sales commissions, overhead and performers), about $2000 a week. And that's without counting the money we made selling magic and hypnotic stuff at our booth right next to the stage. We also sold a ton of shows to locals (mostly magic and clowning for smaller parties, where we got a commission on each). In all, it was a decent way to make some nice money without too much effort.

Another little "perk" I regularly include in my negotiations is a letter of recommendation. I explain that I'm trying to break into their market, and I'd be willing to knock $200 off my price if they'd be willing to put in writing, on their letterhead, what they thought of the show. Once they agree, I then add a paragraph to my contract to the effect the "client agrees to send out a letter, on company letterhead, to Howard, placed in the mail no later than one week after date of performance in which client agrees to put in writing their feelings concerning the show".

One last obvious place to do some fancy negotiating is with travel arrangements and expenses. You can usually get companies to agree to pay for your airfare easier than you can get them to send you the money. Airfare usually falls under a different budget, somewhere in the "general costs we pay to move VIP's, sales associates and others around" account. Granted, if you get them to pay for your expenses you can rake up Frequent Flyer Miles quickly, which eventually adds up to another "perk", but in most cases I just let them do travel arrangements. I will, however, every now and then, when I think the negotiating is getting tough, make a "deal" like, "if you can get me a deposit for 50% of the cost by the end of the week, I'll go on and pay for my own travel." This works good when you feel comfortable driving (and they're seeing a $300 airfare suddenly disappearing). What they don't know is that I charged them $1800 instead of $1500 and that if you shop around, you can usually get airfare much cheaper than these guys usually pay for.

Before closing an article on negotiating, I have to include the one cardinal rule that will either make or break every negotiating meeting. NEVER LOSE YOUR WALKING POWER. The moment you feel you must sell a contract, that instant you lost your negotiating leverage. The second you start equating any single contract with paying your rent or feeding your kids, you've placed yourself in a position that can only lead to $100 shows where you agree to sweep up afterwards. Set up a savings account or credit card or something that gives you enough security to guarantee that the instant the client drops below what you consider a fair pricing level, you can nicely explain that you really don't think you're going to be able to do the show. You may end up losing the show, but you'll be amazed at the number of clients that give in when they find out what your bottom line really is.

If you can negotiate, you'll be successful regardless of where you go. If you can't, then you're out of business until you sell yourself to someone who can.

Effective Press Releases

If you had all the money in the world, but couldn't write an effective press release, your promotional efforts would be greatly reduced. Yes, you could pay for a full page ad in the local paper, and you could even write it in an editorial style, but after all was said and done, your ad would still be just that, an ad. Most would look at it as an attempt to sell something, and would accept it with the proverbial grain of salt. A well written press release, on the other hand, literally puts words in the mouth of a third person. It tells an "impartial" reporter what to say about your show. It's the single most effective way to have a respected person in the community (the reporter) say good things about your show.

Unfortunately, it's precisely the fact that it's so effective that makes it difficult to make them work. A typical editor probably receives 8 to 10 press releases a week. I know when I was entertainment editor for Dawn Magazine (out of Southern California), I used to get at least 20 or more weekly. Most of them got little more than a glance and ended up in some file somewhere under "if we ever run out of things to write about". But some did make it, and this article is about what it took to get free publicity.

There are three basic variables that determine the effectiveness of a press release. The first is newsworthiness. Is it something the world wants to know? Is Neil Diamond doing a concert in town? Will a world record be broken? Will the local homeless benefit from the performance? Things like these make the job of a news editor simple. Instead of having to run around town looking for information the readers of the paper are interested in, the press release provides the editor with a ready made story. We'll talk more about making your story newsworthy in a moment. The second variable that makes press releases get noticed is quality. How well is it written? How good are the accompanying pictures? Is it sharp and to the point? Is it written in such a way that makes an otherwise dull topic seem fascinating? The final, and possibly most important variable in successful press release writing is familiarity. Does the editor know you? Does he or she know your event will be done right? Does he or she feel comfortable trusting your release to adequately reflect what will really happen?

Let's take these one at a time. First, creating news. The easiest way to approach this is to pick up a newspaper and look at the headlines. What do people want to read about? Are they buying papers to find out that the Elm tree down on the corner of main street was trimmed yesterday morning? Are they interested in knowing that Mrs. Smith's cat had kittens? Probably not. They do want to know that little Bobby Anderson was just selected as having the highest IQ in the nation. And they definitely are interested in knowing that your local school system was found to have the highest crime rate in the state. The fact that the Vice President will be doing a talk on our involvement in the middle east will probably merit a second page mention and the results of the readers pole of "most liked" businesses in the community will also make the cut. These are the stories you are competing with. If you are a well known local celebrity getting ready to do a show that the community is interested in attending, then simply sending out a press release might get you noticed. But to most of us, "creating news" will require becoming a "press agent".

You don't hear a lot about them, mainly because they prefer to work in the shadows of their clients. But out there, hidden behind most larger media events there's at least one good press agent running around making it all come together. They're the "guerilla troops" of the advertising industry. They are relatively unknowns like George Evans.

George was well known in the entertainment industry as one of the top press agents of his time. He was hired by an unknown Vegas lounge singer called Frank Sinatra. According to Kitty Kelly in her unauthorized biography of Sinatra, "His Way", George attended one of Sinatra's concerts looking for something that could make him unique. Something that could become a media grabbing calling card that could promote him to stardom. As he sat in the audience, he saw a girl near the front row toss a red rose up at Sinatra. Another girl near him moaned "Oh, Frankie". According to Kelly, Evans decided that a theater full of moaning, rose throwing girls might catch the media's attention. As the story goes, Evans hired a group of girls and paid them each $5 to jump and scream and yell, "Oh, Frankie, Oh, Frankie!" when Sinatra sang a slow song. "He drilled them in the basement of the Paramount (where Sinatra was performing), directing them to holler when Frank bent and dipped certain notes. 'They shouldn't only yell and squeal, they should fall apart,' Evans said... Two of the girls were coached to fall in a dead faint in the aisle, while the others were told to moan in unison as loudly as they could."

The scheme worked. Girls on vacation were given free tickets by Evans, and security guards were given ammonia to carry "just in case". The theater hired an ambulance to wait outside. A few calls to local columnists and pictures of girls being carried out on stretchers was all it took to take a relative nobody and make him world famous.

"We hired girls to scream when he sexily rolled a note," Jack Keller, one of George Evan's partners recalls, "The dozen girls we hired to scream and swoon did exactly as we told them. But hundreds more we didn't hire screamed even louder. Others squealed, howled, kissed his picture with their lipsticked lips, and kept him a prisoner in his dressing room between shows at the Paramount. It was wild, crazy, completely out of control." And it worked beyond anybody's wildest expectation. Of course, not all of us can use this gimmick. Women yelling wildly at one of my shows might add to the comedy relief, but not much more. But there are other ways. Years ago I learned how to swallow swords and walk on fire. Just sending in a picture of me with a sword down my throat or with a group of seminar attendees walking on fire is enough to guarantee getting articles published in most smaller papers. Back when I was looking for a lot of free press, I used to open my show with a quick sword swallowing act, as a demonstration of how much you can do if you can control your mind. Another "press agentting" bit I used quite successfully was to go to a local retirement center and offer to hypnotize any of the residents who would like to take a trip back to their childhood. A bit of time regression, a couple well choreographed pictures and I was well on my way to a front page in the local paper heralding me as the "miracle worker" who was appearing at the XYZ theater later on this week. I have also had a few occasions where I'd call local police agencies a month or so before a major show, explaining that I was going to be in town and if they needed help solving any rough cases, I'd like to volunteer my services. Again, a carefully done time regression and a few choice quotes from the chief was a definite shoe in for local coverage. I've also offered a free two hour course for wellfare mothers-to-be on how to use hypnosis in childbirth. Just announcing the course would be offered is enough to get plenty of local coverage.

Several years ago I was four walling an auditorium (renting the space and putting the production on from scratch). I organized a seminar that was going to take place the Saturday morning of the week I was appearing. By itself this didn't carry much weight. However, when I guaranteed to cure phobias of all kinds in less than 15 minutes each, and offered several community scholarships for individuals that could offer the best reason why their phobias should be treated free of charge, things went crazy. I ended up with several weekly update articles in local papers, a few call in radio and television appearances, and sold out shows and seminar, all for very little out of pocket expense.

I've heard of people doing hypnotic "bits" where individuals are hypnotized for the entire afternoon prior to a show (at, say, a mall) during which time they think they are fishing or watching television, oblivious to passing spectators. I've also heard of people being hypnotized over the air (you have to be careful with FCC regulations here), while sitting in a public place. I myself have offered demonstrations of the "power of the mind" to cure illnesses and experience hightened mental abilities. Anything the average person might be interested in hearing about can qualify you for a "news event" and get your press release published. Not all "news events" have to be staged, however. Calling a local charity and offering to give them a portion of your door is a news item. Coming up with unique twists here can work wonders as well. A few years ago I put together a Halloween event for a city where we did a city wide scavenger hunt that ended at our carnival where the prizes were all awarded on the day of the show. We put together a small haunted house and I did a hypnotic show in the next room. We contacted the local Red Cross and set up a "Dracula Blood Drive". The nurses all dressed up like vampires and offered free admission to either my show or the house for a pint of blood. Every so often Dracula made an appearance and helped keep the atmosphere "alive" (sorry, I couldn't resist). The city paid us a set fee for organizing the event and local scout troops volunteered labor to run the function. We even found a sponsor that gave us half our ticket price for each pint of blood that was donated.

Even a catastrophe can be converted into a media blitz if you can keep your wits about you. A few years ago I was hired by the then fledgling "Singles Magazine" to help them orchestrate a good media campaign. We put together a "Miss Legs" contest where we were going to look for the best looking legs in the country. Girls had been competing locally at clubs around the country. My crew and I were going to then go around and help select the lucky legs in each state that would accompany their owner for the national competition that would take place at Universal Studios in Hollywood. One of our first stops was in a mid west (bible belt) town. We were busy decorating when we found out that several of the local religious groups had organized a protest. About a hundred people gathered in front of the club and started chanting and picketing about 2 hours before the club doors were scheduled to open. I called the local cops and explained that they were blocking access to the club. The police came by and provided us with a free police blockade (and plenty of free local coverage). The mob outside grew as curious locals watching the 6 o'clock news came out to either participate or watch from the sidelines. I noticed one of the signs being carried announced "we don't want a meat market in our town". That spurred my imagination. Most of my crew were actors and models from the L.A. area, very flexible, capable types that could make any plan work. I gave each of them a $100 or so and had them drive across town and buy all the ground beef they could. They were each also told to buy a wheelbarrow. About 1/2 hour before showtime, these "disgruntled citizen" types came rolling their wheelbarrows down the main isle. They started shouting "we don't want a meat market" while throwing ground beef at the front of the club. It worked. All these otherwise "reserved" religious types suddenly broke out into a frenzy. They rushed all the local stores, buying all the beef that was available, and proudly displayed themselves acting foolishly in time for the "live coverage" on the evening news. We got swamped. All the locals that didn't want to be associated with the mob had no problem walking down the isle to the club. In fact we not only sold out that show (probably to the kids of the people yelling outside) but the event made national news and we pre sold every other function in that state long before spending a penny in promotions. Before I start getting hate mail here, I should say that all of this happened during my younger, "wilder" days. Since then I have settled down quite a bit and currently I'm very active with the church I go to. I don't think I'd join the mob protesting the contest, but I also don't think I would currently agree to promote a "Miss Legs" contest if asked to. I just include this as a way of showing just how powerful press agenting can be.

Another quick story along these lines that happened this past Christmas season. I was hired by a club in Kansas to do a series of 3 shows during the course of a week. I had done plenty of shows for them before and had never had a problem. Just as I was about to leave my house to take the 4 hour drive up to Arkansas City from Oklahoma City where I now live for my first show I got a frantic call from the club owner. It turns out that Kansas is one of the two states where it is illegal to do "hypnosis" for "entertainment purposes". I guess Oregon is the other. Some religious type had complained to the local District Attorney, and the club owner had been warned that if the show went on, the club owner, any volunteers that came on stage and I would all be arrested for knowingly breaking the law. I had about 5 hours till showtime to think of something. In looking around, I was told of another hypnotist who had actually been arrested for doing a show during a State Fair about 50 miles North of this town.

Almost as an afterthought it dawned on me that the law was very specific about how hypnosis couldn't be used for "entertainment" purposes. All I had to do, was change the purpose of my show. As long as I was doing the show with another purpose in mind, it would be legal. I called a local hotel and arranged to rent a room to hold a seminar. I walked on stage, as scheduled (to a sold out house) and explained that I was not permitted to use hypnosis for entertainment, but that I was going to demonstrate what the mind is capable of and hopefully anybody interested would sign up for my seminar. I even printed up some last minute seminar applications and brought along a poster of the brain and a laser pointer to ad an air of "science" to the event. It worked. The cops who came down to arrest me were handed applications to the seminar. They called in to their legal department and were told to leave. They also left the next two sold out shows alone as well. As an added bonus, we had a sell out seminar that made me quite a bit of money with relatively little out of pocket efforts on my part. The "package" was so successful I've even considered offering it again, in the same town, while the local media is still dying to meet the "guy who took on the law". As a side note here, to be fair, the DA did decide to press charges. We were told that it would cost us a fine of $50 for "breaking the law". Both the club owner and myself are interested in having them prove we did "break the law", however, so we've scheduled a jury trial for this coming month. I'll let you know how it goes.

A hint that might help here in creating "news" is to remember that not many of us are impressed by our neighbors. When you hear that the guy next door is going to do a magic show it doesn't ring as dramatic as hearing that the guy from "Hollywood, CA" will be performing to help support XYZ. If you take the time to travel a little ways from your hometown, being a "celebrity" is a lot easier. A few years back, I used to have an office in Los Angeles and another one in Vegas. Whenever I performed in L.A. I used to announce that I was from Vegas. The Vegas crowd was much more impressed when the club brought in a performer from "Hollywood".

The second way to get a press release published is to do it up right. When I was getting press releases at Dawn Magazine, at least a quarter of them were sloppy, obviously self seeking, poorly written ads. Statements like "It's the very best rock group to ever perform in America" were quite common, and guaranteed I wanted nothing to do with them. A well written press release should be formatted like an article submitted by a freelance writer. It should be double spaced (it gives an editor room for notes). It starts with a half page or so of "white space" that includes nothing but the title, and gives the editor room to do his own general notations about where and when he thinks he might use the article. It has to be lively and timely. Magazine press releases need to arrive at least 2 months before publication date (so editors can plan for deadlines). A newspaper usually needs about 2 weeks advance notice. Always give yourself a "rider" paragraph or two at the bottom of the article. "Wrap up" type paragraphs that can be dropped without hurting the rest of the article. These are great when an editor is a bit short on room and has to decide if he feels like re writing your entire article or simply dropping a paragraph at the end. I usually use catchy but unimportant statements like, "It's been 27 years since Howard Morgan first walked on stage to hypnotize audience volunteers. At his upcoming show, audience members can expect not only the experience of a full time professional, but the chance to participate in a show where guests are the real stars. Take a moment to mark your calendars for this limited engagement." I can almost always expect editors to drop this paragraph, which makes them feel important, but pretty much guarantees they print the rest of the article without much editing. Write the article the way a reporter would, in the third person, complete with "Mr. Morgan tells us that...." type quotes and all.

What kind of pictures you include can also go a long way. I mentioned earlier how my sword swallowing pictures help a lot. Pictures of people dancing wildly, sleeping limply, or shooting imaginary guns all spur the imagination and seem to get noticed. We used to call them "Hey Bertha" pictures. The kind of picture that would make someone stop reading the paper and call out "Hey Bertha, you gotta see this one". As a rule of thumb, if the picture doesn't grab your attention without a caption or at the very least, tell a complete story, it probably shouldn't be used with a press release. Pictures can be 5 by 7 or 8 by 10 black and whites (unless you know your material is so powerful it's almost sure to merit a front, color page). Make sure it's a picture and not a good copy. Some of the bulk "picture" companies actually do copies. Most computers also use copy or "halftone" technology. When you copy a copy (the way an editor will have to when using it), you create something called a moray effect. It's a set of intrusive lines that appear when dots collide or something. They make it very difficult to use the picture. A typical press release should have some objective warmth about it, where you're from, why you chose to do hypnosis, some of the funny things that have happened, etc. It should almost downplay what you're selling. A simple paragraph near the end along the lines of "Jack Smith will be performing live at the SpellBreakers lounge on Friday and Saturday nights, Aug. 12 and 13 at 8 P. M.. For ticket information and reservations contact the club at: (609) 538-9988." should be enough "plugging". The total word count on a press release is rarely over 1200 words.

Finally, a point that can either make it or break it for a good press release is the kind of relationship you have with the media. This begins by you opening a general "information" file at their office. Whenever I received a press release that looked promising, the first thing I always did was go to my files to see if I had any "information" on the act. This information usually came from one of two sources. Either I had clipped other articles or general info about the group sometime in the past (something that happened quite rarely) or the group's promoter or press agent had sent me a general info package. Get a list of every major paper, magazine, radio and television station in the town where you want to become "famous". Call the print media and find out who the city editor, the entertainment editor and the feature editor are. Call the radio and television stations and find out if they have any programs that bring on guests. If they do, get the name of the producer of the program. It's the producers job to find interesting material for the show. Also find out who the news editor for the various news programs is. After you have your list of "Media VIP's" place it on a mailing list in your computer or somewhere. Begin by sending them each a package containing as many pictures as you can, a general biographical sheet, an article that briefly describes what makes your show unique and anything else that might help introduce yourself. I find that it also helps to mail all of this in a standard sized file folder. I go out and buy a bright colored folder and place a fancy Avery name label on it. That way, every time the editor opens his or her file the first thing they'll always look at is my name.

Follow this up with all the PR you can muster up. Mail them each invitations to any public shows you might be doing, and don't forget the holidays. I always send out Thanksgiving day cards instead of Christmas. It beats the crowd, gets noticed much more, and if the recipient might have forgotten you at Christmas, they now have a month to ad you to their list, making them feel like they know you. Send out regular press releases every time you do something special, but don't overdo it. The goal of all the smaller "did a show at the Boy Scout Camp" kind of releases isn't to be published. They are simply new excuses for the editor to have to open your file and insert another piece of paper. Every time he does, he reminds himself that he should look into your show some day. Now, when the big day comes, he won't feel he's promoting an unknown.

Two last little promotional tricks I find work well for me are a VIP show and plenty of thank yous. I usually find a local hotel with a large banquet room and offer to do a show for free for their employee holiday party if they'll agree to allow me to bring in 30 or so guests which they'll feed, etc. Most hotels jump at this deal. I then send out special invitations to all the local media types. One year I had bronze key chains made out in the shape of Broadway Show Tickets (they cost me about $5 each). I mailed them out to the media, explaining that they needed to show these "tickets" at the local Hilton in order to come to my "by invitation only" show. Another slant I used to use on this theme in Los Angeles is I would donate a show to a hotel in exchange for a 200 or so person auditorium. I would then contact some of the better know performers around town and invite them to perform at a special promotional show. In exchange for their free performance they were allowed to bring in, say, 50 people. With each of us bringing in 50 or our best clients, 30 or 40 of the local reporters and media types and a few close friends, we basically would end up with a great audience that would enjoy an evening of close up magic, incredible balloon decorations, a live band, a portrait photographer and caricature artist offering their services for free, an opening comic and my stage hypnotic show. It didn't take long for word to get out that this was the party to go to. Clients started asking if they would qualify for our Christmas party if they hired me to do a seminar.

Obviously sending out thank you notes to the editor or producer goes without saying. A very effective trick I use whenever I get free airtime of any kind for a charitable event, is I find out where the local FCC office is and I mail them a letter telling them about the coverage and thanking the station for their efforts. I also send a copy to the station with a small post it note attached explaining when the letter was sent. By law all radio and television stations are required to run a certain percentage of free time for charitable organizations. These are the "public service announcements" you see at 2 in the morning. These extra time slots are carefully monitored by the FCC. At least once a year, FCC inspectors will listen to the station for a week or so and count the PSA's that were run. They then call the station manager and sit down to compare log books. Imagine the manager's reaction when the FCC inspector comes in with a sheet of airtimes, a regulation book and one letter from you thanking them for the 23 minutes of free time they gave you. Try this, it works. I'd be willing to bet you money that if you take the time to write the FCC, you'll suddenly find the station bending over backwards to help you promote any charitable event you happen to be associated with.

One final way to get all kinds of free press is to offer to do the "live remotes" for radio and television stations at a discounted rate. Basically, whenever the station is hosting live remote events, you can show up and do a show. This works better for small crowd shows like magic or clowning, but some events can be offered where you do a street performing version of your hypnosis. The DJ will spend a week plugging the fact that they are going to be at "Bob's Ford" on Friday, and use you as a draw, constantly plugging the fact that "Tom Smith will also be there, hypnotizing volunteers and adding to our mayhem". They'll also spend a lot of time interviewing you before and during the event. Back when I used to use this technique, I used to offer to do live remotes in exchange for free air time. How could they refuse? Basically they would promote their event, using my name. They would then do their event, featuring my show. And then, for the next 3 weeks, the same station would run advertising for my services. Considering that they did live remotes at least once a month, and that having free live entertainment helped them sell these to their clients, my ads pretty much ran daily year round.

Use your head, be consistent and professional, and before long you'll find your in laws will finally accept that Hypnosis isn't just "another phase you're going through".

Scheduled Progress

Several months ago I mentioned in an article here that it was important not to sell yourself short. That it was up to you to set your fees high enough to establish the fact that you were a professional. I must have hit a responsive note. I got swamped by emails asking me to help performers figure out how much their shows were really worth. Unfortunately, its not that simple. So in response to the many requests, I'm going to try and lay out a formula that's worked well for me, and several entertainers I represented back in my agent/manager days.

First of all, you need to start with your show. It doesn't matter how long you've been doing it, or how much work you've put into it, it needs improvement. That's not to say you don't do a good show. What I'm really saying is that the quality of any show is always changing. Either you are actively involved in making it a better show, or time is taking it's toll and little by little the quality of your performance is deteriorating.
I'm a member of a club in Los Angeles that's dedicated to helping "preserve" the quality of stand up performing. It's a pretty exclusive club. To get in you have to be nominated and voted on by a panel and they only accept individuals who have either been professional entertainers in the past, or are currently making their living on stage. Many of the old vaudeville acts are members. You'll find a lot of the old tap dancers and ropers from the soap box western movies. You'll also find plenty of the old vaudeville types. Some of the original Key Stone Cops are members as are Johnny Carson and Ed McMahon. It's a great place to meet some of the

"greats" and get one on one advice on your show. The club meets once a month and a different performer is invited each month to "do their thing". And almost without exception, all acts fit into one of two categories. You have those who have continued to fine tune their acts over the course of the years, acts that obviously shine. Timing is right, clothing is sharp and response is great. Then you have the "has beens". And not all of them are in their 70's. Many of the young performers with just 5 or 6 years experience fit neatly into this category. They get up there and go through the motions of repeating a bunch of lines they obviously memorized several years ago. There's no energy, no excitement, just a recorder pumping out punchlines. And their clothes reflect their lack of concern. Old, worn out tuxes and unpolished shoes. And we all wait together for the end of the show to save us.

Now I'm not saying these acts aren't "good". What I am saying is that they obviously aren't as good as they were back when the guy was pushing to reach the top. They obviously reflect his arrogance and contempt. (I'm not trying to be sexist here, but the "Variety Club" is still a "mens only" group with a sister club that meets elsewhere). He's "made it" so he's just going to sit back and let his reputation take over. If you hang out in the Vegas and Reno scenes, you know exactly what I'm talking about. Many of the all time "greats" have let themselves go.

One of my youth idols was Pat Collins, the "Hip Hypnotist". For many years she did a show that could sell anywhere. She brought along her own 4 piece band and burst out into spontaneous song as she performed. She had a magical way of blending vaudeville and hypnosis. For a while there, she owned The Celebrity Club in Los Angeles, where she regularly featured hypnotic acts. Her act was tight, and every show was different. And working her club was a real honor. Not because it was a big club, or the pay was great, but just because you got to rub shoulders with someone as talented as she was. Not long before she died I went down to see her doing a lounge act in Vegas. It broke my heart. Where once there had been a fresh, excited lady, sharing the joys of exploring the mind with you, now there was a performer who was obviously struggling to make it through the show. Her lines were stale and her smiles obviously fake. And you could almost feel the anger when you didn't laugh at lines that had worked so well for decades. Somewhere as she got older, she decided to stop pushing for the top. She allowed herself to coast, and if it hadn't been for her reputation, chances are, nobody would have hired her.

And it's an easy trap to fall into. As your reputation grows, and more "fan's" keep telling you how good you are, it's easy to decide you've finally "made it". That's when apathy starts to set in, and you're usually the last person to find out. It's a problem faced by many actors doing long running stage productions. You can only say "To be or not to be" so many times before your mind starts going into neutral. To avoid that destructive trap, most actors work hard at "falling into character", and then "experiencing the plot". Each show is an excuse to relive the love and anger. To really become just a little more like Romeo. Hopefully, before long, the character becomes so real that he stops acting and starts living the life of a shunned Capulet. When actors talk about their character, they always find themselves referring to it in the third person. Comments from actors, talking about their characters like "she has a temper and feels a bit insecure about her job" or "he's a real pain to live with" reflect the separation actors make with their characters.

Developing a "persona" is just as important when doing a stand up act. We know where the highlights of our shows are. We need to look forward to them and savor the excitement each time, as if it were the first. And we need to constantly pick at details, the way we did when we were scared to walk out there. Are our fingernails trimmed? Have we polished our shoes? Is our music appropriate for the show? We also need to continue to stretch. Experiment with new lines, add new bits every now and then. Try different twists in our pretalk. Try being more animated or maybe do a show experimenting with being a bit more mysterious. And learn to be honest with yourself. Don't just add something because you like it, watch for audience response and reaction.

Personally, I videotape every show I do. Even the shows where the client has paid to videotape themselves and where I know I won't sell any tapes, I videotape the show for my own records. And as I work my way through the show, I watch for reactions. If nobody laughs at a line I think is "tried and true", I make a mental note of it and go try to figure out why in front of my television after the show. If I happen to say something that somehow gets a great response, I dissect it in front of a monitor later on to try and figure out why, and if I should leave it in. Now don't get me wrong here, I'm not saying I do everything right. As I write this piece I find myself remembering the number of times I walked out on stage with a wrinkled pair of pants on or shoes that had obviously been scuffed and scratched in a trunk somewhere during a long run of shows. And I'm the first to admit that when I'm tired, or preoccupied, I've often resorted to letting the show do it's own thing, coasting on my memory to deliver the lines and go through the basic motions. And looking back, I can't help but wonder how somebody who paid $22 to watch the show must have felt. In fact, there's probably a large group of people running around the country today that over the years have watched me during one of my off nights and have gone back to Bono, Arkansas or wherever to tell the neighbors I wasn't worth watching. And all because I didn't take the time to leave the rest of the world behind and get ready for my time on stage.

But tightening up the show, and continueing to push upwards is just the first step to succeeding. If you know you have an act worth watching, then you need to tell someone. You need to believe in your act enough to start promoting the daylights out of it. I've spent a lot of time talking about promoting your show in previous articles, so I won't become redundant here and repeat myself, but make sure you're sending out quality promo materials to the right people. And do it on a consistent basis. If your prospective client isn't getting something from you at least once every 2 or 3 months, chances are, they don't even know you exist. Oh, they'll glance at what you mail them, but it will probably end up in a very large filling cabinet along with thousands of other hopefuls.

Finally the last "secret ingredient" in the formula for success is pricing. Exactly how much should you charge? I devoted a whole article, not that long ago to the fact that how much you charge reflects the kind of show you do. And that's true. But reality also dictates that if you charge too much, too soon, you're still going to need to keep your day job. So on one had you have a hypnotist willing to do shows (actually, more times than not, begging to do shows), at $100 each. That's like offering to do a magic show for $10. Few birthdays would find that hard to afford, but even fewer would be willing to take the risk. Anybody who sells themselves that cheap must not be too good. A $500 show, on the other hand, sounds like a safe bet, if you can afford it. The problem is, most of the people willing (and able) to pay that kind of money, are also considering several other professionals as they do their planning. So we get right back to the quality of your advertising and the depth of your background. Just how many references can you produce? How sharp is your demo tape? Without a good one, you really aren't even in the running. Personally I not only have 5 good demo tapes that cater to most of my markets, but I own my own video editing equipment and constantly put together new, updated tapes to send out with my promotion.

Once you are sure you have both those components well under control. You know you have a show that is constantly moving upwards and you have a good quality promotional package. You're ready to set your price. And the formula is really not that difficult. You need to do enough shows to comfortably pay your bills and continue to promote the show. At the beginning you need to realize that at least half your income is probably going to go back into promotion. Remember, it's the promotion that guarantees your growth. Without it, even Neil Diamond would be sitting at home waiting for phone calls. You have to believe in yourself, and your show, enough to be willing to put all your money and efforts into it before you can expect to get a penny out of it.

Begin by figuring out how much you're monthly bills are (and you might as well accept the fact that at this point you need to cut back on luxuries as much as you can), and then double that amount. The number you end up with is probably a fairly accurate estimate of how much money you need to make monthly to stay on the right track. Next you need to figure out how to make it.

You could try to sell one show a year for $48,000. If you do, I'd like to read your column. Or you could try to convince 480 clients a year into buying a show for $100. Again, you would not only run yourself ragged, but you'd also quickly gain a reputation of being a "cheap" act. In fact, you might as well accept the fact that any show sold for under $500 will be regarded as "cheap" in today's market. So let's suppose you decide to settle for $500 a show (to begin with). That means, in order to make your budget, you'll need to sell at least 96 shows a year. Again, you aren't going to do this unless your allowing yourself the $24,000 a year promotion budget. In essence you're aiming at making a $250 profit from each show you do.

Of course that also means it's costing you $250 to sell each show. But don't let that scare you. Because the truth of the matter is, you aren't spending $250 per show. What you're really doing is selling next years shows. You're giving yourself enough exposure so that next year you'll be able to continue to do 96 shows, but now you'll have enough people calling to be able to raise your price up to, say $600 a show (and take home $350 each). Now you've developed a working formula. You've accepted the fact that a good working year, for you, involves roughly 100 shows (that rounds out to 2 to 3 a week, although most of them will probably happen during holidays and extended runs like fairs and/or casino shows). Accept the fact that success in show business almost always means traveling. As you get more expensive, you're going to discover that fewer and fewer local markets can afford you. If you really are growing, it won't be long before you'll need to start flying out to where the markets are. Of course, by that time you'll be making enough to afford the travel (and you'll usually tack on expenses in the negotiation anyway). But it means time away from home, it means missing your daughters little league game and not being able to join the local bowling team. Be sure you're ready to grow before you set the process in motion.

Another consideration you might want to keep in mind here is that in order to really get this ball rolling, you'll need to send out enough promotional material to get the original 100 shows going. To do that, you need to understand that the first several shows will probably go entirely into promotion. And at that time you'll probably be depending on Kinkos or someone else to do the work, which means you're paying premium price for the stuff. This might be a good time to start negotiating trades with local printers for promotional materials, etc. It may mean you also need to make sure you either have some money saved up to pay bills or you find a job that's flexible enough to allow you to do shows when they come up. A good job might be a sales job, where you're rated on results rather than scheduling. Just be sure you're not stuck calling the same clients to sell them office furniture and hypnotic shows. Getting enough shows to get moving (at the start) is the real "test of fire". That's where the men (and women) are separated from the boys. Hang in there and you'll soon find yourself rubbing shoulders with the pro's. This starting time might also be a good time to spend a lot of time on the phone trying to sell the show before you have much to back it up with. You might also try getting a few local agents to promote for you. Get used to rejection, it's part of the business. The Beatles were kicked out of Deca Records because "guitar music is on it's way out". The director of the Grand Ole Opry told Elvis to go back to driving trucks, because his offbeat style had no chance in the real world.

If you set your goal at doing, say, 100 shows a year, the pricing takes care of itself, and enough people out there are seeing your show to insure a steady growth of your reputation. With a consistent 100 shows a year, it won't be long before people will start talking about you, and it won't take long for them to start calling. Be sure you pick up all the letters of recommendations you can along the way (go back and read my article about "The Very Best Advertising") and let others tell your story for you. As soon as 200 people a year are calling, wanting to fill in the same time slots, you can afford to raise your price, explaining to old customers that you really can't afford to turn down clients willing to buy shows at $800 (or whatever). If you toss in enough bartering "extras" with your package, where, say, you agree to "knock $200 off the cost is you let me place a full page ad in your club newsletter" you can afford to offer the show at $1000, knowing you plan on only making about $800 per show. If your advertising budget stays at $250 per show, you're now walking home with $650 each plus a bunch of bartered perks. Again, I believe one of the "Promoting the Show" articles covers this area pretty thoroughly. Eventually, you'll find yourself accepting more shows at a higher cost. Once you've set your rate at, say $1000, you might try doing 150 shows instead of just the 100. Again, you're real goal here is to be sure you keep the steady income coming in. It should have nothing to do with your pride (and being able to brag to mom that you once sold a $5000 show). If you work the system, and allow for growth to take it's natural course, it won't be long before you'll get there. If you're killing yourself to sell the high ticket show, you'll soon talk yourself right out of business.

One other cost I usually factor into my growth is commissions. Whereas I refuse to sign an exclusive with any one agent, at this point I have 6 agents that are all competing for my time. I let them do a lot of the calling and promoting, and I simply sit back and fill in my calendar, but I never stop promoting myself. I now spend about $1200 a month sending out packages, taking out ads in trade journals and targeted publications (business journals, caterers magazines, etc). My promotions guarantees me enough clients so I can comfortably tell agents (or prospective clients) that I feel comfortable knowing I can make, say, $1500 for a show (my current "lowest price"). If they can't match that, then I probably won't do business with them. Without my own advertising, I'm pretty much stuck accepting whatever they think my show is worth. I'm usually pretty generous with my commissions. Whereas tradition says I should offer 10 - 15%, it isn't rare for me to offer 20%. I regularly offer my $1500 show to agents for $1200. The advantage to offering higher commissions is that the next time that agent gets a call for a bigger program, they'll end up calling me long before they'll consider anybody paying them, say, $150 for the same show. Remember, I'm in this for the long run. Keeping agents happy is a guaranteed way to make sure you don't go out of business.

But my commissions are not limited to agents. I plan on spending about 20% of my income thanking someone for getting me every show I do. Every now and then, with old friends, I give them the $300 or whatever commission in cash for referring a show to me. But most of the time, when an individual gets me a show, I enjoy getting creative and finding a $300 gift to give them as a "thank you". Many of these "gifts" are actually items I traded for. I regularly say "thank you" by giving away a weekend for 2 in Vegas, good any time, with a ticket to a nicer show. Truth is, I still have favors I'm calling in with Casinos from shows I did in exchange for a reduced fee and "a two night stay, any time, for me or anybody I'd like to give it to, and tickets to whatever your main show is at the time". Or I might pay to have them and their spouse get picked up by a limo and taken out to dinner at a $50 a plate restaurant in their home town they would have never paid for themselves. People remember that kind of thing long after the thrill of $300 that got shuffled into the bill paying budget is forgotten. I also send out a ton of fruit baskets and nice advertising specialty items during thanksgiving. "It's just a little token of my thanks for the way you helped make this a great year for me", I'll usually include with the package.

So the trick, in a nutshell, to being successful in stand up entertaining is simple. Be sure you're show is worth far more than you're currently making, be sure you tell the people who can buy it, and aim at doing enough shows, at a reasonable price, to get your name out. As demand grows, so will your price tag and the number of shows you do. And some day, when you look back at it all, you'll agree with virtually every "successful" performer I've ever discussed it with, that the time you spent "playing the market", when you wondered how the bills were going to get paid, but were willing to risk it all on a single mailing, was the most exciting period of your life.

Making Money Raising Money

I got an E-mail recently from a reader asking about fund raisers. I started to answer it and realized that it's a topic we all have to deal with at one time or another, and that, if done correctly, can become a big money maker for us. So I decided to write this month's column about it.

Getting calls from organizations trying to put on fund raisers is a normal part of being in the entertainment industry. The basic pattern is simple. The home for battered children is trying to build a new wing and wants us to do a show (where they plan to charge admission) to raise money for the project. It's a cause we believe in and we almost feel guilty saying we want some money for doing the show. So it usually ends up becoming one of those "good deeds" we do for free. After all, it's just 90 minutes of our time, isn't it?

Or is it? Unfortunately, if we start thinking of it as just "a bit of my time", it won't be long before the rest of the world will start thinking of it that way as well. Fund raisers do talk to each other, and the better your show is, the more the chances that you'll start getting calls from everybody in town asking for free shows.

I made that mistake when living in Los Angeles. I agreed to do a free show for a hospital (like they don't have money!?). Two things happened. First, it didn't take long for word to get around town, and I was stuck with a phone ringing off the hook with all kinds of other "great" causes wanting a handout. Secondly, when I arrived at the hospital for the show, I discovered they tended to treat me the way you would expect a "Free" show to be treated. When a company pays $4000 for one of my shows, not only will they have everything I requested there, but they'll usually assign someone to make sure any loose ends I need dealing with get covered. My hotel room is usually top grade, and without requesting it, I can usually expect to be flown out first class. In the minds of the client, I'm a $4000 investment. They can't afford to throw away their money because they used a second rate sound system.

The hospital (and almost every other "free" show I've ever done) kind of shuffled me around, making me sit in a corner of the auditorium until my "turn" on a long list of PR speeches by all the hospital administrators and the like. Even the posters to this event, where I was promised top billing, proclaimed in bold letters, across the front: "XYZ Hospital Yearly Fund Raiser". Somewhere buried in the small print on the bottom, between "recognition of employee of the year" and "details of upcoming hospital plans" was a small line that read, "entertainment by hypnotist Howard Morgan". Obviously, a show that seemed so unimportant to the promoters tended to be non consequential to the audience as well. It took longer to get them going and volunteers were harder to come by. In short, not only did I not make any money, but it turned out to be one of the harder shows to do (so much for the "think of the exposure you'll get" argument).

Now I'm not trying to belittle doing all you can to help a worthy cause. The way I've worked myself around this dilemma is to pick a couple charities I feel good about (children's causes and the disabled) and dedicate my time to helping them out. In Florida I ended up serving on the then Governor Graham's (he's now a Senator for the state) 5 man advisory committee for the disabled. I lobbied in Tucson and Southern California for them as well, helping change transportation and employment laws in both. I'm a member of the Optimist club, a service organization that works primarily with children causes (they call themselves the "Friends of Youth"). If any other organizations call asking for a free handout, I simply explain that I dedicate what little free time I have to these two causes.

Even when dealing with these two causes, I usually make it clear ahead of time, that I can't afford to give away my shows. I am, however, willing to help in the planning, coordinating, etc. of events for free. I make a decent income as a promoter for corporate events and functions, so letting these groups see me in action actually helps establish my reputation as an "idea" man. Another affiliation that also helps in this area is the United Way. I usually volunteer as a "Loaned Executive" to help them coordinate and brainstorm events. Again, word gets out quickly that I can usually come up with an innovative, working solutions to most scenarios. Two of my ideas have gone on to win top awards, which also helps me sell a lot of "extra" work. If you're old enough to remember the "Hands Across the Country" event Kenny Rogers spearheaded back in the 80's, it was based on a "Hands Across the County" project I brainstormed for the San Diego United Way. Basically, my "volunteer" time actually helps me promote myself as a promoter, writer and press agent, each of which help pay the mortgage.

When the children, disabled or United Way need me to do a show, I usually set up a rather innovative way of doing it. I agree to do the show for $500, provided they give me a "charitable donation" receipt for the $1000 balance. Basically I'm donating my time. These tend to add up by the end of the year. Adding 4 or 5 thousand dollars in write offs at the end of the year definitely helps. The fact that I'm associated with specific causes also guarantees me plenty of community recognition, which again translates into shows, articles in local papers, more local radio guest spots and a shoe in the door at many of the larger companies when I'm calling about Holiday events, etc.

And there are definite advantages to associating yourself to a cause. Because you spend so much time with the same people, you start establishing networking basses. I probably get 3 or 4 shows a year from referrals I make through these associations. And it also allows me time to identify sponsors interested in the causes as well. When mingling at the social events or when organizing functions, names invariably pop up of people who believe in the cause. I keep these names on file, ready to pull when needed. Whenever one of these organizations needs a show, I recommend to them that they contact some of these individuals to see if they're willing to "sponsor" the show. Basically, Coca Cola will pay the $500 cost of my show in exchange for including their name on all the posters, programs etc. Basically "Coca Cola proudly presents" is tagged, in tiny letters, at the top of everything that announces "The Hypnotic Comedy of Howard Morgan." Not only does it get the show to the cause for free, making Coca Cola look like the good guys who made it all possible, it also establishes a relationship with Coca Cola that may become a sponsored run for some other cause in the future.

That doesn't mean I don't do other charitable causes, though. Most professional entertainers who do these "charity" causes, charge for them. It's only the beginners that are willing to give them away. If I find a cause that I feel is worthwhile, I explain to them that my show usually goes for no less than $1500, but that I'll be willing to do their show at half price, if they are willing to make certain guarantees. Then I put in writing every detail I'm looking for. They must have a sound system with no less than a 200 watt output. I use my own wireless mike, so I specify the kind of plugs they must have. They must assign a person during my show to help with music (or the CD player needs to be where I can get to it from the stage). They must have a place set aside for me to wait till I'm announced away from the crowd (unless it's a dinner event or other social function where I'm invited to join in and don't mind explaining what Hypnosis is 20 or 30 times). I also request that they do the same "charitable donation" process for the extra $750.

In all charity shows, I also include, in writing, a clause to the effect that "client agrees to write a letter, on their company letterhead, explaining their feelings regarding the show. This letter is to be mailed no later than one week after the completion of the performance." I explain to the client that I'm interested in their input, whether positive or negative, concerning the show. Over the course of 30 years, and probably 70 or 80 letters, I've never had anybody say "you were terrible" about a show they got at a discount. I've got a ton of great letters of recommendation from all kinds of organizations I can add to my portfolio whenever needed. I also make a point of mixing with the crowd after the show, which allows me to hand out a bunch of business cards and collect them from interested parties for future follow up (see my column from July of last year on Effective Networking).

One last way to handle these "call in" requests is to agree to take a percentage of the door. Most of the larger rock stars use this method for handling charity cases. Of course, they don't have to worry about not being adequately promoted and ending up taking home 25% of $100. A way around this is to ask for a guarantee. You're guaranteed at least, say, $300, and then, if your 25% goes over the amount, you keep whatever the total comes out to.

So far we've dealt with shows that come from outside referrals (people calling you), but that's only half the equation. There are several promoters and/or entertainers that make a lot of money representing charitable organizations. Years ago I remember my first exposure to this concept. I was a member of a Press Agenting club in Los Angeles (Press Agenting is about getting the press to give you free publicity - kind of the "media gimmick" version of an advertising agent). One of the other guys was busy doing what he called "Charity Shows", and asked if I could do 15 minutes of magic for one of his Los Angeles events. I agreed and showed up an hour or so before the show to a 500+ auditorium. Plastered in large letters behind the performing area was a large "Just Say No" or something sign. At about 15 minutes to showtime there were 2 people sitting on the front row. I asked Ron why he had such poor turnout. He laughed and told me not to worry, they'd do just fine. About 3 minutes before the MC made his way on stage, there were about 30 people in the room. Again Ron seemed okay.

The show started on time, to an audience of 35 or so people. Each of 6 of us did our "thing" for 15 minutes. After the show, Ron invited me to dinner, explaining he wanted to celebrate another "successful" program. At dinner he explained that one of the larger charities had agreed to accept 20% of any ticket sales he made during his show in exchange for the right to use their name. Ron lined up shows all up and down the West coast, hiring professional telemarketers to call the more affluent neighborhoods and sell tickets at $10 each. He explained that they had actually oversold this show. They had sold about 550 tickets. Most people were more interested in giving a donation to the "Just Say No" program than they were in the show itself. Basically, tickets were mailed to a ton of people, but only a small percentage were ever expected to show up. Ron joked about making $2000 or $3000 clear profit for shows being done for audiences of just 30 or 40 people. It's all legal, and it guarantees a worthwhile charity a $1000 or so profit per show. In Ron's case, he was doing a show a week (every Saturday night, each in a different area), so his cause was getting $50,000 or so a year from him, probably their main source of income. His total expenses boiled down to $600 or $700 for performers, $1000 or so for the charity, another $600 or $700 for the telemarketers and maybe $200 for the room. At $10 a ticket, he only had to sell 260 people to pay his bills. Everything after that was pure profit. A crew of 10 telemarketers calling for 8 hours a day, averaging a call every 2 minutes, allowing for one hour lunch, means they're making 2100 calls a day. 260 sales in a week isn't that unreasonable. Ron started his marketing a month before the show was to arrive in town.

This, obviously, is a major undertaking, but I've successfully used the basic formula on individual shows. On one of these events, I vaguely remember I booked an 800 or so seat auditorium and agreed to give a local charity 25% of my profit from a show. I then hired telemarketers to sell 1000 tickets. I also sent out press releases and recorded PSA's (public service announcements) for local radio stations. Basically, the telemarketers were added to a normal promotion package. Posters around town, guest appearances on local stations, newspaper adds, etc. ended up selling 500 or so tickets. The telemarketers sold their 1000 (of which 100 or so showed up) making our total take for the show 1500 sales at $8 each ($12,000). After giving the charity their $3000 (they loved it, and gave me a placard of thanks) and $1600 to the telemarketers, I took home a $7400 profit.

Another "fund raising" package I've worked quite successfully included a package where I sold magic shows at $100 each to a group of schools as school assemblies. During the show I promoted (and showed a demo tape) of the hypnotic show that I was going to do at a larger auditorium several weeks later. All kids took home a brochure promoting the large "show". It's the only way to advertise legally through the school system, which virtually saturates a neighborhood. One of the local school organizations (PTA, Boosters, etc.) then are allowed to sell tickets and keep half the take. I go on to do several other schools around town, all promoting the one larger show as a fund raiser for their cause. If you figure each school has 800 or so students, each with 2 parents and probably at least one sibling, you're effectively promoting to at least 1200 kids and another 1200 or so adults per show. Once word gets out around school that the "cool" kids are going to the show, you have a troop of personal promoters out there begging their parents to buy tickets. At $6 an adult and $4 a kid, if only 10% of the possible sales go through, you're still getting 120 kids and another 120 adults. If you're getting $2 a kid and $3 an adult, that works out to $600 or so profit per school. And this estimate is way low. If you do 10 or 15 assemblies around town, selling $600 to $1000 per school, making $10,000 profit is not unreasonable. You'll need to deduct $400 or $500 to rent an auditorium and hire door people, etc. Your sub total will then come to roughly $9,500. Add to that $100 each for the assemblies, you're now up to $10,500 to $11,000 profit.

But it doesn't end there. Remember, you now have an auditorium with roughly 3000 people in it. That's a lot of energy. If you take an intermission and offer tapes, CD's, posters, T-shirts, etc. it shouldn't be hard to add another $2000 or so in profit. Be sure to include plenty of gimmicky stuff for the kids (rulers with your name on it, spiral disks, magic kits, etc.). Have sellers go up and down the aisles and set up plenty of tables. If you sell refreshments as well (check for needed permits and maybe hire a caterer to handle the details). That should end up adding another $2000 or $3000 to your take. If you want to really clean up, find a local charity interested in taking a part of the profit and do the telemarketer thing also.

Just a added note here, in closing. I've been at this over 30 years. I've had my share of successes and failures and have made it a lifetime quest to study programs that have been successful for others. About the only two qualities that seem to be needed to succeed at these or any other well planned package, is vision and dedication. If you can really see through all the possible flaws with a package, and come up with good tools to overcome them, it's then only a matter of going for it with all you have. It takes being willing to dedicate plenty of time and money up front, based on the insight of what's coming. Yes it's a gamble, but if the event is carefully planned out before beginning, the odds are far better than Vegas, the lottery or even the stock market, and the rewards are measured not only in money, but also in momentum that will make the next event easier to sell and produce.

Negotiating with Club Owners

By
Howard Morgan

Most of you know (from previous articles) that I recently made Oklahoma City my home. Originally the plan was to use it as a central USA base from which I could fly to shows around the country at affordable rates. Soon after arriving (after doing a few local shows) I discovered a steady local following. In fact, I decided to create a local, steady income which will keep me from having to be on the road 10 or 11 months out of every year. To do this I started looking around for local clubs where I could book weekly shows, and as I did so, I couldn't help but think many of you are probably in similar situations, so I decided to take you through my adventures and give you a few ideas on setting up local, steady, work. Hypnosis definitely lends itself to weekly performances. If you are capable of rotating material in and out of your show, a steady, weekly gig works itself. People see the show and decide they'd like to volunteer, so the next show they come back, and bring friends as moral support. Unlike stand up comedy, where listening to the same show, with the same punchlines, can get old very quickly, hypnosis changes every show. New volunteers, new bits and different audiences all make the show new and exciting every time. If you're experienced with more than one routine (if you can do, say, three good shows without repeating your material), a weekly show works great. There's something about knowing that "every Thursday night" there'll be a show at the club. It makes it easy for your followers to keep track of where you are.

Dr. Dean did quite well in San Diego for many years doing weekly shows, as did Pat Collins in Los Angeles. Flip Orley, I've been told, actually shut down a comedy club in Texas by doing weekly shows. From what I was told, he was hired to do weekly show, which ran for over a year. He was very successful, keeping a steady crowd of loyal followers. A year later, when he decided to call it quits, the club suddenly discovered that everybody in town was exited about hypnosis, and nobody came out when comics started taking the stage. I haven't actually talked to him about this, so this may all be rumor, but I've heard it from 2 different sources (including a Comedy Club owner) and the scenario is very possible. One other consideration you need to think about is the quality of your show. Doing weekly local gigs is a very high exposure, quick fame kind of deal. There's no way to run the program I'm about to explain and not end up "famous" in your town. The problem is, what are you going to be famous for? If your show is mediocre, it won't be long before all your neighbors will know you're a so-so performer. If your family lives in your town, it won't be long before you'll start embarrassing the folks. So before you start exposing yourself, be sure you have something to show.

My first impulse, in looking for a local venue, was to go down to the local comedy club and offer to work one of their off nights. After all, they do have their own steady clientele and I'm sure I could keep the room full. But the more I thought about it, the more I felt that idea wouldn't do what I'm trying to do. The best you can do at a comedy club is fill the house, and they do that regularly. At best you can be another good "one nighter" on their books. Because the comedy club already monopolizes all the prime time nights (whatever your local market can bear - usually Wednesday through Saturday, or sometimes weekends only), you'll be forced to take the off nights and try to compete with the full houses their getting on weekends.

In my case, I definitely cannot afford to plan on a weekly weekend show. I do far too many corporate shows each year where I make anywhere from $2000 to $4000 a show to fly in on Friday or Saturday night, do my 90 minute thing and then leave. There's no way a weekly gig can compete with this. So the Comedy Club setting might have worked. A very serious consideration for me, however, was that if I worked an established club, ultimately it wouldn't be my show. People would be coming to see "a hypnotist" down at the Comedy Club. I'm interested in being a star in my own right. I want local businesses to think of me when they plan their holiday parties and conventions. I want to establish a firm base for me to do seminars and private consultation. So at least for me, the logical solution was to find a nice looking club, with the potential to grow, and work together with them at making the show a big deal around town.
My first step was to "scope out" the local club scene. I looked for the parts of town where people went for "a night out". In Oklahoma City, there's one area that really fits the bill. Just East of the downtown area is a neighborhood called "Bricktown". It still has the old colonial charm about it. Brick roads, rock warehouses and plenty of big name clubs (Old Spaghetti Factory, etc). In fact, the local Comedy Club happens to be in

this area as well. A lot of promotion has gone into the "Bricktown renewal" project lately, including a riverwalk area that's become quite popular. The busy "party crowds" that walk the area every night make this a natural area for a regular show.

Your town may have a downtown "party district" or some area where the evening crowds gather. If so, try to work close to that. It's a lot easier talking someone into walking into a club they've passed lots of times than it is to get them to drive across town to a building in the middle of a residential area, to go see a show they're not familiar with. Even in showbiz, the first three priorities are "location, location, location". Another very serious consideration is the kind of image you want to promote. If you end up doing a show at a tiny local pick up joint, you're never going to get the classy theater crowd (your main possible, repeat customers, people who are used to going out regularly to be entertained).

As you get organized, and know the area of town you want to work in, you need to consider the bigger picture here. My goals are all long range. If I can get a steady local following, it'll be worth a fortune to me. If I can get 150 people in a room to see the show, I know I can plan on selling anywhere from $160 to $240 dollars worth of video tapes at every show (at $20 each, and I deliver them the following week). I can also plan on selling $40 to $60 worth of self help CD's ($20 each). When I do local seminars, it won't be hard to fill the room with 30 or 40 people, at $40 to $80 each, to stop smoking, overcome stress, deal with anxiety and depression, etc. I'll also be able to plan on doing at least one private session per show, at $100 an hour. So if I can somehow get 150 people in a room to see my show, I can plan on making an average of $350 or so just in "extras" weekly. This is without counting corporate shows and city events I'm sure to book from the high exposure in a small town. Knowing this, I walked down the Bricktown area ready to negotiate. My real goals weren't as much to "make a killing" at a single show as they were to get a big crowd and have a quality location where we could grow. In my case, I got lucky. The first place I walked up to was a large, nice restaurant/club called the Bricktown Brewery. It's kind of a TGI Friday's feeling spread out over two floors with plenty of floorspace. Downstairs they have a nice restaurant while upstairs houses the bar and pool hall. They have a larger concert stage where they regularly bring in nationally recognized rock stars. They also have a banquet area that can grow from an intimate 50 or so room to about 300 by moving out partitions. I knew I would probably start small (and would look tiny in a 600 person auditorium), but I wanted enough room to grow. I really wanted this room, so I made him an offer he'd have a problem refusing.

When you negotiate with club owners, there are far several areas you can negotiate in. You can obviously ask for a flat rate, say $500 a night to perform. If you do that, the club owner is taking all the risk and is going to be saddled with not only your $500, but also the cost of promoting your show. If he feels you can draw a good crowd quickly, he may go with it, but unless you're a well known local celebrity, he probably won't be interested in sticking his neck out just because you think it'll work. Another option is to work for the door. You set the door charge and you keep whatever people pay at the door. This package assumes you'll be promoting the show. Yes, the club will probably put your posters up and include you in their local newspaper ad but the heavy promotion will rest on your shoulders. Without having a start up income from the door (it won't be there until after you've promoted), this usually means you're spending a lot of your own money up front trying to get things going. Another option (not used much anymore, but still available) is to take a portion of the drink tab. Every club has a tally sheet that tells them how many drinks were sold per night. They typically make most of their money here. I know of performers that agreed to let the club take the door and they worked exclusively for 50% of the drink tab. This might be a harder sell, but it does tend to spread the responsibility of promotion evenly. One last note to keep in mind when negotiating, you can usually plan on making a lot less per show if you plan on working long term. Comedy clubs typically pay me anywhere from $400 to $600 a show (for the exact same show corporate clients will pay $4000 for). How can I afford it? Well, when you figure I'm doing anywhere from 6 to 10 shows a week at the club that usually guarantees me no less than $2000 a week. If I'm doing that many shows, you better believe I'll make at least that much again over the course of the week in "extra" sales. Knowing I'll work the same club once or twice a year at that rate makes it worthwhile. When negotiating a weekly show, my goal is to stay here for 3 or 4 years. I don't really care if I make a fortune the first night out, as long as I allow for growth and work in a good promotion package.

Keeping all of this in mind, I approached the club owner with a simple offer. I'd work one of his smaller banquet rooms to begin with and as we grew we could expand it out. I agreed to take 1/2 of the door and a $200 guarantee. Basically, if 10 people walked in the door, the club would pay me $200. If 50 people came in, at $8 a person (which is what we're charging before the show), I'd still break even and get half of $400. Every person over 50 guarantees me either $4 (if they buy their tickets before the show) or $5 if they pay $10 at the door. This gives me a base income, and plenty of room to grow. I didn't tell the manager that I was planning to help him promote (that would only talk him into moving his advertising money to another one of the shows he has coming in weekly). I made it very clear that it was up to the club to do the promoting, and then, as soon as the contract was signed, I started working on a mailer to my 600 person mailing list (people who have seen my show and requested to be on my list) in this area. We opened our initial 6 show "trial" package on the 4th of July weekend, with plenty of outside competition and ended up with about 80 people. I took home $200 plus another $150 from the overage crowd. I sold 4 video tapes ($80) and 1 private stop smoking session ($100). That evening I ended up with $530. Not a fortune, but not bad for a start up project.

Two weeks into our trial, a guy who happens to own a club in a smaller town about 2 hours drive from here came up after a show to see if I'd be interested in doing a package at his club. We worked out a flat $500 a week deal (I'll still get the extras) for a trial 6 week run.

The Bricktown deal went okay, but not great. We grew to about 130 people, but ended up fighting a lot of other events and local happenings during the summer months. I knew coming in that I had a few Club shows scheduled for August, so we had already decided, before beginning, that we'd take a couple months off in August and Sept. We both agreed, however, that we were getting some good momentum, so we decided to start up again in the fall. At this point I'm scheduled to do a larger Halloween show, followed by weekly shows through the end of the year. Between the two clubs, I use up my Wednesday and Thursday nights and make $1000+. It frees up my weekends, so I'm plugging the corporate shows real hard now.

To promote these local shows, the first step is to make sure you keep track of everybody who sees your show. They're you're best customers. To this end, I offer a self hypnotic CD ($20 value) as a door prize at every show. I then keep the names and add them to my local mailing list. I also did a couple promos where I offered free show posters (which I sell for $10) to anyone who would fill out a demographic questionnaire. Stuff like "Where do you usually go for entertainment?, How often do you go out for shows?, Where did you hear about tonight's show?, Where do you usually look to find out what's going on around town? Are you interested in finding out about upcoming seminars and programs by Howard Morgan? What kind of programs would you like to find out more about?" Basically, I get all the information I need to promote seminars, upcoming shows, etc. to each person.

I also sent out a press release to the local paper that jumped on the chance to promote a different kind of show that was going to take place locally for an extended period of time. One of the local radio stations jumped on the chance to have me go in and hypnotize a couple of their people on the air. In fact, that interview was so successful, that a week later, when I was scheduled to do a public show in Virginia, I got a call from a station out there that had heard "through the grapevine?!" about the interview and wanted to know if I'd do one for them as well.

As far as I see it, my goal locally, this year, is to become a household name. If I can accomplish that, I can easily open up a successful local practice and more than make up for the sacrifice in seminar, private therapy and CD sales. To do this, I'm mounting up a pretty heavy local promotion package. I've become a marketing consultant for the local United Way (a job I did successfully for several years in Southern California, that quickly gives me a local reputation as a guy who gets things done). I'm also in the process of negotiating a deal with the local Chamber of Commerce (that also serves as our local Convention and Visitors Bureau) to do a show for one of their mixers in exchange for two years membership. The package is great! I do a show for the owners of all the local businesses (an audition?) and then I mingle for 2 years, handing out business cards and discussing doing shows and seminars for their company. I also get listed in the convention guide and get notices of any events coming to our town. And part of the deal is that I've agreed to "lower my rate" if they'll let Bricktown Brewery co sponsor the show. So basically, I'll do a show "brought to you by Bricktown Brewery" where I'm permitted to hand out flyers to everybody advertising my weekly shows there. Bricktown will be delighted, the Chamber will feel like I've done a great job of working with them, and I'll end up with a good steady local business.

I also went down to a local gym and traded a show for a years membership. Again, I'll be standing in front of 200 or so people who can all afford the luxury of a club membership (most are upper management or owners somewhere). Again I'll agree to do the deal if I can let Bricktown Brewery "sponsor" the event. Plenty of health conscious people (future seminars? Certainly several new clients). I'm also sure to get at least a couple corporate shows out of the deal, and I end up with a year's membership in the city's best club to boot!

Before opening night on Oct. 31, I'm running around town doing several college shows (again "sponsored by Bricktown Brewery") and even a mall show where I'll be allowed to solicit mailing list participants. In fact, by the time I'm through doing all these "sponsored shows", where I'll offer door prizes in exchange for addresses, my local mailing list, of people who have seen my show, should be up to 1500+. And I made a profit while doing it!

A couple weeks before the show I'll start hiring a couple high school students (at $5 an hour) to stand on street corners around Bricktown and hand out flyers advertising the upcoming shows. I'll also place a large 8 foot by 12 foot banner in front of the place each night I'm performing announcing "Here Tonight, The Hypnotic Comedy of Howard Morgan" followed by some bio material. That should help get some walk in traffic (it'll probably cost me $500 and pay for itself in two weeks).

Finally, I'm setting up CD sales racks in all the local health food stores, health clubs and even some medical clinics. Whether or not I sell anything isn't that important. I offer to set them up on consignment. Basically, if they agree to leave them on a certain spot, I'll agree to pay them so much per CD that gets sold, with no money down on their part. An easy sell that gets my name all over town as an "authority" in hypnosis.

The trick to making this work, if you're trying, is to plan it all out ahead of time and ride the momentum. Remember, the general public has a very short memory. You might have a feature article come out in the local paper and the local radio station may run you for a couple hours, still, a month from now you'll be a vague memory. You need to be sure you keep track of the people that see you (mailing list) and send out newsletters and special offers, etc. from time to time. Put it all together just before your show (notice how little we're hearing about the presidential elections coming up in Nov? Watch and see how busy it gets 2 weeks before the event).
In my case, when I was based in Los Angeles, I did a lot of trading with Food and Beverage Directors at local hotels where they'd get my show at a discount (or free) in exchange for them giving me a banquet room with meals once a year around thanksgiving. I'd then invite all the people that had hired me (local business owners, etc) to a special appreciation ball (usually held in November, around Thanksgiving, early enough to fill any empty holes in my holiday schedule). I'd also invite anybody that had come to more than one of my shows to be my guest (talk about feeling important! These guys usually became groupie types). Finally I'd invite any prospective clients (local agents, event coordinators, destination management companies, etc). I would usually find a local band or good Disk Jockey and allow him to bring in, say, 50 people, in exchange for 5 hours of his services (before the show dinner music, during the show show music and after show dance music). I'd have a balloon company do balloon arches and table settings in exchange for mention in the program and 40 or so people. We'd end up with quite a production for a crowd of maybe 400 which everybody would remember (and try to return to next year). I'm not sure if Oklahoma City will have a big enough clientele to pull one of these off, but maybe your town will.

Find out how local theater promotes themselves. You want to become a "theatrical event", so get yourself listed in the local directories and web sites. Get good at networking (I wrote a column a few months back about that) and start giving out business cards. It's up to you to let them know you're in town, and you need to do it quickly.

Whatever else you do, buy yourself a bulk mailing license and be sure to mail out a week or so before opening night to all the locals who have seen your show. If you can buy a local theater list and mail out a classy looking brochure to them, you should get a good response from that as well.

It takes work, but then that's why every corner in America doesn't have a hypnotist doing regular shows!

WORKING THE HOLIDAYS

Yes, believe it or not, this is the time to start getting organized for the holidays. I'm now starting to get several calls a week to fill the 6 holiday slots available this year (three weekends)in December before X-mas.

If you haven't already gotten yourself organized for the Holidays, or if you're tired of doing the $600 shows and want to make this Holiday season a big money maker, I thought I'd take a moment and walk you through the process I've used (and so have several of the entertainers I've managed in the past) quite successfully.

It's all about supply and demand. If only one person is interested in your show during the holiday season, you might as well accept whatever they want to pay you and be thankful you were able to stuff your stockings for free. If, on the other hand, you're interested in making the Holidays one of the financial highlights of your year, you need to create enough demand so you can ask for higher wages. Imagine the position you'd be in if, say, 15 different companies all wanted your show, but you only have 6 time slots available to offer. It shouldn't be too hard to ask for high wages.

Let's begin with some of the givens.

1) Every major city in the country will have upwards of 100 company holiday events going on this December.
2) Almost every one of them will try to fit it into one of the 6 Friday/Saturday time slots in December.
3) Every one of them is interested in making theirs a memorable/entertaining event.
4) Most of these events are being coordinated by secretaries and/or

committees that consider "putting it together" an intrusion into their already busy schedule.

5) The traditional (and readily available) entertainment used by most are exactly the same (i.e.band (or DJ), pictures, food and maybe, among the more creative, a comedian or singer.

If you think about the options available to them, and what you have to offer, it would be hard not to create a very large demand for your time. The process of putting it together consists of 4 basic steps. Of course, I'm assuming you have a good show. If you don't, I should probably warn you that it would be a good idea to stop everything and make sure you're going to be ready by December to really wow them. If not, you should probably store this article somewhere until you're ready to "expose yourself". Getting good clients to hire you, and then doing a second rate show, is a sure formula for performance suicide. Word will get around town quickly, and whatever you made this year will probably be the sum total of your long term income from performing. I regularly get calls from people who paid $600 for a show last year and feel they were jipped. They don't mind paying me $1500+, because they want to be sure they don't get stuck with someone whose show drags or is in poor taste.

If you're sure you're ready to "tackle the big time", here's the "secret 4 step formula":

1. YOU NEED TO PREPARE YOUR PROMO MATERIAL

If you're a working professional you probably already have most of what you're going to need. Be sure everything you have is first rate. Imagine you are bidding for these shows against Elvis Presley and Neil Diamond. Remember that long before the dicission maker ever meets you, or even gets to talk to you, they're going to see your material. Nowhere in the entire process is attention to detail more important than in your promo material. Your promo package should include, as a minimum:

a)A good Demo Tape; This is a working must. Do a good show and, if possible, hire a professional to tape it. Be sure they use High 8 or Super VHS (at a minimum) cameras, and if possible, have them use 2 cameras. One should be set up on a tripod from a good vantage point(covering the entire stage) and the other one should be hand held by a good camera man (or woman) who zooms in on individuals for reaction and moves around to get different angles shots. Later on you're going to edit out about 10 minutes worth of video from these two tapes, so you want it to be fast moving and interesting. Back before I bought my own equipment and started videotaping all my shows I usually expected to pay somewhere around $200 for a videographer to shoot the a show. If you sell copies of the video to people in the show, it's not hard to recoup a good portion of this (if I don't sell 8 to 10 videos at $20 each after a show, I know I did a so-so job).

If you can afford it, and you plan on doing several shows this year, it's well worth the investment to buy your own camera(s). I invested about $2000 in two cameras and usually bring along a person to run the second one. I'll pay my cameraman (usually a college student or unemployed friend) $35 a show, plus expenses (they love the free travel). The cameras paid for themselves within a month, and I probably average a good $100 profit per show. I've also accumulated close to 2000 videotapes of past shows to draw from for future demo tapes. I make a point of rating each, right after the show, so I know if it's a good show, worth using in promo material.

Once you end up with the masters, you then need to get them edited. Some of the bigger cities have editing booths you can rent and do it yourself (they usually have a technician show you how to use the equipment). This will probably cost you $35 or so an hour and take about 4 or 5 hours to complete (unless you know how to use the equipment and come knowing what you're going to put on your demo tape in which case you should be able to whip one out in no more than a couple hours). If you have a professional do it, it again saves time and makes things move faster if you ask to sit with him while he edits and you walk in with a written list of points in the show you wish to include.

A little trick you'll find very helpful here is to remember, while doing your show, to always repeat what is about to happen just before you wake your subjects up. Basically you can take as long as necessary to tell subjects that when they wake they're going to be celebrities, but just be sure you again repeat, as you're finishing off, "and at the count of three, when you awaken, you're going to know you are a celebrity at a special awards banquet...". Doing this makes editing much easier. Instead of trying to splice together some difficult setup so people watching the video will know what you're doing, each "bit" can be introduced as you get ready to do it.

As you put your video together, try to make it as fast moving and entertaining as possible. Watch MTV carefully, and write down concepts that make some person standing up there singing a song worth watching. Do you like the way they segway (slide from one scene to another)? Do you enjoy the camera shifting from one angle to another? What makes you feel entertained? Once you have a good idea how to do a rock video, then you need to move on to the real test. What makes television commercials sell? In particular, commercials for upcoming shows. Go see (or rent) a movie and take notes on what makes the "upcoming attractions" commercials interesting. Did you like the way the narrator talked before you saw any pictures? Do you enjoy listening to the same music playing low in the background through the entire commercial? This only works if you don't have music of your own in your show. If you do, you might pick out a "theme" music you start with and then fade into at the end of your tape, as you scroll up your name and number. How does the commercial grab your attention?

Take the time to learn from the pros. Back when I ran my agency, I really had to struggle to make it through all the "home video" type "demo tapes" I used to get. When I got a good one, you better believe it quickly jumped to the top of my list. Once you know what you want in your video, go do it.
And be sure you do it right. A good video is well worth thousands in future profit. If at all possible, keep it under 10 minutes. You can buy blank video tapes that are 10 minutes long pretty cheaply, which weigh less (for mailing) and look more professional than a 15 minute demo on a 90 minute tape). If it must go longer (remember, most of the people watching aren't going to be willing to sit through 20 minutes of advertising), they also sell 20, 30 and 45 minute tapes.

As you're finishing, be sure to scroll up a quick contact number a la "John Smith can be reached personally to discuss availability or bookings at: (555) 555-5555". Make a list of any agents you work with regularly, and make up masters including their numbers as well, with a caption to the effect of..."John Smith is available through Empire Entertainment at (555) 555-5555". Then be sure you make up one copy with no scrolled number at the end. That's for agents that call and ask for a demo tape (and will eventually make their own copies to send out).

Once you've canned several masters, have the editor copy them back on to your High 8 or Super VHS camera (if you own one), so you'll end up with a good master to make copies from in the future. Remember as you make copies, that every generation looses definition. This means that if you copy from your High 8 master on to a normal VHS tape and then you copy from this VHS tape to another, the third and forth generation will look pretty grainy and broken up. I make a point of never sending out anything that's more than 2 generations old. It makes for clean, crisp, television quality promo material.

Be sure you also print up some good looking labels to place on your video tapes. If you don't own a computer of your own, it's well worth it to go down to your public library (if they have Microsoft Word or Adobe Pagemaker) and make up some labels. Copy them to disk (very few libraries have color printers) and then go print them out, on Avery or Neato video tape blanks down at Kinkos (you'll pay $12 an hour plus $2 or $3 a copy (for each sheet of 10 to 15 labels), and probably be ready to leave in 30 minutes. Again, print up some with your phone number and a sheet or two for each agent you work with. Also print up some generic labels. Agents love it when you put their number on your material (it guarantees they'll mail it out long before the rest of the guys).

Once you've finished the editing process, be sure you have 30 or so video tapes with your number on it made and ready to mail out. I always buy decorative sleeves. I use black glossy sleeves with window cuttouts which allow the tapes to be seen from the top and cost me about 10 cents each at a bulk video distributor. You can usually find these guys in most larger cities by calling local videographers and asking where you can buy video sleeves. While you're there , be sure to pick up mailing boxes as well. You'll pay 10 to 25 cents each here as compared to $1.50 at the post office. Don't skimp. You're package may end up costing you as much as $10 each by the time you mail them out, but considering you're trying to sell a $1500 product, you can well afford it.

b)The second part of your promo package is the Bio Sheet. This is a list of where you've worked, what kind of credentials you have, etc. Theoretically this is a resume type sheet, in practice, I go out of my way to avoid making it look like a resume. I print up a folder type mailer (on an 11/17 sheet) that looks a lot like a classy newsletter. It has articles about "Why a Hypnotist is the right choice for your event", etc. and buried inside it lists shows I've done this year and quotes from satisfied clients (whenever a client says they like my show, I always answer with, "you know, it would really help me promote future shows if you'd be willing to put that in writing on your company letterhead". I've now got upwards of 100 letters in virtually every conceivable industry to list from). I also include the interesting facts about my background (over 150 television appearances nationally, 30+ years of captivation audiences around the world...etc.).

Personally I own a Hewlett Packard 1120 copier which lets me print 11 X 17 sheets easily and has more than paid for itself in shows I got from impressed agents and clients. If you don't own one, you can print on a normal 8 1/2 X 11 sheet and fold it booklet style to get away from the boring flyer look.

c) The third item you need to be sure to include with every promo package is a headshot. Make it fun to look at, but close enough to your face so they can see your personality. If you need to get some pictures taken, again, be sure to get them done professionally. Be sure also, to specify, before you begin, to the photographer, that you're an entertainer and would like a photo without their stamp on the back. Basically, those little "Alpha Photo" stamps on the back of pictures constitute a copyright mark and you won't be able to get them copied in bulk without permission from the photographer (and if he won't let you take the picture without the mark, he'll certainly not agree to let you copy it without charging you extra in the future).

A cheap way to get a good picture is to find an "Expressly Portraits" shop at a larger city near you. They usually do a basic sitting fee of $8 and then offer copies of any prints you like for $12. I always tell them ahead of time that I need to get a non copyrighted head shot, and have never yet had much problem convincing the manager to make an exception in my case. They are betting you're going to buy all 6 or so shots they take of you (and raise your cost to $100 or so), but if you plan on just walking out with a single show, you'll end up paying a total of $20 for a good studio sitting.

I've found over the years that most of their studios have at least one quality professional working for them. If you ask ahead of time, you can usually get that person to take your shot. An added bonus of going with Expressly Portraits is that they print your shot within an hour while you shop, so you won't have to wait a week or two to get it. Once you have the shot, order 100 or more copies. I use ABC photo out of Springfield, MO. They do a good job, get the shots out within 2 weeks, and can add copy on the bottom if you need it. They actually print out Litho copies which nowadays are as good as real prints (the photo process that used to be used by newspapers sometimes created a Morray Effect [slight distortion] when a copy of a copy was made. With computers on the scene, most papers have no problem printing from Litho copies).

d).The final item you'll need in your promo package is a good business card. Actually, no, you don't need a good business card. If you plan on working as a professional entertainer, you better be sure you have a GREAT business card. Remember this is the first thing someone sees (in most cases) that represents you. It's the item you give out when networking, and it's the one piece of your promo package that will be removed and placed somewhere else (usually among another 100 or more in a roladex somewhere). You better be able to stand out as someone who doesn't cut corners if you plan on asking for $1000 to cover 90 minutes of your time.

2. ONCE YOU'VE PUT TOGETHER YOUR PROMO PACKAGE

You'll need to figure out who to mail it out to. Remember, you've gone out of your way to spend money doing it right, so be selective about who gets it. You're going to go bankrupt quickly if you mail 1000 of these $10 babies out to every business in town. Go down to the largest public library in your town and ask for the Social Science area (smaller libraries usually mix this department into the Reference section). Ask a librarian for a list of local employers. Most towns have a yearly magazine, usually printed by the local newspaper or the Chamber of Commerce, that lists the larger employers in the area. You'll usually find a list of the 50 or (if you're lucky) 100 top employers in the area. Copy down their names, phone numbers and mailing addresses. If you don't recognize the name, you might also want to list what they do. Personally, when I'm marketing to a new town, I simply photocopy the entire page(s) that contains that list. Any employer that hires more than 50 people will probably be doing something for the holidays, and most employees will bring along a spouse, so you can plan on at least 100 people in the room.

Once you have your list, get on the phone and start calling. Ask the receptionist if the company usually does a holiday event (don't call it X-mas, some Jews find that offensive). If the secretary says yes, ask if she knows who's in charge of coordinating it. If she does, ask to speak to that person, if she doesn't, ask to talk to personel (they usually get saddled with this task).

Once you get through to the person in charge, find out when their event will take place (write it down, so you won't continue to solicit a show that's on a date you book elsewhere!). Ask if they normally do any form of entertainment at these events. Notice I'm not asking "would you like entertainment?" If you get a no to that question, anything else you say is simple harassment. If they say they do, tell her you do a Comedy Stage Hypnotic show and would like to mail her a free Demo tape and information about your show. If she says no, tell her you do a lot of holiday events, and if she's willing to consider adding entertainment to her evening, you'd like to send her a demo tape and info. Be sure to mark the people who haven't traditionally done entertainment, because it's going to take more effort to sell those. If they don't already have a budget allocated for entertainment, finding an extra $1000 or two might be an issue.

If the person asks how much you charge, tell them you usually ask for $1000 a show (or $1500 or, in some cases more. Personally, I regularly sell holiday shows at $2500 to $4000 each). If she doesn't cringe at the price, ask if that's going to be a problem. If it is, and you really want to do the show, you might consider negotiating some barter arrangements into the contract. I do it a lot. Not that long ago I negotiated with American Airlines to do a local show for the $200 they had budgeted for entertainment and
10 tickets for 2 (without expiration dates) good for anywhere around the country. That's 10 round trips anywhere. The next year, I simply tacked $400 to $500 on to every out of town show I had for airfare and pocketed a good $4000 from that show.

Along with your promo package, you should send out a cover letter that reminds the person of your conversation and casually mentions that considering you only have 6 open spaces for the holidays, these dates do go quickly and, unfortunately, you're forced, by policy, to honor the first person to send out a deposit to hold a date (I ask for 50% and never have a problem getting it).

Once you mail the package, call back in a week to make sure it arrived. This is a very critical point in the process. DON'T TRY TO SELL ANYTHING HERE. You're only purpose is to check and see if they got your package (and to casually, by hearing your name again, remind them to look it over). If this call takes more than 2 minutes, you'll probably be labeled as a nuisance that's going to continue to call and pester them and end up finding your $10 investment in a dumpster somewhere.

During this call, ask how long they feel it'll take to review your information. If they say it'll be several months, you might mention that you'll be glad to talk to them when they're ready, but chances are those dates will be booked within a month or so, so if they're interested they might want to consider talking it over sooner.

Finally, once you know when they expect to have looked over your information, casually mention, "well, if you don't mind, I'll call you on Friday the 9th to see how your meeting went". That'll put pressure on her to be sure to bring up your show during their meeting. Otherwise you'll get shuffled around until there's nothing else to talk about, two or three meetings from now. If you're talking to someone local, you might consider asking for a personal appointment. I often walk in and take 30 minutes to play the demo tape and discuss the event, and how I can make it more interesting.

3. THE FINAL STEP TO THE PROCESS IS TAKING ORDERS!

Simply call back and find out if they're interested. If you have an even halfway decent demo tape, several should be. Remember, you should have mailed out to at least 40 companies, which means it doesn't matter if they say no. In fact, you probably don't want to do a show for a company that isn't interested in considering you. You'll probably get treated badly and the audience will probably be disrespectful. With 40 packages sent (about $400 investment and maybe 4 or 5 hours of your time, after you're finished making up the promo package - which you're going to need to promote from now on), you are pretty safe assuming you'll sell all 6 slots. At $1000 each (if you charge less, you're either not interested in tightening up your show, or you're under selling yourself), that's $6000. You just made a $5600 proffit, which more than paid not only for your promo mailing, but even for the cameras and time involved in getting a quality promo package together. Have fun, make money, you can send commission checks to:

Howard Morgan.

Email:howardmorgan@witty.com
Web Site http://www.HowardMorgan.com/

Besides his 25+ years as a performer, Howard also lists, to his credit, 3 years as a Casting Director for Newport Pacifica Films out of Los Angeles, 2 years as a stunt coordinator and stunt man for the National

Association of Stunt Actors, and 18 years experience as an

Agent/Promoter with his own company, The Merlyn Arts Group. He's a writer, lecturer, actor and all around lousy cook.

Krisztina Hall

Using Language Patterns in Hypnosis

1 In my four years as a professional stage hypnotist I have had the opportunity to really learn the do's and don'ts of giving effective suggestions. You might think that what you say to the subject doesn't matter, but let me tell you it does. Remember, the subconscious mind often interprets thinks quite literally and more simply than the conscious mind.

2 In giving suggestions, your objectives are to: 1) make it really clear what you want the subject to do; and 2)have the subject want to carry out the suggestion that you give him/her.
When giving a suggestion to the subconscious mind you must realize that the subconscious mind is more readily accepting of a positive suggestion than a negative one. When I say positive or negative suggestion, I am NOT referring to whether it is good or bad BUT how it affects their mind.
A good example of a negative suggestion is: "don't think the color blue." Automatically, the subject will think the color blue because this is the only information their brain has to work with. This is the opposite of what you probably meant. First they think of blue then they have to "NOT" do it. Many people will think of blue with an X over it or think of a different color afterwards.
Another way to have someone "not think the color blue" is to say it as a positive suggestion: "think the color red." This way the subject knows exactly what to do and there is no disputing what you want. They will think of a specific and different color.
However, there are uses for negative suggestions. For example: if you have a subject that is a polarity responder. A polarity responder is a person who will almost always do the opposite of what you say. If you say "black" they think "white," if you say "white" they think "black." In this case, you could suggest to him/her "Don't relax

now" or "You can't go into hypnosis." As a result, they will cooperate and go into hypnosis.

The key is to make sure you say what you want them to do rather than what you don't want. For example, it will be easier for a subject to "see the audience naked" than to "see the audience with no clothes on." People will understand both versions but it is easier for them to follow a positive suggestion.

3 So how do you make it easy for subjects to carry out your suggestions?

Early in my career, I found out that one of the words that should never be used on stage, is the word "TRY", unless you really want the subject to fail at something. I still hear a lot of stage hypnotists who use this word many times a night.

When you say to a subject "Come up here and TRY to get hypnotized," you pre-condition the subject to fail at getting hypnotized. The word TRY renders failure. For example, when you tell a friend, "I'll try to be there," what is the likelihood of you showing up? Not very likely, is it? Whereas if you tell your friend "I will do my best to be there," you are very likely going to make it. Do you notice the difference?

The word "TRY" puts doubt in your subject's mind and actually sends them the message that they are likely to fail. My guess is that when a hypnotist is using the word "TRY" a lot, this is an indication that THEY are not confident in their ability or that they have doubts as to whether the suggestion will work.

However, if you really WANT your volunteer to fail at something, use the word "TRY". Let me give you an example: On stage, when I give my induction, I say to the volunteers: "And as you sit there... think of your hands... and as you do... they become like lead weights... So heavy that the harder you TRY to lift them... the heavier they get." Now, if I had said that they can't lift the hands, they would have felt challenged to prove me wrong. By emphasizing the word "TRY," I am indirectly and powerfully suggesting that they will fail at lifting their hands. If you want them to fail, use TRY. If not, leave it at home and speak with confidence.

4 I could talk about the benefits of learning to use language patterns for a long time, but I won't because I could end up writing a novel :-). I just want you to see how using language effectively can really

influence the success of your show. You can use even use language to get rapport with your audience and volunteers, to make subjects want to volunteer for your show, plus much more.

5 If you would like to know more about using language patterns, please feel free to e-mail me with your questions.

Canada's Original and Best Female Stage HypnotistI am available for bookings across the US and CanadaDrop me a line:_ info@FemaleHypnotist.com and visit my web page:http://www.femalehypnotist.com/.

Geoffrey Ronning

How to Book Corporate Hypnosis Shows

- So, why are so many people so interested in working this market? First
  you have an abundance of prospects that need your service. Any company or association event is considered a corporate show. This event may be a trade show, a sales meeting, an annual dinner, a holiday (don't make the mistake of calling it a Christmas) event, appreciation dinner, a bi-yearly retreat, etc. Any event that is comprised of professional in a related way (company or association) is considered a corporate event!

- Now how many of these are available in your market? More then you can ever work... there are literally thousands available in my market!

- Where you are located may be different, but rest assured that wherever

  you are located, there is an abundant amount of business. And, because the corporate market has a need for quality entertainment, you will find that travel expenses are a common necessity they are willing to absorb for your high quality show. Travel will take you outside your local market and introduce you to even more business. So your local market is only the beginning, your starting point.

- So here you are thinking (or at least you should start to realize) every group, be it an association or company, has a potential need for your

  services. Think about it. Open up the phone book and begin to understand how much potential business is out there. It is staggering how much business there is available to you, and for the most part, your prospects are required to purchase entertainment. Your service is not optional, it is required!

- What is needed to be successful in corporate entertainment is to have a

  system in place to work this market correctly.

- The first step is to size up your competitors, the other types of entertainment available to the corporate world. Don't get discouraged
  when you do this! Remember, the uniqueness of your hypnotic show makes it attractive for many corporate groups.

- Your main competitors for the headline entertainment will be magicians,
  comedians, murder mysteries, bands and casino nights.

- Let's look at these competitors more closely. Please understand I love all artists and appreciate others talents, but I'm talking about how to service the customer and obtain the booking. You will need to understand your strengths and weakness as well as those of each of your competitors.

- Below are the general thumbnail views of prospective meeting planners.
  These comments are based on thousands of conversations I have had with clients and prospective event planners over the years. Remember, these our the general feelings by your prospective clients about the following competitors you have.

- 1. Magicians are passé. Magic is often times viewed as "children's" entertainment by many corporations. I know this is not true, but it is many prospects perception. In addition, many corporations have had

numerous magicians in the past and want something different! That is
you.

- The strength of magicians is they are safe entertainment.

- Please understand I'm not voicing my opinion, but that of your prospective client. Personally, I enjoy magic .

- 2. Comedians are risky. That is the perception of many corporations because unfortunately for the comedians, and fortunately for us, some
ignorant comedians have taught them that! Comedians are a different
group. The pros understand the business but there are so many amateurs and they work so cheap that they hurt their own market. The corporate market is not where you want to be doing any racial or sexist material. They require clean, non- offensive entertainment!

- The strength of comedians is everybody enjoys laughing.

- 3. Murder mysteries are unique. In my experience with clients, the murder mystery sounds like a lot of fun and is an attractive option for
their entertainment. Unfortunately though, smaller groups are typically not satisfied with the murder mystery and end up sorry if they go with
it . The basic concept is great! But sometimes delivering on the concept is difficult.

- The strength of murder mysteries are they are unique, novel.

- 4. Bands are loud and not diverse enough. That is the general attitude. Many corporations feel "safer" with a DJ Besides that bands have less
repertoire then a DJ. DJ's can play a variety of music, interact, get people participating and keep the evening on course and they don't

typically take breaks.

- The strength of bands is they can be a marquee name that their audience
  is familiar with.

- 5. Casino nights are making a comeback, but very similar to the murder
  mysteries, the results are often disappointing to the clients. Many grow
  bored gambling, particularly with money that is not real. More importantly there is no coherent group experience.

- The strength of casino nights is they can be exciting and novel.

- Those will be your main competitors, now lets look at what your offering.

- Your Hypnosis Show

- Now, a Hypnosis Show is unique! You are providing an audience participation show that will have their entire audience laughing and enjoying their program. They will be able to watch their friends, family and co-workers up on stage. There is no other type of entertainment that is as exciting or intriguing to watch! Everybody will enjoy your type of entertainment!

- Look at the above strengths of each of your prospective competitors. Most all of their strengths is a strength of your act! You have the majority of them all covered plus much more.

- You are so far ahead of the others that as long as you have a system in place to generate interest you will have a full schedule of gigs! We know, corporate entertainment is where the bulk of our business comes from.

- About 2 years ago we relocated from Nevada. We basically had to restart our business in this market and have been very successful doing so. We are now the premier stage hypnotist in the market and we are making an executive living with the system we put into place. It relies on a systematic approach that we have used for years, one that has benefited from constantly tweaking and testing to increase its booking power. If your not constantly testing your methods consider starting, it will increase your business.

- So, let's get down to the exciting fun and talk about the steps necessary to book the corporate gigs. These are the steps from beginning to end we use.

- 1) Create prospects list. You need to determine specifically who your prospects are. By this I mean you must create a list of companies, their addresses, company size and the contact person who hires entertainment that potentially will book your show. There are many ways to do this including:

- a) cultivating leads from the phone book
  b) purchasing a corporate event planners list
  c) getting a copy of your states directory from American Business Directories
  d) getting a specialty lists from a list provider
  e) referrals from previous shows

- 2) Create interest in your Hypnotic Show.

- There are 5 ways to create interest in your service from your corporate

  prospect:
  a) phone
  b) mail
  c) advertising
  d) internet
  e) fax
  Each has its benefits and its weaknesses.

- 3) Provide documents that sell your program.
  a) brochure
  b) sales sheets
  c) video

- These do the job of representing your show. If you know how to create them, your business will explode.

- 4) Book your show.
  a) follow up
  b) professional courtesy
  c) Service and Sale. There is no room for pushy manipulation techniques when dealing with corporations. The service and consulting approach will book the shows.
  5) Paperwork.
  a) send out the agreement immediately
  b) bank the deposit and enjoy the benefits from proper investing!

- 6) Performance
  a) work the show
  b) create at event spin-off business.
  Experiment with techniques to create the spin-off business at your completed shows. The main technique we now utilize is very powerful, the people we have taught this to have tripled their referrals! This is so good....my wife even was caught off guard with it the first few times I used it. A friend, a stage hypnotist from Cleveland attended 4 of our shows in June of this year and could not believe the leads we generated. He had learned the technique in our booking corporate programs but had not put it into play. He is now!

- 7) Thank You's
  a) follow up and demonstrate your professionalism and
  b) creates after event referrals

- Those are the steps. If you follow them logically you will have more business than you know what to do with.

- Next issue we will look at the specifics of finding your prospects. We will talk about the different techniques, different roadblocks, costs and the numerous options you have at your disposal. But don't wait till next issue. Follow the above steps and go out and get booking!

- The Holiday season is booking up now and you can fill your calendar using the above steps in no time! Print the steps out and follow them logically.

- Go get those corporate holiday shows! Write me with your success stories. I would love to hear from you.

- For more information about the business of Stage Hypnosis including promoting, booking, increasing your business, pro issues and a free Stage Hypnosis E-Zine visit:

http://www.stagehypnosiscenter.com

Boost your Business and have the good fun,

Geoffrey Ronning

Geoffrey Ronning
Corporate Booking Continued

- Welcome back to booking corporate shows. This session we are going to cover the specifics of finding your prospects. We will talk about the
different techniques, roadblocks, costs and the numerous options you
have at your disposal.
The first thing we need to ask ourselves, is what constitutes a good prospect? A good lead has to have the following:

- 1. The name of the company
  2. The name of the person(s) who plans the company events
  3. The mailing address
  4. The number of people in the company and the size of events that are planned

5. What time of year they use entertainment at their company events
-

holiday parties, sales retreats, etc.

- Surprisingly, the phone book can be the best place to start building
your list of leads if you can invest the time to call each business and
get the above information. This is also the most inexpensive route to

cultivate leads. There are thousands of listings in the phone book for

different businesses. What you have to be careful of is that you
aren't
wasting your time, promotional material and money on one man
operations that won't be able to use your services. The best way to
utilize the phone book is to go through and pick out businesses that
you recognize.
It is also helpful to look at the ads that are in the phone book. As a
general rule, the larger the ad, the more money and employees the
company may have.

- If you just go through the phone book and enter all of the businesses
in
you data base, you don't know the number of people in the company
or whether that company has a budget for your services. Doing a
mailing off of a list cultivated from the phone book may result in a
huge waste of time and money if you don't call and get the above
information and make your prospect list complete. If you have the
time to invest to make the calls and get the information the phone
book can provide you with an outstanding prospect list.

- Another option is the American Business Directory for your state and
any other state you may be interested in working. These volumes
contain the businesses in the state you are interested in, but also give
you the specifics of the businesses such as the number of employees
and their financial information. It also breaks the businesses in your
state down by profession, by city, major employers in your area, and
manufacturers by city and product. This is an extremely helpful tool
in helping you generate leads. The American Business Directory
now comes on a disk or CD as well so that you can put it directly
into your computer. This is an excellent starting point to the

beginnings of a successful data base, and it can be purchased for $300.00-$600.00 when you purchase the book and CD. When using this list, remember to keep it up to date and make note of any changes in the addresses and contact names.

- You now have a great data base for businesses in your target area. Most of the businesses will use an event or meeting planner when planning
their company functions, whether it is the sales retreat or the company
holiday party. You want to make sure you are reaching the event planners as well in your area so that they are aware of your services and can suggest you to their clients.

- Again, this can be done through the phone book, but again, this can be a waste of time and money. Some meeting planners may specialize in
children's shows or Tupperware parties, not corporate work, which is
where you want to target yourself. The best source for corporate meeting planners is, oddly enough, the Directory of Corporate Meeting Planners. It is published yearly and will give you the data to contact key decision makers and an alphabetical list of companies and meeting planners that you want to target to offer your services.

- Another great resource for acquiring a list of meeting planners is through MPI, or Meeting Planners International. Usually each area has their own chapter, and information about them can be found on the web.

- Any association that you join, such as the Chamber of Commerce, is going to provide you with leads. If you are interested in playing casinos, join a gambling association. This is an excellent way to fine tune your mailing list to a the market you are interested in marketing to.

- Many companies, or a mailing list broker, specialize is "specialty lists." You tell them the criteria of what type of list you want, and they will supply it.

- We highly recommend keeping all of your data bases separate. The
  information that you are going to send to a corporation is not the
  same
  information that you would send to a event/meeting planner.

- Your best source for potential leads are the people that have seen your
  show before. Many times after a show, your audience members will
  come up and ask for a business card. It is fine to give them one, but
  also get their information as well. After you fill their requests for
  either promotional material or a phone call, add them into
  whichever data base fits them. If they are from a corporation, then
  go ahead and put them into your data base with other corporations.
  If they are an
  event/meeting planner, put them in that data base.

- The fail proof method that we use to generate leads at the end of a
  show
  can be found in the program, "How to Book Corporate Shows with
  Your Hypnotic Entertainment." We rarely walk away from a
  corporate show with less than 5 new leads.

- Using these resources you can put together some great data bases, now

  lets discuss what roadblocks you may run up against.

- The first roadblock, believe it or not, is our economy at this time.
  The economy is great and there are a lot of jobs available out there!
  People are not staying in one job for any great period of time as they

  can always find one that will pay them more. This plays havoc when
  you are trying to keep your data bases current!

- It is very possible that you can talk to a person one week, and the next
  week they will not be at that company. You will find that your
  mailings will come back with notes that a certain person is no
  longer at that company, or you may receive a fax on it. Always try
  to get the name of the person that has taken your old contacts place.
  Keeping the data bases updated is a constant job and one that you
  cant let slip,
  especially if you are using the data bases to their fullest potential

and you are always working your lists.

- This roadblock can also be a huge bonus to you. As people move from

    company to company, they give you the opportunity to perform for
    their new company, which increases your data bases and income.
    This recently happened to us! Out of the blue a woman who used us
    at her company holiday party last year called us for the holiday
    party this year for her new company.

- Another roadblock is modern technology. As wonderful as it is, we
    have found one particularly annoying drawback. If you purchase a
    CD or disk containing lists of business and meeting/event planners,
    there is a
    chance that they disk or CD may "expire." This means that you
    cannot use the CD or disk after a certain date, usually one year after
    you
    purchase it, requiring you to purchase a new and updated version.
    We
    have had this happen to us, so a word of advice: when buying a CD
    or
    disk, ask a sales representative from the company if it will expire
    after a certain amount of time. Another good idea is to load the
    whole
    disk on your computer all at once.

- The last roadblock you can run into, except when using the phone
    book, is money. All of the lists and books available out there have a
    cost,
    and it us usually not very cheap. If you afford to get a good list from

    a list broker or any other of the resources we have mentioned, you
    will have a great beginning to growing your business and your
    income.

- So, as you can see you have many options to creating a list of prospect

    or prospective clients. In general the lower/free ways to go are
    going
    to provide you with more work to do on your own, the lists you

purchase will eliminate that work for yourself. You need to determine what is the best route for you at this time. In either case, you will have the prospects you need to book your show! Go gather those leads and let's start booking!

- Next session we will cover the methods used to get those prospects interested in your hypnotic show and the benefits and drawbacks of each method.

- This article is an excerpt from the program: "How to Book Corporate Shows with Your Hypnotic Entertainment."

- It has been edited to provide the maximum amount of information while protecting our markets from competitors.

- In other words, due to the internets indiscriminate availability, certain powerful techniques could not be revealed here that are presented in the volume available to purchasers of the whole program. his way we can control the distribution of our actual program and make it available only in markets outside of ours.

For more information visit:
http://www.stagehypnosiscenter.com

"Hypnosis On Tour"
By Hypnotist Marc Savard

The "Joy and Pain" of touring with a full production are exactly that. I currently tour with approximately 6000 lbs of Sound and Lighting Equipment, Props, Tour Bus, Production Crew, and many other 'special effects'. I consistently get involved in conversations with other hypnotists and entertainers about the value involved with such a production. Do the headaches outweigh the kick-ass performance? In my opinion, these are what I consider the pros & cons; you make your own decision from there.

Pros:

The second an audience member walks into a venue that my production gear is set-up in, they immediately separate my performance as a high quality act as opposed to a performance in an openly lit area such as a gymnasium or hall. The performance has not yet started, yet I am better in some people's eyes. This may or may not be true, but at this point we can all agree it is irrelevant. Like Gil Boyne would say, "What is expected tends to be realized." Give the people the expectation of a HUGE show; they will walk away having seen a HUGE show. This also applies to what you wear, your opening announcement, your diction, etc. These all give the audience an idea as to what they should expect. Even more importantly, it gives the buyer an idea. That is where I noticed the biggest advantage of touring with gear. You can charge more. You get what you pay for. Now don't misunderstand me when I say that I expect people to pay for production, and that is how we determine price for a show. You'd better be as good if not better than what you told the buyer you were. The show is the show. Production is used to ENHANCE the performance, not to replace the hypnotist's weaknesses.

Cons:

Cost and Labor. Cost is cost. You get nothing for free and buying cheesy DJ effects does not cut it. I currently carry an extensive lightshow including and not limited to 8 automated lights that are fully programmable and run by a desktop PC. The lighting cues are responsible for scene changes to general atmosphere and everything in between. The sound system I carry is VERY punchy and has got crystal clear sound with LOTS of juice pushing it. Shure Beta 58 wireless microphones and all. Too much crap to even bother naming. Cost is the least of your worries.

Labor, Labor, Labor. Union technicians are Union technicians. Enough said. In a theatre where your performance is stationary is one thing. But touring with Union techs, is a completely different ball game. So you decide to tour with punks that can operate some sound and lighting gear. You begin to get unqualified people, your performance reflects it, and in turn defeats the purpose of why you got the production equipment in the first place. Cheap labor turns out to be a babysitting course. It takes a long time to find the right people that care about the product you put on, and WANT to be a part of it. Once you do, keep them happy, and keep them around. The production value increases, and then the gear is worth it. I've been lucky enough to find that a few years ago, and now my performance reflects it. My team and I are exactly what I have been looking for, and have been touring with a very successful stage show for the past 5 years. This came at a price. It takes a while to get everything the way you expect it. The headaches and problems that can arise can and will last a long time. Is it all worth it? 5 years ago, I would have said No. Today I say yes. I suppose I can compare to the people that say, "Money is not the most important thing in life." Aren't they usually the people that have the money?

CollegeBooker

by
Sam Hawley

When approaching a college booker find out two things:
A- Is this the buyer (who can get a check cut and sign a contract) or
B- Is this the college associate who fields the phone calls and "shops price" from an outside desk and lets the buyer know who they think is cool?

For A go onto the big sell. Tell them the six W's and H.

1.WHO you are and WHO you've presented for. Give specifics and numbers. Ask for their FAX number and offer to FAX letters of reference if they'd like to see them. Put your material on disk or better yet CD ROM or DVD. I have a source for that if you are interested. (PS they are cheaper to mail out and make YOU look cutting edge.)

2.WHAT it is PRECISELY that you do (For a great many bookers the word mentalist is lost. Say Hypnotist or Psychic Entertainer they can attach meaning to that.). Keep this short and to the point. (Just the facts or FAX ma'am)

3.WHERE you have presented this type of show and for HOW MANY. Most college shows are given for handfuls of curious or non-socially active (read homebody) type students and the number count! The last show I gave for a local college was well over two hundred and fifty students. That sounds small I guess but the next highly attended show packed in a whopping 68 kids and twelve of them were there because they were pledges and were holding the fans for their big brothers/sisters. Did I mention that the college had an enrollment of less than 1200 students?

4. WHEN do they usually need a great act to either draw extra media attention or give prospective students and their folks a great family show? Mom and Pop days or Orientation days are great times to pitch for the local schools. They have no idea how to promote this so offer to be a gangbuster for them. If you're a reader then offer to work with the campus security to draw students into "staging areas where they can be picked up by their "guides" for the tours and registration. Move them into less crowded areas when one area gets too packed or draw them into the lunchroom for food. Recently I was booked to do palmistry and "fun fortunes" (remember the name as there will be a test later) at the University of Tennessee (huge school). I had such a group of parents gathered around that the kids were having to elbow their way in. I moved out under a tree in the center of the dorm quad and sat under the shady branches causing the rest to sit in a circle around me. Elizabeth Riggs (John's lovely wife saw this and cracked up. She said that it looked for all the world like Bible shots of Jesus and his street sermons. (Remember that SHE said it not me!)

5. WHY they should book you rather than BARFO the human regurgitate for their Sweetness Party. Have a list of the top three reasons that they NEEDED your show. Only Three. (Any more and you're bragging.)

6. WHOA NELLIE why am I soooo expensive? Because you need to know that colleges are just full of folks who look at gigs being offered and say (insert HAAVAHD accent hear) " Well Muff, he khant be ahll that good, he willing to work for $_____." Folks it's happened to me believe it. I once offered a show to the same local college where I am now being booked three years in advance at what I thought would be a fair rate $600. They took a pass for a magician who drew 31 kids and cost them 950 bucks plus travel and hotel. Their cost per student $35.50. I sell them my show for $1250 and (I live here so they get the whole enchilada for one rate) and

their cost is only $5.00! Which one do you think they want. Prove the cost with the math it works. (BTW I do ask for and get travel and lodging expenses for the out of town gigs)

7. HOW do they get me. They get a 15% discount for booking me within ten business days of the initial call. This gets them motivated to book quickly.

I also offer an extra five percent if they have a local (to them) school call and book a show in concert with them. The other school gets a slight break on the price as I am already there and I get to double dip with a built in referral.

For B's --find out A's name in casual conversation and call them later.

Sorry about the extreme length but I have been really quiet for a while and needed to catch up. I have several other sure fire methods for doing killer college shows so if you want more let me know.

Email <u>Myndmage@aol.com</u>

NOTE = That now concludes the excellent contributions from James Szeles "Hypno-Stage"

Give Your Hypno Show A Ninja Flow

Author: Professional Entertainer Jimmy Graham

(25 Year Entertainment Industry Veteran & President of PartyMix Entertainment Services. Providing Hypnotist, Mentalist, Motivational Speaker, Singer, Musician, MC & DJ Services For Corporate, Fundraisers, Festivals & School Events)

Full Time 6 Figure Income Entertainer & Entertainment Coach

No B.S. Real World Entertainment Career Coaching That Works!

Website - www.getlivegigs.com **Get Live Gigs.com**

I don't wan't to admit it but after years of being a professional touring comedy stage hypnotist, I have a real hard time convincing myself to go see another hypnotist's show anymore.

As one who always went out and supported a fellow entertainer, whether it was musician freind or a comic at an open mic night, I love live entertainment, want to see great entertainment and it feels good just to get the hell out of the house!

I remember the first time I saw a Mike Mandell hypnotist show back in the late 90's. I was amazed seeing people get hypnotized and had never laughed so hard in my life.

Since that time until I became a touring pro, I had only seen two more shows and the entertainers I saw are legendary stage hypnotists still working today, Sailesh and Tony Lee.

Thier shows set the bar for what I considered to be an entertaining hypnosis show.

Once I decided to become a professional stage hypnotist, I met and trained with my first mentor, Attila J. Khun.

His shows were astounding!

To watch him standing on stage in front of almost 4000 people at the Yukon Days Festival in Alberta, completely in command, dropping volunteer after volunteer instantly and then producing a show that held everyone's attention for 90 minutes was simply inspirational.

Then I travelled to Las Vegas and saw a few more hypnosis shows.

That's when I began to notice that all stage hypnosis shows were not equally entertaining.

One of the hypnotist shows I got to see was Marc Savard.

As of this writing, he performs nightly at the Hard Rock Cafe and his show was non-stop entertainment and a total theatrical performance from start to finish.

The other guy (who will remain nameless) also performed regularly on the strip but his show was not that impressive.

As time went on, I would hear about a hypnotist coming thru my area and would go out to support the show.

Even though some of these hypnotists were names that I recognized, it became evident that there are hypnotists that do shows and then there are entertaining hypnosis shows.

So what's the difference?

In my mind, it's one word... FLOW.

Great hypnosis shows flow like a Broadway play.

From the opening curtain to the closing bow, there must be a natural rhythm to the show and natural progression that leads to a climactical conclusion.

There must be drama, emotion and suspense and scenarios that provoke the drama, emotions and suspense.

There should be some twists and thematic events that re-occur once or twice in the show when the audience least suspects it.

And when it's all done, the audience should be able to take home both memories of the most fun they've ever had and a positive message as well.

So how do we create a masterful stage hypnosis show?

Step One

First of all, one must realize that there are two audiences you are playing to.

The audience in front of you and the people that sign your paycheck.

A great show is one that the organizer will be proud of while still being entertaining to the audience.

Case in point, unless your doing a fratboy house party where their paying you to make a volunteer run around believing thier pants are on fire, stay away from ANY controversial skits.

Some of the audience members of Fortune 100 and 500 companies I work for may want to see this too, but I know the event organizor absolutely does not, so to ensure re-bookings and great referrals, my shows are squeaky clean.

Step Two

To have an entertaining show, you must BE ENTERTAINING.

From the moment you walk on stage, all eyes are on you.

Most people decide within five seconds whether they like you or not and if you fail this most important first test, you will have an uphill battle to create an entertaining show.

You must exude confidence from the very start. The best way to do this is SMILE.

Smiles create confidence within you and project confidence to the audience.

When you launch into your pre-talk (for those of you starting out, this is a brief explanation of what is about to happen in your show), you MUST be funny.

Unless your doing a highschool, college or fair (where all you need to say is "C'mon Up"), you should construct a 2-5 minute comedy routine that is disguised as a pre-talk.

Your in the "make with the funny" business, so it's imperative to get your audience laughing and loosened up as quickly as possible.

If you find yourself unable to write funny jokes into your pre-talk, find a local comedian to work with to help you.

Step Three

Design your show to FLOW.

Let's face it, 90% of all the working stage hypnotists do the same ten to fifteen skit ideas in their show so if your just starting out, don't worry, you won't get sued for doing the same routines.

It's like watching your hometown bar bands, they all play the same top-40 hit songs as well.

Why?

Because those are the songs that the audience reacts to best.

It's the same with hypnosis shows. I still do the age old "See the Naked Hypnotist" skit because EVERYONE loves it!

The most important difference between hypnotists doing the same skits and hypnotic entertainers who use these skit ideas to create a great flowing show is this...

It's the SPIN you put on the skit idea.

I do the "Naked Hypnotist" bit, but I have a whole twist to it. I do the "Beach Skit" but there is a completely unexpected twist to it. I do a "SuperModel/BodyBuilder" skit but there's a surprise ending to it.

This is where drama and suspense come into play. There must be a payoff or conclusion to your skits.

The best way to come up with the payoff ideas is to ask yourself "why" or "what if"?

If you have someone lose their bellybutton... big deal!

So they lost thier bellybutton, your audience will be left with... "so what".

Ask yourself, "what happens next AFTER they lost thier bellybutton?"

That's when the funny will start to come out in your shows.

Are you starting to get the idea?

Everything old is new again if you take it in a whole new direction.

Step Four

Now that you have your skit ideas and put a twist on them, it's time to

FLOW.

Whats your main theme?

Is it a vacation? A cruise? A day at a festival?

What kind of adventure are you taking your subjects on?

Whatever it is, if you structure it properly, your audience will get it even if you don't actually tell them.

So many stage hypnotists I've seen simply suggest a scenario to thier subjects, let it play out and then end it by saying..." and the scene fades.. SLEEP!"

Their show is simply a series of one act skits with sleep periods in between.

This becomes as entertaining as watching paint dry.

You do not need to put everyone out after each skit. Once their hypnotized, they'll stay in hypnosis as long as you want them too if you know proper induction and deepening techniques.

Think about how you can transform from one skit into the next that makes sense and builds upon your theme.

Whatever your theme is, there must be a beginning, middle and climactic end like all good movies.

Here is a VERY BASIC example of a plot outline...

Beginning

Your plot should always start off on a happy note like enjoying being at the beach, on vacation, etc.

Middle

Now maybe there is a movie theater close by that the subjects can go to. They start watching a movie that has funny, sad, scary then embarrassing moments in.

End

Then they go to a concert and get onstage to play with their favorite band and meybe even become the stars of the band.

Now, think of all the scenarios that could happen within these three sections.

What could happen to the subjects while they are on the beach?

What kind of scenes would they see at the movie? What else would they do at the movies?

What could happen on the way to the concert? What would happen at the concert? What would happen after the concert that would be very memorable for the entire audience to close your show?

Now, how can you make each situation seemlessly flow from one skit to the next?

Watch hit TV comedy shows. You will get plenty of ideas.

Step Five

Once you have developed your show, always do the same show!

Don't keep switching it up.

Major touring rock bands do exactly the same show night after night so that it flows seamlessly.

You should do the same until you start working for repeat clients or are working back to back shows at the same venue. That's the only time you should switch it up.

By doing the same show, you will develop a comedic sense of timing that will start showing up on it's own.

Remember to use the lines that continually make people laugh because if they worked in Manitoba, they will probably work just as well in South Dakota.

You'll also probably make mistakes that will be funnier than your original ideas. If so, KEEP THEM!

My best material in my shows are from ideas that totally went off track.

Keep whatever makes people laugh and lose what doesn't.

Step Six

Your Closing Thoughts.

You want to end your show on a high note and leave your audience wanting more. They might want you to keep going but don't.

When I first started, my 90 minute shows sometimes went 2 1/2 hours because I was having so much fun.

The problem was, I didnt notice the audience starting to lose interest around the 2 hour mark!

Once I was finished, all they wanted to do was get home.

If your show is 90 minutes, leave yourself about 5 minutes to give your "post-talk".

You want to keep it short but informative about your hypnosis programs for sale and souvenir DVDs of the show they just witnessed.

This is the moment you want to transform from "funny guy" to "Trusted Authority" and promote the benefits of your hypnosis products.

Personally, I also convey a message of self improvement and setting higher standards for one's life for the betterment of themselves and their families, but that's just me.

Step Seven

Now plant yourself as quickly as possible at the exit and greet everyone!

Shake their hand, give them a contact card or better yet, give them something free in exchange for their contact information.

The more people you build up in your data base, the faster and larger your fan base and stage hypnosis business will become!

Display all of your audio hypnosis programs and sell them at a discount for multiple copies.

Make sure you get their contact information and follow up!

Step Eight

Now for the most important part of your show.

Make sure you thank the people who hired you!

Leave them with a great impression of you and send a thank you card a week later with a DVD copy of their show as a gift to them.

This will go a long way in your re-booking practice!

If your now interested in learning more strategies to increase the BUSINESS of your "show", contact me at getlivegigs@gmail.com

Get Live Gigs

Discover How To Get Top Paying Shows
& Become The Go-To Choice For Entertainment!

www.getlivegigs.com

Hypnotherapy and Stage Hypnosis Are Not Alone

David John Pack

I began studying hypnosis in 2008. I have never really stop learning hypnosis since then, even though I have done a fair share of hypnosis. I believe that all branches and/or theories of hypnosis benefit from learning what the others know.

Website: **DavidJohnPack.com**

Email: **hypnosis@davidjohnpack.com**

Get some of my hypnosis mp3s for free at DavidJohnPack.com/free (NOTE: You will have to sign up to my newsletter to get access to the code to get them for free.)

Types of services/products/courses I offer: I offer mp3s for self-improvement as well as for fun. I do stage shows. At the time of this book being printed, I do not offer any 'formal' courses, but will be selling short ebooks on various hypnosis technics and such soon.

When I was first introduced to hypnosis in 2008, I thought all hypnosis rounded down into two types: therapy and stage. As I continued in my studies of hypnosis, I ran into uses of hypnosis that didn't fall into either of these two categories very well. Over time I've come to find a third type that tends to receive less attention from both the stage and therapy communities. This type is recreational hypnosis.

Before going farther into looking at recreational hypnosis, I'll give a quick summary of the three different types of hypnosis I'll discuss.

Therapy/Beneficial Hypnosis

The intent of this type of hypnosis is to help a person to make permanent, positive changes in their life.

Examples of Therapy/Beneficial Hypnosis:

Overcoming Fear

End Addiction

Lose Weight

Form a Habit

Stage/Street/Show Hypnosis

The intent of this type of hypnosis is to entertain the viewers, crowd, or audience with hypnotized subjects, (or feats of hypnosis).

Examples of Stage/Street/Show Hypnosis:

Hallucinations (positive or negative)

Make Believe

Cluck like a chicken

Their shoe is their cellphone

"Simon says"

Recreational/Self-Entertainment Hypnosis

The intent of this type of hypnosis is to give the person being hypnotized a fun experience.

Examples of Recreational/Self-Entertainment Hypnosis:

Virtual Reality

Lucid Dreams

Hallucinations (positive or negative)

Make Believe

As you probably noticed, hallucinations and make believe are on both the stage list and the recreational list. The key difference between what defines them as different is who it is intended to entertain. In stage hypnosis, since it is intended to entertain the audience, the suggestion is chosen based on what will bring out a funny reaction. In recreational hypnosis, since the audience is the person who is hypnotized, suggestions are made based on what the individual will find enjoyable.

For example, stage hypnosis might suggest that the person is trying to find cover from a rain storm, versus in recreational hypnosis, where the person could be suggested to believe that their favorite fictional character is in the room with them. Although the second one could be used in a show, it would likely not be very entertaining for the audience. This doesn't mean there aren't suggestions which are both stage and recreational hypnosis at the same time.

(I don't want you to misunderstand; stage hypnosis is fun for many people who want that experience of being on the stage doing silly and random things.)

Does Recreational Hypnosis Have a Place in Hypnotherapy?

I know many gut reactions to recreational hypnosis is that it is a complete waste of the power of hypnosis (many say the same of stage hypnosis). This is true to an extent. While neither stage nor recreational hypnosis directly help people make changes in their lives, they both are capable of convincing people of the power of hypnosis when used correctly and ethically.

One of the ways I use recreational hypnosis, is my website (davidjohnpack.com), I offer some free hypnosis mp3s. Some of the mp3s are for self-improvement, while the other free mp3s are recreational hypnosis. This way a person can try at least one hypnosis session and see personally that hypnosis does work.

You can get these free hypnosis mp3s at DavidJohnPack.com/free (NOTE: You will have to sign up to my newsletter to get access to the code to get them for free.)

(Author's Note: Although much recreational hypnosis found on the internet is erotic hypnosis, the two are NOT inherently the same. If a hypnosis session made it so that all the cups of water you drink for the next hour are like beer for you, would be recreational hypnosis. On the other hand, a hypnosis session that helped a person to increase their sex drive would be erotic hypnotherapy, not recreational hypnosis.)

Website: **DavidJohnPack.com**
Email: **hypnosis@davidjohnpack.com**

HYPNOTHERAPY SCRIPTS

By: Steve G. Jones

About Dr. Steve G. Jones

"If you want to make a positive change in your life, Steve G. Jones can make the difference. He did with me." Tom Mankiewicz, Writer of **"Superman the Movie"**

Imagine living the life you deserve to live! A life in which YOU have unlimited wealth, focus, and confidence. You see endless, exciting possibilities and you feel so good about it. Steve G. Jones has devoted his life to making sure you achieve this goal easily. He has focused his genius on developing thousands of self-help products to launch you powerfully in the direction of ultimate success. New opportunities await you, so start your journey now.

"I have started using Steve's techniques in my practice." –Dr. George Thoduka, MD Internal Medicine

"I have tried other hypnosis recordings, but I have found yours to be very powerful in reaching the subconscious mind of my patients."
Dr. Irina Webster, MD

He is a member of the National Guild of Hypnotists, American Board of Hypnotherapy and president of the American Alliance of Hypnotists. Steve is a former member of the board of directors of the Los Angeles chapter of the American Lung Association. In order to keep up with the very latest in research, he regularly attends training conferences.

Dr. Steve G. Jones, Ed.D. is a board certified Clinical Hypnotherapist who has been practicing hypnotherapy since the 1980s. He is the author of 25 books on such topics as hypnosis, the law of attraction and weight loss. Steve has also created over 9,000 hypnosis audio recordings and 22 different online certification programs, which are sold in over 140 countries.

In the mid 80's, Steve began study at the University of Florida. His primary research focus was cognitive psychology, understanding how people learn. Much of his early research was published in psychology journals in late 80's. Meanwhile, he continued practicing hypnosis outside of academia on a regular basis.

From 1990 to 1995, he was fortunate to counsel families and individuals. During this time he finished his degree in psychology at the University of Florida and went on to graduate studies in counseling. Steve has a bachelor's degree in psychology from the University of Florida (1994), a master's degree in education (M.Ed.) from Armstrong Atlantic State University (2007), a specialist degree (Ed.S) in education (2009), a doctorate in education (Ed.D.) at Georgia Southern University (2013) and has studied psychology at Harvard University.

Dr. Steve G. Jones sees clients for a variety of conditions. Among them are: weight loss, anxiety, smoking cessation, test taking, phobias (such as fear of flying), nail biting, road rage, anger management, IBS, general wellness, pre-surgical and pre-dental pain control, natural childbirth, and many others.

In business settings, he is regularly called upon by sales teams to boost salesperson motivation. His straightforward techniques have significantly and consistently increased sales.

Dr. Steve G. Jones also works extensively with Hollywood actors, writers, directors, and producers, helping them achieve their very best.

Steve has been featured on Bravo's Millionaire Matchmaker as both a hypnotherapist and a millionaire. Additionally, Steve has been interviewed on CNN, ABC, NBC and CBS.

"Steve G. Jones has had a tremendous impact on my career. I came to him to overcome a fear of selling and to improve my public speaking skills. He worked with me on my self confidence and helped me become comfortable in front of people. Working with him has helped me become more relaxed and confident. He also helped me decide to write a book so that I could share my experiences with others."
Michael McMillan, **MBA**, **Harvard Business School**

Unlimited Wealth by Steve G. Jones

You are unaffected by negativity and retain the ability to enjoy all of the warmth and joy that life has to offer. You are totally detached from negativity. You are open and receptive to love. You do not complain. You accept other people as they are and you do not expect them to change. You are patient, calm, and harmoniously centered at all times. You let go of all fear based emotions such as blame, jealously, guilt, and possessiveness. These negative emotions are now a part of your past and you open yourself, open yourself to receive all the good things life has to offer. You accept all good things into your life. You know that you are worthy of receiving all good things in your life. You allow yourself to receive good things. You do not block good things from entering your life. You are worthy of receiving them. You allow money to come to you. You allow money to come to you. You allow money to come to you. You now have a flow in your life and money is actually attracted to you and you allow it to come to you. You do not stand in the way of money flowing toward you. You allow it to come to you. You know it is for you. And you know that you will use it for the greatest good. You allow it to come to you. You now realize that you have the ability to create in your life unlimited wealth, unlimited wealth. Your wealth will be without limits. You allow money to flow to you and it does. It flows to you easily and effortlessly because you are now open and receptive to all good things. You keep your mind calm like water. You remain centered at all times. Physically relaxed, emotionally calm, mentally focused, and spiritually aware and money flows to you. You now realize that you will have unlimited wealth. You will have all the wealth you desire and you let this happen easily and effortlessly. You are comfortable with wealth.

Unlimited Motivation by Steve G. Jones

Imagine that nothing holds you back from reaching your goal and becoming the successful person that you want to be. Imagine a perfect kind of day. A day that you awaken to and you just know its going to be the kind of day where everything is just right. Everything just falls into place. Your feelings are good. You feel at peace. You feel content. You have been comfortable and protected within the boundaries that you yourself have created. You have been comfortable and safe and now you choose to expand your comfortable space. Just imagine yourself pushing back the barricades, pushing back the barricades you created and instead you are expanding your horizons, expanding your goal, reaching forward higher and higher, feeling comfortable with your new goals. Feeling comfortable with your expanded boundaries. You feel safe, secure, and pleased that you have the control and power within you to change. To change your limitations and be the successful person you want to be. Your feelings are good. You feel at peace. You feel content. Now just imagine taking this special day and placing it a little bit in the future, a day or two, a week, a month, just a little in the future. Imagine that you have resolved many conflicts, many problems and they are now in the past. Imagine a smile on your face. You are at peace, content, and you have found solutions to problems and resolved them. You are now free of past burdens. You are confident, self-assured. You feel centered and strong. Now, just imagine a goal or a project that you would like to accomplish. See yourself with all minor goals aside and just focus on one goal or project. See yourself with energy into your work. See yourself complete it. You see new opportunities. You see new challenges that are more exciting than the old ones. You see yourself with renewed energy. You are enthusiastic, you focus, you concentrate, and new ideas develop from the old. New energy and positive feelings emerge. You are successful. You reach your goal. Imagine yourself worthy of all good things that life has to offer. Reaching your goal is very beneficial to you and as you continue to reach the goals in your life, see them as positive events, positive to you, your family, friends, and people you work with. Imagine the goals in your life, see them as positive to you, your friends, your family, friends, and the people you work with. Imagine yourself putting energy into reaching your goals and becoming the successful person you deserve to be. Reflect for a moment on other positive goals you have already reached. These goals were good for you and all those around you. Now see yourself become successful. You are happy. You are sensitive to others. You are helpful and your success is positive for all. You are comfortable in your success. You use your success in the most positive and worthwhile ways. You deserve to be successful. See it, feel it, you are successful. Your mind is clear. You see yourself as the intelligent, creative and beautiful person that you are. You have many choices, many options, and whatever you choose to do, whatever direction you take, know that it will be positive for you. Your success is a positive event for you and all those who touch your life. Every choice you make and any path you choose is absolutely right for now. Now just see yourself clearly in the near future with many positive directions and choices and bring this image into the present. See yourself resolving problems. See yourself confident and successful with many wonderful and positive paths to choose from and you know you can continue your success. You can continue to make choices that enhance your life.

Reducing Stress Using Hypnotherapy and NLP

By Suzanne Gardner-Cuthbert, GQHP, CHBPP, AAMET,

Website: *www.suzannegardnercuthbert.com*

Email: *suzannegardnercuthbert@gmail.com*

About the Author

Suzanne Gardner-Cuthbert is a qualified Clinical Hypnotherapist, Stress Management Consultant, EFT and NLP Practitioner and a mum to three children.

Suzanne first became interested in hypnotherapy when preparing for a home birth for her third child. Suzanne spent her pregnancy educating herself about natural childbirth. Suzanne learnt a number of relaxation, visualisation and self-hypnosis techniques that she used during labour. Suzanne experienced the benefits of these techniques and was then inspired to learn more about hypnotherapy. Suzanne trained as a Clinical Hypnotherapist and later completed a training course in Hypnosis for Childbirth.

Suzanne is the founder of Suzanne Gardner-Cuthbert Hypnotherapy, a service that provides hypnotherapy and other alternative therapies in East

Yorkshire. Since 2007, Suzanne has been helping clients to overcome their issues and to achieve their goals and desires. Suzanne specialises in the area of stress management, fears and phobias and hypnosis for childbirth.

To help many more people, Suzanne was inspired to take her career into a new direction and has commenced the development of self-help products. Suzanne is the author of the e-book The Stress Survival Guide for Parents.

If you would like to subscribe to the Suzanne Gardner-Cuthbert Hypnotherapy monthly newsletter, go along to the website at **www.suzannegardnercuthbert.com** and sign up to receive a newsletter that includes the latest news and developments at Suzanne Gardner-Cuthbert Hypnotherapy, informative articles, free life changing tips and free self-help guides.

The Stress Response

Stress is both a psychological and biological response that happens when a stimuli (a stressor) triggers the stress response (also known as the fight or flight response). The stress response is a survival mechanism that gives the body additional resources to enable a person to deal with emergencies and dangerous situations. When the stress response is activated, stress hormones are released into the body. These stress hormones give the body additional resources to deal with the threat.

Many centuries ago, the stress response enabled the cavemen to survive. It provided the cavemen with the resources they needed to stay alive. These additional body resources gave the cavemen what was needed for them to fight wild predators, or to flight (run) quickly away from them.

We do not encounter emergencies and dangerous situations often in modern day life, therefore, we activate the stress response by our own triggers created by the pressures and stresses of modern day life.

Techniques that produce a deep level of relaxation such as hypnosis and breathing techniques create a relaxation response and switch off the stress response.

Using Hypnotherapy and NLP for Stress Management

The following hypnotherapy relaxation script can be used to help a client relax and de-stress. Using a hypnotherapy relaxation script at the client's first session will help the client to reduce the level of stress that has been building. This script also instructs the client to go back to their beach visualisation and use it when they need to unwind, switch off or reduce stress.

A relaxation script

Close your eyes and take 3 slow deep breaths…. Breathe in through the nose and out through the mouth…..

Starting at your head, relax your facial muscles by imaging the muscles in your forehead relaxing…. letting go of any tension that is stored there…. Now imagine this relaxation spreading to the muscles in your cheeks…. imagine the muscles relaxing…. and becoming limp and loose….. And this relaxation is now spreading to the muscles in your jaw…. let go of any tension that is stored there….You are drifting into a deep state of relaxation…. This wave of relaxation is now moving down to your neck and shoulders…. Imagine that the muscles in your neck and shoulders are relaxing…. becoming loose…. Allow any tension that has been stored in your neck and shoulders to drift away…. As this relaxation deepens, imagine this relaxation spreading to the muscles in your arms…. imagine the muscles in your arms becoming loose and limp…. Now imagine the muscles in your fingers relaxing….. And as you drift deeper down…. you are becoming more and more relaxed…. Notice how your muscles in your back are relaxing easily…. becoming loose and limp…. And now imagine your stomach muscles relaxing….. And this wave of relaxation continues to muscles in your thighs…. imagine these muscles relaxing…. and becoming limp…. and loose…. Relaxing further still…. you move on to the muscles in your calves…. imagine them relaxing…. and becoming so loose…. And to the muscles in your feet…. imagine the muscles are relaxing….

Using the power of your imagination…. imagine yourself walking along a sandy path…. and with each step you take along this path…. you feel more and more relaxed…. And as you walk along the path you come to some steps….You stand at the top of the steps…. and as you walk down each step…. you count the number of steps down…. You take the first step down…..

10… you are becoming more and more deeply relaxed….

9…. letting go of any tension….

8…. drifting into a deep state of relaxation….

7…. drifting deeper and deeper….

6…. drifting further down….

5…. deeper and deeper….

4…. drifting into a deep state of relaxation….

3…. nearly there….

2…. allowing a deep state of relaxation to flow through the body….

1…. drifting 10 times deeper into a relaxed state…. Now you are completely relaxed…….

You now step on to the sand of a golden beach…. Maybe a beach you have visited before….You walk across the warm golden sand…. to an empty red and white striped deckchair…. You sit down in the deckchair …. Feel what it feels like to be sat in the chair…. How relaxed and calm you feel…. Take a few moments to feel the warmth of the sun on your face and body…. and take a moment to hear the noises around you…. What can you hear?....You gaze into the sea….Take notice of the different shades of blue and green….. And whilst you are gazing into the sea…. you hear the seagulls circling above in the sky….You look up and watch them circling around and around…. and as you watch them circling around and around…. you become more and more deeply relaxed…. Become aware of how calm and relaxed you feel….You feel peaceful…. with not a care in the world…. So calm and relaxed…. Feel the texture of the sand underneath your feet… feel the warmth of the sand…. notice how comfortable you feel sat in your deckchair…. you feel at peace…. so calm…. and so relaxed…. In your mind you say to yourself three times "I am calm and relaxed"…."I am calm and relaxed"…."I am calm and relaxed"….Take a few minutes to enjoy this wonderful relaxed feeling….

(Pause for a few moments to allow the client to relax)

Ok that's good…. And at any time in the future…. when you feel you need to switch off, unwind and release stress you can come back to this beach visualisation…. and enjoy this level of relaxation…. All you have to do, is to close your eyes if is safe to do so…. and take 3 slow deep breaths…. and then visualise your special beach.

It's now time to come back to the here and now…. I am going to count slowly from 5 to 1…. and when you reach 1, you will open your eyes and come back to the room…. Let's begin….

5….

4…. beginning to wake up

3…. your body senses are coming back to normal

2….

1…. wide awake open your eyes

Creating a New Way to React to Stress

After using an induction and deepener of your choice the following script can be used to teach the client a diaphragmatic breathing technique. Breathing techniques switch off the stress response and can be used in situations where there is a need to remain calm or to regain calmness. Breathing techniques can also be used for relaxation.

This script also uses a mental rehearsal technique, to enable the client to form a new behaviour pattern, so that they will react and respond calmly when future stressful situation are experienced.

<u>Script</u>

I would like you to take a moment to concentrate on your breathing…. Slowly breathe in through your nose and out through the mouth…. you are to breathe from your diaphragm, the lower chest area….The area in-between the top of the stomach muscles and the upper chest.

Breathe slowly and deeply from your diaphragm…. When you breathe in, I want you to push your stomach muscles out, hold this breath for a moment, up to the mental count of 3…. And now slowly exhale through your mouth, pushing your stomach muscles in…. And again, Inhale slowly through your nose, pushing your stomach muscles out, hold for a moment, up to the mental count of 3…. and now slowly exhale through your mouth, pushing your stomach muscles in…. And repeat this breathing technique one more time….That's good….I would now like you to return back to your normal breathing….

Using the power of your mind…. I would like you to imagine, how you currently react and respond when you are stressed…. Perhaps imagine a recent situation that has stressed you out…. Run this scene in your mind…. With this image in mind, make this image a still picture…. step out of the picture so that you are looking at the image and seeing yourself…. turn down any sounds you hear…. drain the colour out of this imagine and replace it with black and white…. Reduce the image in size, so that the image is becoming smaller and smaller…. And as this image is becoming smaller…. the image is moving further away…. until the image has completely disappeared….

Now I would like you to run this scene again but this time I would like you imagine reacting and responding in a new way…. Reacting calmly by using the breathing technique I have taught you…. and responding positively to the situation.

Run this scene in your mind, seeing the scene as if you was looking out from your eyes…. And when you reach the end of the scene, I would like you to run this scene over and over again from the beginning to the end.... and continue to repeat this for the next few minutes....

(Allow the client a few minutes)

Ok that's good....you have now mentally rehearsed a new way of reacting and responding when a stressful situation happens.... When you experience a stressful situation for real, you will find that you will react calmly.... and as you have imagined here today.

(Terminate the trance)

Techniques and Strategies to Help a Client Deal with Their Stressors

When a client is facing a stressful situation or circumstance, there are two approaches that can be used. If the situation or circumstance is within the client's control, then making a change or several changes could either improve, or resolve the situation. Where the situation or circumstance is beyond the client's control, the client will need to change their thoughts, feelings, and the meaning they give to the situation or circumstance.

Ask the client what is creating stress for them. The client may have one stressor or several. Make a note of the client's stressors. Working with one stressor at a time, ask the client to take a few minutes to think about what they can do within their own power to bring about a change to the situation.

If the client has come up with a solution for their issue, ask them to visualise how the stressful situation is at the moment before making changes. With this image in mind, the client is to make the scene a still picture. Ask them to step out of the picture, so that they are looking at the image and seeing themself. The client is to turn down any sounds that they hear from the picture and drain the colour out of it, replacing it with black and white. The client is then to reduce the image in size, so that the image is becoming smaller and smaller. And as this image is becoming smaller, the client is to imagine the image moving further away, until the image has completely disappeared.

Now using the power of the mind, the client is to visualise their solution, as if the change or changes have already taken place. What would they see? If the situation had already changed. What would they hear? How would they feel? The client is to step into the picture and see the image as if they were looking out from their eyes. They are to make the colours on the image brighter, make the image bigger and closer.

When a situation or circumstance is not within the client's control

If the client doesn't have a solution because the situation or circumstance is not within their control, ask the client how the situation makes them feel? What colour is the feeling/emotion? What shape is the feeling/emotion? How big is the feeling/emotion? What texture is the feeling/emotion? Where in the body do they feel the feeling/emotion?

Ask the client to change the colour of the feeling/emotion to a colour they like. Then change the shape of the feeling/emotion. Then change the texture, to a texture they like. They are to imagine the feeling/emotion shrinking in size. Shrinking until it is very small. And to imagine moving the feeling/emotion from where they feel it in the body. The feeling/emotion continuing to move until it is out of their body and floating away.

Replace the negative feeling/emotion with a feeling of calm. Ask the client what colour represents calm to them. On the inward breath, the client is to imagine breathing in this colour of calm and to image the calm energy flowing into every area of the body, radiating into to every muscle, tissue and cell.

Repeat this process from the beginning, for each of the client's stressors.

•*The Power Of Career Re-Invention*

James E. Graham C.H. | www.lifepowermastery.com
lifepowermastery@gmail.com

How many times have you heard the phrase... *"Dont re-invent the wheel"* ?

If you or your clients have been faced with career challenges in life, this sage advice may have been given to you by some well meaning friend or relative.

While this may work for baking blueberry pies, it may not apply when things are not going so well in your own universe and your in desperate need of a new result.

While we accept that life can be full of hurdles, major life challenges can sidetrack or even disable our clients and maybe even some of us... especially in the area of career.

I've had some great conversations with a couple of close friends recently who were faced with major career challenges.

My friend Jeff had been trained in the antique business at a very young age by relatives who taught him everything they knew.

He started buying and selling antiques when he was 16 with his uncle and by the time he was 25, he was travelling the USA promoting huge, three day antique shows at fairgrounds and making big profits.

Life could not be better for Jeff as he made more money than he could imagine, met thousands of interesting people and travelled throughout the country.

Then internet auction sites became popular.

Suddenly the huge show attendances dwindled, antique dealers went out of business and buyers simply went online to find new treasures.

While he also shifted to an online business model, he saw the market was now over saturated and knew the antique business was no longer a profitable career choice.

Then my good friend Kim contacted me about starting a new business venture, we also had a lengthy talk about life challenges that had effected both of us.

Even though I've watched her accomplish many achievements, she revealed to me a recent major life challenge that had wiped out her successful administrative career and virtually paralyzed her from working for many months.

Unfortunately once she regained her health, her position was no longer available and she too realized that the only way out of her predicament was to re-invent herself as well.

During our conversations, I told Jeff and Kim about my most major career challenge.

Up until 2009, I had made a great living as a full time entertainer, disc jockey and musician.

Due to changing lifestyle and economic factors, the live music business had become virtually extinct and weddings and corporate entertainment events have been decreasing year after year for DJ entertainment.

I love entertaining and have been an entertainer my whole life!

Yet here I was, facing possible career extinction myself.

I knew I needed to find something new if I was going to continue to prosper or simply keep the bills paid.

Al of us came to the conclusion, either conciously or subconciously, that we could either keep trying Benjamin Franklin's version of insanity - aka doing the same actions over again and expecting a different result or hit the reset button and *"re-invent the wheel"*.

Once we accepted that doing the "same ole, same ole" was no longer going to work, the process of re-invention was set in motion.

We all admitted being a little fearful of the unknown but also being faithful that the subconcious mind would attract new success that was available for the asking.

The only thing that mattered was that we HAD TO take action and go after it. (*Admitting that your in a "do or die" situation will tend to light a fire under your butt!*)

The funny thing is... once you start the process of re-invention, incredible new ideas will suddenly come to mind.

New conversations will take place, new opportunities will spring up and new people will enter your life to help you in your quest.

As you open your mind up to new possibilities, you'll be amazed at how many new possibilities start showing up in your life.

The great artists, musicians and actors have always known this.

My favorite actor, Johnny Depp is a master at self re-invention. Look at all the roles he has played. From a swashbuckling pirate to freaky kid with scissors for hands. He constantly re-invents himself with success.

Madonna is a master of self re-invention as well. Every album she ever produced portrayed a total different character and changed musical styles and success followed.

So what happened after Jeff, Kim and myself decided to boldly set out on a new uncharted course?

Jeff took his marketing skills and started his own consultation firm, helping companies find other companies to do business with.

Kim used her administrative and people skills to launch her own business.

And I took my entertainment and motivational skills to become a nationally known touring comedy hypnotist as well as a motivational career coach, author and speaker.

I also now create motivational hypnosis programs that help people lose weight, stop smoking, improve their confidence, memory, concentration and even their golf game.

Was our "career re-invention" a miracle?

Well yes and no.

To the people who simply witnessed the transformation it was. But to us, it was simply re-focusing our minds and intentions on what was truly possible.

None of us did anything but keep an open mind to success and had faith that our new ideas would lead us down a new, adventurous and prosperous path.

Focusing on new possibilities and being open to the truth that the subconcious can be programmed to attract the successful results that we desire is everyone's magic ability.

Also, it was the conscious acceptance of what was not working and releasing the ego feelings of loss about letting go of something that had long since served it's purpose.

Our lives are constantly growing and evolving whether we choose to acknowledge it or not.

Most of that growth comes from accepting all challenges as something to learn and grow from, not to be afraid of.

Helping clients or personally do something as life changing as re-inventing yourself can be a little scary but with the right positive attitude, it can become incredibly exciting as well.

No matter whether your age is twenty four or eighty four, re-invention will get your blood pumping, your mind racing and give your life new purpose and meaning.

And isn't that the way our lives should be lived anyway?

Hypnotic Memoirs
By David Shipman

A bit about me

I am a consulting Hypnotherapist working from Kirkcaldy in Fife, East Central Scotland.

I've had an interest in Hypnosis ever since I was a boy. I can remember reading American comic books, and at the back, amidst the adverts, for sale was a Hypnosis Disc.

I can still remember the excitement of wanting to own one of those magical items. Unfortunately they were only for sale in the United States and thus required dollars to buy, something not readily available to me at that time.

Some years later, as part of a youth group, we were asked if we could decorate the bedroom for an older couple who lived locally. On meeting the couple I found out that the gentleman, Mr Rankin, was a retired stage Hypnotist who used to go by the name 'Ran King'. He would often tell me stories about the things he would do on stage as well as the therapy work he carried out, both of which I found fascinating.

When we finished decorating the bedroom, Mr Rankin gave me two books on Hypnosis which I still have to this day:

Hypnotism by Albert Moll, first published in April 1889.

Hypnotherapy by M. Brenman & M. Mcgill, 1947.

Both books were a bit hard going for a teenage boy, but again my interest in Hypnosis was kindled.

After I left school and started work, Hypnosis was put on the back burner for the next twenty years or so. Throughout that period, however, I still had a keen interest in Hypnosis and read as many books as I could find on the subject.

During that period I found out that James Braid, one of the leading lights in Medical Hypnotherapy, was born in a small mining village just fifteen miles from my home. Coincidence or what?

It was in 1984 that I took my first course in Hypnotherapy – Hypno Analysis, under the tutelage of Neil French, the founder of The Institute of Analytical Hypnotherapists.

I followed this up by training with Wilf Proudfoot, the founder of the British Guild of Hypnotist Examiners, now known as the UKGHE.

I opened my own practice in Tolbooth Street, Kirkcaldy in 1986 and I am still there today.

Group Sessions

In the early days, when I was trying to get myself known, I started teaching self-hypnosis evening classes at schools in the local area.

There were five classes, if memory serves me right, all well attended.

Not only was I teaching a class that allowed me to pass on my knowledge to others, it was also a learning process for me.

It was amazing to see the different ways in which people responded as they went into the hypnotic state. Some would be slumped in their chairs, others sitting stiff as ramrods, and some becoming so relaxed they really did not want to open their eyes when asked to at the end of the session. Often it was easier to leave them in the relaxed state and allow them to become alert in their own time, rather than pushing them to open their eyes.

The classes ran once a week for the duration of six weeks and lasted for two hours apiece. A short break was offered half way through each class. Most of the class would pick up the self hypnosis techniques fairly quickly, and more importantly, practice them at home. However, when they came along in the evenings the majority preferred to be led into the deep relaxation by yours truly.

One of the easiest ways to do this was to tell a story as you went along whilst having them make the images in their own minds, perhaps swimming with dolphins, drifting along in a hot air Balloon (always making sure that they only went to a height that felt comfortable to them, even if that was only three feet of the ground.) and always putting suggestion into the stories creating calmness and confidence.

What I found amazing was that as the classes went along, it would be a different story each week, none of them pre-planned.

I soon became aware that with my eyes closed I also was slipping into the altered state and the images were presenting themselves into my mind.

At the end of the class the general consensus was how real the images appeared as the story went on, and in all honesty that was the way it seemed to me. As I related the story to the class it was as though I was there, telling them what was happening as I experienced it.

Although I would take the class through a new self hypnosis technique each week, it was inevitable that the question of 'when are you going to take us on a new story?' would arise.

It was fun for us all, but it also made me realise how the subconscious could mistake imagination for reality, even though it was the subconscious releasing the imagery into my mind.

The week before the class ended I was persuaded to put a story type induction on to an audio cassette along with the background music so those who had attended could listen to them at home. I sold these at the end of the course for a minimal £5.00. The cassette always started with 'Hello, it's David here again' and the contact number for the office just in case anyone had a presenting problem they would like to get rid of.

Of course it was inevitable that the cassette would be shared with the family and friends of those who had attended, thus spreading the word about myself, my business and where I could be found.

At the end of one of the six weeks I was asked if I would be willing to do some inductions on a one to one basis. There were about ten people who wanted to take part, and to make it more interesting we decide to do a different induction for each person. When you have not done it before it is quite difficult to think of ten inductions, one after the other, then something strange happened. I started to do inductions I had never seen or heard of before, tipping them forward on to my shoulder, spinning them around, in all honesty I can scarcely remember what we actually did, but every one of the volunteers went quickly into trance. It was later as I was sitting down thinking about this that I realised that it didn't really matter what type of induction you come up with, it is the expectation of going in to a trance that causes them to respond to what you do, they actually put themselves in to the trance state because it is what they expected to happen.

One of the group sessions I was asked to take was at a centre for people with disabilities. Quite a few were in wheelchairs, others sitting on chairs around the room. Again I did one of the imagery inductions followed by a deepening technique. As the session went on, the staff that were not participating were hurrying around the room catching people who were sliding on to the floor and falling forward onto the wheelchair trays. At that point it seemed like a good time to terminate the session.

As the folk started to return to full awareness, the room was buzzing with everyone talking about their experience whilst in a hypnotic state. One of the most incredible things was the amount of people who not only felt really good, but also found that a lot of the physical discomfort they had experienced from sitting in the chairs for prolonged periods of time had also been greatly reduced, or in some cases, had gone all together. We all knew that this would only be a temporary relief, and this was probably the only time I would give the backup cassettes away for free. In fact for a year or two after, I would get a call from the centre asking if they could have a few more cassettes for new members.

As my name got around I was asked to give talks to Rotary clubs, Probus groups, Pharmacists, even HMRC, and Women's guilds etc. This inevitably resulted in some new clients coming along.

In the beginning I would use Hypno analysis to work with the problems clients were coming along with. This would take up to around eight sessions to get the result required. However, as the years went by, new techniques that would get the result much quicker, and without delving in to the clients past and turning over bad memories, began to emerge.

Nowadays I tend to specialise in working with **Phobias**, **Stress** and **Panic attacks**, although a lot of people tend to come along to stop smoking or lose weight.

In days gone by it was smoking secession that used to bring in most clients. Nowadays it is weight control.

Past life regression

On occasions you do get a client coming along that asks to be regressed to a previous life. I always tell them that there are different ideas on what regression actually is.

One school of thought is that they do not actually go back to a previous existence. They simply start to relive things that happened at an earlier time in their life that lay submerged in the subconscious, e.g. stories they were told as youngsters started to emerge as reality in the hypnotic state.

Another train of thought is that by using the wrong wording, the hypnotist can unwittingly start to lead the client in to imagery that again appears real to them.

I was once asked to do a past life regression for a spiritualist group, and after asking for a volunteer a lady came forward asking if I would work with her.

She slipped easily in to the relaxed state and was asked to let her thoughts go back through time, as if there was no such thing as time, back through the years that had past, back to a time before this time, and to give a small nod when she was there.

I asked if she was inside or outside, what she could see, and if she was by herself or with someone. To cut a long story short, she saw herself as a male missionary doctor called James, in a small village in Africa in the eighteen hundreds. She was trying to improve hygiene in the village and help children who had come down with some illness.

It was now time to come forward and to return to the present.

After opening her eyes, every one was eager to find out what she had been doing, did it appear real to her etc.

After a cup of coffee and a slice of cake it was time for me to go.

Just as I was leaving she came across to thank me for the experience and to tell me that ever since she had been a little girl she had wanted to be a missionary working in Africa. According to her, she now knew how it felt to be one. A real past life experience or someone's subconscious releasing memory's as reality?

There was another regression where a lady saw herself standing on a cliff side overlooking the waters, waiting for her fisherman husband to come home, but with a feeling deep inside that the sea had claimed him and she would never see him again. She became quite upset at that point and was swiftly brought back to full awareness in the present.

She started to tell me more about herself, how her ancestors came from a fishing village in Ireland and of the stories her grandparents would tell her about the place and the people who lived there, how hard their lives would have been. The memories seemed very real to her and it was almost as though she could remember it happening.

Fears and Phobias

It is quite amazing the fears that people come along with.

Snakes, Dogs, Birds, Spiders, Going outside, Going in to small spaces i.e. a lift or the middle of a row in a theatre, just to name a few.

Although there are no snakes to speak of in the UK it really is astonishing how this phobia pops up every now and again.

I had a young woman come along with a morbid fear of snakes that had now started to incorporate worms. She found it almost impossible to step on earth or grass in case a snake or worm was lurking around waiting on her.

She came along for a few sessions where I used Hypno analysis to go back in to her past memories.

She eventually recalled going to the zoo as a schoolgirl and visiting the reptile house that she found to be quite scary. On the way home in the bus a couple of boys sitting behind her had purchased rubber snakes and placed one on the back of her seat, telling her not to move as there was a snake crawling over the seat towards her. As she turned round to look they let it drop on to her lap at which point she freaked out until her friend sitting next to her picked it up and showed her it was made of rubber. Being quite upset she went in to her school bag for a tissue and low and behold the second snake had been placed in the bag, this time she went into hysterics until one of the teachers came along and got her settled.

Something as simple as a school boy prank had years later developed in to a phobia that was disrupting a young woman's life. When I say a young woman, she was in her thirties and had long since blocked the memory of the initial cause.

It came as a surprise to her as she recalled the event from her past and remarked 'I can hardly believe something as stupid as that has caused me so much disruption for such a long time.' After leaving the office she came back about an hour later to tell me that she had gone for a walk in the park and to let me know that there were no snakes lurking about.

She sent a note a few weeks later to say the fear had completely gone

And she was happily working in her garden with a complete disregard to the worms.

Quite a few years later another lady with a fear of snakes turned up to say that her husband, a sales man, had won a prize holiday in Thailand for best sales. Unfortunately, the prize also included a guided tour through a serpent temple - apparently this was a place where the snakes were seen as holy and could slither anywhere they wanted in the temple.

She could recall as a youngster having her photo taken with a snake lying across her shoulders and was absolutely terrified.

With new techniques, using the fast phobia release, the fear was taken away and the memory was left as nothing more than what it was, a harmless memory.

I received a very nice card from her, sent from Thailand, saying that they had been to the temple and she had had no bad reaction to the snakes slithering around her feet whatsoever.

Weight Control

With obesity on the increase in the western world, more and more people are turning to Hypnosis to assist in losing weight.

There are many reasons people put on weight, bad diet lack of exercise,

And an increase in the consumption of processed foods,

Worry, Upset, Boredom, Frustration and Stress, eating to quickly, All of those things and more are reasons that cause people to over eat.

When we eat our body releases endorphins into the brain that make us feel good, if we eat fast the feel good factor passes quickly so we feel the need to eat more.

However if we can take twice as long to eat our food we keep the good feeling, enjoy the food and do not have the urge to eat more.

All of the reasons mentioned earlier Worry, Upset, Boredom, Frustration, Disappointment and Stress, are feelings we hope to alleviate by having something to eat even although we are not hungry.

With the use of hypnosis we can train the subconscious to respond to these negative feelings in a more positive way by introducing new thought processes to change the way we think about food. It is one of those problems that can take more than one session, however the results can be impressive.

And then there is the other end of the spectrum.

People who do not eat enough as they see there body image as being overweight even although everyone else sees them as a normal build.

(We are not talking Anorexia here. That is a medical condition that hypnosis can help with but only with their Doctors consent)

Then there are the ones who will only eat a particular type of food e.g. will only eat pasta, one young boy would only eat Tomato soup with bread and butter.

This tends to happen more often with youngsters but hypnosis can be very effective in dealing with this (A Parent needs to be in the room if the child is under age)

Motivation& Self Belief

Some people find it difficult to motivate themselves for various reasons, they are afraid to step out of their comfort zone in case things don't work out.

They talk themselves into believing that they are not good enough to achieve the things they would like to achieve.

They let others talk them down, what happens if it does not work out every one will laugh at you. The list goes on.

At one of the evening classes where we spent a lot of time building

Self esteem there was a young woman who would turn up for every class. At the end of the six week course she came across to me and said that she had never felt herself good enough to do things she really wanted to do, she had been working in the schools as a classroom assistant, but had always wanted to be a teacher.

As the evening classes had gone along she had decided there was no good reason why she couldn't be a teacher so she had applied for a place in teaching college and had been accepted, she is now working as a primary school teacher. It really is having the courage to take the first step.

Two or three years ago another lady came along she had a fear of driving and had failed her driving test two or three times. She came along for a few sessions and felt she was now ready to sit the test again.

A couple of months later I had a letter from her saying how thankful she was for helping her change her life. She had passed her test, left her husband who was always putting her down, and she was now a college student.

She had realised on passing the test that she was capable enough to do all The things she always wanted to.

(Hope her ex never finds out she came to see me.)

If we mix with people who are always negative about things we come to accept this as normal and get nowhere. If however we mix with people who are always upbeat and encouraging we come to believe that all things are possible

(If another person can do it so can you).

(What your mind can conceive and believe then your mind can achieve)

(The only thing stopping you is **FEAR. F**alse **E**vidence **A**ppearing **R**eal)

Public Speaking.

It can be quite daunting for some people to stand in front of a group and give a talk, surprisingly even someone who comes across as being very confident can fall into this category.

It appears to be that because they are the centre of attention and all eyes are upon them there is that little voice in their head saying don't mess this up you will look like a fool, what if I forget what I was going to say everyone will laugh at me. It is that old adversary FEAR raising its head again (**F**alse **E**vidence **A**ppearing **R**eal). Even although they have spent hours going over what they want to say, have their presentation all laid out they start to freeze with the negativity going on in their head.

There are some easy ways to deal with this. One off the clients I had along recently was a school teacher and although she stood in front of classes every day the thought of giving a talk in front of colleagues filled her with dread, although she was recognized as a competent teacher when she went along for interviews for promotion she would go to pieces, her stomach would churn she would forget what she was going to say and feel her eyes welling up. By using the techniques below she made a major change she was up for three interviews and was feeling relaxed about it.

Imagine

Just before you go on, picture yourself sitting in the audience looking at yourself on stage, see yourself looking calm and relaxed and watch as you smile at the audience notice how comfortable you feel as people smile back, see yourself looking and talking calmly and confidently to the people sitting there

Then imagine that you are merging with that you on the stage, see what she sees, feel how she feels and realise that when you step onto the stage you are going to respond in the same way as that imaginary you.

Eye contact

When standing in front of all those people make eye contact with one person and smile, because you are standing back from them, the people round about the one you are smiling at are not sure if you are smiling at them so they will smile back it is instinctive to smile when someone smiles at you.

There is nothing better to help you relax than to see friendly faces.

As you start your presentation keep making eye contact with different people around the room and smile.

You will find that by doing these simply exercises you can quickly relax as you begin your presentation in that calm confident manner and talk as though you were talking to a best friend.

Frequently asked questions

Q). What is Hypnosis?

A). Hypnosis is a very gentle form of therapy entirely natural and for the most part very relaxing.

It works like a bridge between the two parts of your mind, the conscious and the sub-conscious, allowing you to make the alterations necessary, to bring about the changes you require.

Q). What can Hypnosis help with.

A). Hypnosis can help with a variety of problems

Anxiety, Stress, Phobias, Smoking, Weight control,
Insomnia Pain control, Childbirth and many other problems
associated with the Mind.

Q). Do I fall asleep or blackout

A). No, in the Hypnotic state you are very relaxed whilst fully aware of
what is happening, you are able to open your eyes any time you feel you
need to.

Q). Can I be made to do things I don't want to do

A).No-one can be made to do anything they don't want to do.
In hypnosis, as in the normal waking state, you always have freedom of
choice.

Q). Can everyone be hypnotised

A). everyone of normal intelligence who is not under the effects of
drugs or alcohol can enter into the hypnotic state.

Q). what happens at the first session

A). at your first session the type of therapy required will be discussed with you along with an explanation of all it entails.

You will then be gently led into a very enjoyable relaxed state where you can begin to make the changes required.

Q) How many sessions will I require

A) Smoking cessation can usually be done in one session, most other problems will require more than one session the number of sessions will vary for each individual and everyone is assessed, one session at a time.

There are various techniques used with Hypnosis, i.e.

Hypno-Analysis, Suggestion therapy,
Neuro-Linguistic-Programming, regression therapy and
VCDTTM and to name just a few.

Hypnosis Can Help!

VCDTTM

is a Fast Way of Freeing Yourself from Phobias, Anxieties, O.C.D. and Stress.

It has been used to help people overcome problems such as,

Phobias, Smoking Cessation, Losing Weight, Food Addictions

Stress, Anxiety, Panic Attacks, Obsessive Compulsive Disorder and many other problems associated with the mind it can literally transforms people's lives.

It can be used as a stand alone therapy, or in conjunction with other techniques, depending on the presenting problem.

VCDT was developed by Nik & Eva Speakman Celebrity Life Coaches & Stars of the TV documentary 'A Life Coach Less Ordinary'

I am one of only a few people in the world personally trained in VCDTTM by Nik and Eva, the founders of this technique.

For further information /look at the website

www.hypnosisfife.com

A Short History of Hypnosis

Hypnosis is one of mankind's oldest healing therapies there are hieroglyphics from ancient Egypt thought to relate to it.

The Egyptian and Indian Priests used hypnotic skills to induce altered states in the sleep Temples to aid healing. This was also used in the Greek healing Temples that were dedicated to Hypnos the Greek God of sleep.

James Braid is the man credited with bringing Hypnosis onto a scientific basis. He was a Scottish surgeon from Ballingry in Fife working in Manchester, and is regarded by many as the father of modern day hypnosis. Braid became interested in what known as Mesmerism when watching a demonstration by a French Mesmerist. He examined the physical condition of mesmerized subjects and found that they were,

in a different physical state.

He started to study mesmerism, and realized that in the altered state, people were much more open to suggestion, which when used in a proper manner could prove to be highly effective in changing belief systems, and to bring about positive change in their lives.

It was Braid who first used the word Hypnotism naming it after 'Hypnos' the Greek god of sleep. Later when he realised that hypnosis was not actually a sleep state, he tried to change the name to monodisim, but by that time hypnotism had caught on and the new name never really took of.

For further information /look at the website
www.hypnosisfife.com

The Battle for Your Mind !

Written by Dr Daren Armstrong

I'm a fully qualified and professionally trained member of The Association of Professional Hypnotherapists & Psychotherapists, as well as being fully qualified, in a number of other disciplines such as pain control, NLP and life coaching.

I've spent the past 10 years researching the workings of the human mind and more recently the latest, cutting edge, technologies available for fast, effective, subconscious reprogramming.

Proud Creator of 'Direct Neurological Association' Programming. *The* most Advanced subconscious reprogramming system available, that actually allows, you to *become a **Master** Programmer* of your subconscious mind in 7 Days. So you CAN Be, Do and *Have* Anything and Everything you desire. Visit http://www.dna-programming.com

Many years ago a famous personal development guru said "If you don't take control of the garden of your mind, then weeds will grow"

Many years ago you may have been able to think of your subconscious mind as a garden. Now, just as most of us no longer work the land for a living, there are no gardeners of your mind. Your mind is **no longer** a garden.

Just as the world has evolved, just as technology has evolved in quantum leaps, we too have evolved, our minds have taken a quantum leap from a garden to a super highway.

It is no longer useful to know a bit of gardening, to know how to feed your good thoughts and keep the weeds (your bad thoughts) at bay. The power of positive thinking and all that.

Our minds have now evolved, WAY beyond that, to work more like the technology, we are now accustomed to, they work more like a super computer.

It is no longer effective to potter around the garden of your mind, planting seeds, fending off the weeds, greenfly and slugs. Hardly a battle.

NOW your subconscious mind is being bombarded with programs, just like all computers, we also **need** programs, to operate.

You have a program that determines your eating habits, your buying habits,what you do for a living, how and what, you do in your spare time, How you react in any given situation, in fact EVERYTHING you do is determined by the programs, run by your subconscious mind.

So unless you can program your own subconscious computer, it is running other peoples programs, meaning you have virtually no control over your life.

If they are not your own programs, you are running, they have to be someone else's.

But Who's ? …........................

There are those who know how to program your subconscious mind and do so, very effectively, whenever they wish. These are the *Intentional programmers*, More about them later.

There are those that program you, that don't know they know, how to program you and don't even know they are, programming you. These are the *incidental programmers*

And finally there are the *Internal Programmers*. Yes that's YOU....... You program YOU, just not consciously. So you don't know, you know how, or what programs you are installing.

Have you ever stopped to ask yourself why you eat what you eat, why you watch the TV programs you watch or why you react in a certain way in a given situation, even though sometimes, you wish you had reacted differently.

Have you ever asked yourself why you believe ? What you believe ? Whether it is your religious beliefs, the beliefs about, what you are capable of, your political or financial beliefs. I would hallucinate not.

The chances are that, unless you are your happy, healthy, ideal weight and are totally aware of everything that enters your ears, eyes and, your mind regarding health and nutrition, chances are, you have no idea, or a best a vague inkling for the primary reasons why you eat, what you eat or how and when you decide, what to eat. That's because it is controlled by a program and if it's not your program, if you didn't <u>write</u> it and you didn't <u>install</u> it. It's someone else's !

The same is true for the TV programs you watch, how you react in any given situation and your beliefs about your abilities(limitations). If they are not your programs, if you didn't <u>write</u> them and you didn't <u>install</u> them then........They are someone else's !

EVERYTHING you do is a set of instructions (a Program) carried out by your subconscious mind that compels you, to do everything you do. My assumption is that you didn't <u>write</u> any of them, you didn't <u>install</u> any of them. So they are ALL Someone Else's !

Hence 'The Battle for your Mind '. All these programs have been put there by one of the Three programmers Battling for your Mind.......

(I). The *Intentional Programmers* – These are by far the most effective of ALL the programmers in the battle for your mind. They are experts on the workings of the mind and know how to utilise all the psychological tips, tricks and technologies to <u>write</u> the programs, and make them so effective.

They are also experts on the most powerful installation methods of all, utilising hypnosis and NLP. After all its no good having a highly effective program, if you don't <u>install</u> it properly. Just like a computer, it won't work.

At present these are the **Master** *Programmers* and you are running more of their programs than anyone else's. These include the media – TV, film, radio, newspapers and magazines. All advertising media and people of influence.

(II). The *Incidental Programmers* – These don't actually write programs, they just install programs that have already been installed in them. Its like swapping a file from one computer to another they don't actually write the program. These include your parents, teachers, friends relatives and peers. These people have programmed you but don't know they have, and you probably didn't know they had either. Until Now. Its *true.*

Your parents, the first hypnotists you ever met, not programmers, they install programs not write them, and are largely responsible for your beliefs and limitations, as most of the programs installed by your parents, purely to protect you, and for your own good, concerning your self belief and limitations were installed before you were 8 years old. And these programs are usually, almost carbon copies of their beliefs and limitations.

It is common in therapy to see many people running the programs of limitation installed by their parents and many more who had issues with talking or reading in public, limitations, placed upon their abilities from programs, installed years ago, by their well meaning school teachers.

(III). The *Internal Programmers* – These are the voices inside your head and every time you say " I " or " I AM " you are programming your subconscious mind.

" I AM no good at tennis, football, golf " or whatever, " I can never remember names ", " I could never do that " etc.

Every time you say them things to yourself the program is executed and your subconscious mind makes sure, you are, what you said you were. I have taught people who said they had bad memories, to have fantastic memories.

We just created a new program that is effective at instantly recalling memories and installed that instead of the old one they were running previously.

So what can I you do to win this battle of *My Mind* and *breakthrough* ALL my limitations. So I CAN <u>Be</u>, <u>Do</u> and <u>Have</u> ANYTHING and EVERYTHING I desire ?

I'm sorry to say there is no easy way, no quick fix or pill you can take. You have got to **learn to program** your own mind. Learn to *WRITE* your own *programs* and then <u>install them correctly.</u>

Knowing HOW to do it, is *easy.* Its just, doing it that is the challenge. Just look at the **Master** *programmers*. Do what they do, and you will have highly effective, perfectly installed programs.

The thing is to, *do what they do,* you would have to study in depth, Psychology, Hypnosis and NLP all to master level and beyond. I know from personal experience that can take years and cost thousands. I would highly recommend it though, for those of you with the inclination.

The other way is to catch yourself running these wrong programs and correct them repeatedly so that the new behaviour or thought becomes a habit.   This is effective and time consuming as you more or less have to repeatedly deal with one issue at a time. Its called Personal Development or self help.

Another effective method of programming is Self Hypnosis. This installs programs into your subconscious mind and, *it works*, however it lacks the installation precision, Powerful psychological technologies and total subconscious compulsion used by the ***Master*** *programmers* to make **them** the most effective, available.

The programs installed by the *Incidental Programmers,* quite possibly before you were 8 years old are in your *DNA* as it was so long ago the *Programming* took place.

This was before a crucial part of your brain had developed. So You feel you have virtually no control over them. You are what you are. "This is me, its what I'm like" and you are absolutely right ! It is what you are like, its in your *DNA*. I call this *DNA Programming.* This is the sort of *Programming* you see in therapy all the time its fears, phobia's and limitations in all their various guises yet fundamentally, all the same.

They are all installed by the *Incidental Programmers* and are possibly in your *DNA,* if the *Programming* was installed early enough. The good news is *When* you learn to *program* your own subconscious mind you will be able to change your *DNA Programming* easily and effectively.

It doesn't really matter what method you choose. Just chose one. The *right one,* for you, and stick with it. Its *important* only that you *learn* to *program* your own mind. Instead of leaving it for someone else to do for you.

I believe as the battle for our mind continues the ***Master*** *Programmers* who spend billions and billions creating these programs for our minds and will continue to spend billions more on research to constantly improve their effectiveness, will continue to improve, exponentially, taking over more, and more, of our minds.

The time to start is NOW ! They are not too far ahead, yet. The battle can still be won. Start TODAY, Start NOW exploring the steps, to learning, how, to program YOUR own mind. So you can <u>Be</u>, <u>Do</u> and <u>Have</u> ANYTHING and EVERTHING, you Deserve.

Dr Daren Armstrong - http://www.dna-programming.com

<u>HYPNOSIS : Reality V/s Myth</u>
- <u>Dr. Kruti Parekh</u>

<u>About Dr. Kruti Parekh</u>

Dr. Kruti Parekh , has researched extensively on the Mind for 9 years and has developed a special presentation that would explain the "Science of Mind" & how we can to empower our minds. She has researched on the mind through books like Bhagwad Geeta , Upanishads ,Vedas etc . and prepared a special presentation that will "CHANGE THE WAY YOU THINK" She has also penned down a book named "<u>Beyond the Threshold of Mind</u>" . She has also developed a Special concentration card that Helps you achieve thoughtless meditation in few seconds .

Kruti Parekh has transformed lives of thousands of people in both national and international arena in Countries like USA , Canada, Europe Middle-east , China and India . She has trained people from all fields and sections of society , ranging from Doctors, Engineers , Lawyers , Managers to Students .

Different people have different needs. Every individual absorbs only what they need to know the most. Kruti also caters to individual Clients in case of special needs.

Kruti Parekh's has specially designed , fun based, intellectual and highly engaging workshops with experimental learning , Demos and practical exercises. She also customizes workshops to concentrate on specific issues in an organization.

www.krutiparekh.com

When you hear the word **HYPNOSIS ….**, you picture the mysterious figure, the hypnotist, popularized in movies, comic books and television. This Mysteriously looking man ,waves a pocket watch back and forth in front of a person's eyes , guiding the subject into a zombie-like state. Once hypnotized, the subject obeys, no matter how strange or immoral the request, muttering "Yes, master".

This popular representation bears little resemblance to actual hypnotism, of course. In fact, modern understanding of hypnosis contradicts this on several key points. Subjects in a hypnotic trance are not slaves to their "masters" -- they have absolute free will. And they're not really in a semi-sleep state -- they're actually hyper attentive.

Our understanding of hypnosis has advanced a great deal in the past century, but the phenomenon is still a mystery of sorts. There is a universal belief that hypnosis is a form of unconsciousness and you can control people under its influence , but that is not entirely true.

Generally people at large have a very confused idea about the term Hypnosis . There have been various explanations given by people and audiences by various performers , to suit their demonstrations and ideas .

Hypnosis is defined as "a special psychological state with certain physiological attributes, resembling sleep only superficially and marked by a functioning of the individual at a level of awareness other than the ordinary conscious state."

Persons under hypnosis are said to possess very high level of focus and concentration with the ability to concentrate intensely on a specific thought or memory, while blocking out sources of distraction.

Hypnosis is usually induced by a procedure involving a series of preliminary instructions and suggestions. Hypnosis, if delivered in the presence of the subject is called self suggestion or may be self-administered as autosuggestion.

When hypnotism is used for therapeutic purposes is referred to as <u>hypnotherapy</u>.

The hypnotized individual appears to follow the communications of the hypnotist and seems to respond in an uncritical, automatic fashion, ignoring all aspects of the environment other than those pointed out to him by the hypnotist.

He sees, feels, smells, and otherwise perceives in accordance with the hypnotist's suggestions, even though these suggestions may be in apparent contradiction to the stimuli that impinge upon him.

Can *You really* Be Hypnotized?

The experience of hypnosis can vary dramatically from one person to another. Some hypnotized individuals report feeling a sense of detachment or extreme relaxation during the hypnotic state, while others even feel that their actions seem to occur outside of their conscious volition. Other individuals may remain fully aware and able to carry out conversations while under hypnosis.

While many people think that they cannot be hypnotized, research has shown that a large number of people are more hypnotizable than they believe.

Some facts :

- 15% people are very responsive to hypnosis
- Only 10% of adults are considered difficult or impossible to hypnotize.
- Children are more likely to get hypnotized than adults
- People who can become easily absorbed in fantasies are much more responsive to hypnosis

If you are interested in being hypnotized, it is important to remember to approach the experience with an open mind. Research has suggested that individuals who view hypnosis in a positive light tend to respond better than the others.

Hypnosis Myths

Myth 1: When you wake up from hypnosis, you won't remember anything that happened when you were hypnotized.

While amnesia may occur in very rare cases, people generally remember everything that occurred while they were hypnotized.

Myth 2: Hypnosis can help people remember the exact details of a crime they witnessed.

While hypnosis can be used to enhance memory, the effects have been dramatically exaggerated in popular media.

Myth 3: You can be hypnotized against your will.

Despite stories about people being hypnotized without their consent, hypnosis requires voluntary participation on the part of the patient.

Myth 4: The hypnotist has complete control of your actions while you're under hypnosis.

While people often feel that their actions under hypnosis seem to occur without the influence of their will, a hypnotist cannot make you perform actions that are against your values or morals.

Myth 5: Hypnosis can make you super-strong, fast or athletically talented.

While hypnosis can be used to enhance performance, it cannot make people stronger or more athletic than their existing physical capabilities.

21 Myths and 30 Truths of Hypnosis
By Antonia Harrison

Many people have false, misconceived ideas about hypnosis which prevent them from seeking natural help with issues or problems which may have been limiting their lives for years. I would like to put your mind at rest about these "myths" and then give the truths about hypnosis and many of the problems that can be solved quickly and naturally.

The Lifestyle Liberator

"Freedom to live without bad habits, addictions or fears"

www.EnglishSkypeHypnotist.com

I combine Clinical Hypnosis with NLP Results Coaching and Personal Development to give a unique personalized approach to the issues that are holding you back from living the life you were born to live. I run online coaching in modules which can be tailored to suit your needs where and when you have the time. I see clients one-to-one anywhere in the world over Skype and run workshops and training in groups, including Public Speaking Confidence for Women.

For your own free version of this chapter as an illustrated downloadable e-book, visit **www.21HypnosisMyths.com**

21 Myths of Hypnosis

1. Hypnosis is a strange, unnatural state. No, it is a totally natural state and one we all go into several times a day e.g. waking up and falling asleep, daydreaming, watching TV and driving. It is an altered state of awareness in which the brain relaxes from Beta brain wave down into Alpha or Theta brain wave. This has been recorded on EEG measuring.

2. The hypnotist has control over you. No, that is a belief caused by too many bad films. Pure Hollywood. I can't force someone to stop smoking if they adamantly want to remain a smoker, no matter how much their partner wants them to or if the boss is paying. Going into hypnosis requires co-operation so if someone does not want to be hypnotised, they won't be. Simple as that.

3. The hypnotist will make me say or do embarrassing things like in a stage show. Anyone who volunteers to go on the stage of a stage hypnosis show knows that they will be asked to say or do ridiculous, funny or embarrassing things yet they still go up. They are usually the first to buy the DVD of the show because they are aware of what they do but not how they do it so want to see the show they created. The hypnotist uses screening tests to find the best candidates for the show who will usually have the ability to achieve a deep trance. Stage hypnosis is entertainment. Clinical Hypnosis or Hypnotherapy is to help a person be rid of unwanted habits, addictions, fears or help them overcome a stress-related health problem or improve in some area of their life. A deep trance state is not necessary. The key word here is "help" them, not embarrass them.

4. Hypnotists have special powers. I wish! A hypnotist is someone who has learned to lead someone into a hypnotic trance via use of an induction followed by a deepener to deepen the state of trance. That can be learned. Hypnotherapy is using that hypnotic trance for the person's benefit to help them overcome a problem. I see hypnotherapy as a practical skill combined with creative intuition to know the direction to go for therapy. Some hypnotherapists combine hypnosis with other skills such as:

- NLP (Neuro Linguistic Programming)

- Psychotherapy (study of schools of thought e.g. Freud, Jung, psychoanalysis, Counselling, Adlerian & Family Therapy etc.)

- TimeLine Therapy (have the person go out of their body and go back in time to when a problem was created or go forward in time to see future behaviour, goals achieved etc.)

- Solution Focussed therapy is aimed at helping you to realise your own potential to help yourself. It brings about a change of mind that enables you to free yourself from problems and be much happier.

- EFT (Emotional Freedom Technique – tapping on certain parts of the body).

- Hypnosis by itself is undoubtedly the most powerful technique on the planet for effecting change and is enough on its own. Some therapists just like to add techniques if they believe they are in the person's interest.

5. Only stupid or weak-minded people can be hypnotised. Not at all. In fact, the higher the IQ the better the person is as a subject for hypnosis. Being able to visualise or imagine things or scenes is beneficial in hypnotic trance. The ability to concentrate and be creative is very useful for hypnosis.

6. Some people can't be hypnotised. As hypnotic trance is a natural trance which we all enter daily, clearly everyone can be hypnotised. Whether everyone "wants" to be hypnotised is another matter. A hypnotist requires some co-operation e.g. the person should close their eyes, focus on deep breathing and start to physically relax. If someone does not want to solve their problem or has been taken to a hypnotherapist against their will, the chance of solving their issue is slim.

7. Hypnosis is like going to sleep or being put "under". The word "hypnosis" comes from the Greek Hypnos which means sleep. Unfortunately, this was not a good name to select as generally anyone who is in hypnotic trance is not asleep. I say generally as the idea is to stay awake and not fall asleep but should the person fall asleep it does not matter as the hypnotist is talking to their subconscious mind which is always awake. This is the part of your mind which wakes you e.g. if there is an intruder in your house or will wake a mum if her baby is in distress.

Hypnosis is a heightened sense of awareness, concentration, focus, and hearing. When deprived of one of our five senses, another sense tends to compensate. It therefore makes sense that with your eyes closed, you may hear better. You may hear outside sounds such as traffic as a little louder than the hypnotist hears them. However, they won't disturb you because the deep state of mental and physical relaxation is just not bothered by outside sounds. A dog can keep barking and you will stay deeply relaxed. *"Contemporary research suggests that hypnotic subjects are fully awake and are focusing attention, with a corresponding decrease in their peripheral awareness." (Wikipedia)*

8. You can get "stuck" in hypnosis. No, you can't. As it is a natural state of being in a different brain wave, you come out of it just like when you are daydreaming. If the hypnotist stops talking, you will either emerge from hypnosis to see why the talking has stopped or fall asleep due to your very relaxed state. If you fall asleep, you will just "sleep it off" and waken fully.

9. You forget what was said in a hypnosis session. This is generally untrue. In some cases amnesia may occur if uncovering a particularly traumatic memory which was long-forgotten and deeply buried. The person may not be ready to remember that memory so it is safer to keep the can of worms closed. Mostly a person remembers what was said and even what they said, although not every word and may have been aware of their mind wandering during the session. This is all perfectly normal.

10. If you can hear the hypnotist talking, you are not hypnotised. No. Hypnosis is an altered state of waking consciousness which means you are awake and will therefore hear what is said. Your mind may wander and you may even fall into slumber but your subconscious mind will hear every word and act upon the positive suggestions given in the session. As hypnosis is a heightened state of awareness, you will be aware of the hypnotist's voice and outside sounds.

11. You lose track of time in hypnosis. Actually, this is true. You probably know that the left-hand side of the brain is the rational, thinking, timed side whilst the right-hand side is the creative, dreamy, untimed side. At least for a right-handed person. This means that if you lose yourself in painting, sculpting, sewing etc., you are likely to lose all sense of the time because you enter into a different state of awareness. The same happens in hypnosis. People often comment that their session seemed to last 15-20 minutes and are surprised to find it lasted 40-45 minutes. The beauty is that 20 minutes of hypnosis can leave you as refreshed as 7-8 hours of sleep.

12. What if the hypnotist has a heart attack or dies? You will naturally bring yourself round from the trance, just as you do when daydreaming. In fact we usually include a sentence like, "Should anything happen to me or anything occur which requires your immediate attention, you can bring yourself safely back into full wakening consciousness by counting from one to three." PS. Please dial emergency services and call an ambulance!!!

13. Hypnosis can be dangerous! Life can be dangerous. Seriously, hypnosis is totally safe. It is a state of mental and physical relaxation in which positive, useful suggestions are given to help the person with their problem. No harm can occur.

14. The hypnotist could make me commit crimes or bad acts. Thanks Derren Brown. He broadcast an elaborate experiment called "The Heist" in which the volunteers committed petty crimes right up to an armed raid of a security van. Derren is a very talented entertainer who creates jaw-dropping stunts. Sometimes he explains how he sets up his subjects, often using subliminals and word suggestions. No one can be made to commit or say anything against their values and beliefs. Any hypnotic suggestion which contradicts these values would shock a person back into full waking consciousness.

15. I could reveal sensitive or private information against my will. No, no-one can force you to reveal your bank card PIN numbers or your family's secrets. Usually, you don't have to say anything in hypnosis and if you don't want to, you won't. Simple.

16. Hypnosis can be used as a lie-detector test. If only this was true, every accused criminal could be hypnotised to find out whether they are guilty or the victim of the crime could reliably give evidence of what really happened. It is used sometimes to help reveal forgotten details of crimes or traumas.

17. Repeated hypnotic inductions weaken the mind - Repetitive inductions actually strengthen a person's mental abilities to achieve their goals and release fears, limitations or discomforts. Learning self-hypnosis is enormously beneficial.

18. Hypnosis is addictive. No, but the beneficial feeling of being deeply relaxed both mentally and physically is obviously attractive.

19. You shouldn't hypnotize children. Any parent knows that children live in at least a semi-trance state. They have a great imagination and enjoy the visualization enormously. Most children love the fantasy of flying on a magic carpet which is my favourite induction for children. Others could centre on their favourite TV characters, scoring the winning goal for their favourite football team or flying on a cloud. Children respond very well to positive hypnotic suggestions. Generally, it is best if they are at least seven years old so that they can concentrate on the session but they can also be hypnotized whilst playing and with their eyes still open. Hypnotherapy with children is a skilled area.

20. The Bible bans hypnosis or this is the Devil's work! This is absolute nonsense and comes more from a fear of the unknown than common sense. Some misguided believers even told me that when you relax under hypnosis, the Devil can come in to your mind. Think about it. If that was true, the Devil would enter every time you relax into sleep, relax in front of the TV or a film, relax into a warm bubble bath, relax under the sun, etc.

There are no specific references to hypnosis in The Bible. The Old and New Testament specifically speak against sorcery, witchcraft, spirit channelling and other religious practices. However, they are all specific practices whereas hypnotic trance is a completely natural state which we all enter daily. Some hypnotists practice past life regression. I personally do not believe in this and as I also believe that I attract clients who are meant to work with me, I have never been asked to take someone into past life regression. Regression within this lifetime can have excellent therapeutic outcomes and I do use this technique when I think it is appropriate and after discussion with my client. I would never seek to inflict my beliefs on anyone.

21. Hypnotists use a swinging fob watch or pendulum to put someone into trance. I don't and don't know any hypnotist who does. We are back to films on this stereo-typed image. Whenever I meet someone who finds out that I hypnotize people, they also joke about "..not looking into my eyes". Reality is that we talk people into a hypnotic trance using our voice.

Oh, we don't wear purple jackets or cloaks either! Well I don't anyway.

●**You've read the 21 Myths now read the 30 Truths and Positive Uses of Hypnosis.**

1. Hypnosis is all about relaxing to a deep level. Many people think they cannot relax or have never really relaxed to a deep level until they experience hypnosis. The first time will be pleasant but the person is not sure what to expect and is still holding back in some way. From the second time onwards, people report how much deeper they can go.

About 5% of the population can enter really deep state hypnosis which is necessary for surgery without anaesthesia. Some can even be trained to enter Nth Stage where breathing goes down to 2 or 3 beats per minute. Most people with training can go deep enough for childbirth without pain control called Hypnobirthing (I did, twice), dentistry and learn pain control for chronic pain. Having said that, even in a light trance we can achieve results with many issues, even regressing to past events. I am just saying that a deeper trance is necessary for some aspects of clinical hypnosis.

2. All hypnosis is fundamentally self-hypnosis. The hypnotist leads you with his/her voice but you have to allow yourself to go into hypnotic trance.

3. Hypnosis provides an increased response to suggestions. Although it is not a physical barrier, there is said to be a Critical Faculty between the conscious and subconscious mind. By bypassing the Critical Faculty, with the person in deep relaxation, the subconscious is receptive to positive suggestions. The reasoning, evaluating and judging part of your mind (conscious) is bypassed. The subconscioius does not process negatives so suggestions must always be positive e.g. instead of saying "you will not eat snacks", say "you will enjoy a full feeling without any need to snack between meals." It also prefers pictures hence we use so many visualizations and metaphors.

"The unconscious mind is decidedly simple, unaffected, straightforward and honest. It hasn't got all of this facade, this veneer of what we call adult culture. It's rather simple, rather childish... It is direct and free."

(Dr Milton H. Erickson - founder of modern hypnosis)

4. Hypnosis has the ability to bypass the strong mental defences in a person's conscious thinking. You know consciously why you want to be rid of a bad habit or give up an addiction. You have every good motive to do so but somehow you can't. That is because your subconscious mind is controlling your conscious mind and you are not even aware of the subconscious messages which rule every thought, action, behaviour and belief you have. Hypnosis works direct with this much larger subconscious mind. This is the level where change must occur for it to become permanent.

"The conscious ego cannot tell the unconscious what to do." **- Dr Milton H. Erickson**

5. In hypnosis, your brainwave changes from Beta Wave to Alpha Wave or even Theta Wave. Beta brain wave is the normal, awake state of the brain with conscious activity, alert, ready for physical activity, able to operate machinery, have a conversation, make quick decisions and able to feel positive and negative emotions e.g. excitement but also anger, fear, tension.

Alpha brain wave is the early stage of relaxation although the person may still be alert but not fully focused. As the person relaxes physically and mentally, they are passively aware of their surroundings and feel a sense of well-being and tranquillity. When I say passive, you might be daydreaming so miss your turning when driving. As such, it is a level of trance which is an altered state of consciousness. Realising you have missed the turning means you are back in Beta. Alpha state is the state necessary for most hypnosis e.g. changing habits, eliminating fears, improving confidence etc.

In Alpha, the doorway between the conscious and unconscious/subconscious is opened which also means memories otherwise pushed deep become easily accessible. This is why we can take someone back, in this lifetime or otherwise, depending on the person's belief system, in what we call "regression". Alpha state allows creativity to flow. You can imagine yourself performing without any thinking limiting your achievements.

Theta brain wave is the level of deep relaxation which brings tranquillity but also creativity and accelerated learning. The unconscious, or subconscious, mind cannot distinguish between reality and imagination so this is the state where we can visualize what we want to achieve e.g. a slimmer figure looking good, or playing a sport consistently well, charismatic public speaking and the unconscious mind will re-program whatever is necessary to make this a reality. This is an optimal trance state for hypnosis with heightened imagination and receptivity to suggestion, possibly deep day dreams or lucid dreaming. It is a normal state that we experience from pre-sleep all the way into REM sleep. We therefore go into Theta state every day.

6. Hypnosis is recognized medically. It has been recognized by the American Medical Association and used in the field of medicine since 1958. The United States Government defines it as:

> *"The bypass of the critical factor of the conscious mind and the establishment of acceptable selective thinking."*

Although hypnosis is not yet available free of charge on the UK's National Health Service, many GPs and specialists refer patients to clinical hypnotists. Reimbursement is available through BUPA if the hypnotist has a BUPA number.

7. Hypnosis can be quicker and more cost-effective than traditional therapy.

Comparison of Hypnotherapy Success Rates

Hypnotherapy 93% Success Rate

Only 4 sessions

Behaviour Therapy 72% Success Rate

Only 22 sessions

Psychotherapy 38% Success Rate

Only 600 sessions

Source: Psychotherapy – Theory Research and Practice Volume 7, Number 1

8. Hypnosis has an effect on the serotonin and dopamine levels in the brain. Technically what appears to be happening in hypnosis is that the balance of chemical neurotransmitters such as serotonin and dopamine change dramatically both during hypnosis and afterwards, the latter apparently as a direct response to suggestions during hypnosis. The act of entering hypnosis, often induced through calming, meditative practice appears to increase serotonin levels (feel-good, inner peace neurotransmitters) and this primes the brain for acceptance of hypnotic suggestion, whilst dampening conflict responses. At the same time, dopamine levels (alertness, excitation neurotransmitters) are reduced. After hypnosis, dopamine levels rise, but depending on hypnotic suggestion, reuptake of serotonin may be inhibited.

9. Hypnosis really helps in stress management. Stress, anxiety and worry: at least one of these probably applies to just about every member of the population, even young children. We may not be able to remove the cause of the stress but it is about how we react to it, whether *it* controls *us* or whether we can learn to handle the cause effectively. Drinking wine to forget might be a strategy but it is not a healthy strategy. Swallowing tranquillizers or anti-depressants is another road which may give temporary relief but again is not the best way. For the chemical reasons explained above, hypnosis is a totally natural way of learning to cope with stress which cannot be avoided in the modern world.

10. Hypnosis can help you overcome a phobia quickly without extensive CBT (Cognitive Behavioural Therapy). If you are arachnophobic (scared of spiders), CBT will require introducing you to small spiders, then bigger ones and even bigger ones. You will have to take them home, study them and let them crawl over you. I was arachnophobic and the thought of undergoing that treatment was far worse for me than running away from spiders. My fear was so bad that I would scream if I saw a tiny money spider and my family called them "Freds" because even the word scared me.

One day I realised my young son had copied my fear so I decided to do something about it. I put myself into self-hypnosis and applied a technique we use called "de-sensitisation". Within just a few minutes I was able to look at a book of spider photos. I visited a session with the "Spiderman" at my son's school and held a tarantula in my hand. No screaming, no clanging heart and no fear. I now take the spiders out calmly. I still don't like them because I think they are ugly but I am not afraid of them anymore. I overcame the fear using hypnosis. One week after doing this, someone rang me who was going to work in Africa and had a terrible fear of – you've guessed it – spiders. She was also scared of grasshoppers and cockroaches. She thought she might have to turn down a dream job but with two sessions from me she overcame all the fear and is now happily coping with life in the African wild.

I also use the NLP technique "Fast Phobia Release" which is another 15 minutes technique using association (seeing the problem with your own eyes) and disassociation (seeing you as a third person having the problem).

It is rational to be afraid of certain things like sharks when swimming in a shark-infested sea but irrational in a swimming pool. That is when a fear tips into becoming a phobia. Often they are debilitating affecting daily life such as claustrophobia (enclosed spaces), agrophobia (open spaces), germs or water.

11. Hypnosis can help you overcome the fear of public speaking. No more clammy hands, sweating, anxious heart-beating and squeaky voice. Just calm, confident, self-assured speaking. I used to blush if I had to speak in a business meeting of three people. Now I actually enjoy speaking in front of a group and am delighted to help others move from fear to fun. As well as overcoming the physically unpleasant symptoms of fear, I will teach you techniques to enhance your speaking and communication skills. Even a bit of warm-up I learned in speech therapy to ensure you speak crystally clear.

I also helped an opera singer with her stage fright. She did not want to depend on beta blockers and chose to control her nerves with self-hypnosis.

12. Hypnosis can eliminate your fear of heights, fear of flying or many other fears . e.g. clowns, insects, animals, balloons, lifts/elevators, bridges, thunderstorms, needles, blood, MRI scans, using eye drops or contact lenses. Some of these fears prevent people from seeking much-needed medical treatment or going to the dentist. Using the desensitisation method mentioned above, a long list of fears can be dealt with at the deep subconscious level. Now you can buy that penthouse apartment or fly to Australia.

Then there are the intangible fears which really can prevent us from living a full life. These include fear of failure (and success), fear of being alone, commitment, conflict, rejection and the unknown. We can challenge those fears and with some of my techniques, have you on the way to a bigger, brighter future.

13. Hypnosis helps you with Weight loss by changing the way you think about food at the deep unconscious level.

Why Diets, Slimming Clubs and Low-Fat Foods Keep Adding on the Pounds...

FORGET DIETING...

Diets only work in the short term. The US$ 40 Billion diet industry knows that yet they keep allowing you to waste your money. You might lose a few pounds but then you put even more weight back-on. Yo-yo dieting!

FORGET STARVATION...

If you restrict your calorie intake you starve your body and become obsessed with eating. Starving your body slows down your metabolic rate so you actually lose weight at a snail's pace.

FORGET" LOW-FAT"FOODS & "LIGHT" DRINKS

"Low-fat" foods and "light" drinks only make your body hold on to the weight. The artificial sweeteners in these drinks raise blood sugar thereby worsening the effect on diabetics and lead to a host of chronic illnesses. Fat is not a bad word as your body needs a certain amount of fat for essential functions. The hidden sugar and salt are far worse.

FORGET DIETING CLUBS

Dieting clubs are great for mutual support but they focus on calorie counting and ultimately want you to buy their brand of restricted foods. Go for friendship, not for their system.

I offer the amazing new Gastric Band Hypnosis – all the benefits of gastric band surgery but without any of the side effects. "Imagine" your stomach reducing to the size of a golf ball without anaesthetic, scars, pain or time off work. This is Virtual Gastric Band. I didn't believe it but it has been available for about four years now, has been in clinical trials with the NHS and works. The best result so far is an amazing eight stone!!!

14. Stop Smoking in One Session. The NHS have a quit smoking programme which takes time and centres on nicotine replacement products. You remain addicted to nicotine which is totally not necessary. Rather than have you focus on smoking and obsess with cutting down, I can stop you smoking in just one session! This will be without cravings or withdrawal symptoms. Recently a woman came for my single stop smoking session. She went away a non-smoker and we kept in close contact so that I could give her any support she needed. Her boyfriend decided to stop at the same time by himself using willpower. He cannot stop thinking about cigarettes, still has 2-3 per day and is feeling rough. She stopped the EASY way for a small investment whilst he is still a smoker.

15.**Hypnosis can rid you of unwanted habits.** Many are not seriously limiting your life but may be annoying, perhaps more to others around you than to yourself e.g. nail-biting, thumb-sucking and bedwetting (children or adults), persistent skin picking or scratching, teeth grinding (bruxism), mouth or cheek chewing, restless leg syndrome, nervous tics, blushing, knuckle cracking, nervous cough or swallowing, excessive blinking, rocking (Rhythmic Body Disorder Relaxation), night tremors and bladder control (stress incontinence).

Hypnosis can help with compulsive habits or disorders. Gambling, lying, internet porn, shopping (Oniomania) – think of the money you will save!, stealing, Kleptomania (hoarding), hair pulling (trichotillomania), Tourette's Syndrome (involuntary swearing), OCD (Obsessive Compulsive Disorder) although I stress that OCD is a difficult disorder to treat fully.

16. Hypnosis can help with addictions in a positive way. 12-step programmes have been around for a long time and obviously work but they keep the person fixed in the addiction e.g. repeatedly saying, "My name is xxxx and I'm an alcoholic." No, xxxx used to be an alcoholic but hypnosis can give the freedom to put that behaviour in the past and adopt a new behaviour.

When I conduct my "Stop Smoking in one session of hypnosis", I remind the smoker of all the hazards which they are leaving behind but focus on their new, healthy life and the new behaviours. I say that calling themselves an "ex-smoker" reminds them of being a smoker rather than the more positive "non-smoker". Other addictions frequently treated are chocolate, sugar, caffeine (yes, you can live without tea and coffee J), cannabis, tranquillizers/anti-depressants, even hard drugs like cocaine or heroine. Also, problem addictions such as gambling and pornography. The internet has led many people down the dark paths of addictions eg online gambling, cybersex and social media addiction. While the internet has opened up ways of communicating to the whole world, the apparent anonymity encourages people to be untruthful in internet dating, cybersex and so much more.

17. **Hypnosis can help you control your alcohol drinking or stop altogether.** Some people know they have a problem with binge drinking, drinking alone or just want to be in control of their alcoholic intake and enjoy a couple of drinks rather than waking up with a thick head in someone else's apartment. It takes guts for someone to admit they have tipped into alcoholism but I don't like labelling anyone. I certainly don't judge someone else's behaviour or life choices. If someone wants help, we can discuss how far they need to go and change the behaviour at the deep subconscious level. If you've had a problem for a long time, don't expect a magic wand to take it away in one session.

18. **Hypnosis can improve memory, concentration and performance.** While in this state of mind, one's focus and concentration is heightened. The individual is able to concentrate intensely on a specific thought or memory, while blocking out all possible sources of distraction. Hypnosis can be used to enhance your performance e.g. improve your mental ability to play better golf; mentally rehearse sporting events; help you to prepare for public speaking in a calm, confident manner. One company specialises

in the teaching of foreign languages to people who are in hypnotic trance.

http://www.naturalnews.com/026978_hypnosis_memory_therapy.html#ixzz2NuvcZjCp

19. **Hypnosis helps with many areas of personal development** e.g. overcoming procrastination, becoming motivated, realizing that perfection can hold you back and generally working on areas which are keeping you from being the person you can be. Living the life you can create. Personal development is my passion and I love to help someone find a world without limits and go forward.

"Who looks outside, dreams; who looks inside, awakes." - **Carl Jung**

20. **Hypnosis can help with Fertility.** Knowing that some physical problem reduces your chance of conception is an all too common situation today. About one in five couples find it difficult to get pregnant and in 10 per cent of those cases, no cause is found. For those who decide to try IVF, the road ahead is painful, stressful and very expensive. Hypnosis aids fertility by working at the deep unconscious level to undo the programming which is causing the physical restriction. There are no guarantees, of course, but more and more fertility doctors are working with hypnotists to relax their patients and give them the best possible chance of conception. Sometimes the problem is not fertility but processing a healthy pregnancy and there again hypnosis can help.

Studies indicate "infertile" women using hypnosis have up to 55% conception success rate as compared to 20% for those not following these methods. Hypnosis has been so successful in fact, that now a specialised field of hypnosis exists, appropriately called HypnoFertility.

21. **Hypnobirthing** is the natural way of giving birth whilst controlling pain without the need of an epidural (risk of back problems later on), pills (baby is born sleepy so may not want to breastfeed), gas & air (not good for asthmatics) or a TENS machine (have to hire beforehand and somewhat awkward to use). Hypnobirthing is a specialized form of hypnosis so look for a hypnotist with this training.

22. **Hypnosis can help with Children's problems** e.g. bedwetting,

thumb-sucking, coping with being bullied, coping with divorce or death in the family, increasing self-confidence, even feeling bigger. As I said above, children really enjoy hypnosis and respond very well. I helped a boy of 8 who was small for his age. He lacked self-confidence, was not coping well at school and was attracting bullying. In one session "flying out of the magic chair on the magic carpet", we changed his self-image. He walked out of the room feeling taller, more self-assured. His mother reported a noticeable improvement in his school work and the bullying just stopped.

Hypnotherapy may be helpful for certain symptoms of ADHD. Teenagers and young people can be really helped with the stress of exam nerves. Hypnosis can make the difference between a pass or fail just by learning to relax and heightening focus and concentration.

23. Hypnosis can lead to improved sports performance. A study of Olympic athletes showed that whether an athlete actually ran a race or imagined that he did so, the neurons in the brain still made the muscles fire. Many athletes and sports people use hypnosis to imagine themselves running faster, driving the golf ball into the hole, volleying the tennis ball harder etc. What we can imagine in our subconscious mind becomes reality.

However, while hypnosis can be used to enhance performance,it cannot make people stronger or more athletic than their existing physical capabilities. It cannot do is the physically impossible e.g. build your arm muscles without the necessary exercise, have you play championship level golf/tennis unless you already have the skill.

24. Hypnosis can help sleep problems e.g. insomnia, falling asleep, staying asleep, frequent nightmares, night tremors, restless leg syndrome, snoring (or sleeping with a snorer).

25. Hypnosis can help depression. Changing negative memory associations into positive associations can dramatically change a person's life. The result of using hypnosis is a healthier perspective on life. Changing a negative association with a memory can have a profound positive effect on people's life and causes a shift in perceptual predisposition.

It has even been suggested that hypnosis can reduce the symptoms of dementia. University of Liverpool (2008, July 29). Hypnosis Shown To Reduce Symptoms Of Dementia. *ScienceDaily*. Found online at: **http://www.sciencedaily.com/releases/2008/07/080728111402.htm**

26. Hypnosis helps with many stress-related illnesses. The Health Education Authority said:

"Research shows that there is more scientific evidence for Hypnotherapy than any other Complementary Therapy...by using hypnosis people can perform prodigious feats of will-power and self-healing."

There are many studies indicating that sensory, circulatory, gastrointestinal, and cutaneous functions can be altered by means of hypnosis. 1. Psychol Bull. 1961 Sep;58:390-419. Physiological effects of "hypnosis". BARBER TX. PMID: 13686786 [PubMed - indexed for MEDLINE]. MeSH Terms. Hypnosis*.

Professor Spiegel, who works at the Department of Psychiatry and Behavioral Sciences at Stanford University in the US, also advised that the National Institute for Health and Clinical Excellence (NICE) should add hypnotherapy to its list of approved therapies for many more conditions. He reported that hypnotherapy is effective with allergies, high blood pressure and post-operative pain, as well as anaesthesia for liver biopsy. Hypnotherapy is already recognised by NICE for treatment of irritable bowel syndrome (IBS).

Professor Spiegel's call was for hypnosis to step out from the shadows and be recognised as a highly effective therapeutic procedure for appropriate condition, and that it slough off its old image as a strange mystical practice.

"It is time for hypnosis to work its way into the mainstream of British medicine," he said, before affirming that there is solid science behind hypnosis and adding: *"We need to get that message across to the bodies that influence this area. Hypnosis has no negative side-effects. It makes*

operations quicker, as the patient is able to talk to the surgeon as the operation proceeds, and it is cheaper than conventional pain relief. Since it does not interfere with the workings of the body, the patient recovers faster, too."

"It is also extremely powerful as a means of pain relief. Hypnosis has been accepted and rejected because people are nervous of it. They think it's either too powerful or not powerful enough, but, although the public are sceptical, the hardest part of the procedure is getting other doctors to accept it."

Skin diseases. *Some skin complaints have even baffled dermatologists when they do not respond to creams, cortisone or other treatments. This can be because the subconscious mind has created a skin problem for a reason which we are not consciously aware of. Or the problem can be stress-related. Typical problems which respond well to hypnosis are psoriasis, eczema, acne, rosacea, hives (urticaria) and warts which literally drop off a few days after hypnosis.*

Irritable Bowel Syndrome (IBS). *Hypnotherapy has been studied for the treatment of irritable Bowel Syndrome.*

Moore, M. & Tasso, A.F. 'Clinical hypnosis: the empirical evidence' in The Oxford Handbook of Hypnosis (2008) ISBN 0-19-857009-0 pp. 719-718

Hypnosis for IBS has received support in the National Institute for Health and Clinical Excellence guidance published for UK health services.[59] NICE Guidance for IBS. (PDF) . Retrieved on 2011-10-01.

At Manchester University, Whorwell's group have found long-term follow-up rates of 95% success with classical, refractory IBS cases who had previously failed with an average of six types of treatment. Certain atypical patients had a wide range of lower rates, but classic-form IBS in patients under 50 had a 100% success. [Prior, Colgan, Whorwell 1990; Whorwell, Prior and Faragher, 1984; Whorwell, Prior and Colgan 1987;

Whorwell 2004]

Cancer. I am in no way suggesting that hypnosis is a cure for cancer. How hypnosis does help is to relieve the person of the fear caused by cancer, help them to relax, help the body undergo chemotherapy, reduce nausea/vomiting and promote a healthy immune system. A colleague of mine is researching the effect of hypnosis on cancer patients and has found very positive outcomes.

The reduction of nausea and vomiting in cancer patients undergoing chemotherapy.4 Barrett, D. (2001). The power of hypnosis. *Psychology Today*. Found online at http://psychologytoday.com/articles/index.php?term=20010101-000034&page=1

27. Hypnosis can help someone with chronic pain. *The management of chronic pain can be helped greatly by learning how to use hypnosis. Psychological approaches to pain relief are well documented, and hypnosis has been widely used for centuries in this area.*

Dr Milton Erickson, one of the world's leading lights in the use of clinical hypnosis, used his skills to manage his own chronic pain from the two bouts of polio he suffered during his lifetime.

One of the problems with chronic pain management is that the brain habituates to pain-killing drugs, requiring higher and higher doses. Hypnosis works in a different way, causing the brain to stop responding to pain signals.

Hypnotherapy has been used by many to manage numerous instances of pain, including irritable bowel syndrome, sciatica, spinal stenosis, burns, rheumatoid arthritis, joint pain, neck pain and a variety of other injuries and illnesses. The basic premise of hypnotherapy is to change the way individuals perceive pain messages in order to reduce the intensity of what they are feeling.

This can be achieved using a number of techniques which may either be used alone or in combination depending on your individual circumstances and the specialist areas of your practitioner. As well as using certain hypnotherapy techniques such as suggestion hypnotherapy, analytical hypnotherapy and *visualisation, some practitioners may also use Neuro-Linguistic Programming (NLP) and Psychotherapy to enhance their treatment.*

Many hypnotherapists will also include self-hypnosis as part of your treatment plan, meaning that they will teach you to practice techniques so that once your sessions have come to an end you will be able to continuing using the skills you have learnt in daily life.

28. *Hypnosis is used instead of anaesthesia.* *Some people are allergic to chemical anaesthesia (ether). Many prefer not to use it as it can take up to a month for the body to rid itself of the effects. I know! Recovery time is faster with less pain and less bruising. I heard a women talk of her foot bone operation using only hypnosis. The NHS was reluctant to allow this so cancelled her operation twice and then required her to sign disclaimers. They wanted to give her pain medication even though she was not in pain and insisted she walk out of the hospital on crutches even though she did not need any assistance.*

At the University Hospital in Liege, Belgium a team of doctors led by Dr. Marie-Elisabeth Faymonville has logged more than 5,100 surgeries by hypnosedation, a technique Faymonville developed that replaces general anesthesia with hypnosis, local anesthesia and a mild sedative. One operation was on the Queen of the Belgians in 2009.

The new interest stems in part from studies showing that hypno-sedated patients suffer fewer side effects than fully sedated ones do. According to Dr Faymonville, hypnotized patients can get by on less than 1% of the standard medications required for general anaesthesia, thus avoiding such after effects as nausea, fatigue, lack of coordination and cognitive impairment. In a 1999 study of thyroid patients, Dr Faymonville found that the typical hypno-sedated patient returned to work 15 days after surgery, compared *with 28 days for a fully anaesthetized patient.*

http://www.time.com/time/magazine/article/0,9171,1174707,00.html#ixzz 2NzJ8JBS6

Dave Elman devised a hypnotic induction with which his students routinely obtained states of hypnosis adequate for medical and surgical procedures in under three minutes. The first heart operation using hypnosis rather than normal anaesthesia (because of severe problems with the patient) was performed by his students with Dave Elman in the operating room as "coach".

29. Hypnosis can prepare the body for surgery and faster recovery. This is more than positive thinking to take away the fear. Disbrow, Bennet and Owings made suggestions of early return to normal bowel movements and reduced hospital stay so much so that an average saving of $1200 per patient was made.

I was in hospital for brain surgery. My surgeon told me I would have to stay for two weeks yet he was so impressed by my recovery after I used self-hypnosis and Tai Chi before my operation, that I was allowed to go home after just six days. Within one month, I was functioning normally again.

30. Hypnosis can help sexual problems e.g. Erectile Dysfunction (ED), premature or delayed ejaculation, vaginisimus, addiction to pornography or masturbation, sexual orientation issues. Some suggest that hypnotic suggestion can help with penis or breast enlargement by regressing to the time of development.

So now you know the truths about hypnosis.

I help people worldwide with Hypnosis On Skype

www.skype-hypnosis.com

Holistic Practices and Hypnotherapy

Alasdair Gordon

Alasdair is a graduate of Edinburgh University. He has worked in the fields of administration, college teaching and personal development. He is a registered hypnotherapist in the United Kingdom (General Hypnotherapy Register) and a Certified NLP Master Practitioner through NLP Highland. Alasdair is also qualified in a number of alternative therapies, including spiritual healing. He achieved a taught doctoral degree (EdD) in change agent studies with Calamus International University (BWI) in 2005.

Alasdair edited Book 2 of Delavar's "The Hypnotists' Bible" that was included in Volume 2 of Dr Royle's "Encyclopedia of Hypnotherapy, Stage- Hypnosis and Complete Mind Therapy".

Alasdair is now retired and living in Hamilton, South Lanarkshire, Scotland (UK).

abghypno@yahoo.co.uk

Virtually unknown as recently as the 1970s, the term "holistic" has now become somewhat of a buzz word. The word is derived from the Greek root *holos* which means "entire" or "inclusive".

Looking at the therapy world today, we could find ourselves confused by the huge – and ever growing – number of approaches that are available. There has also been a tendency, perhaps especially so in the United Stated of America, to take one existing approach and break it down into smaller parts, each one of which then becomes a therapy in its own right.

How can all of these different approaches be right? Does the client put all his trust in colour therapy, crystal therapy, hopi ear candles, reflexology or hot stones to say nothing of the hypnotherapy itself? But even hypnotherapy can be broken down and specialised. There are, for example, past life regression, cognitive hypnotherapy, complete mind therapy and clinical hypnotherapy. Are these approaches (and there are many more) only part of a bigger picture or are they therapies in their own right? In fact, there is no easy answer.

Some therapists will adopt an exclusive attitude, reminiscent of the less positive aspects of conventional medicine, declaring that they alone have the "answer" to the client's problem trough the application of their own dedicated approach.

I write these words without any intended disrespect for conventional medicine, on which we all rely at some time in our lives. Yet, the medical model has not always served us well. When the present writer was a child, the local doctor was treated as little less than a god (which was actually very unfair on him). The doctor would tell you what was "wrong" with you and what he would prescribe. The doctor would tell you when it was time to retire or for you to go on holiday. The doctor could not be asked questions or argued with because that would waste his incredibly valuable time and might hold him back from saving some more lives before dinner-time. This is a stereotype, of course, but like most stereotypes, it contains a grain of truth.

Nowadays, people are usually much less deferential than they used to be towards all of the professions, medicine included. And the medical profession itself has changed in many respects. I remember a doctor telling me how frustrating he found it when a patient tried to place total responsibility for his healing on the doctor. "I'm in your hands, doctor!"

To me, it is crucially important for hypnotherapists to pitch themselves at the appropriate professional level. We are not medical practitioners. We have clients, not patients. We are not qualified to diagnose nor do we offer to "cure" people. We want to assist and support people to achieve their own healing, but that is quite a different matter.

The reputation of the therapist is very important. It can take years to build up a good reputation. Equally, a good reputation can be lost overnight.

Many – probably most of you who are reading this chapter – will be members of some kind of professional association. I pass no value judgement on which one you "should" join. That has to be a personal decision. Also the law and therapeutic practices generally can vary greatly between different countries. However, I suggest it is unwise not to be a member of some organisation that has at least minimal professional requirements.

Professional organisations will normally publish their ethical standards and the only advice I would presume to offer is simply to follow them. It may be superficially attractive to think of oneself as a "loose cannon", but it will not please your association nor will it satisfy your insurers. That is not to say that you cannot be original or creative.

When meeting a client for the first time, it is useful to gather as much information as possible about the client's particular circumstances, taking care not to breach the Data Protection legislation. These details should include such medical details and treatment received as the client is willing to share. Remember that a hypnotherapist is not qualified to diagnose physical or mental illness or disorder. That includes depression which (in the UK) can only be diagnosed by a qualified practitioner.

You may well form your own opinion of what is "wrong" with the client but it is advisable to be very cautious in what you say.

There is nothing wrong – indeed it is good practice – in asking the client if his medical practitioner is aware that he is seeking hypnotherapy. In general, however, the therapist has no right to approach a client's doctor without that client's express permission. If a client seems in doubt as to the suitability of hypnotherapy for his particular issue, you can suggest that he talk it over with his medical practitioner before proceeding further. In practice, few will take up the opportunity at this stage but in this litigious society, it is a useful safeguard.

It is also worth pointing out to a client that hypnotherapy has been used and developed by a number of distinguished doctors in the past, including James Esdaile, James Braid, John Elliotson (who invented the stethoscope) and, more recently Milton Erickson. It is also worth pointing out that the British Medical Association ("BMA") recognised hypnosis as a valid therapy as long ago as 1955.

If a client declares that he is epileptic, suggest that hypnotherapy is not appropriate for him. Other subjects who are unsuitable for hypnotherapy are people with an active psychotic illness or a current suicidal state. It would be unprofessional to attempt hypnosis on any client who is clearly under the influence of alcohol or illicit drugs. Also if a client has lost memory syndrome, hypnotherapy is probably best avoided.

Client confidentiality is important and whatever is disclosed in the session(s) must remain totally confidential. Confidence could only be broken if the therapist had good reason to believe that the client was posing a serious risk to himself or someone else. If in doubt, consult the guidelines of your own professional association.

Although attitudes are changing and hypnotherapy has become much more main stream in the United Kingdom, there is still a fair degree of ignorance and suspicion. Many otherwise sensible people still equate hypnosis with some form of sinister manipulation or even with the occult. It is worth emphasising to a new client that hypnotherapy is complementary to conventional medicine and not in opposition to it. At the same time it is worth emphasising that hypnosis has achieved remarkable success in areas where conventional medicine has not proved especially helpful – such as smoking cessation, weight reduction, stress relief, phobia removal and related areas.

It should be remembered that the ability of the mind to affect the physical body has been well documented over many centuries. The mind/body connection is not some recent New Age fad. Recognition of this synergistic link certainly goes back to the time of Ancient Greece and possible even further back. Over the late nineteenth century and throughout most of the twentieth, that relationship seemed to be forgotten by most of conventional medicine. In fact, medicine became much more scientific in that it demanded rational empirical proof for the efficiency of any kind of treatment. No disrespect is intended to science when it is suggested that science cannot answer every question nor can it explain everything that happens in this world.

In more recent times, possibly due to the rising interest in psychology, the capacity of the human mind to influence the body has come much more to the fore and back into the mainstream of medical thinking.

The other side of the coin is that practitioners such as hypnotherapists cannot ignore physical issues that may arise. If someone wants to lose weight but lives on a diet of chips and fizzy drinks it is not out of place for the hypnotherapist to suggest that the client obtain some advice on healthy eating and well as offering weight control hypnotherapy. Similarly, if someone has a major problem with stress, hypnotherapy may be very helpful in achieving relaxation but there may be other issues in the person's family or work life that also need to be addressed.

It is always worth at least attempting to establish a good working relationship with medical practitioners in the area. There are some who will, from time to time, refer a patient for hypnotherapy and, obviously, you want to be top of that list.

So far, we have looked mainly at the relationship between the conventional medical practitioner and the hypnotherapist. But how – if at all – does the hypnotherapist interface with other complementary therapists, of whom there are now many? Is there a place, say, for integrating other approaches into your own practice?

Opinions of this matter vary greatly. There are those hypnotherapists who take the purist line. In other words they offer hypnotherapy and absolutely nothing else. To offer more would compromise their professionalism. I respect that view. We must all do what we believe is right for us. My own personal approach would not be purist, but I say that with a degree of caution.

Sometimes, you will also come on a client whom you wish to refer on to someone else. This should not be done lightly or as a matter of course but, in certain cases, it can be appropriate. An example might be suggesting that a client with a weight problem might also wish to meet with a dietician as part of the overall treatment of the condition.

But, for hypnotherapists who do not take the purist approach how far is it possible – and reasonable – to offer more than hypnotherapy? The first word of warning is to check that you are adequately insured. Most indemnity insurances will allow you to add a number of additional therapies to your basic cover. Some will ask to see evidence of your qualifications. In my view, it is unwise anyway to offer any therapy without at least a piece of paper to back it up. Diplomas vary greatly in quality and standard but if they are issued by any reputable training organisation they are usually an adequate basis to start your practice. The real learning, of course, is always in the doing.

It is certainly helpful to any hypnotherapist to have some training in NLP. Whilst hypnotherapy and NLP frequently run in to one another, there are NLP techniques, such as the Fast Phobia Cure, which are extremely useful in practice. It is maybe worth pointing out that NLP officially is not, and does not claim to be a therapy. It is worth finding out if there is an NLP Practice Group in your area. These groups tend to meet about once a month to exchange information and experience and to demonstrate techniques.

As a therapist, I personally favour what might be called the toolbox or integrative approach. If my carefully prepared hypnotherapy script does not seem to be working for that client, what else might be appropriate and could I offer it? In the paraphrased words of Milton Erickson, remember that there are no difficult clients, only unresourceful therapists.

What works for one person may not work for another. So, someone of a sceptical frame of mind may not be impressed if you offer, say, Angel

Therapy. Such a person may respond more positively to Cognitive Behavioural Therapy or even Life Coaching.

I also suggest that you do not, at least publicly, advertise too many therapies or approaches you might offer. The public will tend to be suspicious of someone who appears to be a jack of all trades. You also might give the impression of being desperate to take your clients' money under any circumstances.

What you, as therapist, feel comfortable in offering has to be a very personal matter. Do ensure that you feel competent in what you offer. There is nothing more off-putting to a client than to have a therapist who does not appear to be entirely competent or confident.

So, assuming g that you decide to have more than one string to your bow, how do you know when to use different approaches?

I suggest that the initial consultation cannot be overrated in importance. Not only can you gather important factual information about the client, but you can also establish professional rapport. The client will become more confident in the therapist as he opens up and shares. The therapist will also become more aware of where his client is "coming from".

Obviously this feedback will be helpful in framing an appropriate script. It may be that one client will expect what might be called the "full works" – induction, deepener, suggestions – involving quite a deep trance. Other clients may favour a more conversational Ericksonian approach. The ability to make such assessment comes with experience.

However, I would like to conclude this chapter by suggesting that, of all people, a hypnotherapist should be willing to listen to his own intuition. We believe that the subconscious often holds the remedy for our clients and that it is an incredibly powerful factor. Similarly, let us not be afraid to listen to our own intuitive feelings when we are supporting clients and want to choose what is best for them.

Perpetual State Theory
By Brian Stracner (HypnoSwami)

Brian is a professional individual of clinical, personal, and academic experience. He has a keen knack for relating with people, and building new friendships. This is a person who you can say "has been there." Brian feels this enables him to understand his students' and clients' needs.

www.NorthStateHypnosis.net

www.NationalSchoolofHypnosis.com

Perpetual State Theory

There is no doubt that personality and behavior development is a complex subject. Many professionals struggle to persuade that life is a simple scale relying heavily on simple, one sided views of reality. However, there are many grey areas between the spectrums of black in contrast to white. One common example is seen through the nature versus nurture debate. However, a possibly more important debate is the one between state versus non-state hypnotic theories. The author proposes that, just as in the nature versus nurture debate, both aspects are relevant. However the author also proposes that, everyone is already hypnotized to behave in the manners that they carry out. Thus Perpetual State theory is born.

Everyone is Hypnotized

Personality and behavior is not only learned through modeling others, it is also developed through examples, metaphors, direct, and indirect feedback from internal as well as external suggestion. A hypnotist could view life as one long series of hypnotic inductions and suggestions, and how the individual relates to the feedback develops into the personality and behavior.

In 1774 Benjamin Franklin and Antoine Lavoisier sought out to see whether the first clinical hypnotherapist (Anton Mesmer) was actually utilizing magnetic forces to heal clients, or if the phenomenon was something else entirely (Herr, 2005). This was not only important to assess whether or not Mesmer was using magnetic forces, this is also an important marker in history since it was the very first controlled clinical trial (Herr, 2005). This valuable historic study found that, Mesmer's healing abilities resided in the art of suggestion, not magnetism. Unfortunately, instead of focusing on the power of suggestion as an important facet of healing, Mesmer was debunked and lived an obscure life from the traumatic realization that there was no special power associated to the treatments he conducted. Furthermore, to assert the point, everyone is always subjected to variant levels of suggestion. In turn, since suggestion is at the core of Mesmerism (what we now call hypnotism), every single living being on earth is hypnotized into their personal reality.

State Versus Non-State Theories

Somewhere within state versus non-state debate there is an argument of whether or not trance is necessary to achieve hypnotic phenomena. However, if one keeps an open mind, the studies conducted about hypnosis do not actually lead one to believe that trance is a special state that must be induced by an operator. In fact the complete opposite can be seen in many pre-induction talks of state and non-state theorists. A few examples that Cheek and LeCron (1968) stated were: "Whenever we become absorbed in what we are doing, we slip into hypnosis," and "Any strong emotion may produce hypnosis (p. 6)." Not only are these statements commonly made by lay hypnotists around the globe, but have also been confirmed by arguments made by Spiegel and Spiegel, Edmonston, Hilgard, Kihlstrom, Kirsch, Parry, and a myriad of others, all who have conducted a plethora of research providing a huge amount of data in regards to what hypnosis is (Kirsch & Jay, 1995). Seeing that any strong emotion can induce hypnosis, compared to how many strong emotions a person experiences in a lifetime, compounded how those suggestions affect the individual personality and behavior of a person shines a bright light on the realization that every single person is in fact hypnotized into who they have become on every level of being. In turn, this would also mean that hypnosis is not an arcane power to be wielded by an operator at all, or simply utilizing manipulative psychology and conditioning. Instead, it would mean that everyone is already hypnotized, and can also be de-hypnotized and hypnotized into changing personality traits and behaviors.

People like to believe that they have free will; that they are able to choose what they think, and do. People like to believe that they have control over their lives and their destiny. The fact is that because people live in a society with a specific culture and influences by the media, their "decisions" are not the result of choice, but the result of a set of beliefs and morels that they did not choose. These beliefs and mores were produced by outside sources and each person has been convinced of their veracity. The truth of these beliefs is not the result of careful deliberation, but the result of a steady stream of messages that people gradually accept as fact. Because of this, each of us lives in persistent hypnotic- like state. All of us are already living with a set of mental parameters created by social hypnosis. Thus, the current view that there are State theories and Non-State theories of hypnosis begs the question. By definition, we are all already living in a hypnosis-like consciousness. It is not possible to hypnotize the already hypnotized.

State Theory holds that one experiences an altered state of consciousness and Non- State theory holds that one is able to respond to a suggestion without being in special state of mind (Walley, 2013). Each of these theories points to something that is true about the human consciousness yet neither is true enough in and of itself. The influences most people experience each day produce a third kind of hypnotic state, what I call "Perpetual State" (PS). PS is the result of culture, media and other social influences. These result in a steady stream of suggestions and influences which create a seemingly free conscious state. In effect, each is the product of the suggestions heard directly or indirectly in everyday life. A PS is very similar to the idea of Determinism. This idea states that all events are caused by another (Hoefer, 2010).

To illustrate the connection between Determinism and PS, imagine a person who is trying to decide whether or not to go to college. Determinism would argue that the choice this person ultimately makes can be predicted by looking at the events which preceded him. So, for example, if this person's parents went to college, it is a family expectation, and it will increase the chances of a successful career (something this person values), then it is likely that these factors will cause the person to decide to go to college. PS is similar in that the "causes" of Determinism are replaced with "influences" or "suggestions". There are many such factors in each person's life that contribute to PS.

One element of PS is culture. Each person is born into a particular culture with its own ways of explaining phenomena and of dealing with the interactions among one another. As we grow, we accept this situation as a reality. Most, if any, never question cultural expectations unless they are influenced by another source which causes a conflict between two possible realities. When this happens, one reality is rejected for another. For many, it is a cultural expectation that they marry, get a good job, and have a family. This is something that is not ever questioned for most people. Instead, it is just something that is done. People who experience this are indeed experiencing a PS. They have been influenced by the suggestions of their culture to act in a certain way at certain points in their life.

Another element of PS is the media. The media is such a strong part of PS that hundreds of television shows and articles have been written about the influences of media on individuals, society and criminal behavior (Sage Publications, 2009). Madison Avenue depends on this influence. The media and PS are so intertwined that certain populations, such as young girls, are endangered by the media's influence. This is seen in the area of body perception. Young girls ages 9-15 are susceptible to taking suggestions so literally that it causes serious medical conditions such as bulimia (PBS, 2003). Additionally, the media affects the buying behavior of consumers worldwide and nearly all possible space on TV, the Internet, on city streets and vehicles is purchased for ad placement. The advertisement industry is huge with larger corporations in the US spending 3-5 billions of dollars a year on advertising (Laya, 2011). Companies do this because they know that influences of advertising work. They intrinsically understand that a PS is how people live and function. Part of how advertising works is its relation to peer pressure.

Peer pressure is a powerful influence on people's values and decisions. This is true of teenagers deciding to try drugs and corporate men deciding which golf club to join. The media takes advantage of this element of human nature and uses it to create a second level of messages given to others through their peers. If one's peer group is buying Apple iPads, it is extremely unlikely that they will by a Kindle HD. Between the imagery and suggestions provided by Apple advertising and the values of one's peer group, the suggestions and influences are nearly insurmountable. A PS is created which decides that this person will purchase an Apple iPad. If needed, this person will go into debt to have it, or, in rarer cases, they will steal one (Sage Publications (2009).

The idea that any of us can be placed in a hypnotic state is true. What is misunderstood is the fact that we all are always in a PS. We are all already determined to believe certain things and to behave in a certain way. Perhaps it is possible to change some of the influences on our beliefs and values through additional hypnosis. But people need to understand that they are not undergoing hypnosis for the first time! They have been in a persistent state of hypnosis and going for more hypnosis is like being alive and trying to get more "life". It is not really possible. Certain elements of life and hypnosis can be adjusted perhaps, but no one undergoes hypnosis as a new experience.

References:

Cheek, LeCron (1968). Clinical Hypnotherapy. New York: Grune &

Stratton

Herr, H.W., (2005) Franklin, Lavoisier, and Mesmer: origin of the

controlled clinical trial.

Department of Urology, Memorial Sloan-Kettering Cancer Center, New

York, NY 10021, USA. Sep-Oct;23(5):346-51.

Retrieved PubMed February 13th, 2013 From: PubMed - indexed for

MEDLINE PMID: 16144669

Kirsch, I., Jay. (1995) The Altered State of Hypnosis: Changes in the
Theoretical Landscape. American Psychologist. APA Inc. Vol. 50. No. 10.
846-858. 0003-066X/95

Hoefer, C. (2010). "Causal determinism". Stanford Encyclopedia of
Philosophy. Retrieved from

http://plato.stanford.edu/entries/determinism-causal/

Laya,P. (2011). "Do you pay enough for adverstising? One big corporation
spend a jaw-dropping 4.2 billion last year". Business Insider. Retrieved
from

http://www.businessinsider.com/corporations-ad-spending-2011-6?op=1

PBS (2003) "Eating disorders and the family". Retrieved from:

http://www.pbs.org/perfectillusions/eatingdisorders/preventing_media.html

Sage Publications (2009). The influence of technology, media and popular
culture on criminal behavior. Retrieved from

http://www.sagepub.com/upm-data/19507_Chapter_10.pdf

Walley, M. (2013) "Hypnosis and suggestion: exploring the science behind
hypnosis". Retrieved from:

http://www.hypnosisandsuggestion.org/scientific-theories-of-
hypnosis.html

The Battle For Your Mind

Mass Mind Control Techniques In America

By Dick Sutphen - https://richardsutphen.com/

Persuasion and Brainwashing Techniques Being Used On The Public Today Reformatted for WWW display and distribution by Dynamic Living

I'm Dick Sutphen and this tape is a studio-recorded, expanded version of a talk I delivered at the World Congress of Professional Hypnotists Convention in Las Vegas, Nevada. Although the tape carries a copyright to protect it from unlawful duplication for sale by other companies, in this case, I invite individuals to make copies and give them to friends or anyone in a position to communicate this information.

Although I've been interviewed about the subject on many local and regional radio and TV talk shows, large-scale mass communication appears to be blocked, since it could result in suspicion or investigation of the very media presenting it or the sponsors that support the media. Some government agencies do not want this information generally known. Nor do the Born-Again Christian movement, cults, and many human-potential trainings.

Everything I will relate only exposes the surface of the problem. I don't know how the misuse of these techniques can be stopped. I don't think it is possible to legislate against that which often cannot be detected; and if those who legislate are using these techniques, there is little hope of affecting laws to govern usage. I do know that the first step to initiate change is to generate interest. In this case, that will probably only result from an underground effort.

In talking about this subject, I am talking about my own business. I know it, and I know how effective it can be. I produce hypnosis and subliminal tapes and, in some of my seminars, I use conversion tactics to assist participants to become independent and self-sufficient. But, anytime I use these techniques, I point out that I am using them, and those attending have a choice to participate or not. They also know what the desired result of participation will be.

So, to begin, I want to state the most basic of all facts about brainwashing: In the entire history of man, no one has ever been brainwashed and realized, or believed, that he had been brainwashed. Those who have been brainwashed will usually passionately defend their manipulators, claiming they have simply been "shown the light" ...or have been transformed in miraculous ways.

The Birth of Conversion: Brainwashing in Christian Revivalism in 1735.

Conversion is a "nice" word for brainwashing...and any study of brainwashing has to begin with a study of Christian revivalism in eighteenth century America. Apparently, Jonathan Edwards accidentally discovered the techniques during a religious crusade in 1735 in Northampton, Massachusetts.

By inducing guilt and acute apprehension and by increasing the tension, the "sinners" attending his revival meetings would break down and completely submit. Technically, what Edwards was doing was creating conditions that wipe the brain slate clean so that the mind accepts new programming. The problem was that the new input was negative. He would tell them, "You're a sinner! You're destined for hell!"

As a result, one person committed suicide and another attempted suicide. And the neighbors of the suicidal converts related that they, too, were affected so deeply that, although they had found "eternal salvation," they were obsessed with a diabolical temptation to end their own lives.

Once a preacher, cult leader, manipulator or authority figure creates the brain phase to wipe the brain-slate clean, his subjects are wide open. New input, in the form of suggestion, can be substituted for their previous ideas. Because Edwards didn't turn his message positive until the end of the revival, many accepted the negative suggestions and acted, or desired to act, upon them.

Charles J. Finney was another Christian revivalist who used the same techniques four years later in mass religious conversions in New York. The techniques are still being used today by Christian revivalists, cults, human-potential trainings, some business rallies, and the United States Armed services...to name just a few.

Let me point out here that I don't think most revivalist preachers realize or know they are using brainwashing techniques. Edwards simply stumbled upon a technique that really worked, and others copied it and have continued to copy it for over two hundred years. And the more sophisticated our knowledge and technology become, the more effective the conversion. I feel strongly that this is one of the major reasons for the increasing rise in Christian fundamentalism, especially the televised variety, while most of the orthodox religions are declining.

The Three Brain Phases: The Pavlovian Explanation

The Christians may have been the first to successfully formulate brainwashing, but we have to look to Pavlov, the Russian scientist, for a technical explanation. In the early 1900s, his work with animals opened the door to further investigations with humans. After the revolution in Russia, Lenin was quick to see the potential of applying Pavlov's research to his own ends.

Three distinct and progressive states of transmarginal inhibition were identified by Pavlov. The first is the equivalent phase, in which the brain gives the same response to both strong and weak stimuli. The second is the paradoxical phase, in which the brain responds more actively to weak stimuli than to strong. And the third is the ultra-paradoxical phase, in which conditioned responses and behavior patterns turn from positive to negative or from negative to positive.

With the progression through each phase, the degree of conversion becomes more effective and complete. The way to achieve conversion are many and varied, but the usual first step in religious or political brainwashing is to work on the emotions of an individual or group until they reach an abnormal level of anger, fear, exitement, or nervous tension.

The progressive result of this mental condition is to impair judgement and increase suggestibility. The more this condition can be maintained or intensified, the more it compounds. Once catharsis, or the first brain phase, is reached, the complete mental takeover becomes easier. Existing mental programming can be replaced with new patterns of thinking and behavior.

Other often-used physiological weapons to modify normal brain functions are fasting, radical or high sugar diets, physical discomforts, regulation of breathing, mantra chanting in meditation, the disclosure of awesome mysteries, special lighting and sound effects, programmed response to incense, or intoxicating drugs.

The same results can be obtained in contemporary psychiatric treatment by electric shock treatments and even by purposely lowering a person's blood sugar level with insulin injections. Before I talk about exactly how some of the techniques are applied, I want to point out that hypnosis and conversion tactics are two distinctly different things--and that conversion techniques are far more powerful. However, the two are often mixed...with powerful results.

How Revivalist Preachers Work

If you'd like to see a revivalist preacher at work, there are probably several in your city. Go to the church or tent early and sit in the rear, about three-quarters of the way back. Most likely repetitive music will be played while the people come in for the service. A repetitive beat, ideally ranging from 45 to 72 beats per minute (a rhythm close to the beat of the human heart), is very hypnotic and can generate an eyes-open altered state of consciousness in a very high percentage of people. And, once you are in an alpha state, you are at least 25 times as suggestible as you would be in full beta consciousness.

The music is probably the same for every service, or incorporates the same beat, and many of the people will go into an altered state almost immediately upon entering the sanctuary. Subconsciously, they recall their state of mind from previous services and respond according to the post-hypnotic programming.

Watch the people waiting for the service to begin. Many will exhibit external signs of trance-- body relaxation and slightly dilated eyes. Often, they begin swaying back and forth with their hands in the air while sitting in their chairs. Next, the assistant pastor will probably come out. He usually speaks with a pretty good "voice roll."

The "Voice Roll" Technique

A "voice roll" is a patterned, paced style used by hypnotists when inducing a trance. It is also used by many lawyers, several of whom are highly trained hypnotists, when they desire to entrench a point firmly in the minds of the jurors. A voice roll can sound as if the speaker were talking to the beat of a metronome or it may sound as though he were emphasizing every word in a monotonous, patterned style. The words will usually be delivered at the rate of 45 to 60 beats per minute, maximizing the hypnotic effect.

The Build-up Process: Inducing Altered States

Now the assistant pastor begins the "build-up" process. He induces an altered state of consciousness and/or begins to generate the excitement and the expectations of the audience. Next, a group of young women in "sweet and pure" chiffon dresses might come out to sing a song. Gospel songs are great for building excitement and involvement. In the middle of the song, one of the girls might be "smitten by the spirit" and fall down or react as if possessed by the Holy Spirit. This very effectively increases the intensity in the room. At this point, hypnosis and conversion tactics are being mixed. And the result is the audience's attention span is now totally focused upon the communication while the environment becomes more exciting or tense.

Assured Continuation: Fleecing the Flock

Right about this time, when an eyes-open mass-induced alpha mental state has been achieved, they will usually pass the collection plate or basket. In the background, a 45-beat-per-minute voice roll from the assistant preacher might exhort, "Give to God...Give to God...Give to God...."

And the audience does give. God may not get the money, but his already-wealthy representative will.

Bonding by Fear and Suggestion

Next, the fire-and-brimstone preacher will come out. He induces fear and increases the tension by talking about "the devil," "going to hell," or the forthcoming Armegeddon. In the last such rally I attended, the preacher talked about the blood that would soon be running out of every faucet in the land. He was also obsessed with a "bloody axe of God," which everyone had seen hanging above the pulpit the previous week. I have no doubt that everyone saw it--the power of suggestion given to hundreds of people in hypnosis assures that at least 10 to 25 percent would see whatever he suggested they see.

Testimony: Creating Community Spirit

In most revivalist gatherings, "testifying" or "witnessing" usually follows the fear-based sermon. People from the audience come up on stage and relate their stories. "I was crippled and now I can walk!" "I had arthritis and now it's gone!" It is a psychological manipulation that works. After listening to numerous case histories of miraculous healings, the average guy in the audience with a minor problem is sure he can be healed. The room is charged with fear, guilt, intense excitement, and expectations.

Miracles

Now those who want to be healed are frequently lined up around the edge of the room, or they are told to come down to the front. The preacher might touch them on the head firmly and scream, "Be healed!" This releases the psychic energy and, for many, catharsis results. Catharsis is a purging of repressed emotions. Individuals might cry, fall down or even go into spasms. And if catharsis is effected, they stand a chance of being healed. In catharsis (one of the three brain phases mentioned earlier), the brain-slate is temporarily wiped clean and the new suggestion is accepted.

For some, the healing may be permanent. For many, it will last four days to a week, which is, incidentally, how long a hypnotic suggestion given to a somnambulistic subject will usually last. Even if the healing doesn't last, if they come back every week, the power of suggestion may continually override the problem...or sometimes, sadly, it can mask a physical problem which could prove to be very detrimental to the individual in the long run.

The Grey Area of Legitimacy

I'm not saying that legitimate healings do not take place. They do. Maybe the individual was ready to let go of the negativity that caused the problem in the first place; maybe it was the work of God. Yet I contend that it can be explained with existing knowledge of brain/mind function.

A Game in Which the Rules Keep Changing

The techniques and staging will vary from church to church. Many use "speaking in tongues" to generate catharsis in some while the spectacle creates intense excitement in the observers. The use of hypnotic techniques by religions is sophisticated, and professionals are assuring that they become even more effective. A man in Los Angeles is designing, building, and reworking a lot of churches around the country. He tells ministers what they need and how to use it. This man's track record indicates that the congregation and the monetary income will double if the minister follows his instructions. He admits that about 80 percent of his efforts are in the sound system and lighting.

Powerful sound and the proper use of lighting are of primary importance in inducing an altered state of consciousnes--I've been using them for years in my own seminars. However, my participants are fully aware of the process and what they can expect as a result of their participation.

Six Conversion Techniques

Cults and human-potential organizations are always looking for new converts. To attain them, they must also create a brain-phase. And they often need to do it within a short space of time—a weekend, or maybe even a day. The following are the six primary techniques used to generate the conversion.

Isolation Intimidation, Deprivation and Indoctrination

The meeting or training takes place in an area where participants are cut off from the outside world. This may be any place: a private home, a remote or rural setting, or even a hotel ballroom where the participants are allowed only limited bathroom usage. In human-potential trainings, the controllers will give a lengthy talk about the importance of "keeping agreements" in life. The participants are told that if they don't keep agreements, their life will never work. It's a good idea to keep agreements, but the controllers are subverting a positive human value for selfish purposes.

The participants vow to themselves and their trainer that they will keep their agreements. Anyone who does not will be intimidated into agreement or forced to leave. The next step is to agree to complete training, thus assuring a high percentage of conversions for the organizations.

They will usually have to agree not to take drugs, smoke, and sometimes not to eat...or they are given such short meal breaks that it creates tension. The real reason for the agreements is to alter internal chemistry, which generates anxiety and hopefully causes at least a slight malfunction of the nervous system, which in turn increases the conversion potential.

The "Sell It By Zealot" Technique.

Before the gathering is complete, the agreements will be used to ensure that the new converts go out and find new participants. They are intimidated into agreeing to do so before they leave. Since the importance of keeping agreements is so high on their priority list, the converts will twist the arms of everyone they know, attempting to talk them into attending a free introductory session offered at a future date by the organization. The new converts are zealots. In fact, the inside term for merchandising the largest and most successful human-potential training is, "sell it by zealot!"

At least a million people are graduates and a good percentage have been left with a mental activation button that assures their future loyalty and assistance if the guru figure or organization calls. Think about the potential political implications of hundreds of thousands of zealots programmed to campaign for their guru.

Be wary of an organization of this type that offers follow-up sessions after the seminar. Followup sessions might be weekly meetings or inexpensive seminars given on a regular basis which the organization will attempt to talk you into taking--or any regularly scheduled event used to maintain control. As the early Christian revivalists found, long-term control is dependent upon a good follow-up system.

Wearing Down Resistance

Alright. Now, let's look at the second tip-off that indicates conversion tactics are being used. A schedule is maintained that causes physical and mental fatigue. This is primarily accomplished by long hours in which the participants are given no opportunity for relaxation or reflection.

Increasing Tension

The third tip-off: techniques used to increase the tension in the room or environment.

Introducing Uncertainty About Identity

Number four: Uncertainty. I could spend hours relating various techniques to increase tension and generate uncertainty. Basically, the participants are concerned about being "put on the spot" or encountered by the trainers, guilt feelings are played upon, participants are tempted to verbally relate their innermost secrets to the other participants or forced to take part in activities that emphasize removing their masks. One of the most successful human-potential seminars forces the participants to stand on a stage in front of the entire audience while being verbally attacked by the trainers. A public opinion poll, conducted a few years ago, showed that the number one most fearful situation an individual could encounter is to speak to an audience. It ranked above window washing outside the 85th floor of an office building.

So you can imagine the fear and tension this situation generates within the participants. Many faint, but most cope with the stress by mentally going away. They literally go into an alpha state, which automatically makes them many times as suggestible as they normally are. And another loop of the downward spiral into conversion is successfully effected.

Jargon

The fifth clue that conversion tactics are being used is the introduction of jargon--new terms that have meaning only to the "insiders" who participate. Vicious language is also frequently used, purposely, to make participants uncomfortable.

Lack of Humor: No Release, No Resistance

The final tip-off is that there is no humor in the communications...at least until the participants are converted. Then, merry-making and humor are highly desirable as symbols of the new joy the participants have supposedly "found."

Not Always a Bad Thing

I'm not saying that good does not result from participation in such gatherings. It can and does. But I contend it is important for people to know what has happened and to be aware that continual involvement may not be in their best interest.

Over the years, I've conducted professional seminars to teach people to be hypnotists, trainers, and counselors. I've had many of those who conduct trainings and rallies come to me and say, "I'm here because I know that what I'm doing works, but I don't know why." After showing them how and why, many have gotten out of the business or have decided to approach it differently or in a much more loving and supportive manner.

Many of these trainers have become personal friends, and it scares us all to have experienced the power of one person with a microphone and a room full of people. Add a little charisma and you can count on a high percentage of conversions. The sad truth is that a high percentage of people want to give away their power--they are true "believers"!

Cults: A Captive Course in Stockholm Syndrome

Cult gatherings or human-potential trainings are an ideal environment to observe first-hand what is technically called the "Stockholm Syndrome." This is a situation in which those who are intimidated, controlled, or made to suffer, begin to love, admire, and even sometimes sexually desire their controllers or captors.

But let me inject a word of warning here: If you think you can attend such gatherings and not be affected, you are probably wrong. A perfect example is the case of a woman who went to Haiti on a Guggenheim Fellowship to study Haitian Voodoo. In her report, she related how the music eventually induced uncontrollable bodily movement and an altered state of consciousness.

Although she understood the process and thought herself above it, when she began to feel herself become vulnerable to the music, she attempted to fight it and turned away. Anger or resistance almost always assures conversion. A few moments later she was possessed by the music and began dancing in a trance around the Voodoo meeting house. A brain phase had been induced by the music and excitement, and she awoke feeling reborn.

The Only Hope of Immunity

The only hope of attending such gatherings without being affected is to be a Buddha and allow no positive or negative emotions to surface. Few people are capable of such detachment.

The US Marines as a Brainwashing Cult

Before I go on, let's go back to the six tip-offs to conversion. I want to mention the United States Government and military boot camp. The Marine Corps talks about breaking men down before "rebuilding" them as new men--as marines! Well, that is exactly what they do, the same way a cult breaks its people down and rebuilds them as happy flower sellers on your local street corner.

Every one of the six conversion techniques are used in boot camp. Considering the needs of the military, I'm not making a judgement as to whether that is good or bad. IT IS A fact that the men are effectively brainwashed. Those who won't submit must be discharged or spend much of their time in the brig.

Steps in the Decognition Process

Once the initial conversion is effected, cults, armed services, and similar groups cannot have cynicism among their members. Members must respond to commands and do as they are told, otherwise they are dangerous to the organizational control. This is normally accomplished as a three-step Decognition Process.

Alertness reduction

Step One is alertness reduction: The controllers cause the nervous system to malfunction, making it difficult to distinguish between fantasy and reality. This can be accomplished in several ways. poor diet is one; watch out for Brownies and Koolaid. The sugar throws the nervous system off. More subtle is the "spiritual diet" used by many cults. They eat only vegetables and fruits; without the grounding of grains, nuts, seeds, dairy products, fish or meat, an individual becomes mentally "spacey."

Inadequate sleep is another primary way to reduce alertness, especially when combined with long hours of work or intense physical activity. Also, being bombarded with intense and unique experiences achieves the same result.

Programmed Confusion

Step Two is programmed confusion: You are mentally assaulted while your alertness is being reduced as in Step One. This is accomplished with a deluge of new information, lectures, discussion groups, encounters or one-to-one processing, which usually amounts to the controller bombarding the individual with questions. During this phase of decognition, reality and illusion often merge and perverted logic is likely to be accepted.

Thought Stopping

Step Three is thought stopping: Techniques are used to cause the mind to go "flat." These are altered-state-of-consciousness techniques that initially induce calmness by giving the mind something simple to deal with and focusing awareness. The continued use brings on a feeling of elation and eventually hallucination. The result is the reduction of thought and eventually, if used long enough, the cessation of all thought and withdrawal from everyone and everything except that which the controllers direct. The takeover is then complete. It is important to be aware that when members or participants are instructed to use "thought-stopping" techniques, they are told that they will benefit by so doing: they will become "better soldiers" or "find enlightenment."

Thought-Stopping Techniques

Marching

There are three primary techniques used for thought stopping. The first is marching: the thump, thump, thump beat literally generates self-hypnosis and thus great susceptibility to suggestion.

Meditation

The second thought stopping technique is meditation. If you spend an hour to an hour and a half a day in meditation, after a few weeks, there is a great probability that you will not return to full beta consciousness. You will remain in a fixed state of alpha for as long as you continue to meditate. I'm not saying this is bad--if you do it yourself. It may be very beneficial. But it is a fact that you are causing your mind to go flat. I've worked with meditators on an EEG machine and the results are conclusive: the more you meditate, the flatter your mind becomes until, eventually and especially if used to excess or in combination with decognition, all thought ceases. Some spiritual groups see this as nirvana--which is bullshit. It is simply a predictable physiological result. And if heaven on earth is non-thinking and non-involvement, I really question why we are here.

Chanting

The third thought-stopping technique is chanting, and often chanting in meditation. "Speaking in tongues" could also be included in this category. All three-stopping techniques produce an altered state of consciousness. This may be very good if you are controlling the process, for you also control the input. I personally use at least one selfhypnosis programming session every day and I know how beneficial it is for me. But you need to know if you use these techniques to the degree of remaining continually in alpha that, although you'll be very mellow, you'll also be more suggestible.

True Believers and Mass Movements

Before ending this section on conversion, I want to talk about the people who are most susceptible to it and about Mass Movements. I am convinced that at least a third of the population is what Eric Hoffer calls "true believers." They are joiners and followers...people who want to give away their power. They look for answers, meaning, and enlightenment outside themselves.

Hoffer, who wrote "The True Believer", a classic on mass movements, says, "true believers are not intent on bolstering and advancing a cherished self, but are those craving to be rid of unwanted self. They are followers, not because of a desire for self-advancement, but because it can satisfy their passion for self-renunciation!" Hoffer also says that true believers "are eternally incomplete and eternally insecure"!

I know this from my own experience. In my years of communicating concepts and conducting trainings, I have run into them again and again. All I can do is attempt to show them that the only thing to seek is the True Self within. Their personal answers are to be found there and there alone. I communicate that the basics of spirituality are self-responsibility and self-actualization.

But most of the true believers just tell me that I'm not spiritual and go looking for someone who will give them the dogma and structure they desire. Never underestimate the potential danger of these people. They can easily be molded into fanatics who will gladly work and die for their holy cause. It is a substitute for their lost faith in themselves and offers them as a substitute for individual hope. The Moral Majority is made up of true believers. All cults are composed of true believers. You'll find them in politics, churches, businesses, and social cause groups. They are the fanatics in these organizations.

Mass Movements will usually have a charismatic leader. The followers want to convert others to their way of living or impose a new way of life--if necessary, by legislating laws forcing others to their view, as evidenced by the activities of the Moral Majority. This means enforcement by guns or punishment, for that is the bottomline in law enforcement.

A common hatred, enemy, or devil is essential to the success of a mass movement. The Born-Again Christians have Satan himself, but that isn't enough--they've added the occult, the New Age thinkers and, lately, all those who oppose their integration of church and politics, as evidenced in their political reelection campaigns against those who oppose their views. In revolutions, the devil is usually the ruling power or aristocracy. Some human-potential movements are far too clever to ask their graduates to join anything, thus labeling themselves as a cult--but, if you look closely, you'll find that their devil is anyone and everyone who hasn't taken their training.

There are mass movements without devils but they seldom attain major status. The True Believers are mentally unbalanced or insecure people, or those without hope or friends. People don't look for allies when they love, but they do when they hate or become obsessed with a cause. And those who desire a new life and a new order feel the old ways must be eliminated before the new order can be built.

Persuasion Techniques

Persuasion isn't technically brainwashing but it is the manipulation of the human mind by another individual, without the manipulated party being aware what caused his opinion shift. I only have time to very basically introduce you to a few of the thousands of techniques in use today, but the basis of persuasion is always to access your right brain. The left half of our brain is analytical and rational. The right side is creative and imaginative. That is overly simplified but it makes my point. So, the idea is to distract the left brain and keep it busy. Ideally, the persuader generates an eyes-open altered state of consciousness, causing you to shift from beta awareness into alpha; this can be measured on an EEG machine.

"Yes Set"

First, let me give you an example of distracting the left brain. Politicians use these powerful techniques all the time; lawyers use many variations which, I've been told, they call "tightening the noose."

Assume for a moment that you are watching a politician give a speech. First, he might generate what is called a "yes set." These are statements that will cause listeners to agree; they might even unknowingly nod their heads in agreement. Next come the truisms. These are usually facts that could be debated but, once the politician has his audience agreeing, the odds are in the politician's favor that the audience won't stop to think for themselves, thus continuing to agree. Last comes the suggestion. This is what the politician wants you to do and, since you have been agreeing all along, you could be persuaded to accept the suggestion. Now, if you'll listen closely to my political speech, you'll find that the first three are the "yes set," the next three are truisms and the last is the suggestion.

"Ladies and gentlemen: are you angry about high food prices? Are you tired of astronomical gas prices? Are you sick of out-of-control inflation?

Well, you know the Other Party allowed 18 percent inflation last year; you know crime has increased 50 percent nationwide in the last 12 months, and you know your paycheck hardly covers your expenses any more. Well, the answer to resolving these problems is to elect me, John Jones, to the U.S. Senate."

Embedded Commands

And I think you've heard all that before. But you might also watch for what are called embedded commands. As an example: On key words, the speaker would make a gesture with his left hand, which research has shown is more apt to access your right brain. Today's media-oriented politicians and spellbinders are often carefully trained by a whole new breed of specialist who are using every trick in the book--both old and new--to manipulate you into accepting their candidate.

The Power of NLP

The concepts and techniques of Neuro-Linguistics are so heavily protected that I found out the hard way that to even talk about them publicly or in print results in threatened legal action. Yet Neuro-Linguistic training is readily available to anyone willing to devote the time and pay the price. It is some of the most subtle and powerful manipulation I have yet been exposed to. A good friend who recently attended a two-week seminar on Neuro-Linguistics found that many of those she talked to during the breaks were government people.

Interspersal Technique

Another technique that I'm just learning about is unbelievably slippery; it is called an interspersal technique and the idea is to say one thing with words but plant a subconscious impression of something else in the minds of the listeners and/or watchers.

Practical Examples

Let me give you an example: Assume you are watching a television commentator make the following statement: Senator Johnson is assisting local authorities to clear up the stupid mistakes of companies contributing to the nuclear waste problems." It sounds like a statement of fact, but, if the speaker emphasizes the right word, and especially if he makes the proper hand gestures on the key words, you could be left with the subconscious impression that Senator Johnson is stupid. That was the subliminal goal of the statement and the speaker cannot be called to account for anything.

Persuasion techniques are also frequently used on a much smaller scale with just as much effectiveness. The insurance salesman knows his pitch is likely to be much more effective if he can get you to visualize something in your mind. This is right-brain communication. For instance, he might pause in his conversation, look slowly around your livingroom and say, "Can you just imagine this beautiful home burning to the ground?" Of course you can! It is one of your unconscious fears and, when he forces you to visualize it, you are more likely to be manipulated into signing his insurance policy.

Shock and Confusion

The Hare Krishnas, operating in every airport, use what I call shock and confusion techniques to distract the left brain and communicate directly with the right brain. While waiting for a plane, I once watched one operate for over an hour. He had a technique of almost jumping in front of someone. Initially, his voice was loud then dropped as he made his pitch to take a book and contribute money to the cause. Usually, when people are shocked, they immediately withdraw. In this case they were shocked by the strange appearance, sudden materialization and loud voice of the Hare Krishna devotee. In other words, the people went into an alpha state for security because they didn't want to confront the reality before them.

In alpha, they were highly suggestible so they responded to the suggestion of taking the book; the moment they took the book, they felt guilty and responded to the second suggestion: give money. We are all conditioned that if someone gives us something, we have to give them something in return--in that case, it was money. While watching this hustler, I was close enough to notice that many of the people he stopped exhibited an outward sign of alpha--their eyes were actually dilated.

Subliminal Programming

Subliminals are hidden suggestions that only your subconscious perceives. They can be audio, hidden behind music, or visual, airbrushed into a picture, flashed on a screen so fast that you don't consciously see them, or cleverly incorporated into a picture or design. Most audio subliminal reprogramming tapes offer verbal suggestions recorded at a low volume. I question the efficacy of this technique--if subliminals are not perceptible, they cannot be effective, and subliminals recorded below the audible threshold are therefore useless. The oldest audio subliminal technique uses a voice that follows the volume of the music so subliminals are impossible to detect without a parametric equalizer. But this technique is patented and, when I wanted to develop my own line of subliminal audiocassettes, negotiations with the patent holder proved to be unsatisfactory.

My attorney obtained copies of the patents which I gave to some talented Hollywood sound engineers, asking them to create a new technique. They found a way to psycho-acoustically modify and synthesize the suggestions so that they are projected in the same chord and frequency as the music, thus giving them the effect of being part of the music. But we found that in using this technique, there is no way to reduce various frequencies to detect the subliminals. In other words, although the suggestions are being heard by the subconscious mind, they cannot be monitored with even the most sophisticated equipment.

If we were able to come up with this technique as easily as we did, I can only imagine how sophisticated the technology has become, with unlimited government or advertising funding. And I shudder to think about the propaganda and commercial manipulation that we are exposed to on a daily basis. There is simply no way to know what is behind the music you hear. It may even be possible to hide a second voice behind the voice to which you are listening.

The series by Wilson Bryan Key, Ph.D., on subliminals in advertising and political campaigns well documents the misuse in many areas, especially printed advertising in newspapers, magazines, and posters. The big question about subliminals is: do they work? And I guarantee you they do. Not only from the response of those who have used my tapes, but from the results of such programs as the subliminals behind the music in department stores. Supposedly, the only message is instructions to not steal: one East Coast department store chain reported a 37 percent reduction in thefts in the first nine months of testing.

A 1984 article in the technical newsletter, "Brain-Mind Bulletin," states that as much as 99 percent of our cognitive activity may be "non-conscious," according to the director of the Laboratory for Cognitive Psychophysiology at the University of Illinois. The lengthy report ends with the statement, "these findings support the use of subliminal approaches such as taped suggestions for weight loss and the therapeutic use of hypnosis and Neuro-Linguistic Programming."

Mass Misuse of Subliminal Programming

I could relate many stories that support subliminal programming, but I'd rather use my time to make you aware of even more subtle uses of such programming. I have personally experienced sitting in a Los Angeles auditorium with over ten thousand people who were gathered to listen to a current charismatic figure. Twenty minutes after entering the auditorium, I became aware that I was going in and out of an altered state. Those accompanying me experienced the same thing. Since it is our business, we were aware of what was happening, but those around us were not.

By careful observation, what appeared to be spontaneous demonstrations were, in fact, artful manipulations. The only way I could figure that the eyes-open trance had been induced was that a 6- to 7-cycle-per-second vibration was being piped into the room behind the air conditioner sound.

That particular vibration generates alpha, which would render the audience highly susceptible. Ten to 25 percent of the population is capable of a somnambulistic level of altered states of consciousness; for these people, the suggestions of the speaker, if non-threatening, could potentially be accepted as "commands."

Vibrato

This leads to the mention of vibrato. Vibrato is the tremulous effect imparted in some vocal or instrumental music, and the cyle-per-second range causes people to go into an altered state of consciousness. At one period of English history, singers whose voices contained pronounced vibrato were not allowed to perform publicly because listeners would go into an altered state and have fantasies, often sexual in nature. People who attend opera or enjoy listening to singers like Mario Lanza are familiar with this altered state induced by the performers.

Extra-low Frequency Vibrations (ELFs)

Now, let's carry this awareness a little farther. There are also inaudible ELFs (extra-low frequency waves). These are electromagnetic in nature. One of the primary uses of ELFs is to communicate with our submarines. Dr. Andrija Puharich, a highly respected researcher, in an attempt to warn U.S. officials about Russian use of ELFs, set up an experiment. Volunteers were wired so their brain waves could be measured on an EEG. They were sealed in a metal room that could not be penetrated by a normal signal.

Puharich then beamed ELF waves at the volunteers. ELFs go right through the earth and, of course, right through metal walls. Those inside couldn't know if the signal was or was not being sent. And Puharich watched the reactions on the technical equipment: 30 percent of those inside the room were taken over by the ELF signal in six to ten seconds.

When I say "taken over," I mean that their behavior followed the changes anticipated at very precise frequencies. Waves below 6 cycles per second caused the subjects to become very emotionally upset, and even disrupted bodily functions. At 8.2 cycles, they felt very high...an elevated feeling, as though they had been in masterful meditation, learned over a period of years. Eleven to 11.3 cycles induced waves of depressed agitation leading to riotous behavior.

The Neurophone

Dr. Patrick Flanagan is a personal friend of mine. In the early 1960s, as a teenager, Pat was listed as one of the top scientists in the world by "Life" magazine. Among his many inventions was a device he called the Neurophone--an electronic instrument that can successfully programm suggestions directly through contact with the skin. When he attempted to patent the device, the government demanded that he prove it worked. When he did, the National Security Agency confiscated the neurophone. It took Pat two years of legal battle to get his invention back.

In using the device, you don't hear or see a thing; it is applied to the skin, which Pat claims is the source of special senses. The skin contains more sensors for heat, touch, pain, vibration, and electrical fields than any other part of the human anatomy.

In one of his recent tests, Pat conducted two identical seminars for a military audience—one seminar one night and one the next night, because the size of the room was not large enough to accommodate all of them at one time. When the first group proved to be very cool and unwilling to respond, Patrick spent the next day making a special tape to play at the second seminar. The tape instructed the audience to be extremely warm and responsive and for their hands to become "tingly." The tape was played through the neurophone, which was connected to a wire he placed along the ceiling of the room. There were no speakers, so no sound could be heard, yet the message was successfully transmitted from that wire directly into the brains of the audience. They were warm and receptive, their hands tingled and they responded, according to programming, in other ways that I cannot mention here.

Technological Tools for Mass Manipulation

The more we find out about how human beings work through today's highly advanced technological research, the more we learn to control human beings. And what probably scares me the most is that the medium for takeover is already in place. The television set in your livingroom and bedroom is doing a lot more than just entertaining you.

Before I continue, let me point out something else about an altered state of consciousness. When you go into an altered state, you transfer into right brain, which results in the internal release of the body's own opiates: enkephalins and Beta-endorphins, chemically almost identical to opium.

In other words, it feels good...and you want to come back for more.

Recent tests by researcher Herbert Krugman showed that, while viewers were watching TV, right-brain activity outnumbered left-brain activity by a ratio of two to one. Put more simply, the viewers were in an altered state...in trance more often than not. They were getting their Betaendorphin "fix." To measure attention spans, psychophysiologist Thomas Mulholland of the Veterans Hospital in Bedford, Massachusetts, attached young viewers to an EEG machine that was wired to shut the TV set off whenever the children's brains produced a majority of alpha waves. Although the children were told to concentrate, only a few could keep the set on for more than 30 seconds!

Most viewers are already hypnotized. To deepen the trance is easy. One simple way is to place a blank, black frame every 32 frames in the film that is being projected. This creates a 45-beat-perminute pulsation perceived only by the subconscious mind--the ideal pace to generate deep hypnosis.

The commercials or suggestions presented following this alpha-inducing broadcast are much more likely to be accepted by the viewer. The high percentage of the viewing audience that has somnambulistic-depth ability could very well accept the suggestions as commands--as long as those commands did not ask the viewer to do something contrary to his morals, religion, or selfpreservation.

The medium for takeover is here. By the age of 16, children have spent 10,000 to 15,000 hours watching television--that is more time than they spend n school! In the average home, the TV set is on for six hours and 44 minutes per day--an increase of nine minutes from last year and three times the average rate of increase during the 1970s.

It obviously isn't getting better...we are rapidly moving into an alpha-level world--very possibly the Orwellian world of "1984"--placid, glassy-eyed, and responding obediently to instructions. A research project by Jacob Jacoby, a Purdue University psychologist, found that of 2,700 people tested, 90 percent misunderstood even such simple viewing fare as commercials and "Barnaby Jones." Only minutes after watching, the typical viewer missed 23 to 36 percent of the questions about what he or she had seen. Of course they did--they were going in and out of trance! If you go into a deep trance, you must be instructed to remember--otherwise you automatically forget.

In Closing...

I have just touched the tip of the iceberg. When you start to combine subliminal messages behind the music, subliminal visuals projected on the screen, hypnotically produced visual effects, sustained musical beats at a trance-inducing pace . . . you have extremely effective brainwashing.

Every hour that you spend watching the TV set you become more conditioned. And, in case you thought there was a law against any of these things, guess again. There isn't! There are a lot of powerful people who obviously prefer things exactly the way they are. Maybe they have plans for...?

Explosive Secrets Revealed to Ensure Smoking Cessation Success!!

By Harley Street Hypnotherapist & NLP Lifestyle Coach

Rob Martin DHP DCMT DNLP

Rob Martin is also known as Robert Phoenix. With many years of experience & *Expert Training*, Rob has been taught amongst others by *"The Man that taught Paul McKenna"* Hypnotherapy - Mr Andrew Newton & Dr Jonathan Royle PhD.

"I wholeheartedly recommend Rob for Weight Loss, Smoking Cessation & Stress related issues..." says Dr Lisa Smith, General Practitioner – UK.

Rob qualified as a Hypnotherapist in 2004 & has trained in the USA as well as the UK. He has Diplomas & Certificates in many areas of Hypnotherapy & NLP including a Non Accredited Doctor of Philosophy in Hypnotherapy & Advanced Master Practitioner Certificate in NLP.

In 2011 Rob set up the International Academy of Advanced Clinical Hypnosis & the Institute of Advanced Clinical Hypnotherapy [UK] to help share best practice in the industry & is also a member of The Association of Complete Mind Therapists & The Royle Institute of Hypnotherapy and Psychotherapy & also is a Certified Professional Hypnotherapist - issued by the Institute for the Advanced Study of Hypnotism, St. Charles, Illinois, USA .

Each year Rob successfully helps 100's of people one to one & online to

Stop Smoking, Lose Weight, Eliminate Stress & Anxiety, Eradicate Phobias, Boost Confidence & Enhance their Sports Performance & his services have been approved for promotion in GP's Surgeries in London & South Wales, UK.

Rob is also a Trainer & teaches various courses at his training venue in Newport South Wales.

As part of his course work for his Doctor of Philosophy Rob also qualified in the Field of Advanced Stage Hypnosis & is a Member of The Professional Organisation of Stage Hypnotists.

Rob continues to help clients worldwide & is available for Consultations Globally either in person or online.

For further information on Rob's services:

Email: HarleyStreet@London.com

Tel: International 44 7970 625 343 / UK 07970 625 343

Websites:

www.GlobalHypnotist.com www.HarleyStreetClinic.net
www.WalesHypnosis.com www.ReikiGuy.com www.iach.org
www.iaach.com

Training Courses & Products:

https://www.facebook.com/pages/Advanced-Hypnotherapy-

Training/542475612452617

Facebook: www.facebook.com/robert.phoenix2

Youtube: globalhypnotist

Twitter: HypnotherapyMan

Skype: Robert.phoenix69

ooVoo: robertphoenix

Join My Contact List & receive a complementary FREE Gift!

For your <u>FREE</u> gift simply Email me with the Heading - "I WOULD LIKE TO CLAIM MY HYPNOSIS FREE GIFT"

To <u>HarleyStreet@London.com</u>

If you are a Hypnotherapist whether Clinical or Stage you are probably asked regularly by smokers for your help in aiding them to quit.

Smoking & weight loss are the 2 key areas you need to _ensure you are a success_ because every success in these 2 areas becomes a walking advert for you.

You may help clients with issues such as Stress, Anxiety, Confidence etc… but most of these clients will remain silent about how you helped them overcome their issues. Non-smokers or clients that lose weight with your help will tell many others & be a fantastic visual reminder to all those that they come into contact with.

In this chapter I will focus on Stopping Smoking & *reveal the secret of my success* in helping smokers to quit which if you put into practice yourself, can rapidly propel you into becoming known & respected as an authority on Smoking Cessation Hypnosis in your Practice area.

Most successful Smoking Cessation Hypnotherapists claim to have a 90% - 95% success rate but incorporating what I am about to share with you this could rise to 98% - 99%.

So what is your secret to having almost 100% success with helping clients to quit smoking Rob?

I am glad you asked & this is worth the wait – I know we are already about to leave page 3 and I still havn't revealed my secret but I can assure you that you need **pay attention** to my **unique** method of Smoking Cessation because this is the very **first time** I have ever **revealed** this and this information alone is **worth a fortune!**

The secret to having an almost perfect smoking cessation success rate is revealed on the following page so hold on to your seats:

I suggest to clients that there is ***no addiction*** to cigarettes & tobacco!

Yes you read that right. There is NO addiction to cigarettes & tobacco. By the end of the pre-talk my clients are totally convinced that what I am telling them is 100% total reality.

If you would like near to 100% success with clients that see you for stopping smoking then use your time in the pre-talk to change the clients perception of smoking addiction and reinforce that what they have is a simple habit that is about to be broken.

So let's take a look at the pre-talk which plants this seed & changes the Smokers perception of addiction & habit:

I first develop rapport with the Client by introducing myself politely, shaking their hand, smiling & using eye contact.

I will try to have 2 different chairs or a chair & a couch in my therapy room. I use the one chair to talk with the client during the pre-talk & then sit them in the other chair which should be comfier or ask them to lie down on the couch when I am ready to begin Hypnosis.

I also ensure there is a reasonable level of mood lighting during the pre-talk & then lower the lighting level as we begin Hypnosis.

This enhances how relaxed the client will be when they are about to become hypnotized.

In the pre-talk with my clients I ask all the standard questions such as "is it **your decision to quit** today?", "Do you have reasons to *stop smoking today*?", "Tell me about those reasons" [Which re-enforces why they want to quit].

Even though the reasons for quitting are generally the same with every smoker I have seen I always show the client I am listening to them. I am nodding my head & looking understanding, leaning slightly forwards & subtly following their body language patterns.

I am matching my tone of voice to theirs & controlling the flow of conversation. I ooze confidence & belief in my abilities and the ability of the client to quit.

And then I ask the question:

"Do you think you have a habit or an addiction?"

Most clients will either reply that they have some form of addiction or that they have a bit of a mix. On the occasion the client says they just have a habit I tell them that _they are right_ as there is _no such thing as addiction._

Clients that believe they have an addiction are then asked:

"When you go to bed at night do you have to wake up regularly through the night _JUST TO SMOKE_?"

Most clients giggle and say **"no"**. Some will say that when they wake up for <u>some other reason</u> they may smoke. If they do say yes this will be why they smoke so simply confirm this with the client. They may be stressed & simply can't sleep or get up to go to the bathroom in the night.

The FACT is I have never in my years as a Hypnotherapist ever had a client confirm they do wake up regularly through the night just to smoke.

The client is then asked a question that makes them immediately question whether there is any addiction to cigarettes & tobacco:

"Don't you think that if you did have a chemical dependency you would have to wake up through the night – but you don't."

All clients have to agree with this suggestion as it's extremely logical.

I then immediately embed the suggestion to the client that "It's *JUST* a habit."

"If you do one thing with something else over a period of time we create a habit or ritual. It is when we do these things that we reach for a cigarette & smoke."

"This is why the amount of cigarettes we smoke in a day can vary depending on what we are doing – It's a habit!"

"This is why different people smoke different amounts rather than all of us smoke the same amount as each other day in day out – Because it's *just a habit*. This is why some people wake up one day & ***just decide to quit*** – If there was addiction this would not be possible. There is no addiction it's *just habit*."

I then ask the client "Does ***this make sense***?"

They <u>always</u> say yes!

Unless your client has a low IQ they will arrive at the conclusion that what you are saying is logical & makes total sense.

You will notice the embedded suggestions in my conversation.

I then share the following with clients to make them aware of the power of conditioning which in turn reinforces even deeper the suggestion that smoking is not addictive:

The power of Conditioning

Conditioning is a very powerful tool - The mind cannot tell the difference between something that we imagine & something that is real so how we think & what we think plays a vital part in our belief systems especially when we think about how difficult or how easy something might be to do such as stop smoking.

Let's look at a few examples:

Case number 1 - Roger Bannister

In the 1950's Roger Bannister broke the 4 minute mile record. Before he broke the record it was categorically stated that no human could ever run that fast. Over the years many ran close to breaking that time but no one could run faster. Athletes were conditioned that it could not be broken & a psychological barrier created. Within weeks of Roger Bannister breaking the 4 minute mile record others around the world began breaking it too. The psychological barrier that had been created was no longer there.

Case number 2 - The Victorians

The Victorians believed that if you were on a train that travelled faster than 25 mph your face would peel off! This may sound laughable now but at the time that was what was believed. These days with all the challenges on the railways any one that uses the trains probably wishes they did travel faster than 25mph… ;)

Case number 3 – Christopher Columbus

I'm quite certain that when Mr Columbus was setting sail to find new lands & treasure "Watch out for that edge!" could be heard from people around the dockside.

At the time watching out for the edge of the world would have been sound advice… That's what people were conditioned to believe so who in their right mind would challenge this & suggest the world was in fact round.

Case number 4 - The Circus Elephant

Many, many years ago when a baby elephant was introduced to the life of the circus, to stop it from escaping a very small peg was knocked into the ground & a thin piece of rope attached to one leg of the baby elephant. This was adequate to stop the baby elephant from escaping. After a while the baby elephant would come to the conclusion that he/she could not escape & subsequently stopped trying. Years later when the elephant is fully grown the same sized peg & thin rope was used. This was because the elephant believed that it was not strong enough to snap the thin rope or pull the little peg out of the ground. It had been conditioned to think that it can't break free!

[I may use a few or all of these analogies depending on the time.]

I then ask the client the following:

"Question - Who has the most to gain from the conditioning that smokers have been subjected to over the years?"

They may say the Tobacco Companies or may not know but whatever they say I share the following story with them…

"The following is a little story I have pondered over for quite a few years…

If I owned a tobacco company & one day reports began to surface that smoking could be harmful to health I would probably panic that all my customers would quit.

With my knowledge of how the mind works I would pay for reports to be created with embedded suggestions – such as "smoking is addictive", "It's really HARD to quit", "You will go through withdrawal", "you will go cold turkey", "You will have CRAVINGS!" "It's easier to quit using heroin!"

I would send these reports around the world to Governments who would no doubt hand them to their Health Services & Organisations. They in turn would repeat these suggestions to the public. The public in turn are likely to believe what is being said to them as its coming from people in authority & at a time when people didn't really question anything that was presented to them.

Thus the myth populates & grows – Quit Smoking programmes are created around this myth that smokers need help to quit their addiction & help to suppress their cravings. More & more quit smoking products are introduced onto the market as another money spinner & to reinforce the myth that a smoker needs all the help they can get to quit…

Back in the real world smokers have indeed been conditioned to think they are addicted to cigarettes & tobacco & that they need to go through withdrawals & fight cravings.

But we have already established that you are not addicted to cigarettes & tobacco so what could it be that you may have physically experienced if you have tried to quit in the past?

It is simply a **<u>DETOX PROCESS!</u>** Your body is clearing out all the toxins & poisons it has accumulated. Yes smokers have been lied to in a way that then makes it a lot harder for them to quit…

Detox *sounds nice* doesn't it – Almost like a walk in the park on a summers day, something to look forward to, a cleansing.

Withdrawal & cold turkey & cravings on the other hand feels like preparing to climb Mount Everest in the middle of winter in just a pair of shorts!

If you need an injection one nurse may say to you "Sorry but this is going to hurt!" And as she sticks the needle in it really does hurt! Another nurse may use a different approach. She may smile & say the words "just a slight scratch!" Before you know it it's all over & all you feel is a very slight scratch.

As we are conditioned so becomes our reality - As I mentioned earlier the mind cannot tell the difference between something you imagine & something that is real so your conditioning really does become your reality.

This leads to the result of all the conditioning which is that smokers crave cigarettes & tobacco but there cannot be cravings as there is no addiction - you are simply detoxing.

This is the reason how some smokers after many years of smoking one day simply wake up & decide to never smoke again. Their psychological barrier disappears, the **years of conditioning evaporates** with the barrier & they never smoke again.

If smoking was addictive in any way, shape or form this really would never be possible.

If you reached for a cigarette you would start the detox process from square one which is why you should not use any nicotine replacement products – They are all designed for you to fail by keeping your mind on the false suggestion of addiction.

Quitting smoking is that slight scratch, it's that walk in the park on a summers day.

Does this all make sense…"

[The client always answers yes!]

"So you realise that up until now, the only thing that has stopped you from quitting smoking is your belief system which had been conditioned to make you think you were in some way addicted to cigarettes & tobacco.

But this is not the case. There is real power in knowledge & you now have the knowledge that I have shared with you.

Does this all make sense to you & is there anything about what we have discussed that you would like to ask me about?"

Answer any questions the client has. Many say they have no questions as everything said makes complete sense.

Finally before moving on to asking what the client knows about hypnotherapy I tell them:

"Give away or destroy all of your cigarettes & tobacco, bin your ash trays, do not use any nicotine replacement products instead destroy or hand them to someone & simply walk away from this disgusting habit and **never smoke again!"**

The job of convincing the client that addiction was a myth is now complete.

I have had clients at this point give me their cigarettes & tobacco, shake my hand and tell me they no longer need hypnosis as they don't smoke!

But if they don't and they are still sat in front of you it's now time for you to explain to them how hypnosis works and then use your Stop Smoking Hypnosis Script to seal the deal and make them a confident, healthy, happy non-smoker!

The information contained in this chapter may be used by Practicing Hypnotherapists & NLP Practitioners on a one to one basis with their personal clients to aid Smoking Cessation.

The information enclosed in this chapter must not be taught or included in any other training or teaching material whether written, audio / verbal or video without the prior consent of the author.

COMPLETE MIND THERAPY (CMT)

By Dr. Jonathan Royle

Well my dear student, our time together is almost at an end, and your initial education in all areas of hypnosis is almost complete.

Now the reason I say "initial" education is because you will learn far more from the university of life and through the medium of hands on practical experience than any training course could ever teach you.

That is not to say that your academic study should end. Indeed at the rear of this, the final manual you will find a recommended reading list which you are advised to follow in order to further your studies as you also put the contents of this course to use and therefore start to earn as you learn.

This course in Complete Mind Therapy will without doubt, through its unique combination of audio tape, video tape and printed instructional material have taught you more about the stage hypnotism and mind therapies industry than many, if not most all so called established stage performers and therapists will ever know about the subject, so I assure you that you may proceed with the greatest of confidence in your new found skills at all times.

Prior to teaching you the concept and operation of a Complete Mind Therapy session, I would urge you to consider the very true fact that personal hands on training with an experienced expert of their craft is by far the easiest and most effective way of learning a new skill and hypnosis is no exception.

As detailed in the rear of the course prospectus as a student of the Complete Mind Therapy Course, discounted personal one to one training courses with me your head tutor, Alex Leroy are available in order that you can learn through hands on demonstrations, exercises and experience.

Those of you seriously wishing to pursue a career in stage hypnosis and/or hypnotherapy are without doubt advised that eight hours in my company (from 10am until 6pm) on the day of your choice would not only be the learning experience of a lifetime but would also be an excellent chance to ask me any questions you may have.

So in short, your hypnotic success, competence and knowledge are 100% certain if you follow this 12 step plan as follows:

1. Read, study and absorb all 12 CMT course manuals

2. Watch, study and absorb both the CMT course videos

3. Listen to, study and absorb all 12 CMT audio instruction tapes

4. Complete and return your test paper and await your results

5. Upon receiving your successful exam results your diplomas are issued

6. You are then granted membership to the Association of Professional Hypnotherapists and Psychotherapists

7. You are also granted membership to The Professional Organisation of Stage Hypnotists

8. Start your advertising campaign and begin to earn as you learn

9. At this point, when you can afford the fee of £97, you are advised to

order your personal copy of The Hypnotist Bible by Delavar, which in itself is a complete advanced training course in both stage hypnosis, hypnotherapy and related subjects, written by the man who taught me, your teacher, amongst many others, including a certain top television hypnotist

10. Continue to earn a substantial income and earn as you learn

11. When you have saved sufficient funds, eight hours of personal one to one training in my company, at the rates shown in the rear of the course prospectus, would be an excellent investment

12. Continue to earn as you learn by way of the recommended reading list, as detailed at the rear of this manual

By following this 12 point guide to success, you will undoubtedly become one of Britain's most knowledgeable and expert hypnotists, able to enjoy an income and lifestyle that others only ever dream of.

And don't forget that at all times our unique video support service as described in the prospectus is available, along with our full customer support service, which is but a letter, phonecall or fax away.

To remind you the direct contact telephone for the Mindcare Organisation UK is: **07050 377 579.**

All correspondence can be sent to: The Mindcare Organisation UK, c/o Prospect House Publishing, Prospect House, P.O. Box 12, Huddersfield, England, HD8 9YP.

We encourage all course students to both follow our 12 point guide to success to the letter and also to keep us posted on your continuing success within our fascinating industry.

We look forward to receiving videos of your shows and details of your success with therapy clients and with your permission would like to make these examples available to your fellow colleagues and course students.

Now without further ado, I shall explain the concept of Complete Mind Therapy. As I do, please bear in mind that whilst the printed content of this course may seem to have been heavily dominated with Stage Hypnotism training, in fact, each and every method, ploy and technique you have learned throughout this course is of use both on stage and within a therapeutic context. So please remember this most important point at all times.

What follows is the structure of a one hour complete mind therapy session, which when followed in this order will produce excellent results at all times.

Use this format for all your one hour long Complete Mind Therapy sessions and due to it's unique structure you will be able to treat any and all problems presented to you with just one single one hour session and the audio tape which you give the client on completion of their session.

THE COMPLETE MIND THERAPY SESSION STRUCTURE

1   Advertise to obtain your clients

2   Client shows up for session

3   Get the relevant fee off them now

4   Obtain rapport over a cup of tea

5   Obtain total belief and expectancy by your professional office and personal appearance

6   Ask the client to answer all pre – session questions

7   Do follow your thumb with your eyes, suggestibility test and anchor the cure to successful completion of this test

8   Induce trance via physical relaxation method and then counting backwards from 300 method

9   Deepen trance via staircase of relaxation

10   Deepen further by image of bed/sleep

11   Deepen further by dream/blackboard method

12   Ego strengthening therapy

13   The Necessary therapy

        A.   Anchor good time of life feelings to finger and thumb action

        B.   Ruler to 100% confidence

        C.   Ruler to 100% willpower

        D.   Ruler to 100% self image/esteem

        E.   Ruler to 100% relevant to actual problem the client has

F.   T.V set get rid of the past visualization

G.   Mirror stare to instil new feelings and behaviour as reality

H.   Direct suggestion therapy

I.   Pain and pleasure suggestions

J.   Repeat of direct suggestion therapy

14   Implant major post hypnotic suggestion

15   Awaken the client from trance

16   Give them their tape and any other information

17   Say goodbye to them and prepare for your next client to arrive

These are the 17 sections which go together to make the whole, which is a Complete Mind Therapy session. The structure is such that we have combined together the most effective elements of counselling skills, psychotherapy, suggestion therapy, aversion therapy, creative visualisation, noesitherapy, sports psychology and in fact all 14 areas which this course teaches are combined with an emphasis on neuro linguistic programming or as it is sometimes called neuro associative conditioning (N.A.C.), to give us a one hour long approximately session, which is so effective, that in my personal experience, only one session is necessary to cure the clients problem forever. If they do need some back up therapy later, they can then of course just listen to the audio tape which you have given them. I shall now explore each of these 17 separate sections which make up the whole and explain how to carry them out for greatest success.

ADVERTISE TO GET CLIENTS

Advertising has been touched on before but here is some further advice.

By far the most effective way to obtain clients is by word of mouth advertising, which will be generated for you at no charge by past clients which you have successfully treated, but of course you need some clients first for word of mouth advertising to start happening.

Upon passing the exam which leads to you receiving your diplomas for this course, you are advised to obtain a black and white matt finish photograph of yourself, apparently hypnotising someone in the usual cliched stage hypnotist manner. This is then sent along with a press release typed in double spaced format on single sided white A4 paper, explaining that after a comprehensive course of study, with the Mindcare Organisation UK, you have passed exams and have now been accepted as a member of both The Association of Professional Hypnotherapists and Psychotherapists and The Professional Organisation of Stage Hypnotists. Whilst now being the ONLY Complete Mind Therapist in your local area able to help people with all their habits, fears, phobias, emotional problems, pain control and other areas. This photograph and press release bearing your contact details are sent to the features editors and news editors of all your local and regional newspapers and magazines, often leading to a large write up promoting your business, which costs you nothing whilst generating lots of clients. This approach can also be used with local and regional radio and TV stations, leading to feature interviews on their news and entertainment shows, which costs you nothing and leads to more clients. Those who are ambitious can do this on a national level with TV radio and press, leading to stardom, appearance fees and more clients for your business. Talk shows such as Kilroy, Vanessa, This Morning and many others are always looking for interesting guests and subjects to feature and this may as well be you.

The general rule of thumb, is that on a local/regional level you do all TV, radio and media interviews for free. Whilst those on a national level will always involve all your out of pocket and travel expenses being paid, along with an appearance and/or interview fee being paid to you also.

The next best way to get clients at NO cost, is to offer FREE lecture demonstrations of your hypnotic skills to local women's groups, lions clubs, Masonic lodges and other special social clubs of these kinds. Doing these FREE lecture demonstrations costs you nothing and will usually lead to many sales of your audio hypnotherapy tapes on the night and also to bookings for your sessions in person.

Another excellent way to get started at NO cost, is to offer some local venues a FREE stage hypnotism show, which both gives you a chance to rehearse your new stage show and the show itself will lead to paid bookings for other shows, sales of your hypnotherapy tapes on the night and of course, bookings for personal one to one sessions.

Handing your business card to each and every person you meet by way of introduction will rapidly get your name circulated around the community and ultimately lead to many bookings. With business cards available as cheaply as £25 for 1000, from companies advertising in Exchange and Mart, this also is a practically no cost way to get your business kicked off.

Other low cost and effective ways to obtain clients, include having some A5 size leaflets advertising your services printed, then visit all your local libraries and place a folded up leaflet into each and every book on the shelves of the self help, psychology and health sections. People borrowing these kinds of books tend to have problems and/or health complaints they wish to sort out and as such, are red hot leads for you to target, very often leading to bookings.

A classified advert in your local and regional papers, whilst being very cheap to run, can generate 100's of clients, especially if the advert is worded as follows:

FREE HYPNOTHERAPY AND PSYCHOTHERAPY, AVAILABLE FROM ESTABLISHED PROFESSIONAL MIND THERAPIST. FOR FREE SESSION CALL XXXXX XXXXXX. SINCERE HELP FOR ALL PROBLEMS.

This advert of 20 words is placed under the Personal Services section of the Classified adverts. As the advert offers the reader a free session, you will get loads of calls and when the potential client calls you explain that most therapists take around three sessions to treat people at an average of £40 per session, which would cost them around £120 at least. However, as a special offer, if they book now, they can have a FREE session of Complete Mind Therapy, which is so powerful and effective that only one session is needed, which immediately saves them around £80 at least. On top of this instant saving, you'll give them the session FREE of charge, just so long as they purchase the back up audio "Hypnotheratape" for the special price of just £39.95. This means you end up getting just 5p less than the normal cost of your sessions anyway and most all callers will book, as they think they are saving lots of money, getting something for FREE and getting a discount on the back up tape. Which means all in all, they feel they are getting a bargain and so book there and then. Believe me, this classified advert offering FREE sessions will generate you your income of a substantial nature on a weekly basis. Each advert placed will pay for itself many times over, so the more local and regional papers you advertise in, the more money you'll make in the shortest space of time possible. As mentioned before, in the long term, it's worth having a display advert in your local areas Yellow Pages. This display advert, should be as big as those which other therapists are running and there are a few things which will ensure you get all the business. These are, to have a photo of yourself upon the advert as it adds a personal human touch, mention upon the advert your Professional Association memberships, state that you offer FREE Complete Mind Therapy sessions for ALL problems and offer them a FREEPHONE number to call you on. People will always call a freephone number first before paying for a call, especially if it's on the advert offering FREE therapy sessions, which of course, yours will. The final thing to improve your advert response, is to name you business something such as, ABC Hypnotherapy, so that your business appears at the top of the alphabetical list and so is seen first. You are also advised to obtain your FREE lineage entries in both you local Thompson Local Directories, and within the Yellow Pages, as again, this costs nothing for a lineage ad and it does generate some extra enquiries.

It's also worth writing to your regional head office of both B.U.P.A. and your areas N.H.S area healthcare authority, requesting that you are granted a B.U.P.A. and N.H.S. provider number respectively. They will send you all necessary forms and there is no charge to obtain your provider numbers, which once obtained and listed on all promotional materials, helps to attract more clients, as B.U.P.A members will know they can claim on their healthcare insurance to pay for the session. Also doctors will know they can refer people to you on the N.H.S. as you have the N.H.S. provider number. Bearing this in mind, once you have obtained both provider numbers, which costs nothing, it is worthwhile sending a letter of introduction, along with your advertising leaflets, to all the doctors and dentists surgeries in your area, who may then refer clients to you and so increase your business.

A little common sense will reveal numerous other no cost or low cost advertising methods, which do lead to 100's of clients. A last few examples to set you thinking on the right track are as follows:

· Place cards on supermarkets "For Sale" boards, using the FREE sessions ploy detailed earlier.

· Place cards on newsagents notice boards all over your local area, again using the FREE ploy.

· Send leaflets advertising driving test nerves therapy, to all the driving schools and instructors in your area, offering to wholesale them audio hypnotherapy tapes, which they can then sell on at a profit to their clients, thus also helping to increase the level of their pass 1st time success rate, as the students will not be nervous during the test.

· Leaflets sent to travel agents, offering cure your fear of flying sessions, with a cover letter pointing out that any clients they obtain for you will cure their fear and so will want to go on a holiday which involves flying, which means the holiday will cost more and so as the travel agent, they will get more commission on the deal which means by being your unpaid salesman they are increasing their own profits.

These are just a few examples of ways to get clients at little or no cost to yourself. But with a little imagination and common sense, 100's of other ways of obtaining clients at little, or no cost to yourself will present themselves to you, if you think along the lines I've already illustrated.

To sum up on advertising, in the rare event of potential clients replying to your adverts and then not booking there and then on the phone, I would suggest you take their name and address and send them your advertising leaflet, by first class post, as quite often, when they receive this, it's enough to spur them into action, so that they do call back and book a session rather than never hearing from them again. One last point is, that by contacting you in the first place, the client has admitted to themselves they have a problem and so are now making a commitment to change things for the better and so they are already 95% of the way to a solution and just need a trigger to success and that is where we therapists come in. We give the client permission to heal themselves and through the therapy, motivate them to a successful outcome. This combined with the large element of the placebo effect coming into play, as quite simply if they book a session with you, they obviously believe you can help them and expect it to work, or why else would they contact you? Upon taking the booking off the client, take their name, address and telephone number and inform them that if they have to cancel, for any reason, they must give you at least 24 hours notice, or else the full fee will be payable anyway, just like going to the dentist. This stops timewasters and compounds the belief in the clients mind that you're a busy and successful professional. Should they not show up for the session, send them an invoice on a letterhead, headed "Litigation Department", demanding the £39.95 fee and without doubt, you'll get payment by return of post.

CLIENT SHOWS UP FOR SESSION

AND

GET THE RELEVANT FEE OFF THEM

AND

OBTAIN RAPPORT OVER A CUP OF TEA

AND

OBTAIN 100% TOTAL BELIEF/EXPECTANCY

Having booked their session, the client showing up is an important point in their treatment, as they have then made a real commitment to solve their problem. You greet them at your office door and shake them firmly by the hand, whilst looking them directly in the eye, which both gets instant rapport and puts you in control. They see you dressed smartly and professionally which compounds their belief and expectancy levels in your ability to cure them. Having got the client to sit down you say, "Just as when you go to a gypsy, they say cross my palm with silver, well I've got to say cross my palm with £39.95, please, as none of us like talking about money and by getting it all out of the way now, it means we can then concentrate on what's most important today, which is YOU and us solving your problem today."

This both puts them at ease as they perceive your main priority is them and also, it means you've already been paid, which is both a lovely feeling and also a most powerful part of the therapy itself. You see, when the client parts with the money, it's really serious commitment to their own success and concrete's their belief and expectancy levels to a height such that success is 100% guaranteed, as they must believe you can help them and they must expect the treatment to work as why else would they either contact you, book a session, show up and/or pay the fee up front, unless they expect to get the end result of being cured. Bearing this in mind and the power of the placebo effect, combined with the therapeutic power of your caring bedside manner it would almost matter little what treatment you actually gave them now, as the end beneficial result of them being cured would no doubt be the same anyway, however, the CMT session, which they receive, is so powerful and effective in its therapeutic content, that success is 100% guaranteed, if the clients belief and expectancy levels are total.

The diplomas they see hanging on your office wall, together with the book shelf of impressive looking psychology books, all compound the belief and expectancy thing even further. Your office should contain a black leather reclining chair for the client to lie in, a black directors chair for you to sit in at your desk, upon which should be a desk lamp. Your diplomas are displayed, framed upon the wall and you have 2 tape recorders, one of which is positioned behind the clients chair will play the relaxation music for the session later, whilst at the same time, the one upon your desk, to which is connected a microphone, records the entire session from the point of asking the client to close their eyes and starting the induction, until having awoken the client, which should be 45 minutes maximum, so one side of a 90 minute tape will be sufficient and as your voice and background music are picked up by the microphone the end result is a tape which bears your voice over the top of the relaxation music which will be highly effective when listened to. Giving the client a cup of tea instantly puts them at ease and helps relax them and then you can answer their general questions prior to moving onto asking them the pre-session questionnaire, which follows:

ASK CLIENT LIST OF 16 PRE-SESSION QUESTIONS

What follows are the 16 questions which you ask the client to answer, honestly, directly and in detail, before you start the actual hypnotic induction process. The answers given will help you carry out the session with the greatest of success for the reasons detailed after each listed question that follows. The fact you use their answers, which are personal to them, as part of the therapy makes the session seem far more personal to them, especially as you try to use their name a lot, as a persons name is, to them, the sweetest thing in the entire English language. It also means that as you feed the personal information they have given to us by the questions asked back to them as part of the therapy as it is personal to them and they can relate to it so well this explains why the concept of Complete Mind Therapy is so successful. The 16 questions to ask are as follows:

1) **What is your name?**

This is so we can call them by their first name throughout the session

2)   Your address please?

This is just for future reference, as in future you may wish to contact clients to see if they will participate in TV and/or radio show broadcasts.

3)   You telephone number?

Again just for reference as in question 2

4)   Your date of birth?

By knowing this, we can work out the clients age. (Never ask their age outright).

5)   What's their problem?

Obviously asked so we know what we're treating

6)   How long have you had this problem?

Using this piece of information and the clients D.O.B. we can work out what age the client was when the problem started

7)   How do you feel this problem started?

Whilst the way they feel the problem started may not exactly be correct, just so long as it's what they at this time consciously believe to be correct, then we can use this information to erase connections with the past during therapy.

8)   What do you feel I need to do for you today to permanently cure this problem?

Again the answer they give, however daft, will when acted upon, provide the ideal way to cure the patient. This is because, if they feel doing XYZ would cure them, then they believe that if you did XYZ they would be cured. So by doing XYZ they will be cured, as this is what they have convinced themselves needs to be done for a cure to be achieved.

9)   What is the final outcome you wish to achieve from today?

Whilst you may think, for example, that a smoker would say to stop smoking in reply to this question, this is not always the case. They could just as easily say that by stopping smoking today they wish to become healthier and be able to go swimming again like they used to. In other words, the answer to this question very often reveals something we can feed back to them later as an incentive to achieve their goals.

10)   What was the best experience of you entire life, a time you felt confident, proud, loved and on top of the world?

Their answer is later used for the finger and thumb good times feeling connection technique.

11)   What was the worst and most emotionally painful experience of your entire life?

This answer can be used later in the pain/pleasure section of therapy by having them imagine how they felt then etc. and linking it to the thought that any continuance of past actions will make them feel just as bad as they did then whereas avoidance of past actions makes them feel as good as, if not better as their reply to question 10

12)   Who's the one person you love most in the entire world?

By getting the persons name, you can refer to them directly during the pain/pleasure section of the therapy by way of having the client imagine how upsetting it would be to this named person they love so much if they were to have continued smoking and killing themselves. Until they saw each other no more or indeed if the habit/problem had continued making them so stressed and anxious that the person they loved so much feels driven away from them and grows to hate them. As the client loves this person so much there will be strong emotional connection with any thoughts about this person and needless to say the client will wish to avoid upsetting them at all costs and because of the scenario just given to them, the only way to avoid upsetting them as far as their subconscious mind is concerned is by ending their habit/problem etc. once and for all.

13)   Are you on any medication for this problem?

Here, a copy of the medical reference book PIMMS is useful, as you can look up the drugs name, revealing exactly what the drug is prescribed for, what its side effects are and indeed, by having prescribed it, what the clients medical GP seems to think the real problem is, which may not always be the same as that being presented to us by the client and so we can ensure our therapy targets the correct problem as well as the clients perceived problem if necessary.

14)   Is there a history of this problem within your direct family?

This really just gives us more of an idea why this client has got this particular problem in the first place

15)   Have you tried any other alternative therapies to cure this problem before?

If they answer yes, ask which and then make it clear to the client that the treatment you will give them is the most powerful and effective of its kind. Hence it's called Complete Mind Therapy. This is done to remove any doubts they may have instilled in them due to past failures and helps to concrete their belief and expectancy levels in the treatment working 100%

16)   Have you got any questions for me before we begin?

Should the client have any questions, it's just a matter of using your common sense to answer in a manner which puts their mind at ease and ensures they totally believe this treatment will change their life.

Then you get the client to sign and date the bottom of the questionnaire below a printed statement, which says:

I (THEIR NAME HERE) OF (THEIR ADDRESS) DO HEREBY DECLARE I AM OVER 18 YEARS OF AGE AND CONSENT TO (YOUR NAME) TREATING ME WITH HYPNOSIS AND COMPLETE MIND THERAPY.

Once the client has signed such a statement it will be far harder for any legal claims to be made against you for malpractice. Where wishing to treat children and/or those under the age of 18 you must have their parent sign a statement saying:

I (THEIR NAME) OF (THEIR ADDRESS) DO HEREBY DECLARE I AM THE LEGAL PARENT/GARDIAN OF (CLIENTS NAME) AND DO HEREBY GIVE MY CONSENT FOR (YOUR NAME) TO TREAT THEM WITH HYPNOSIS AND COMPLETE MIND THERAPY.

Again this is done to cover you 100% legally, as without proof of parent or guardians consent it is illegal to hypnotise these people under 18 years.

DO FOLLOW YOUR THUMB WITH EYES TEST AND ANCHOR THE CURE TO SUCCESSFUL COMPLETION

Here, you get the client to stand upright, feet together, left arm down by their side, right arm stretched out in front of them and right hand clenched into a fist, with their right thumb stuck up directly into the air. You tell the client that on the count of 3 you want them to move their right arm around in a clockwise direction as far as they comfortably can, without moving their feet from the position they are currently in. They are told to stare at their thumb at all times, whilst doing this and indeed should tell you when they have reached the point where it becomes uncomfortable to move any further. You then count to 3 and the client does as they've been told and when they reach the point where they can move no further, you ask them to stare past their thumb and tell you what they can see in the background in line with their thumb, which can act as a marker to how far they got this first time. The client is then told to resume their original position and then told to close their eyes and keep their arm exactly where it is until you say otherwise. You ask the clients to imagine in their minds eye as 100% total reality, that they are once again rotating their body from the hips in a clockwise direction whilst staring at their thumb just like before. However, as anything is possible in their imagination, you want them to imagine being able to move considerably further than before, both without discomfort and with the greatest of ease and they are told to tell you when they have gone further in their minds eye than they previously did in reality. The client is then told something such as:

"Well (their name) that's excellent, you have just achieved something which was once so difficult in a way which has proved so ridiculously easy, thanks to the power of your mind. Now, (their name), believe it or not, if you've used your powers of intelligence, imagination and concentration effectively, then for you this will have become 100% total reality. So on the count of 3 I'd like you to re-open your eyes and repeat the test by rotating your body as far as you comfortably can in a clockwise manner and as you do so, on the count of 3, notice how as those imagined thoughts of but a few seconds ago become a reality for you, how your goal of solving (their problem) which you once thought would be difficult to achieve will also prove to be so ridiculously easy."

You then count to 3, they repeat it again for real and I guarantee you that without fail, the client will be able to move considerably further this time than they did the first time around and as they see with their own eyes, their thoughts of but a few seconds ago become a physical reality, so they come to believe as 100% total reality that the treatment you are about to give them will work and so they are now 99% of the way to solving their problem.

INDUCE TRANCE VIA PHYSICAL RELAXATION AND COUNTING BACKWORDS FROM 300 METHOD

It's now time to get the client to sit down, to close their eyes and to begin breathing deeply and regularly in through their nose and then out through their mouth, as they continue to relax etc., etc. At this point the relaxation music is turned on and you start to record the session, thus making their "back-up" therapy tape as the session continues. You explain to the client that you will mention areas of their body and that upon doing so, you want them to physically tense up all the muscle groups in that body area, whilst at the same time in their minds eye, imagining 2 pieces of rope tied together in knots and that these knots represent the stresses, tensions, fears, and upsets of days and weeks gone by, which are stored in the muscle groups they are physically tensing. Then the client is told you will count from 3 to 1 and that on 1 when you snap your fingers like this (do it as example) they are to instantly relax the muscle groups they were tensing, whilst at the same time imagining as 100% total reality, in their minds eye, that with your click of the fingers the 2 ropes in their minds eye instantly separate. As they instantly untie, so as they become separate pieces of rope, so in reality all muscles in their body becoming so limp, so loose, so relaxed, so heavy and so tired. They are then asked to nod their head if they understand. Then you proceed to do as just stated for the following muscle groups in this order:

A   The feet and ankles

B   Lower leg area and knees

C   Upper leg area and hips

D   Stomach and abdomen

E   Chest area

F   The back and spine

G   Finger tips to wrists

H   Every muscle from wrist to elbows to shoulders

I   The shoulders and shoulder blades

J   The neck area

K   The jaw and cheek muscles

L   The eyelids and forehead

When you've gone through this list and the client, who is listening both to your voice and the background music, has physically tensed up and then physically relaxed all these muscle groups from head to toe, they will, I assure you, feel genuinely relaxed in a physical way, especially as your office will be nice and warm and the room will be dimly lit by only your desk lamp at this point. On top of this the visual imagery of the knots untying helps them to achieve psychological relaxation also, and with both a relaxed mind and body, they are in an ideal state for the therapy to be 100% successful. As you go through the 12 point list of muscle groups, you can link from one group to the next with a phrase such as, "with every breath you take, every noise you hear and every word I say, you relax even more. With each second that passes by." This, along with the "standard phrases" as detailed in the induction's chapter earlier in this course, both help to link nicely from one muscle group to the next and also help to deepen both the physical and psychological levels of the clients relaxation. It can also be good to suggest to them that as each muscle group relaxes, so a feeling of warmth and total relaxation floods their entire body. Having gone through their entire body's muscle groups, you then immediately ask them to start counting backwards from 300 in their minds eye, as you continue to suggest things to them and then link into the induction method as explained in the verbal psychology section, being that of a "subliminal" nature.

DEEPEN VIA STAIRCASE

After continuing with the "subliminal" induction, it's time to deepen the level of trance, here we use the staircase of relaxation as detailed earlier in the course. The client being told that as you count backwards from 10 down to 1, so in their minds eye they will take another step down the staircase they can now see and as this is a staircase of relaxation, they will sink 100 times deeper with each step down they take. Then using the "standard phrases" whilst counting backwards from 10 down to 1 the trance is deepened.

DEEPEN FURTHER BY IMAGE OF BED

Upon reaching the count of 1 with the staircase deepening, it is suggested to the client that at the bottom of the staircase is a beautifully relaxing and comfortable bed into which they are to climb, snuggle up and go fast to sleep, allowing their mind to wander free, allowing your voice to become but a distant sound as they go deeper and deeper to sleep.

DEEPEN FURTHER BY BLACKBOARD

Now tell the client:

"Your now so deeply relaxed and so deeply asleep, that whatever I tell you to do, you would do for your own good and whatever I tell you will happen, will happen again for your own good. However, in order that the work we do together today will be 100% successful in every way, we need your subconscious mind to take you to a level of deep satisfying relaxation, of both mind and body, which will be right for you. Just as your subconscious can be trusted to circulate the blood around your body 24 hours a day, so it can be trusted to take you to a level of relaxation which is going to be for you 100% successful in every way. So I'd like you to...."

You then get the client to imagine that as they've gone to sleep in the bed, they will start dreaming and as they do, they are to dream they are in a classroom, in which is a large blackboard, upon which their name is written in chalk. They are told that in dreamland, when the blackboard is blank they are instantly taken to a depth of relaxation where they can achieve anything and then they are told to imagine rubbing their name out from the blackboard, so that each chalk letter, one by one, is rubbed out and as each letter disappears, so their level of relaxation doubles in every way, until they rub out the last letter. When they relax so completely that your work together today will prove 100% successful as an automatic reflex action.

EGO STRENGTHENING THERAPY

This is where, as detailed in an earlier section of the course, we praise the clients ego, make them feel good about the work you are about to do together and make them believe they are such a wonderful client, with such good powers of intelligence, imagination and concentration, that their success in achieving their goals and aims is 100% assured.

THE NECESSARY THERAPY

A   GOOD FEELINGS FINGER AND THUMB ANCHOR

This technique is to remind the client of the most special and pleasurable time of their life. (See answers to 16 pre-session questions). Tell them then to push the tip of their right forefinger against the tip of their right thumb, thus making a ring, a ring of confidence. As they continue to push their finger and thumb firmly together, they are to notice how confident they feel at that past time, they are to notice how calm and relaxed they feel, how full of will power and ability to achieve anything they are and how, in fact, life seemed so wonderful at the time. They are then told to let go of the image as they separate their finger and thumb. You then tell them that any time from this moment forward, when they feel a little unsure about continuing in their new life as (opposite of what their problem was) they just need to press their finger and thumb together to make the ring of confidence. This will immediately flood their mind and body with all those positive, pleasurable feelings of the past that continuing with their goal will become so ridiculously easy. This incidentally, is called anchoring, as we have "anchored" a thought to a physical action

B   RULER TO 100% CONFIDENCE

C   RULER TO 100% WILLPOWER

D   RULER TO 100% SELF IMAGE/ESTEEM

E   RULER TO 100% RELEVANT TO PROBLEM

The ruler technique is to have the client imagine a ruler in their minds eye and that upon this are the numbers from 1 to 100%. With 100% being the most desirable level to be at in order to achieve everything and anything. It is if you like a measuring stick of confidence or of willpower or of self esteem, or whichever is relevant at the time. But for this example we'll use confidence, you tell them it's a measuring stick of confidence and that it's filled with liquid mercury, just like a thermometer is and that if they take a closer look, they can see then tell us at what level from between 1 to 100% their confidence levels are now at, as this is where the mercury level will be. When they have answered with a percentage, we tell them that they need to be at 100% to achieve their aim with 100% success. So they are to imagine heating up the mercury with a very hot lighter flame, until it's become so hot that it has rapidly risen to 100%, at which point they should indicate by saying yes. You then have them imagine taking a hammer and a nail and hammering the nail through the mercury mark at 100% and through the measuring stick, so that their confidence levels are now permanently locked in place at 100% and can never again fall below this level. Once they've done this you tell them to think of the next ruler, which represents their levels of willpower, then the next ruler, which represents their self-image/esteem and how they feel about themselves. Finally the ruler which, using your common sense, you make 100% relevant to each client's particular problem. In all 4 cases, however, the bizarre mental images are used to get the levels to 100% so that 100% success can be achieved. Don't forget that the more bizarre a mental image is, the more effectively it will be acted upon. Lastly, with reference to the ruler relevant to each client's personal problem, use your common sense, but for example, people wishing to pass their driving test, could have a ruler of nerves control, which means that when it's at 100% they are 100% in control of their nerves and so can pass the test.

F   TV SET GET RID OF PAST VISUALISATION

Here, we get the client to imagine watching a TV set in their minds eye, upon which they are watching themselves as they once were. The volume is still very loud, the colour is very bright and all in all, it's very much a reminder of how they once were, which they no longer need. So first, they are to imagine turning the colour down so low that they can no longer see the picture of themselves as they once were. Then they are to turn the volume down, so much that they can no longer hear how they once were. Now that they can neither see nor hear how they once were, they are to turn the TV set off and once switched off, they are to unplug it from the wall, so it can no longer be fed any power to survive as it once was and lastly as they can no longer see, hear or be as they once were, they are to destroy the TV set in their minds eye, by blowing it up with a huge bomb. As they imagine the TV set blowing up, they are to wave goodbye to how they once felt, how they once acted and what they once did, which is no longer part of their everyday reality.

G   MIRROR STARE TO INSTIL NEW FEELINGS/FUTURE AS REALITY

Having got rid of the past, we now need to instil the future and the clients new reality. They are to imagine staring into a full length mirror, in which they can see themselves as they now are, as a (here insert what they wished to achieve). They are to notice how good they feel within themselves, they are to notice how proud they are feeling as they have now achieved their goal and ambition. They are to notice how much better they look, how much better they feel now they are a confident, happy, healthy, calm and relaxed person with bags of willpower, who has now become a (here what it was they wish to achieve). They are then to imagine turning a key in the frame of the mirror, which freezes the reflection in place forever and just so long as this image remains frozen in place so they will continue to be a (here what the aim is).

H   DIRECT SUGGESTION THERAPY

Here common sense is used, the direct suggestions must suggest clearly that the client has achieved their aim. Examples of direct suggestions are contained within the script outlines given within the advanced hypnotherapy chapter. But in short, clients who want to stop doing something they do now, must be told that they have stopped doing it. Whereas clients who wish to do something they don't currently do, must be told they have started to do it, with the greatest of ease.

I   PAIN AND PLEASURE SUGGESTIONS

Here the principle is to reverse the pain and pleasure connectors in the clients mind. So that by so doing, their behaviour is reversed to that they desire and because the cause of the problem which is the pain and pleasure circuit in their mind relevant to their problem has been reversed. The cause of the problem has effectively been removed and so a cure achieved without the need for long sessions of psychotherapy treatment. Thus getting the same end results within one 1 hour session. Also, as the cause has indirectly been dealt with and removed, there is no chance of symptom substitution, so the client you've stopped smoking has no debris left in his/her mind, which could for example, then cause them to start biting their nails instead.

The 3 steps of pain/pleasure therapy are

1   Get the client to imagine how they were when they had the problem and in their mind connect this to the most awful experience of their life, in order that it becomes painful for the client to think about or continue being as they once were, because it now has painful associations with this awful real life event of the past. (See their answers to questions.)

2   Get the client to imagine how they are now, without the problems of the past and in their mind get them to connect this with the most pleasurable experience of their entire life, so it becomes pleasurable to continue with their new behaviour pattern. Because as they continue with the new behaviour pattern, they are always reminded of this very pleasurable past event and feel just as they did then.

3   Have them think of the person they said they loved most and use the example I gave earlier, of how if they had continued with their problem, they would have ended up dead and/or pushing this loved one away. Either way, the idea is to make it so upsetting to continue with past behaviour, as by doing so, it would remind them that it would upset the one they love so dearly in a way they wish to avoid

and so a strong emotional motivating link is made here.

J   REPEAT DIRECT SUGGESTIONS

Prior to implanting post hypnotic suggestion the direct suggestions are repeated to the client once more.

MAJOR POST HYPNOTIC

Here it is suggested to the client, that everything you have said to them, will remain with them for the rest of their lives and will grow stronger with each second that passes by, from this moment forward. Also they will find that each and every time they listen to the audio tape you will give them, it will be just as, if not more effective, than if you were with them in the room in person at the time of listening to it.

AWAKEN CLIENT FROM TRANCE

Here counting up from 1 to 10, you awaken the client, an ideal therapy awakening is:

On 1 – everything I've suggested to you, growing stronger with each second of each minute of each day of each week of each month and of each year for the rest of your life.

On 2 – from this moment forward you will continue with you new desirable lifestyle as an automatic reflex action as 100% total reality.

As on 3 – from this day forward, you will awaken with an inner warm glow of confidence, a renewed optimism to life and by far a more positive attitude to get things done, whilst also continuing in your new lifestyle, as a confident, happy, healthy, calm and relaxed (their aim here)

As on 4 – finding that each day you have a huge inner reservoir of willpower which can be drawn upon when ever needed and which in fact, you will draw upon as an automatic reflex action whenever that little extra help is needed.

As on 5 – every day in every way, things are getting better and better.

As on 6 – something you once thought would be so difficult to achieve has turned out to be so ridiculously easy.

As on 7 – almost as though each and every muscle group in your body is being filled with energy, vitality, confidence and optimism.

As on 8 – almost as though your whole body is being washed in cool refreshing spring water.

As on 9 – lighter and brighter, coming on up out of it.

And on 10 – wakey, wakey rise and shine.

GIVE THEM TAPE ETC.

They are now awake and so you give them the audio tape of the session, along with an instruction sheet, clearly stating that to ensure 100% guaranteed success, they must listen, (but not whilst driving) to the tape every other day, for the next 28 days. In other words, the day after the session they don't, the next day they do and then it's do a day and miss a day for the next 28 days, as it takes 28 days for new habits to be formed and concreted into the human mind. This also puts the onus on them to commit time to their own success and seems to attach so much importance to the tape that A. they will listen to it as instructed and B. the tape will prove to be just as effective as if you were there with them in person.

SAY GOODBYE TO THEM

It's then time to say goodbye to them and await arrival of next client.

This format is followed 100% to the letter for all problems presented to you, with the only minor changes being as follows.

FOR;

*Habits, emotional problems, general nervous complaints etc.

These kinds of problems are such that the CMT session is conducted 100% to the letter as per example given.

*Fears and Phobias

Here, instead of using direct suggestions twice, the first time you get the client to imagine what they used to be scared of and then you have them make it an object of ridicule. So that the thought of what once scared them now makes them think humorous thoughts making them laugh and as laughter leads to relaxation, they will then feel relaxed when presented with what once scared them. The more ridiculous and bizarre the mental image is that you get them to imagine in order to make the original fear trigger an object of ridicule, by far the more powerful it will be. For example, a person once scared of spiders is told to dress them in wellies, put a silly party hat on it, a big clowns red nose, a bright silly coat and so on, until the image which was once the trigger to their fear becomes so ridiculous, that all that image can now trigger is laughter and/or relaxation. The rest of the session remains the same.

*Sports psychology/peak performance

Where the first set of direct suggestions normally go, we instead have the client run through a successful mental rehearsal of the increased success they wish to achieve in their sport and/or work. For example, mentally we would take a football player through the full match in a matter of a few minutes and as we did, we would have him imagine as reality scoring more goals than ever before. We would have him feel how it feels to be an achiever and we would make him believe in his mind that he had already successfully achieved his aim and so to do it again would be easy. This works and to illustrate, think of Roger Bannister, who first ran the four minute mile, until then no one had got close, but Roger believed he could do it and so he made it his reality and guess what? Once other athletes had seen Roger achieve something they once believed to be impossible, they knew it could be done and within days of Roger having done it athletes the world over found themselves able to run the four minute mile. Such is the power of belief and mental rehearsals.

*Pain control

Again the only change is that instead of direct suggestion, you instead run through instilling the saliva leads to no pain trigger as detailed in the Noesitherapy chapter. With it here being done whilst the client is in trance and then at the end of the session, the client is reminded to get saliva on their tongue and make the affirmations whenever they need instant pain control in the future.

*Illness and disease

Instead of direct suggestion number one, the client is told to visualise a rabbit in their minds eye in a field filled with 1000's of carrots. These carrots are cancer carrots, AIDS carrots or whatever their illness is carrots. They are to imagine the rabbit is so hungry and never loses his appetite and he is rapidly eating up all the carrots, one by one and with each carrot the rabbit eats, so in turn as 100% total reality, the cancer, AIDS virus or whatever, is growing weaker and so in turn they are becoming healthier and healthier.

*Stress Management

Instead of direct suggestions twice, the first time the client is told to visualise the burning fire within them, that has got too hot to handle. Then they must imagine connecting a hose to a tap and aiming it at the fire so to keep it cool. Although it continues to burn it will be at a level where the client will be able to deal with challenges which may arise. Or you can the Noesitherapy fight/flight saliva method. Not for pain control, but rather for stress control and instant relaxation.

*Allergies

Instead of direct suggestion on two occasions, the first time get your client to visualise a Perspex screen across the room and see a clone of themselves becoming "one".

A SUMMARY OF THE KEY POINTS

1   The more bizarre the images, the more effective they will be.

2   The subconscious is abstract and is best reprogrammed through images and not just words.

3   Phrasing suggestions to the subject (are they a visual, auditory, sensual person) helps.

4   Using their name helps a lot.

5   Pain/Pleasure and Fight/Flight is the secret.

6   The CMT session combines all the major areas of hypno/psycho related subjects.

7   Give them a tape at the end of the session.

Well, there you have it.

THE COURSE IN COMPLETE MIND THERAPY.

Congratulations in getting to the end and may you have all the luck in the world with your new venture.

To become a member of The Association of Professional Hypnotherapists and Psychotherapists and The Professional Organisation of Stage Hypnotists and receive your Diploma's simply return your question paper for marking. We will do the rest.

Please also observe the recommended reading list.

Unless otherwise stated, all books on the following recommended reading list are available mail order from:

The A.A. Book Co. Ltd.

Crown Buildings

Bancyfelin

Carmarthen

Dyfed

SA33 5ND

Tel. 01267 211880

OR

The Tao of Books

Station Warehouse

Station Road

Pulham Market

Norfolk

IP21 4XF

Tel. 01379 676000

OR

Via most specialist bookstores.

Stage Hypnotism

New Encyclopaedia of Stage Hypnotism by Ormond McGill £29.99

Hypnotherapy

Hypnotherapy by Dave Elman £23.50

Transforming Therapy by Gil Boyne £27.50

Trance Formations by Richard Bandler and John Grinder £9.95

Psychotherapy/Hypno Analysis

A Guide for Beginning Psychotherapists by Joan S. Zaro and others £13.95

The Book of Hypnosis by Davis Lesser £10.95

Hypnotherapy Explained by David Lesser £10.95

NLP

Frogs into Princes (Bandler and Grinder) £9.95

Reframing (Bandler and Grinder) £9.95

Hypnotic Realities (Erickson and Rossi) £26.00

Using Your Brain for a Change (R. Bandler) £11.99

Past Life Regression

Other Lives, Other Selves by Roger J. Woolger £10.50

Cashing in on Past Life Regression by Richard Webster £29.99

From Magic Books by Post, 29 Hill Avenue, Bedminster, Bristol, BS1

Motivation/Stress Management

Awaken the Giant Within by Anthony Robbins £12.95

Unlimited Power by Anthony Robbins £9.95

Business Side

The Hypnotherapy Resources and Career Guide by Morris Berg and Michael O'Sullivan £17.50 inc p&p.

To – "M. L. Berg" Box BCM 3695 London WC1N 3XX

Consumer Guide to Hypnosis by Christine Kirtley £2.95

Noesitherapy

The Simple Secrets to the Power to Heal by John Howard £12.99
C/O 19 – 20 St. George's Avenue, Northampton, NN2 6JA
Tel. 01604 716817

Sports Psychology

Hypnotic World of Paul McKenna £5.99

Paul McKenna's Hypnotic Secrets £8.99

Creative Visualisation/Self Hypnosis

Self Hypnosis by Charles Tebbetts £5.99

The Magic of Mind Power by Duncan McColl £10.00
D. P. McColl, Pilgrim Tapes, P.O. Box 107, Shrewsbury, SY1 1ZZ

Therapeutic Marketing Advice

Manual of Publicity and Exploitation by Nelson R £19.95
Magic Books by Post, 29 Hill Avenue, Bedminster, Bristol, BS1.

(All prices subject to change)

COMPLETE MIND THERAPY

NON SPECIFIC TREATMENT SCRIPT

© 2002 JONATHAN ROYLE

PROCEED AS FOLLOWS:

01) Use the Progressive Relaxation Induction (PRI) as detailed in CMT course and mentioned again in chapter 21 of CMT course!

02) Towards the end of this Induction say the "Post Hypnotic" of **"AND JUST SLEEP NOW!"**

03) Deepen the trance via the staircase visualization method as detailed in chapter 21 of CMT.

04) Deepen further using get into bed and go to sleep visualization, again detailed in chapter 21.

05) Further deepen using having a dream and wiping your name off the blackboard method as per chapter 21.

06) Say the "Post Hypnotic" again of **"AND JUST SLEEP NOW"**

Then its time for step 07) – Ego strengthening Therapy:

As you relax more completely with every breath that you take, every noise that you hear, every word that I say and every second that passes by, You are now so deeply relaxed, so deeply asleep, that whatever I tell you to do, you WILL do for your own good. And whatever I tell you WILL happen, WILL happen for your own good. Because from this moment forward I am talking directly to your subconscious mind and as you relax more deeply with each word I say and every thought that you think, so in turn every suggestion that I give you, WILL for your own good become 100% Total Reality. You have made a promise to yourself and as you relax more deeply with each second that passes by, so you realize that whilst on the odd occasion it may be OK to break a promise to a friend, that in reality you can NEVER break a promise to yourself. In fact your subconscious mind WILL NOT allow you to break a promise to yourself, you can have 100% faith that your subconscious mind will enable you to achieve everything that I am suggesting to you with the greatest of ease. And as you go deeper and deeper, you notice that the deeper you go, the better you feel and the better you feel, the deeper you will go as you realize now that you can trust your subconscious mind, for just as it makes you breath automatically without any conscious effort, and just as it pumps the blood around your body and keeps you alive, so you can be certain that from this very moment forward your subconscious mind will ensure that every single thing I suggest to you, WILL become your new reality as an automatic reflex action, with the greatest of ease. In fact you will find that something you once thought may be so difficult to achieve will now become so ridiculously easy, as you realize that from this moment forward, you can equal the greatest achievements of life's greatest achievers and that for you, your innermost dreams can and have now become your 100% total reality. Noticing now that with every breath that you take, every noise that you hear and every word that I say, that all the stresses, tensions, worries, fears and apprehensions of days and weeks gone by are leaving your mind and leaving your body NOW!

08) NOW TIME FOR THERAPY SPECIFIC TO PROBLEM

Realizing now that from this moment forward, each morning you will awaken with an inner warm glow of confidence, a renewed optimism to life, a more positive attitude to get things done. You will notice that every day in every way you find it so much easier to deal with events and situations, which once would have bothered you greatly. Realizing now that from this moment forward within you is a large inner reservoir of willpower, self-confidence and self-esteem, which you may draw upon as an automatic reflex action whenever you need to, enabling you to deal with everything and anything there and then, the very moment it happens, you no longer need, want, crave or desire for stressful situations and as such from this moment forward with every breath that you take, you will be able to handle everything and anything that life presents to you with the greatest of ease. Nothing bothers you as it once did and in fact you now realize that just as all of the stresses, tensions, Worries, fears and apprehensions of days, weeks, months and years gone by are leaving your body and leaving your mind NOW! So you realize also that every day in every way your life is getting better and better, your approach and attitude to life is getting more relaxed, more positive and more constructive and in turn your approach, attitude and response to other people, especially those you care for, those you respect and those close to you, WILL BECOME far more positive, far more relaxed and far more friendly and appreciative in every way, shape and form. You realize now as 100% Total Reality that your life is now like a mirror, and whatever you give out to others in life is now reflected back towards you tenfold. So from this moment forward as an automatic reflex action you will find that you will send out positive, peaceful, constructive and loving thoughts, actions and words to all those around you and in turn these things will positively and beneficially be reflected back to you tenfold with each second that passes by. Notice how good it feels to realize that these improvements in your daily life have now taken place and will continue to grow stronger and more positive each and every day. Realizing now that just as you can and WILL now equal the greatest achievements of life's greatest achievers, so in turn you now realize that no one person ever did it all alone and so from this moment forward you will eagerly, happily and positively encourage those around you to help in your aims, actions & desires. You no longer resent or feel shy or in any way negative about accepting help, advice and assistance from others, in fact it makes you happy and proud to know that you can enabling you to achieve whatever you wish to achieve with the greatest of ease. Just as you yourself are a wonderful, valuable and worthy person so you now WILL realize from this moment forward, that the opinions of others, especially those of people you respect, people you love and those close to you are worth listening and responding to in a positive manner, just as your opinions and thoughts WILL NOW BECOME and will remain equally Honest, positive, constructive and worthwhile as all the stresses, tensions, worries, fears and apprehensions of every day situations which once would have bothered you have now become and will continue to be but distant memories and things of the past, as from this moment forward you will awaken each morning with an inner warm glow of confidence, a renewed optimism to life, a more positive attitude to get things done and every day in every way you will now realize that you have within you a large inner reservoir of willpower, self-confidence, self-esteem and patience which you can and you will draw upon as a 100% Total Reality automatic reflex action whenever you find yourself in a situation which once would have bothered you. Realizing now that you reap what you sow in life and as such from this moment forward all the stresses, tensions, worries, fears, apprehensions and obsessions which once may have bothered you are now but distant memories and things of the past as you now continue your life as the Confident, Happy, Healthy, Relaxed Stress free positive minded, Loving, caring, considerate individual that you have now become and will continue to be for the rest of your life, with each and every suggestion growing stronger each second of each minute of each hour of each day from this moment forward, you now realize how short life is and how valuable every second of it has now become to you. You no longer need, want, crave or desire to waste a single moment of your now positively Happy, Healthy, Calm and relaxed lifestyle, instead you now wish to and as a result WILL savor every moment, you now notice more closely how enjoyable it is to be in the company of friends, those you respect, Loved ones and others close to you. Their company, their opinions, their honesty, their help, assistance, advice, love and encouragement are all invaluable to you and as a result you WILL RESPOND to them with the same Honesty, Openness, Positiveness, Warmth, Encouragement and Love in all that you do and at all times you spend together. Your greatest achievement in life now being that you have now become one of those rare few, but very talented and perceptive people who is able to admit their own faults and by so doing grow stronger and happier as an individual and as part of a Loving partnership, in short from this moment forward to you the Past is the Past and what you now find is most important to you is The Future, your positive, happy, healthy, confident, relaxed Future made even more enjoyable, positive and beneficial by those around you who are friends, those who Love you, those who respect you and those who care about you which in turn you will reflect back to them as you continue now to live your life like a mirror and reflect to others the way you wish to be Loved for, Cared for, Respected and assisted in your every day life, which from this moment forward is that of a confident, peaceful, happy, healthy, relaxed, stress free, positive thinking, Loving, caring and considerate worthwhile individual.

09) FINGER & THUMB RING OF CONFIDENCE.

Noticing now that the deeper you go, the better you feel and the better you feel the deeper you will go with every breath that you take, every noise that you hear and every word that I say, as you now allow your mind to wander free as you continue to go deeper down into the world of your dreams and the world of your imagination I want you to imagine and remember that one time in your life when you felt more Happy, more confident, more proud and on top of the world than you have ever done before. It could have been a time when you won an award or just a time on Holiday when you felt you could achieve anything, it matters not just so long as YOU NOW FEEL Happy, Healthy, Relaxed, Calm, Confident & Loving to yourself and to others in everyday life enabling you to live a 100% fulfilling and stress free lifestyle. Now I just want to notice how good it feels to experience these positive and beneficial states of mind and body and as you do realize now that whenever you need to renter this special place in your every day life, whenever you are confronted with the unexpected or those things which once would have bothered or concerned you then now as an automatic reflex action all you need do is push together the tip of your forefinger of the right hand together with the tip of your thumb and instantly this will make your ring of confidence, your ring of willpower, your ring of self-esteem and your ring of patience that will instantly enable you to remain as the Calm, Confident, Happy, Healthy, Relaxed and Loving individual that you have now become and will continue to be from this moment forward. Remembering that your subconscious will remind you as an automatic reflex action to make this ring of confidence with your finger and thumb as and when you need that little extra help in every day life. As you relax deeper and deeper with each second that passes by and every word that I say.

10) RULERS OF CONFIDENCE, WILLPOWER, SELF-IMAGE/ESTEEM, PATIENCE & TRUST.

Realizing now that the personal attributes of self-confidence, Willpower, Positive Self-esteem, Patience and Trust are the only attributes that any individual needs in every day life to remain as a Confident, Happy, Healthy, Relaxed and Loving person, Just as you have now become and continue to be as you live your stress free lifestyle every day in every way getting better and better. So I'd Like you to imagine a thermometer in your minds eye with the numbers from 0 to 100% on it and within this thermometer the level at which the mercury is indicates the level at which your personal levels of self-confidence, Will Power, self-esteem, Patience and Trust are currently at. As you relax more completely with each second that passes by I want you to notice the level that the mercury is currently at and then realize that if we raise the level to 100% then any and all problems you may once have had in your life will no longer ever be able to bother you or effect you and as you realize this as 100% Total Reality I'd like you to imagine heating up the mercury in the thermometer with a lighter or a hot flaming candle so that the mercury gets hotter and hotter, so hot in fact that it starts to rise up inside the thermometer. Up past 30%, up past 40 & 50%, all the way up and past 80% and then notice and just realize in your minds eye that the mercury has now reached 100% and as you notice this realize how much more confident you feel, how you realize now your Willpower is also at a 100%, your self-esteem is higher than it ever has been at 100% and your Patience and trust both of yourself and others is now also at 100% making you a much happier, healthier, relaxed, calm and loving person in every way as you continue to live a stressfree lifestyle. Realizing now that in order to feel this confident forever we need to fix the mercury in place at 100% so imagine now in your minds eye that you have a hammer and a nail and that you are now hammering the nail through the thermometer and through the mercury at the 100% level and rather than leaking out the mercury is now being fixed, solidly, permanently in place so that from this moment forward your levels of self-confidence, Will Power, self-esteem, Patience and Trust are now fixed at 100% enabling you to live your life as the Happy, healthy, Confident, Relaxed, Calm, Loving & trusting individual that you have become and now continue to be as all areas of your life benefit immensely from these improvements every day in every way.

11)- TV SET GET RID OF PAST

As you relax and go deeper, so the deeper you go the better you will feel and the better you feel the deeper you will go as you now imagine in your minds eye a TV set upon which you can see an image of how you once were, just see it clearly on the TV screen the person you once were, notice all those things about yourself that both you and others disliked which are no longer part of you and realize now these things have become and must now remain part of the past. And as you realize this its time to turn down the volume on the TV so imagine doing this now, then just imagine turning down the Colour and contrast so that the image of how you once were disappears completely and now as we realize that image has gone forever, we no longer need the TV set switched on so imagine turning it off, yes that's perfect and now as you relax more just imagine unplugging the TV set from the wall and as you do realizing that you yourself have now said goodbye completely to the past and how you once were as finally just imagine blowing up the TV set with a large bomb, go on that's it just see it being blown up and realize now that these things can Never, ever bother you again now or any time in the future as you relax more with each second that passes by and every breath that you take.

12)- MIRROR TO INSTALL NEW FUTURE

Just imagine now as you relax more completely a full length mirror in your minds eye and imagine that you are standing in front of this full length mirror but rather than seeing the image of how you once were, you are now seeing the image of how you wish to be. Notice how happy and confident you feel about yourself, notice how good it feels to look in the mirror and see yourself exactly as you have on many occasions dreamed yourself to be, notice how much happier you now feel about yourself and as a result how much happier you feel around those you love and how easy it has now become to be open, honest and candid about those things which once bothered you before you became this image of beauty, happiness, confidence and contentment that you now see before you in your minds eye and then as you continue to breath deeply and regularly realizing now that this is no longer a dream, this is in fact 100% Total Reality, it is in fact your New reality and is indeed the person you have now become and will continue to be from this moment forward, as you go deeper, the better you feel the deeper you go and the deeper you go the better you will feel.

13) – PAIN & PLEASURE SUGGESTIONS

Realizing now as you relax further that from this moment forward you find and get the greatest pleasure from making yourself and others happy, from making yourself and others feel Loved, wanted, Needed and appreciated in all that they say and do and that from this moment forward you no longer need, want, crave or desire any manner of painful situation in your life as you continue to be the Confident, Happy, Healthy, Calm, Relaxed and Loving person that you have now become and will continue to be every day in every way. Making others happy makes you happy and seeing others sad makes you sad as you now live your life like a mirror and give out that which you want reflected back to you.

14) – MAJOR POST HYPNOTIC SUGGESTIONS

In a few moments time when I awaken you, everything I have suggested to you and everything that you have suggested to yourself will remain with you in every way and will grow stronger and more positive for you each second, of each minute of each hour for the rest of your life. Each and every time you consent for me to help you re-enter this relaxing and beneficial state you will re-enter this state with the greatest of ease and the very moment that I say "AND SLEEP NOW" that very moment that I say "AND SLEEP NOW" you will instantly and rapidly re-enter this state, and each and every time you re-enter this state it will be 100 times more relaxing, deeper and enjoyable for you in every way, shape and form. As you relax deeper realizing also that whenever you hear my voice on an audio cassette whether consciously or whilst asleep the effect of my positive suggestions upon you will grow stronger in every way enabling you to realize that something you once thought would be so difficult to achieve has in fact proved so ridiculously easy.

15) – AWAKEN FROM TRANCE (IF DAY) OR SEND OFF TO SLEEP IF ON TAPE AT NIGHT.

I'm now going to count from 1 to 10 and on the count of ten everything I have suggested will remain with you at a subconscious level and will grow stronger every second of each day enabling you to continue being the Confident, Happy, healthy, Relaxed, Calm and Loving individual that you have now become and will continue to be from this moment forward....

On 1, Everything I have suggested remaining with you and growing stronger in every way.

On 2, Realizing now that you will awaken in the morning with an inner warm glow of confidence, a renewed optimism to life and a more positive attitude to get things done as you now realize that you have a large inner reservoir of self-confidence, Willpower, self-esteem, Patience, Trust and Honesty within you that you can draw upon whenever necessary as an automatic reflex action.

On 3, Realizing now how much better you feel, how proud you feel about yourself for allowing yourself to come to terms with the problems you once had that no longer bother you.

On 4, Its almost as thought every muscle in your body is now being washed with pure spring water removing all negativity from your mind, from your body and from your life forever,

On 5, Lighter and brighter almost as though you now realize that a huge weight has now been lifted off your shoulders and you are now free to live your life happily the way you once thought may only ever be a dream, but the way which is now for you your 100% Total Personal Reality.

On 6, Normal feelings now returning to each and every muscle group in your body as everything I have suggested is now permanently burnt deep into your subconscious mind

On 7, Realizing now that at a conscious Level only, when you awaken in a few moments time you will remember to forget and forget to remember everything that has been suggested to you, instead allowing it all to be stored to your subconscious mind who will ensure that you act upon it all as an automatic reflex action in your every day life.

On 8, Lighter and brighter now, coming on up out of it, feeling better than you have done in weeks, perhaps even in months, feeling so happy. Healthy, Calm and relaxed

As on 9, Coming on up out of it, Lighter and brighter

And on 10, Open your eyes wakey wakey rise and shine.

END OF PERSONAL SESSION WHICH IS SUITABLE FOR TREATING 99% OF PHOBIAS, HABITS, PROBLEMS ETC

NOTE = The Above information on Complete Mind Therapy was extracted from Volume One and Volume Two of "The Encyclopedia of Hypnotherapy, Stage-Hypnosis and Complete Mind Therapy" by Dr. Jonathan Royle, both of which are available on Amazon.

Www.UltimateHypnosisCourse.com

www.EliteHypnosisBootcamp.com

www.MagicalGuru.com

'Running The Numbers'

by Robert Temple

As hypnotists we are probably one of the luckiest breeds in the world. Not only are we self-employed (and therefore able to dictate our own hours, projects, salary and working conditions) but we are also able to change the lives of ordinary people, every day.

Whether you're a stage hypnotist or a hypnotherapist, chances are that you've been asked to stop someone from smoking or make them 'stop eating chocolate' on more than one occasion.

In fact, if you had a penny for every time you'd had these requests, you'd probably be able to retire, financially free, and simply enjoy the rest of your life on a yacht in the Bahamas.

That's precisely what I want to talk to you about here, today.

I think that all of us have some kind of 'dream' or some big goals which, right now, you may think will never be fulfilled. Maybe you want to buy a $1,000,000 home or drive a Lamborghini.

Perhaps you're looking for that paradise beach lifestyle. Or maybe you'd like to pay off your mortgage and not worry about the bills each month.

Whatever it is that motivates you to be successful and whatever you envision as true 'success', in this chapter I want to empower you and give you the tools that you need to 'make it happen'.

When you started out in hypnosis, chances are you had a couple of things in mind:

1 To change people's lives for the better and make a real difference;

2 To build your own business and make money for yourself, rather than working for 'the man'.

Would you agree?

Well, there is one fundamental 'flaw' with this business model which is limiting you from achieving both of those things to their fullest potential.

There is only ONE of you and only 24 hours in each day so, even with the best will in the world, there are only so many clients that you can consult with per day.

Unless you're charging many thousands of dollars and treating high-end celebrities or business people, chances are you're probably not seeing the kind of dream income that you desired.

Your income will always be obstructed by:

1 The amount of money you can charge per session;

2 The number of sessions/clients you can fit into a day;

3 The number of clients you can actually get per day;

4 The local radius from which you can realistically find clients.

So, without the capital and the business experience to open up a chain of top-notch hypnotherapy practices around the world, chances are your dreams of million dollar mansions are going to remain a far-flung hope.

Wouldn't it be great if there was a way that you could find, attract and treat literally hundreds of clients per day for dozens of different issues or problems, without taking up any of your time.

Imagine if you could be at the beach, in your local coffee shop, browsing the designer high street stores or on a 5* vacation and STILL be able to treat more clients that you ever dreamt possible.

Sounds too good to be true?

Well, it used to be... but it isn't anymore, thanks to an incredible tool.

I am, of course, referring to the INTERNET.

We now live in a world of digital publishing and internet marketing, where literally anything you need is available at the push of a button.

Some of the world's biggest companies are exploding into bankruptcy, whilst regular people are building solid 7-figure businesses from the comfort of their home Internet connection.

As hypnotists, we are in the perfect position to do exactly the same. Whether you'd be happy to make an extra few hundred bucks per month, or whether you're looking to build a multi-million dollar online empire, I urge you to read on - and consider what I'm about to share with you, very seriously.

A couple of years ago, I made the decision that I wanted to raise my fees, work less and make more money. So I set about learning, designing and perfecting a system to generate passive income online, which would allow me to work as much or as little as I wanted.

I soon stumbled across something golden. I realized that you can actually package, market and sell your hypnotherapy skills online for HUGE profit margins as 'downloadable information products'.

Let's face it, there are literally BILLIONS of people around the world who need our help in SOME way, but there's no way we can get them all into our offices for a hypnotherapy session.

BUT, we could easily give them some kind of virtual help, whether that's a hypnotherapy MP3, video training, an eBook or whatever the best medium to package your information is.

I'm sure you've seen those 'big-gun' hypnotists with their best-selling books and audio programs in your favorite high-street book store, right?

Well the truth is that a lot of physical book publishers are worried right now, as more and more people are turning to the Internet to solve their problems.

The cool thing is that ordinary people like me and you can now create their own fantastic products, get them up for sale online and start raking in big cash, for less than $100 and in under a week.

Let's run some numbers...

Imagine you could have a 'Quit Smoking' product, which sells for $67 on-line. If you could sell 10 copies per day, that's $670 in your pocket. Once the 'system' is set up, it takes NO effort to complete those sales.

That's with just ONE product. What if you had 5 of those products.?Or 10?

I call this 'Passive Hypnosis Profits'.

When I discovered this possibility, I knew that I had stumbled onto something that would change my life... and it did.

Over the past few years I've generated over $1.2million in online sales of this kind of information product. Best of all, the overheads and set up costs are super-low and literally ANYONE can copy my success.

Let me tell you, when you have an automated online system selling your hypnotherapy products and generating hundreds or thousands of dollars per day in hands-free income, it's an incredible feeling.

Not only are you helping hundreds of people worldwide to change their lives for the better but you're also making fantastic money along the way.

The truth is, the more money you have, the more resources you have to further spread your skills and help even more people - which, in turn, makes even more money. Cool, right?

All you need to know is the 'system', which I have conveniently broken down into 5 simple, bite-size chunks, ready for you to implement.

Step #1: Choose a topic for your product

This is the simple part. All you have to do is to choose one of your favorite, or most popular, issues that you can treat as a hypnotherapist.

It could be anything from smoking cessation or weight loss to phobia cures and stress/anxiety.

There are literally hundreds of issues which can be easily treated with hypnotherapy, so you can simply pick one of your preferred.

Perhaps there is a particular problem which you've had a great success rate with, or something you have noticed is requested a lot.

Either way, if you can make money from it as a hypnotherapist doing one-on-one sessions, then you can make 100x the money from it as a downloadable information product.

Once you've chosen one, you can move on.

Step #2: Create your product

Most people have never (and will never) create their own product. Why? It's usually because the thought never crosses their mind or they don't think they can.

Truthfully, as a hypnotist, you are probably in one of the most powerful positions to create a fantastic information product effortlessly.

Think about it this way. Every single time you treat a private client for any particular issue, you are effectively creating an audio product, live... which is then instantly gone forever.

You're sitting, in a room, and talking for 60-120 minutes, hypnotizing, treating and re-awakening your clients.

Now, imagine if you were to purchase a simple, cheap $30 USB microphone for your computer or hire a local, basic recording studio for an hour, and you were to do a full hypnotherapy session... for a microphone.

Yes, actually sit down and run an entire session as if your client were there in front of you, but record it all onto a microphone.

An hour or two later, you have your very own perfect information product ready to sell. Simply save it as an MP3 and you're done.

That was easy!

If you wanted to take this a step further, you could also create a manual or video course to accompany the hypnosis MP3, detailing further tips, tricks and tools to help them beat their issue.

Your product could be as simple as a 60-minute audio file or as complicated as an entire multimedia program consisting of books, worksheets, videos, audios, etc.

With the product created, simply give it a snazzy name and it's ready for sale.

Never thought you could make a hit-selling product? You just learned how to do it in as little as an hour. Now what's your excuse?

Go make your product, otherwise you're missing out!

Step #3: Build an automated sales process

Once your product is complete, the next step is to build a simple online sales presence to enable you to convert visitors into customers.

Your online sales system will consist of a few different parts:

1 Sales page - this is a simple web page, which consists of some simple graphics and either a long, scrolling sales letter or a sharp, snappy sales video to sell the visitor on the benefits of your product. It would also have an 'Add To Cart' button, so that your customers can buy the product.

2 Order form - this page enables your customers to actually send you some money for your product. Whether it's $10 or $1000, you need some kind of merchant provider. Fortunately, with companies such as ClickBank, PayPal and JVZoo, who will actually handle your payments for you, this is really pretty easy.

You can simply create a free account with any of these services and create an order form to add to your sales process within minutes.

13 Download page - this is where your customers will be returned after they have purchased your product. It's a simple web page which contains a download link for the MP3, eBook or video course.

This kind of website is often referred to in the internet marketing as a 'minisite'. It's very straightforward to create and can even be entirely outsourced (recommended!) to a professional graphic designer.

If you turn to Google and search for 'Minisite Designer', you'll find a ton of really talented people who can create your entire minisite out for you, while you just sit back and put the individual pieces together.

You'll also need website hosting and a domain name for your product, but you can also find these with a simple Google search.

Step #4: Start driving traffic

With your product and sales process online, you simply need to flood it with traffic. The more traffic you receive to your site, the more sales you'll make and the more money goes into your pocket.

There are literally dozens of ways that you can get traffic to your site, but my personal favorite is to find affiliates and have them promote your product for you.

Affiliates are other internet marketers or information publishers who already have a business in your niche area. For example, if you have created a 'stop smoking' product, then you could search for blogs, product creators, mailing list owners and experts to promote your product to their followers and fans.

They could add a banner to their website or e-mail their subscriber list about your product. If anyone buys it, they receive a commission from the sale.

There are literally thousands of successful affiliates around the world who are hungry for quality products to promote, in every niche or topic you could possibly think of.

It's like having an army of sales people working for you all day, every day, and you only have to pay them when they make you money first. Cool, right?

If you use ClickBank or JVZoo to run your payments (see above) then you already have a built-in and ready-to-go affiliate program to handle all of the sales tracking and commission payouts, too.

Once your system is ready to go, your entire job becomes simply finding and recruiting new affiliates who can promote your product on a daily basis.

I'd recommend spending 20-30 minutes per day just looking for (and contacting) new potential affiliates. Even if you only bring 1 new affiliate on-board each day, that can be enough to generate thousands of sales per month.

Step #5: Rinse and repeat

Believe it or not, it's actually completely possible to have steps 1-4 up and running within 7-28 days, starting from scratch.

So what do you do next? That's easy, you do it again with a new product in a new niche market.

Literally start from the beginning and run through this entire system again. Each time you do it, you'll add a new product to your collection and bump up your potential income.

Why have 1 product making $100 per day, when you could have 10? The more products you have out there, the more money you could make, even if you put less work into each individual product promotion.

Plus, the more you do this, the better and faster you'll become. There is absolutely no reason why you couldn't release a new product every 2-3 months.

If your products sell for, say, $47 and convert at around 5%, if you get 100 visitors to those sales pages every day (this is not an unrealistic figure at all!) then you'll be making 5 sales at $47 = $235 per day.

That's an extra $85,775 per year in hands-free, passive income!

Oh, and that's only with ONE product. Imagine the damage you could do with FIVE or TEN products!

The truth is that the entire world is shifting rapidly to this new, digital marketplace.

People are becoming more and more familiar and comfortable with the idea of online purchases and downloadable digital products every day.

Some people will be buying those products and others will be selling them.

Which would you rather be?

As a hypnotist, you have one of the most powerful abilities to change people's lives and generate huge cash. Please don't limit your opportunities to do this on a global scale.

There is NO reason why you can't build your very own five, six or seven figure online income with the system that I've detailed in this chapter.

I have done it... my students are doing it... and you can do it too.

If you're interested in learning more about this system, you can check out our 100% free coaching on 'Passive Hypnosis Profits' by visiting: http://www.passivehypnosisprofits.com/free/

or http://www.elitehypnosisbootcamp.com/platinum/

FREE VIDEO TRAINING IN HYPNOSIS

For some highly invaluable Video Training in Hypnosis at no cost be sure to sign up for the Free Online Video Training at:

www.EliteHypnosisBootcamp.com

Also be sure to check out the various Training Videos that I have posted up on my You-Tube Accounts and Channels at:

http://www.youtube.com/celebrityhypnotist

And Also At The Link Of:

http://www.youtube.com/hypnotherapycourse

And Then To Keep In Touch and Stay Informed About Exciting New Developments in Hypnosis & NLP And of Course About Forthcoming Live Events Be Sure To Add Me on Social Media

https://www.facebook.com/jonathan.royle

And

https://twitter.com/roylehypnotist/

And Finally For All Your Graphic Design and Professional Printing Requirements Be Sure To Check Out:

http://www.hypnotic-consultants.co.uk/

To Contact Me Personally For One To One Training Or To Book Me To Present A Training Seminar In Your Area

www.MagicalGuru.com

Secrets of Stage Hypnosis – Street Hypnotism - Hypnotherapy – NLP – Complete Mind Therapy And Marketing For Hypnotists

Compiled By: Dr. Jonathan Royle

© 2013 – Dr. Jonathan Royle

www.UltimateHypnosisCourse.com

www.EliteHypnosisBootcamp.com

www.MagicalGuru.com

www.HypnotherapyCourse.net

VERY SILENTLY I CREPT FORWARD, I HEARD A SNARLING GRUNTING SOUND FROM ABOVE ME, NOW I LOOKED UPWARDS, THERE WAS THE TIGER, ITS MOUTH OPEN WIDE SHOWING LARGE TEARING FANGS, THE BLACK PATCHES ON THE ROOF OF ITS MOUTH STOOD OUT WITH STARTLING CLARITY, WITHOUT ANOTHER SOUND, IT LEAPT DOWN TOWARDS ME, I CROUCHED LOWER, AND IT PASSED OVER ME, BEFORE THE TIGER COULD TURN, I LEAPT ONTO ITS BACK, CIRCLED ITS THROAT WITH MY LEFT ARM, AND RAISED MY RIGHT ARM WITH THE LONG DAGGER IN IT, VERY HIGH, READY TO STRIKE INTO THE TIGERS JUGULAR.

THAT SENTENCE HELD YOUR ATTENTION AT THE START OF THE BOOK, THAT IS WHAT A HYPNOTIST DOES, GRABS YOUR ATTENTION THEN HYPNOTISES YOU.

THAT MOST IMPORTANT LESSON WAS BEFORE YOU HAD EVEN STARTED TO READ THE BOOK.

CPSIA information can be obtained
at www.ICGtesting.com
Printed in the USA
LVOW03s1703170716

496677LV00028B/311/P

9 781492 340560